T3-BNO-453

A Light from Eleusis:
A Study of Ezra Pound's *Cantos*

A Light from Eleusis

A Study of Ezra Pound's *Cantos*

LEON SURETTE

Clarendon Press · Oxford
1979

Oxford University Press, Walton Street, Oxford OX2 6DP

OXFORD LONDON GLASGOW
NEW YORK TORONTO MELBOURNE WELLINGTON
IBADAN NAIROBI DAR ES SALAAM LUSAKA CAPE TOWN
KUALA LUMPUR SINGAPORE JAKARTA HONG KONG TOKYO
DELHI BOMBAY CALCUTTA MADRAS KARACHI

ISBN 0 19 812089 3

Printed in Great Britain by
Cox & Wyman Ltd.,
London, Fakenham and Reading

For

Marshall McLuhan

A little light, like a rush light
to lead back to splendour.

Preface

THIS BOOK, unlike most studies that offer a new interpretation of the *Cantos*, starts from the recognition that Pound's epic is more a collection of poetry than a single coherent poem. Even collections, however, may have some unifying features, and it is these that are sought and discovered in the following pages. Many will be familiar to students of the *Cantos*, but recognized here for the first time is the importance of the rites of Eleusis as a paradigm of the *Cantos*' action, much as the Grail Legend is a paradigm of the action of Eliot's *Waste Land*. The reader must not suppose, however, that an articulation of the role of Eleusis will somehow unlock the *Cantos* in the same way that Joyce's *Ulysses* may be said to be unlocked by its parallel to the *Odyssey*. Indeed, the expectation that Pound would some day reveal the key to the *Cantos*' organization, as Joyce had revealed his compositional scheme for *Ulysses*, has been very damaging to studies of the poem. It is an expectation that Pound did nothing to discourage. Even before his release from St. Elizabeth's Hospital in 1958, he was encouraging his students and followers to expect an 'ascension into limpidity' with the promised and final 'paradiso' section of the *Cantos*. I was myself one of those students, writing a dissertation in the early sixties on the assumption that the key might be discovered by an ingenious and assiduous student, even before Pound revealed it.

But he never did write that final revelatory section of the poem. Instead 1969 brought *Drafts and Fragments of Cantos CX–CXVII*, which amounted to a tacit admission of his inability to complete the poem, and even contained two separate palinodes. At that point students of the *Cantos* should have stopped seeking a ghostly poem somehow concealed in a text that grew ever longer but never clearer. It should have been recognized that the scholarly challenge presented by the poem did not lie in the search for some key which would render the cryptic, opaque, and heterogeneous text at once lucid and coherent, but rather in discovering why the poem is so intractable, why Pound could not make it fit his account of what he wished it to be.

At the same time, one must be careful not to dismiss the *Cantos* simply because it fails to live up to expectations fostered by its author. Even though we acknowledge that Pound's modern epic is not quite what he said it was, it is nonetheless a monumental, and sometimes a magnificent, witness to the turmoil of the twentieth century. It is (as Pound told Harriet Monroe epic must be) 'a poem that includes history', but in ways that he never contemplated; for the problematic and truncated text is as much a consequence of his involvement in the political and intellectual history of his day as it is of his *avant garde* poetics. In order to understand that involvement, this study pursues the opinions of those men Pound knew or referred to, or whose influence might have reached him, as well as his own testimony in letters, shorter verse, and the multitudinous prose pieces he wrote to earn his living. Of course, such a study can never be conclusive in its findings—or even definitively concluded—but only through such an approach can we hope to understand how the *Cantos* became the shaggy monster that it is.

The publication of *Drafts and Fragments*, and Pound's death three years later, ended hopes that the poem would be brought to a triumphant and revelatory conclusion. A possibility of discovering some key to the structure and meaning of the *Cantos* has remained, however, for until recently Pound's papers have been in the possession of the family, and essentially unavailable to scholars. They are now in the care of the Beinecke Rare Book Room and Manuscript Library of Yale University and have only just become available to scholars. I have had occasion in preparing this book to examine the fine collection of Pound material held by the Beinecke even before the acquisition of Pound's own papers, thanks to the kindness of Donald Gallup and Peter Dzwonkoski. The new papers were not available until after I had completed the book, but with the permission of Pound's daughter, Mary de Rachewiltz, I have been able to examine a portion of those papers she consigned to the Beinecke.

The papers are as yet uncatalogued, and since the Library, quite sensibly is not anxious to have people riffling through them, one must request to see specific items. Accordingly, I applied to see all the notes and drafts relevant to the first twenty-seven cantos as well as to cantos XXXIX and XLVII. I was able to see photocopies of everything I had asked for.

The photocopies were gathered together in file folders, grouped according to the canto number to which they seemed to be most relevant. The folders contain three sorts of documents: (1) draft versions of cantos or lines for cantos, (2) notes on reading undertaken as background for cantos, and (3) a few handwritten notations on the arrangement of groups of cantos. These last are the only documents I found which address themselves to issues of structure and organization. There are six of them in all; they appear to be casual jottings written at the bottom, in the margin, or on the back of sheets containing other matter.

Although these notes on the arrangement of cantos in no way suggest the existence of some comprehensive scheme such as Joyce had for *Ulysses*, they would repay careful study. It would be irresponsible, however, to attempt any interpretation of the photocopies here since Pound's hand is very difficult to read, and the notes use many abbreviations. A few preliminary observations will be sufficient to indicate that no key to the *Cantos*' structure or meaning is likely to be found in this new material. The notes in question are no more than a column of canto numbers with a matching column of theme or subject labels. In some cases the arrangement of cantos in the notes is not that of the published *Cantos*, and in other cases the notes themselves have been revised—either altering the sequence of subjects, or grouping into one canto subjects that had been divided between two. Clearly these are working notes on the sequence and division of cantos. Invariably they refer to cantos already written or currently being written. They never look ahead to sections of the poem not yet begun, nor do they indicate what principles of organization were being followed. There are no references in anything I saw to a structural role for the *Metamorphoses*, the *Odyssey*, or the *Commedia* even though Pound publicly drew attention to their importance as structural parallels. Nor is there any reference to Eleusis.

Of course, Pound's papers offer an exciting prospect for students of the *Cantos*, and a thorough study of them will improve our understanding of the poem. But it is evident that no key, no scheme will be found. Our only route to an understanding of the *Cantos* is, then, the lengthy one pursued in this book, one in which the poem is followed from its uncertain beginning in 1915 to its querulous termination in 1969. I create, as it were, a biography of the poem, beginning with its earliest contacts with Joséphin Péladan, W. B.

Yeats, and G. R. S. Mead, through the formative influences of James Joyce and T. S. Eliot; the disillusionment of the First Great War; the economic and political revelations of Major Douglas, A. R. Orage, and others; and, finally, the isolation of Rapallo, World War II, and St. Elizabeth's Hospital. As is the case with the life of a man, one can discern a thread of consistent purpose, but not a grand design worked out from start to finish.

The book could hardly have been written without a research grant from the Canada Council and a year's sabbatical leave from the University of Western Ontario. My university has also provided modest financial support over the years, and has generously rescued me from the surprisingly heavy burden of permission fees for quotations from Pound's works. Much of the book was written while on leave spent at Oxford where the resources of the Bodleian Library were kindly made available to me, and where Richard Ellmann's friendly interest made my stay so very pleasant. Early chapters of the book were read and helpfully commented on by my colleagues, D. F. McKay and J. W. Graham. R. J. Shroyer advised me on rhetorical points at crucial stages in the development of the book, and A. M. Young helped me straighten out some tangled prose. I thank them all for their time and advice. If there remain any errors in the text, it is certainly not the fault of the Oxford University Press, whose careful editing discovered an embarrassing number of small blunders. Finally, I want to thank my wife, Valerie, who spent many hours correcting and amending my text.

Part of Chapter III first appeared in a slightly different form in *Paideuma*, part of Chapter IV in the *Hudson Review*, and part of Chapter VIII in *Bucknell Review*. I thank the editors of those journals for permission to reprint the substance of the three articles.

Acknowledgements

Extracts are reprinted from
The Cantos of Ezra Pound: Copyright 1934, 1937, 1940, 1948 © 1956, 1959, 1962, 1970, 1972 by the Trustees of the Ezra Pound Literary Property Trust
Collected Shorter Poems (*Personae*): Copyright 1926, 1952 by the Trustees of the Ezra Pound Literary Property Trust
A Lume Spento and Other Early Poems: © 1965 by the Trustees of the Ezra Pound Literary Property Trust
Collected Early Poems: Copyright 1926, 1935, 1954 © 1965, 1967, 1971, 1976 by the Trustees of the Ezra Pound Literary Property Trust
The Selected Letters of Ezra Pound: 1907–1941: (edited by D. D. Paige) Copyright 1950 by Ezra Pound (Introduction and notes, copyright 1950 by D. D. Paige)
The ABC of Reading: Copyright Ezra Pound 1934
The Spirit of Romance: Copyright © 1968 by the Trustees of the Ezra Pound Literary Property Trust
Guide to Kulchur: Copyright © 1970 by the Trustees of the Ezra Pound Literary Property Trust
Literary Essays: Copyright 1918, 1920, 1935 by the Trustees of the Ezra Pound Literary Property Trust
Pound/Joyce The Letters of Ezra Pound to James Joyce, with Pound's essays on Joyce: Copyright © 1965, 1966, 1967 by Ezra Pound
by permission of Faber and Faber Ltd., London, and New Directions Publishing Corporation, New York. All rights reserved.
Gaudier Brzeska: A Memoir: Copyright © 1970 by Ezra Pound
Pavannes and Divagations: Copyright © 1958 by Ezra Pound
by permission of New Directions Publishing Corporation, New York, and Faber and Faber Ltd., London on behalf of the Ezra Pound Literary Property Trust.
The Chinese Written Character as a Medium for Poetry: by Ernest Fenollosa with a Foreword and Notes by Ezra Pound: Copyright 1963 by Ezra Pound
by permission of New Directions Publishing Corporation, New York, and Faber and Faber Ltd., London on behalf of the Ezra Pound Literary Property Trust, and City Lights Books, San Francisco.

Patria Mia: Copyright 1950 by Ralph Seymour. Copyright renewed © 1977 by the Trustees of the Ezra Pound Literary Property Trust
by permission of New Directions Publishing Corporation, New York, and Peter Owen Ltd: Publishers, London.
The Great Digest & Unwobbling Pivot: Copyright 1952 by Ezra Pound
by permission of Peter Owen Ltd: Publishers, London.
Jefferson and/or Mussolini: Copyright 1935, 1936, 1937 by Ezra Pound
by permission of Liveright Publishing Corporation, New York.
A Vision: Copyright 1938 by William Butler Yeats
by permission of M. B. Yeats and Miss Anne Yeats.
The Selected Prose of T. S. Eliot, ed. Frank Kermode: Copyright © 1975 by Valerie Eliot. Introduction and Notes © 1975 by Frank Kermode.
Collected Poems 1909–1962: Copyright 1936 © 1963 by Thomas Stearns Eliot
by permission of Faber and Faber Ltd., London and Harcourt Brace Jovanovich, Inc., New York.
'Ezra Pound' from *Poetry Magazine:* Copyright 1946 by Thomas Stearns Eliot
by permission of Mrs. Valerie Eliot and Faber and Faber Ltd., London.
Impact: Copyright © 1960 by Ezra Pound
by permission of Gateway Editions Ltd., South Bend, Indiana.

Contents

Introduction

THE persistent impenetrability of the *Cantos* of Ezra Pound—even after more than two decades of commentary—is an intriguing problem for anyone interested in modern poetry. For, however much one may wish to forget about this troublesome man and his impossible poem, he cannot be expunged from the history of the modern movement in poetry. The *Cantos* will remain important to the history of modernism, whatever the ultimate critical estimate of their worth might be, just because they were written by a poet of major talent and major influence. For this reason it is important that we seek to discover how the *Cantos* came to be the singular and puzzling creation that they are. Accordingly, this study is a biography of the poem, a chronological examination of its development from 1915, when it was most probably begun, to the 1960s when the last fragments were written.

The advantages of such an approach are that one can study the entire poem—not just selected portions or aspects of it—and there is no necessity to beg the outstanding critical questions about its coherence and meaning. Not surprisingly, it will emerge that Pound's views and his knowledge were not the same in 1940 as they were in 1915—nor the same in 1930 as they were in 1940. Inevitably, Pound's changing views and knowledge affected the rhetoric, content, and message of succeeding sections of the poem. Indeed, one of its most fascinating aspects is the manner in which Pound uses later sections to revise and alter the import of earlier ones already in print. This practice has not made it easy for those who approach the *Cantos* as an achieved and autonomous poem to discover its principle of organization.

The most prevalent critical assumption among sympathetic readers of the *Cantos* has been that their significance and form are hidden in an iterative and kaleidoscopic pattern for the assiduous and intelligent to discover. This assumption stems from Pound himself, but it was first articulated in Hugh Kenner, *The Poetry of Ezra Pound*

(London: Faber and Faber, 1951). It is also the basic assumption of Walter Baumann, *The Rose in the Steel Dust* (Berne: Francke Verlag, 1967), Daniel Pearlman, *The Barb of Time* (New York: Oxford University Press, 1969), and Christine Brooke-Rose, *A ZBC of Ezra Pound* (London: Faber and Faber, 1971). That such patterns exist is beyond dispute, but the assumption that their articulation is consistent and perfectly controlled is no longer tenable. Kenner himself seems to have abandoned this position in *The Pound Era* (Berkeley and Los Angeles: The University of California Press, 1971) where the *Cantos* are seen to reflect the changing fortunes of the poet.

An alternative critical response to the *Cantos* is one which stresses the poem's didactic message and draws heavily on Pound's prose as a guide to the poem. Harold H. Watt, *Ezra Pound and the Cantos* (London: Routledge and Kegan Paul, 1951) is an early exemplar of this approach, but Clark Emery, *Ideas into Action* (Coral Gables, Fla.: University of Miami Press, 1958) contains a more thorough survey of Pound's prose, and has been more influential. There is a real tension between this approach, stressing the poem's didactic message, and the Kennerian approach, stressing its revolutionary poetic. This tension reflects a genuine conflict of purpose within the *Cantos*, for Pound initially believed that he possessed poetic and rhetorical techniques which would themselves generate significance, but as he became more certain of the message he wished to convey, his interest shifted from form to content. And this tension between didactic and aesthetic interests is made all the more difficult to handle because Pound's didactic message bears on highly emotional political and economic questions. But it is as dishonest to ignore Pound's political, economic, and racial views as it is uncritical to accept those views as adequate justification of the poem.

A third scholarly approach to the *Cantos* is that of largely uncritical explication. The most important contribution in this direction is that of John Hamilton Edwards and William W. Vasse, *The Annotated Index to the Cantos of Ezra Pound, I–LXXXIV* (Berkeley and Los Angeles: The University of California Press, 1957). Although many people have contributed substantially to the poem's annotation, Noel Stock has been in a position to identify its sources more authoritatively than anyone else—*Poet in Exile* (Manchester: Manchester University Press, 1964), and *Reading the Cantos* (New York: Pantheon Books, 1966). The most important contribution to detailed annotations of cantos published later than the *Annotated Index* is to be found in Eva Hesse (editor), *New Approaches to Ezra Pound* (London: Faber and Faber, 1969), and in *Paideuma: A Journal Devoted to Ezra Pound Scholarship* (1972——). Of course, not all of the explication is uncritical. *Reading the Cantos*, in particular, is primarily an evaluation of the poem, and a highly unfavourable one.

All three of these critical approaches begin with the assumption that the *Cantos* represent a single achieved poem of an unusual or even unique type, and therefore with special claims upon our attention. Given the nature of the poem, such an assumption is reasonable enough. But it need not be granted. Most readers who decline to grant the *Cantos* a special status do not write books about them, but there are some important exceptions; George Dekker, *Sailing After Knowledge* (London: Routledge and Kegan Paul, 1963) is the best study of this type. In effect, Dekker edits the poem down to those portions which meet his criteria for poetry, and provides an excellent commentary on them. Donald Davie follows Dekker's lead in this respect in his general study of Pound's poetry, *Ezra Pound: Poet as Sculptor* (New York: Oxford University Press, 1964). This approach has been brought to its logical conclusion in Eugene Paul Nassar, *The Cantos of Ezra Pound: The Lyric Mode* (Baltimore and London: The Johns Hopkins University Press, 1975). Its advantage is that the *Cantos* can be placed within the context of familiar poetic experience, and evaluated in terms of that experience. Dekker in particular is able to maintain a critical detachment seldom encountered in criticism of the *Cantos*. Its disadvantage is that in discarding large portions of the poem, the critic overrules the judgement of the poet himself. Such critical presumption can be justified only by careful study of the entire poem—including its most prosaic and most forbidding passages.

Apart from book-length studies of the *Cantos*, there is also a massive volume of periodical criticism—much of it, but by no means all, dismissive. The case against the *Cantos* has been put so variously and so frequently that a summary of it is scarcely practicable. *Reading the Cantos* will have to stand as representative of destructive criticism of the poem. Stock was for many years a Pound disciple. His disenchantment with the *Cantos* comes, therefore, with all the greater force and weight. In effect, he complains that the poem is wilfully obscure, disunified, and 'nothing like advertised'. So, indeed, it is.

It is also incomplete. Much ink could be wasted in attempts to deny or outflank these charges, but it would serve little purpose. One could point out that the *Faerie Queene* is also wilfully obscure and incomplete, and perhaps even disunified; or that Roman readers complained of the discontinuity and obscure allusiveness of the *Aeneid*. Pound is no Virgil, nor even a Spenser, but he was attempting to write epic. That he failed to achieve his goal of writing a modern epic is neither surprising nor shameful. But it is as a failed epic that one must approach the *Cantos* if one is to understand their beauties and perversities.

It has been said that artistic failures are often more interesting than successes, and that is surely true. But they are seldom more enjoyable. The *Cantos* fascinate, but they do not frequently delight. For this reason the strategy adopted by Dekker and Nassar, of stressing those felicities to be found in the poem, is wise and prudent. However, the strategy adopted in this study is to focus on the fascination of the poem's intricacies, leaving its felicities to fend for themselves.

The organization of the discussion necessarily breaks into two parts, like the poem itself. The early and late chapters are primarily concerned with the nature and provenance of the *Cantos*' rhetoric or poetic, and their *mythos* or 'story'. There is little new to be said about the rhetoric, but the poem's *mythos* has not been properly understood. It has always been recognized that Odysseus is central to the poem's story, but it has not been recognized that Pound has reinterpreted Odysseus' descent in the light of Eleusinian models, creating a bridge between Dante's dream vision of the other world and the Homeric wanderings punctuated by a visit to the Underworld. Odysseus is the link between the world of men and the world of gods, and the varying nature of his encounters with the divine is the key to alterations in the poem's level of expectation in its movement toward revelation.

The middle chapters discuss Pound's use of historical sources, the function of history in the *Cantos*, and the relationship between that history and his economic and political views. Chapter IV offers a reconsideration of Pound's economics in the light of the revolution in economic thinking wrought by Irving Fisher and J. M. Keynes. Earle Davis's study of Pound's economics, *Vision Fugitive: Ezra Pound and Economics* (Lawrence: University of Kansas Press, 1968) is seriously flawed by his failure to take into account the radical change in the climate of economic opinion following upon the work of Keynes and Fisher. It can be seen that Pound's economics are not nearly so wrong-headed and crankish as they have been thought to be. While the economic views of Major Douglas, Pound's economic mentor, were designed to serve politically conservative interests, and led both men into virulent anti-Semitism, and Pound into Fascism, those views in themselves were more correct than prevailing opinion in the 1920s and 1930s. The total rejection of Douglas's theories by orthodox economic opinion accounts for much of the parallel extremism of both Douglas and Pound—although it does not excuse it. Within the *Cantos* themselves, Pound's economic revelations led him to convert his interest in history from a cultural to an economic base, but insisting that the practice of correct economic management coincides with high cultural achievement. This insistence results in some strangely skewed historical judgements.

Finally, this study is in a position to offer a more informed assessment of the later cantos than has been possible in earlier studies, thanks to the very detailed explication of those cantos undertaken in recent years. Despite the remarkable vitality of imagination and continued mastery of poetic resource evident in *Rock-Drill* and *Thrones*, these sections do not significantly advance the poem toward a satisfactory ending. Instead they attempt to get behind the 'ending in adversity', that the *Pisan Cantos* might have been allowed to be, by undertaking a reprise of the poem's history, and by reformulating Odysseus' encounter with the divine. In sum, Pound's late admissions that the *Cantos* were a 'botch' must be accepted as a responsible authorial assessment of the poem. He failed 'to bring it off', to fulfil his intentions. But, at the same time, his failure—like Malatesta's—is monumental.

I · Beginnings

'The problem was to get a form—something elastic enough to take the necessary material.'

Ezra Pound to Donald Hall, 1962.

1. 'THAT GREAT FORTY-YEAR EPIC'

POUND, then an industrious graduate student, spent the summer of 1906 reading in the British Museum, having received his Master of Arts degree from the University of Pennsylvania that spring. He was apparently reading Dante, for he wrote a poem based on the life of one Bertold Lomax, whom he identifies as an eighteenth-century English Dante scholar.[1] The poem is dedicated to Katherine Ruth Heyman, a pianist Pound had met two years previously at Hamilton College. Miss Heyman was fifteen years Pound's senior (which would make her about thirty-five at the time), and could not have been much flattered by the use Pound makes of this age difference in the poem, 'Scriptor Ignotus'[2]: 'Seeing before time, one sweet face grown old,/And seeing the old eyes grow bright/From out the border of her fire-lit wrinkles.' Lomax, we are told, planned to write an epic, but died with the ambition unrealized. In the poem Pound adopts the persona of Lomax addressing his beloved:

> When I see thee as some poor song-bird
> Battering its wings against this cage we call Today,
> Then would I speak comfort unto thee,
> From out the heights I dwell in, when
> That great sense of power is upon me
> And I see my greater soul-self bending
> Sibylwise with that great forty-year epic
> That you know of, yet unwrit[3].

Since Pound was not speaking in his own person in this poem, one cannot assume that he had in mind his own epic, the *Cantos*, the composition of which was not begun for another nine years. Still, when he was asked (in 1960) if he began the *Cantos* in 1916, he replied: 'I began the *Cantos* about 1904, I suppose. I had various schemes, starting in 1904 or 1905. The problem was to get a form—something elastic enough to take the necessary material. It had to be a form that wouldn't exclude something merely because it didn't fit.'[4] It is impossible to believe that Pound had conceived anything like the present poem in 1904 or 1905 when he was still an undergraduate at Hamilton College, but we do know that the date he suggests in the interview coincides with the year he met Miss Heyman. For a man with his capacity for self-dramatization, it is not too much to suppose that he chose 1904 precisely because he met Miss Heyman in that year, and she thereby becomes Pound's Beatrice, just as Lomax's lady organist became his Beatrice in 'Scriptor Ignotus'.[5]

One might be tempted to argue that this little anecdote demonstrates a remarkably enduring consistency of purpose throughout Pound's life. And in a way it does demonstrate his early fascination with the notion of a great life-work. But now that he has died, in his eighty-seventh year without ever having abandoned work on the *Cantos*, no one is likely to dispute that fascination. Rather more interesting is the vitality and suppleness of the metaphorical formulation of his autobiography. That he should in his seventy-fifth year tell his interviewer that he began the *Cantos* in the year he met Miss Heyman flies in the face of all bibliographical and manuscript evidence in order to assert the truth that in that year he encountered his first romantic passion, implying an unspoken analogy characteristic of his cryptic style: as Dante's *Commedia* was in a manner begun when he saw Beatrice at the age of nine, so the *Cantos* were begun when Pound met Miss Heyman at the age of nineteen.

I do not think the news, if such it be, that the *Cantos* were inspired by one Katherine Ruth Heyman will throw any light at all on the poem even if much more were learned about Pound's relationship with the lady than is currently known.[6] What does cast some light on the poem is Pound's capacity to resurrect long-abandoned ideas or incidents in order to shape, or even reshape, the history of his life work. Within the poem itself one finds that this 'tangle of works unfinished' (as it is described in canto 116) is, for all its obscurity, incredibly plastic and malleable in Pound's hands, and that the true form of the poem is created retrospectively as he composes new cantos, holding previous ones in his mind.

Thus if the *Cantos* have any unity—and I believe they do—they have the Gothic unity which Wordsworth ascribed to the whole of his poetic canon in the preface to *The Excursion* (1814). Wordsworth does not pursue the analogy, but a Gothic church was commonly built over many generations, under the direction of various master builders, and frequently with many changes of design and construction techniques in the course of its erection. With the church, as with the *Cantos*, each departure in design or technique would necessarily be made to conform in some respect with already completed portions of the edifice lest the whole collapse. The resultant building may be without form or design in the Aristotelian sense, but represents, on the one hand, a fascinating and ingenious balance of forces, and, on the other hand, a complexity which draws the beholder into its indecipherable detail.

The analogy of a Gothic church can only be suggestive of the *Cantos*' structure, and cannot in any sense justify the poem's modes of procedure. The usefulness of the analogy is that it reminds us that the *Cantos*, composed over a period in excess of fifty years, contain the greater portion of Pound's entire poetic accomplishment, and that if they were approached rather in the manner one might approach the collected poetry of Wordsworth or Yeats, more might be revealed of the nature of Pound's achievement than if one were to approach them determined to discover the sort of articulated design apparent in such works as the *Commedia* or *Paradise Lost*.

Pound has encouraged his readers to believe that sooner or later some articulated design would be apparent in the *Cantos*, but that was never possible—largely because he attempted to embrace contemporary history, and it would not hold still for him. He hoped to create the design retrospectively. 'When I get to end, pattern *ought* to be discoverable,' he told John Lackey Brown as late as 1937.[7] To a significant degree Pound has succeeded in creating such a retrospective design, but it is very different in character from what we ordinarily understand by design, and is achieved only imperfectly because Pound does not avail himself of the resources of revision or suppression of already published work—resources that even Wordsworth and Yeats used in creating their Collected Poems.

2. 'THREE CANTOS', 1917

The only extensive revision of already published portions of the

Cantos has been of the first three cantos published in Harriet Monroe's *Poetry* magazine in June, July, and August of 1917. Pound had been two years attempting to get started on his forty-year epic,[8] but even so this beginning proved to be abortive. 'Canto One' of 'Three Cantos' has been entirely discarded, and the balance much revised. However, it remains the document which tells us most about what he had in mind when he set to work on his epic. Indeed, in the Foreword to *Selected Cantos* Pound himself cites the opening lines of 'Canto One' as 'the best introduction to the *Cantos*':

'Hang it all, there can be but one "Sordello"!
But say I want to, say I take your whole bag of tricks,
Let in your quirks and tweeks, and say the thing's an art-form,
Your Sordello, and that the modern world
Needs such a rag-bag to stuff all its thoughts in;
Say that I dump my catch, shiny and silvery
As fresh sardines slapping and slipping on the marginal cobbles?
(I stand before the booth, the speech; but the truth
Is inside this discourse—this booth is full of the marrow of wisdom.)'[9]

These lines form 'the best introduction' not because the *Cantos* are modelled on Browning's *Sordello* as line one implies—they are not—but because they announce that the poem is to have an 'open form', that it is to be merely a rag-bag intended to contain the thought of the modern world. The poet's primary interest is content, not form.

Pound goes on in 'Canto One', in a Browningesque style very like that of 'Scriptor Ignotus', to indicate that he will be as little frightened by anachronisms as Browning was in *Sordello*:

And half your dates are out, you mix your eras;
For that great font Sordello sat beside—
'Tis an immortal passage, but the font?—
Is some two centuries outside the picture.
Does it matter?
                    Not in the least . . .

Not only will Pound's poem mix eras like Browning's, but he will also move about at will from place to place without any pretence of verisimilitude: 'I walk Verona. (I am here in England.)/I see Can Grande. (Can see whom you will.)'. In their definitive version—not achieved for another eight years—the *Cantos* display an indifference toward the unities of time and place much more flagrant than anything Browning dared, but they retain almost no stylistic or formal influence.

None the less, it is worth pausing over *Sordello* if for no other reasons than that Pound was deeply influenced by Browning in his formative years, and did initially choose *Sordello* as the model for his own long poem. 'Canto One' as printed in *Poetry* reveals that he regarded *Sordello* as essentially a spiritual autobiography:

> You had your business:
> To set out so much thought, so much emotion;
> To paint, more real than any dead Sordello,
> The half or third of your intensest life
> And call that third *Sordello*;
> And you'll say, 'No, not your life,
> He never showed himself.'
> Is't worth the evasion, what were the use
> Of setting figures up and breathing life upon them,
> Were 't not *our* life, your life, my life, extended?

When Pound reprinted 'Three Cantos' in the American edition of *Lustra* later in 1917, he emended this passage, removing all reference to the autobiographical nature of either *Sordello* or his own poem. Obviously Pound had decided some time after submitting 'Three Cantos' to *Poetry*, that his own poem would not be autobiographical, but the uncertainty about just what sort of a poem he *was* writing, apparent in these early beginnings, was never entirely overcome. The *Pisan Cantos*, unexpectedly, pathetically, but unmistakably, revive those latent autobiographical dimensions.

The elision of reference to the autobiographical nature of *Sordello* in the *Lustra* version of 'Canto One', and the later complete abandonment of *Sordello* as a model, indicate a movement away from a personal poem toward a poem concerned with public issues such as economics and politics. This movement was slow in developing. But it was already implicit in the choice of *Sordello* as a model. For *Sordello* is itself a historical poem concerned with the relationship between the private individual—in particular, the poet—and the community. Browning places the stress in his poem on the individual's moral dilemma, not contingent upon historical period. 'The historical decoration', Browning tells us, 'was purposely of no more importance than a background requires; and my stress lay on the incidents in the development of a soul.'[10] It is the 'historical decoration', the 'background', however, that most occupies Pound in 'Canto One':

> So, for what it's worth, I have the background,
> And you had a background,
> Watched 'the soul,' Sordello's soul,
> And saw it lap up life, and swell and burst—
> 'Into the empyrean?'

And elsewhere Pound tells us that Browning, like Ovid before him, 'raises the dead and dissects their mental processes; he walks with the people of myth'.[11] He would appear, then, to have chosen *Sordello* as a model at least partly because of the rather unusual manner in which it approaches the past. In this matter there is a complete consistency of purpose between his first start on the *Cantos* and the poem he actually came to write, for the *Cantos* are unmistakably concerned with the past.

Although *Sordello* is itself a very obscure poem, there is a clear statement of theme within it, and it is much closer to the theme of the *Cantos* than might at first be apparent. Browning states his theme in Book III:

> the fate of such
> As find our common nature—overmuch
> Despised because restricted and unfit
> To bear the burthen they impose on it—
> Cling when they would discard it; craving strength
> To leap from the allotted world, at length
> They do leap,—flounder on without a term,
> Each a god's germ, doomed to remain a germ
> In unexpanded infancy, unless . . .
> But that's the story—dull enough confess![12]

The issue in Browning's poem is that we are, each of us, 'a god's germ' and doomed to remain a germ, that is, an unrealized potential, unless events provide us with the unexpected opportunity to realize ourselves. The issue in the *Cantos* is the same except that the unexpected opportunity—if it comes at all—must be seen to realize the potential of a community, not just an individual. The image of the god's germ come to fulfilment in the *Cantos* is the city:

> Great bulk, huge mass, thesaurus;
> Ecbatan, the clock ticks and fades out

The bride awaiting the god's touch; Ecbatan,
City of patterned streets.
(Canto 5/17:21)[13]

The function of the city as an image of the achieved human community in the *Cantos* will be pursued elsewhere. The point that needs to be stressed here is that the notion of a germ of potentiality struggling to realize itself in a hostile or indifferent environment is absolutely central to the imaginative world of the *Cantos*. If there is any key to the *Cantos*, an awareness of this motif, adapted from the thematic focus of *Sordello*, is that key. The ubiquitous gods and goddesses of the *Cantos* represent, in their manifestations, the bursting of that germ or potentiality 'into the empyrean'.

The philosophy of history which underlies the treatment of the past in the *Cantos* is a corollary of Browning's conception of extraordinary human potentiality seldom realized, and is also expressed in *Sordello*:

Hence
Must truth be casual truth, elicited
In sparks so mean, at intervals dispread
So rarely, that 't is like at no one time
Of the world's story has not truth, the prime
Of truth, the very truth which, loosed, had hurled
The world's course right, been really in the world
—Content the while with some mean spark by dint
Of some chance-blow, the solitary hint
Of buried fire, which, rip earth's breast, would stream
Sky-ward![14]

The task of the *Cantos* is precisely to isolate that truth and loose it so as to hurl the world's course right:

I am writing to resist the view that Europe and civilisation is going to Hell. If I am being 'crucified for an idea'—that is, the coherent idea around which my muddles accumulated—it is probably the idea that European culture ought to survive, that the best qualities of it ought to survive along with whatever other cultures, in whatever universality. Against the propaganda of terror and the propaganda of luxury, have you a nice simple answer? One has worked on certain materials trying to establish bases and axes of reference.[15]

Thus, although the definitive *Cantos* retain only a few scattered references to *Sordello*, Browning's poem has had a profound influence on the rationale of the *Cantos*, and, most particularly, on its formulation of the dynamics of human history. But the problem Pound faced in 1917 was not what the subject matter of his poem should be—it was to be about everything; his problem was 'to get a form'. In 'Canto One' Pound, addressing Browning, wonders aloud if *Sordello*'s form will suit his needs:

> So you worked out new form, the meditative,
> Semi-dramatic, semi-epic story,
> And we will say: What's left for me to do?
> Whom shall I conjure up; who's my Sordello,
> My pre-Daun Chaucer, pre-Boccaccio,
> As you have done pre-Dante?
> Whom shall I hang my shimmering garment on;
> Who wear my feathery mantle, *hagoromo*;
> Whom set to dazzle the serious future ages?

He makes no attempt to answer the question until 'Canto Two' which rapidly surveys a number of Provençal and Spanish stories as if in search of some appropriate hero. (Two of these tales are retained in the definitive third canto: El Cid and Ignez da Castro.) None of them seems to suit until we come to the end of the canto and are introduced to an American whose family had supported him for ten years in Paris to study painting:

> And when I knew him,
> Back once again, in middle Indiana,
> Acting as usher in the theatre,
> Painting the local drug-shop and soda bars,
> The local doctor's fancy for the mantel-piece;
> Sheep——jabbing the wool upon their flea-bit backs—
> The local doctor's ewe-ish pastoral;
> Adoring Puvis, giving his family back
> What they had spent for him, talking Italian cities,
> Local excellence at Perugia,
> dreaming his renaissance,
> Take my Sordello![16]

Nothing more is ever heard of this man who would appear to be introduced only to demonstrate the impossibility of finding any contemporary figure capable of being Pound's Sordello. The exclamation mark concluding the quotation would seem to read: 'What am I to do with material such as this?' In any event 'Canto Two' does not bring Pound any closer to the solution to his formal problem.

'Canto Three' recommences the catalogue of candidates for the role of Sordello:

> Another's a half-cracked fellow—John Heydon,
> Worker of miracles, dealer in levitation,
> In thoughts upon pure form, in alchemy,
> Seer of pretty visions ('servant of God and
> secretary of nature');
>
> . . . . .
>
> Thus Heydon, in a trance, at Bulverton,
> Had such a sight:
> Decked all in green, with sleeves of yellow silk
> Slit to the elbow, slashed with various purples.
> Her eyes were green as glass, her foot was leaf-like.
> She was adorned with choicest emeralds,
> And promised him the way of holy wisdom.
> 'Pretty green bank,' began the half-lost poem.
> Take the old way, say I met John Heydon,
> Sought out the place,
> Lay on the bank, was 'plungèd deep in swevyn'
> And saw the company—Layamon, Chaucer—
> Pass each in his appropriate robes;
> Conversed with each, observed the varying fashion.[17]

Like the anonymous man from Indiana, John Heydon disappears from the definitive *Draft of XVI Cantos* (1925). Heydon, however, has the distinction of being reintroduced into the poem fifty-two years later in canto 91 of *Section: Rock-Drill*—an indication of Pound's long memory, and perhaps of his unwillingness ever to discard anything. Obviously Heydon is introduced in 'Canto Three' as part of the public search for a 'form' or model suitable for Pound's modern epic enterprise. The model provided by Heydon is the dream vision, which is a way of walking with the dead very different from Browning's 'meditative, semi-dramatic, semi-epic story'. Since Pound chose to cite an obscure Restoration astrologer as his model for dream vision rather than Dante's *Commedia* (which he will come to invoke frequently as a model for the *Cantos* in the nineteen-thirties and forties), one may assume that he had not given this particular means of entering the past very serious consideration. None the less, the dream vision is invoked as a possible model at this very early stage, and may well have been the model Pound would have preferred had he not feared comparison with the towering figure of Dante. Certainly Dante never seems to be far from Pound's mind when he attempts to provide some rationale for his poem.

Pound closes 'Canto Three' with a translation of the *nekuia*, or calling forth of the dead, from Book XI of the *Odyssey* and a fragment from the hymn to Aphrodite. This is the third suggested model for the poem, and Odysseus the third candidate for the role of Sordello. And it is, of course, with the translation of Odysseus' calling forth of the dead in the Underworld that the *Cantos* now begin. In finally deciding to begin with the *nekuia*, Pound emphasizes very strongly the retrospective nature of his poem, bringing history, which had been a background in *Sordello*, into the foreground. For Odysseus' visit to the Underworld is a visit to the past in order to learn of the future. The *Cantos*, similarly, involve themselves in an investigation and recovery of the past in order to come to an understanding of the present and future—to learn 'the very truth which, loosed, had hurled/The world's course right'.

3. THE EXAMPLE OF *Ulysses* AND *The Waste Land*

Pound probably sent 'Three Cantos' to Harriet Monroe in April of 1917—at any rate, she had them in her possession by 24 April because Pound refers to them in a letter to her written on that date. In the revision undertaken for the reprinting of them in the American edition of *Lustra*—done in October of the same year—he left them essentially unaltered, and continued to press ahead with more cantos to the end of 1919 when he reported to his father, 'Have done cantos 5, 6, 7, each more incomprehensible than the one preceding it; don't know what's to be done about it.'[18] These three cantos, together with the previously published fourth canto, were sent to the *Dial* and subsequently published there (canto 4 in June of 1920, the rest in August of 1921). But Pound appears to have stopped working on the poem at the end of 1919, for nothing is heard of any cantos beyond the seventh until the 'Eighth Canto' appears in the *Dial* in May of 1922 without any prior reference to it in correspondence.

One can only speculate about the reasons for the temporary cessation of work on the *Cantos*. Certainly the dissatisfaction with what he had so far produced, expressed in the letter to his father, must have had something to do with it. And, of course, the *Cantos* were not consuming all of his poetic energy. He wrote 'Homage to Sextus Propertius' in the latter part of 1918, and 'Hugh Selwyn Mauberly' in 1919. In fact, these two works drew much more critical attention and acclaim at the time than did the cantos he had published, and quite properly so, for they were not only complete poems, but rather better ones.

Although it may not have prevented him from getting on with his own life work, during the years Pound was fumbling with the beginning of his poem, he was closely associated with the appearance of two of the great masterpieces of the century, *Ulysses* and *The Waste Land*. He received the first episode of *Ulysses* from Joyce in December of 1917 in his capacity as literary editor of the *Little Review*, and continued to receive the novel episode by episode through to 'Circe' in 1921. Pound was profoundly impressed by *Ulysses*, and cannot have failed to recognize that Joyce had found, in the technique of 'manipulating a continuous parallel between contemporaneity and antiquity', a solution to the problem of achieving encyclopedic comprehensiveness without sacrificing formal coherence. Forrest Read claims that it was in thinking and writing about *Ulysses* that Pound came to understand how to reorganize the *Cantos* into the form established in *A Draft of XVI Cantos* where 'instead of being merely random evocations of the dead, the poem was now motivated by the fictional pattern of a voyage of discovery and by a traditional epic idea, the *nostos* or return home, which Pound made the symbol of an entire theory of history'.[19]

Read may overstate the crucial importance of *Ulysses* in the reformulation of the *Cantos* between 1919 and 1925, but there can be little doubt that Joyce's novel led Pound to the solution of the Odyssean frame. However, as Read recognizes, Pound uses the Homeric parallel merely as a frame without the close structural correspondence maintained by Joyce. And, of course, the translation from *Odyssey*, XI was already included in 'Canto Three', written and published before he had seen any part of *Ulysses*. For Pound, *Ulysses* was essentially a satiric dismissal of the recent past, and therefore remote from his own conception of the epic task which he saw as the recovery of the past for use in the present:

Ulysses is the end, the summary, of a period, that period is branded by La Tour du Pin in his phrase 'age of usury'.

The reader, who bothers to think, may now notice that in the new paideuma I am not including the monumental, the retrospect, but only the pro-spect.

The katharsis of *Ulysses*, the joyous satisfaction as the first chapters rolled into Holland Place, was to feel that here was the JOB DONE and finished, the diagnosis and cure was here. The sticky, molasses-covered filth of current print, all the fuggs, all the foetors, the whole boil of the European mind, had been lanced.[20]

Pound's involvement in helping T. S. Eliot revise *The Waste Land* must have been at least as important an influence on the *Cantos* as was *Ulysses*. He certainly recognized that Eliot had in *The Waste Land* achieved something on the lines of what he had been attempting himself: 'Complimenti, you bitch. I am wracked by the seven jealousies, and cogitating an excuse for always exuding my deformative secretions in my own stuff, and never getting an outline. I go into nacre and objets d'art.'[21] Eliot had applied the lesson of *Ulysses* to poetry, getting an outline which put a minimum of constraint upon the content of his poem. In 'Canto One' Pound had declared that the modern world needed a Browningesque rag-bag to stuff all its thought in. Eliot recognized Joyce's example as a much better solution to the problem of expressing the heteroclite nature of modernity. He saw Joyce's 'mythical method' as 'simply a way of controlling, of ordering, of giving a shape and a significance to the immense panorama of futility and anarchy which is contemporary history'.[22] Now this was precisely Pound's formal problem as he had described it in 'Canto One'.

Quite apart from the complex matter of Pound's editorial revisions of *The Waste Land*, it is sufficiently obvious that Eliot considerably altered the Joycean technique. In the first instance he chose a model, the Grail legend, which possessed no single, clear formulation, and thus considerably diluted the formal imperatives to which Joyce had submitted himself. In the second instance, Eliot made no effort, either in the early or definitive versions, to maintain a close structural correspondence between his own poem and the declared model, as Joyce had done. And finally, Eliot incorporates allusions to other myths, legends and literatures which have a formal status almost equal to that of the Grail legend. The result is a poem of a puzzling fluidity very different from the lapidary stability of

Joyce's architectonics. *The Waste Land* mimes the 'immense panorama of futility and anarchy which is contemporary history'; *Ulysses parodies* it, and one dimension of the parody is the concealed formal structure of scholastic precision.

The *Cantos*, as formulated in *A Draft of XVI Cantos*, follow Eliot's example in the second and third points. There is certainly no possibility of constructing a table of correspondences between all or any section of the *Cantos* and the *Odyssey*, like that which Joyce used. Nor does the *Odyssey* dominate any section of the *Cantos* as a clearly prevailing point of reference. Pound frequently makes the allusive complexity of *The Waste Land* appear remarkably restrained and straightforward by comparison. Unlike Eliot, Pound does choose a well-known, clearly formulated work of art as his frame, but he begins his poem with a fragment from the middle of the *Odyssey*, clearly indicating that he will use it as a point of reference rather than as an elaborate scaffolding as Joyce had done.

With the examples of *Ulysses* and *The Waste Land* behind him, Pound once again began to turn out new cantos beginning early in 1922. According to reports in correspondence[23] he proceeded quite rapidly until he became stuck once again on what was then canto 9, the first of the Malatesta cantos. Myles Slatin argues that in the long struggle with Malatesta, during which a projected single canto expanded to four, Pound found his structural key 'almost inadvertently'.[24] Certainly the device of grouping a block of cantos around a single individual or historical period, which was to become a characteristic of the poem's organization, was developed with the Malatesta group. Previously he had incorporated history into the poem in a much more fragmented manner as in the three cantos published in the *Dial* in August of 1921 (numbered 5, 6, and 7) which are bound together by the figure of Lorenzo Medici,[25] but which include among others the Provençal figure, Peire de Maensac, Eleanor of Aquitaine, and contemporary figures. But the Malatesta cantos provided him only with a device for blocking cantos into groups on the basis of the continuity of treatment of a single subject as with, for example, the Adams cantos or the Chinese cantos. The 'structural key', if one is to use such a term, was provided by the framing device of allusion to the Odyssey suggested by *Ulysses* and refined or altered by *The Waste Land*.

4. 'OUTLINE OF THE MAIN SCHEME'

Although it is reasonable to assume that Pound felt he had solved his formal problems by July of 1923 when he reported that he had revised the beginning of his poem,[26] he apparently thought that some problems were still outstanding for he took the precaution of labelling the first sixteen cantos a 'draft'. And when he came to describe the formal principles underlying his poem a few years later, he was still hesitant, and even apologetic:

Afraid the whole damn poem is rather obscure, especially in fragments· Have I ever given you outline of main scheme : : : or whatever it is?

1. Rather like, or unlike subject and response and counter subject in fugue.

A. A. Live man goes down into world of Dead
C. B. The 'repeat in history'
B. C. The 'magic moment' or moment of metamorphosis, bust thru from quotidien into 'divine or permanent world.' Gods, etc.[27]

When this letter was written to his father, Pound had already prepared a further eleven cantos for publication (also labelled 'draft' when they were published in 1928). In the same year he had explained the scheme to Yeats who was visiting him in Rapallo so that Yeats could publicize the *Cantos* in 'A Packet for Ezra Pound' prefacing the new edition of *A Vision*. Yeats's description did not please Pound, but would seem to be based on information rather similar to that Pound had transmitted to his father:

For the last hour we have sat upon the roof which is also a garden, discussing that immense poem of which but seven and twenty cantos are already published. I have often found there brightly painted kings, queens, knaves, but have never discovered why all suits could not be dealt out in some quite different order. Now at last he explains that it will, when the hundredth canto is finished display a structure like that of a Bach Fugue. There will be no plot, no chronicle of events, no logic of discourse, but two themes, the Descent into Hades from Homer, a Metamorphosis from Ovid, and, mixed with these, medieval or modern historical characters.[28]

Although Yeats probably confuses the issue a little by referring to the descent from Homer as a theme when it would more properly be described as a frame, he does not appear to have distorted seriously the tentative and rather sketchy plan outlined in the letter to Homer Pound. The mixture of medieval and modern historical characters is described in the letter as a 'repeat in history', suggesting an iterative pattern which Yeats's description misses, and the 'Metamorphosis from Ovid' is there described as a 'bust thru from quotidien into "divine or permanent world"' suggesting some revelatory or paradisal motif also missed by Yeats; but, except for the iterative dimension of the historical motif, the two accounts are equivalent descriptions of the structural principles of the *Cantos.*

Yeats goes on in his account to draw a shrewd comparison between Pound's poem and the painting of Porteous Frenhofer, protagonist of Balzac's *Le Chef-D'Oeuvre inconnu.* Frenhofer worked for years on a masterpiece which he permits no one to see. Eventually he shows it to Nicholas Poussin who is amazed to see an indecipherable chaos of lines and colours redeemed only by the illogical emergence from it of a beautifully drawn foot. Yeats would appear to have heard that Cézanne had identified himself with Frenhofer:

> He has tried to produce that picture Porteous commended to Nicholas Poussin in *Le Chef D'Oeuvre Inconnu* where everything rounds or thrusts itself without edges, without contours—conventions of the intellect—from a splash of tints and shades; to achieve a work as characteristic of the art of our time as the paintings of Cézanne, avowedly suggested by Porteous, as *Ulysses* and its dream association of words and images, a poem in which there is nothing that can be taken out and reasoned over, nothing that is not a part of the poem itself.[29]

Pound has not hidden his *chef-d'œuvre*, but Yeats suggests that his own reaction to it is not unlike Poussin's to Frenhofer's painting, and that the *Cantos* are a product of what he regarded as the aesthetic and intellectual anarchy of modern art.

Yeats's estimate has proved to be distressingly accurate. Like Frenhofer, Pound spent his whole life on a 'great work' which he never finished, and which he was never able to bring into a satisfactory order. Again like Frenhofer Pound has hidden from his readers the title and rationale of his work. He has repeatedly enjoined them to wait until it is finished:

> The first 11 cantos are preparation of the palette. I *have to* get down all the colours or elements I want for the poem. Some perhaps too enigmatically and abbreviatedly. I hope, heaven help me, to bring them into some sort of design and architecture later. (1922)

When I get to end, pattern *ought* to be discoverable. Stage set à la Dante is *not* modern truth. (1937)
As to the *form* of *The Cantos*: All I can say or pray is: *wait* till it's there. I mean till I get 'em written and then if it don't show, I will start exegesis. I haven't an Aquinas-map; Aquinas not valid now. (1939)
[In reply to the question: 'Now that you come near the end, have you made any plans for revising the *Cantos* after you've finished?'] I don't know. There's need of elaboration, of clarification, but I don't know that a comprehensive revision is in order. There is no doubt that the writing is too obscure as it stands, but I hope that the order of ascension in the Paradiso will be toward a greater limpidity. (1960)[30]

It would seem that Pound, like the painter who spends so long on the detail of a landscape that it changes its appearance many times through alterations of weather and season, has continuously laboured meticulously over detail while the modern world he sought to capture changed and shifted before him, preventing him from ever bringing the whole into 'some sort of design and architecture'.

Of course, despite occasional expressions of uncertainty about the formal coherence of the *Cantos*—characteristically in response to direct queries about their form—Pound continued to write and publish sections of the poem. He had seventy-one cantos in print by 1940 only fifteen years after he had published the first sixteen. By contrast, ten years separated his commencement of work on the poem and publication of the first sixteen cantos. It would appear, in short, that he was not much troubled by outstanding problems of formal coherence, but was content to go forward on the basis of the Odyssean frame and the mode of operation he had formulated between 1919 and 1923. He obviously believed or hoped that the poem's coherence would not depend upon some scheme or outline, but upon the matter it contained. His ultimate disappointment is that he was unable to bring his poem out of the dark forest of history into the light, which is history made intelligible and redeemable.

There is no intention in these pages to support an argument that Pound did not know what he was doing in composing the *Cantos*. On the contrary, there is a clear consistency of purpose from the earliest beginnings of the poem to its last fragments. But a work which purports to include history and expose the dynamics of human action, both individual and collective—to be, in effect, the epic summation of the contemporary world—is, by its very nature, impossible to plot out neatly in advance. Pound has himself indicated the nature of his difficulty with some awareness of the Quixotic humour of his predicament:

> An epic is a poem containing history. The modern mind contains heteroclite elements. The past epos has succeeded when all or a great many of the answers were assumed, at least between author and audience, or a great mass of audience. The attempt in an experimental age is therefore rash. Do you know the story: 'What are you drawing, Johnny?'
>
> 'God!'
>
> 'But nobody knows what He looks like.'
>
> 'They will when I get through!'
>
> That confidence is no longer obtainable.[31]

Readers of the *Cantos* cannot expect to learn what 'God' looks like, regardless of any hopeful promises Pound might have made them, but they can learn what the poem looks like if they are prepared to look at it as it has grown, altered, and faltered.

II · Love and War

I. THE POETRY OF INFERENCE

ANYONE endeavouring to discuss the *Cantos* is drawn toward one or several of Pound's verbal tags as a means of focusing attention on salient portions of that 'endless, leviathanic' poem. One such tag occurs early in canto 74, the first of the *Pisan Cantos*: 'To build the city of Dioce whose terraces are the colour of stars'. Such a line arrests our attention and resonates throughout the entire midden heap of Pound's 'gothic' epic, making apparent a continuous line of development rising above what had hitherto appeared merely vagrant and haphazard. However, the vagrant and haphazard in the *Cantos* are not so easily muted as one would wish. The suggestion of yet another key to the interpretation of the *Cantos* must then begin with a caveat, a caution that no door will be opened to reveal an interior of inexplicable splendour. The squalor apparent to all readers of the poem cannot be hidden entirely no matter how cunningly illuminated, nor is there an inner sanctum (the long-anticipated *Paradiso*) bathed in a blinding light to which one can retire. At best one can hope for 'A little light, like a rushlight/to lead back to splendour' (116/797).

The key I am offering for consideration is not of the sort that opens doors, but the sort which gives the musician a reference point from which he can determine the precise value of the musical notes written on the page—although no such precision is to be hoped for with respect to the *Cantos*' notation. The poem can be broken down into isolatable images, phrases, quotations, and references which are repeated and sometimes labelled ideograms by Pound and his critics, but it is not possible to assign each of these a precise value which, when they are taken together, would reveal a carefully articulated structure. In short the *Cantos* cannot be read as an enormously extended imagist poem in which the more intellectually weighted ideogram has replaced the essentially emotional image—

despite the probability that Pound originally imagined that they could be read in just that manner.

He began composing the *Cantos* at just about the time he published *Cathay*, a collection of translations from the Chinese, based on the notes of the American sinologist Ernest Fenollosa. Through his study of Chinese poetry and of Fenollosa's speculations on the effect the Chinese ideogrammic method of writing had on the formation of concepts, Pound thought he had discovered a new mode of poetic composition which would make possible a long poem in imagist rhetoric. The Chinese poetry of Li Po which Pound was translating is extremely reticent, achieving its effect through the articulation of significant detail, rather than by means of direct statement or even metaphor. An example is 'The Jewel Stairs' Grievance' from *Cathay*:

> The jewelled steps are already quite white with dew,
> It is so late that the dew soaks my gauze stockings,
> And I let down the crystal curtain
> And watch the moon through the clear autumn.

There is nothing in this four-line poem that it not direct statement. The only departure from direct, unadorned statement is in the word 'grievance' in the title. That word gives the reader the key enabling him to interpret the poem—as Pound does in the note appended to it:

> Jewel stairs, therefore a palace. Grievance, therefore there is something to complain of. Gauze stockings, therefore a court lady, not a servant who complains. Clear autumn, therefore he has no excuse on account of weather. Also she has come early, for the dew has not merely whitened the stairs, but has soaked her stockings. The poem is especially prized because she utters no direct reproach.[1]

Doubtless Pound hoped that his long poem could be read in the same way he read 'The Jewel Stairs' Grievance'. It is presumably such a manner of communication he has in mind when he wrote that the first eleven cantos were a 'preparation of the palette' as cited above. The poem had to establish its own stock situations and approved or disapproved patterns of behaviour. All that he required was a sufficiently attentive reader and sufficient space to enable him to repeat situations and human figures often enough that their typology would become apparent. Of course, he encountered difficulty from the very beginning. In the first place Pound was not, in the *Cantos*, basing his writing on familiar stock situations as Li Po did in 'The Jewel Stairs' Grievance', and in the second place he was attempting a work of very great length and of great complexity. Some of the poems in *Cathay* run to about seventy lines, but none of them approach the seven hundred and seventy *pages* of the *Cantos*.

All of the poems in *Cathay* depend upon the recognition of some familiar or stock situation for their correct interpretation. The situation repeated most often, for example, is the court poet describing the behaviour of the emperor and his court, behaviour that fails to correspond to familiar but unstated Confucian codes. It would seem axiomatic that if the unstated is to be apprehended at all, it must either be familiar to the reader in the first instance, or be made known to him through some mechanism—whether that mechanism be integral to the work or external to it. The technique of the Homeric parallel which Joyce employed for *Ulysses* is one example of an integral mechanism for making the unstated apparent. The parallel between *The Waste Land* and the Grail legend is a somewhat different example of such an integral mechanism. Allusion to a number of other works is another technique, and one which falls somewhere between the integral and external methods;[2] the greater the familiarity with the works to which the allusion is made required of the reader, the less can allusion be regarded as an integral technique. The clearest case of an external mechanism for the creation of stock situations and characters in modern literature is Yeats's *A Vision*, which, as Yeats himself acknowledged, is much less a philosophical system than a storehouse of stock images and situations upon which he could draw in his poetry.

The kind of poetry Pound writes in the *Cantos* could be labelled the poetry of inference, and it is its inferential dimension that it shares with Joyce and Eliot, and, to some extent, with Yeats. Pound himself has described the *Cantos* in just such a way: 'Am leaving the reader, in most cases to infer what he is getting. Though re two cantos there will be a very narrow margin for error.'[3] The margin of error has proved to be too small for most readers, or the labour of inference too great in the absence of any predominant source of contextual relevance. Nor indeed has Pound always left the reader to draw his own inferences. *Guide to Kulchur* and many economic essays of the 1930s have been written for readers of the *Cantos* even though they are addressed to a larger audience. With the aid of these prose glosses the reader knows what inferences to draw, and is left with the task of working backward from a statement about cultural, political, or economic history to the grounds in the poem which imply that statement. Thus our reading of the *Cantos* tends to become the reverse of what it ought to be: a search for illustrative examples in the *Cantos* of this or that general principle or observation instead of the apprehension of recurrent pattern in the series of particulars.

But the *Cantos* do contain within themselves a coherent and consistent metaphorical structure which thus far has gone almost entirely unrecognized, even though most aspects of it have been noted more or less isolated from one another. In conception and function this 'structure' or complex of associations is very similar to that provided for *The Waste Land* by the declared indebtedness to Jessie Weston's *From Ritual to Romance*. By leaning on her study of the Grail legend, Eliot can proceed, confident that his readers will 'know what's up' when he talks about drought and water. He can also be confident that his readers will recognize the appropriateness of repeated reference to various and unpleasant manifestations of sexuality. All readers of Miss Weston's book know about the intimate connection between vegetative abundance and human male potency in the Grail legend, and can make the rather short imaginative leap from sexual and vegetative health or the lack of it to spiritual health or the lack of it.

The metaphorical structure which permits readers of the *Cantos* to draw inferences from what is represented, as readers of *The Waste Land* do, is necessarily more complex, but not entirely dissimilar. The main point of difficulty with the *Cantos* is that Pound has never told his readers where to look—perhaps because he was frightened by the misuse of Miss Weston's book by so many readers of *The Waste Land*. Another likely reason is that Pound has been much more eclectic in his choice of external sources of metaphorical structure, and has therefore necessarily reformulated what he has borrowed, making it all the more likely that an identification of one or more sources would be misleading. Some of these sources will be examined in the following pages as they gradually manifested themselves during the years 1919 to 1925 when the *Cantos* were still undergoing revision and reformulation. Indeed, they never have ceased to undergo reformulation, but after 1925 the first sixteen cantos were established and were never thereafter altered.

2. THE 1919 CANTOS AND *Agamemnon*

We have seen that Pound apparently became stuck with the *Cantos* some time toward the end of 1919 after he had completed seven cantos. The first seven can be divided conveniently into two groups: the first three published in 1917, and the remaining four all completed in 1919, although only canto 4 was published in that year. The last four remain in the definitive poem with their original numbers, and, except for canto 6, without significant alteration from the form in which they were first published. At about the same time he was working on these cantos, Pound was also studying Aeschylus' *Agamemnon*, for he published a commentary on English translations of that tragedy in the January/February number of *The Egoist* for 1919. His comments are not particularly illuminating for readers of the *Cantos*, but the fact that he was reading Aeschylus' rendering of the working out of war guilt among the Achaeans after the Trojan war draws our attention to certain aspects of these four cantos not always stressed. The 1919 cantos are, after all, themselves written in the aftermath of the 1914–1918 war, and Pound may well have thought that he had other than stylistic matters to learn from Aeschylus.

In any event, canto 4, both in the 1920 *Dial* version and in the definitive version, begins with an evocation of the ruined city of Troy, 'Palace in smoky light,/Troy but a heap of smouldering boundary stones', which is reminiscent of the opening scene of the *Agamemnon*, described by Pound as 'the flash of the beacon fires burning unstinted wood, the outburst of *Troia Achaeoon ousan* [Troy is the Greeks']'.[4] Perhaps these lines were not inspired by *Agamemnon*, but canto 5 cites that play in the midst of a rendering of the murders of John Borgia and Alessandro Medici: 'SIGA MAL AUTHIS DEUTERON!' In the definitive version Pound has returned the phrase to the Greek alphabet, but has made no other change despite the fact that it is a rather strange pastiche made up of the chorus's response to Agamemnon's cry when struck by Clytemnestra, and Agamemonn's own speech. The first word (*siga*: silence) is spoken by the chorus: 'Silence! Who is it that crieth out, wounded by a mortal blow?' The rest is from Agamemnon's anguished cry: 'And once again, ay me! I am smitten by a second blow.' The allusion is cryptic in the extreme, but there can be little doubt that Pound is directing us to think of the two Italian Renaissance murders in the context of Agamemnon's murder.

Canto 7 also cites the *Agamemnon* in the opening transitional passage referring back to canto 6, a capsule biography of Eleanor of Aquitaine:

> Eleanor (she spoiled in a British climate)
> "Ἔλανδρος and Ἑλέπτολις, and poor old Homer blind,
>   blind as a bat.

Elandros and *Eleptolis* are two of the epithets Aeschylus has the chorus apply punningly to Helen of Troy: 'Destroyer of men' and 'Destroyer of cities'. Once again it is clear that the reader is expected to see Eleanor, whose name fortuitously maintains the Greek pun, as an analogue of Helen, or at least, operating under the same auspices as Helen.

If we turn back to canto 4 with Aeschylus in mind, we notice that it is dominated by tales of sexual violation and murder, with the added spice of involuntary cannibalism in the first pair: the revenge of Philomela and Procne on Tereus (Eliot's 'barbarous king'), and the less well known tale of Raimon of Roussillon's vengeance on his adulterous wife, Sérémonde, and her lover, Cabestan. Raimon killed Cabestan, cut out his heart and served it to Sérémonde who threw herself from a balcony when she was told what she had eaten. In the other pair of tales, Diana's punishment of Actaeon for secretly gazing on her unrobed virginal charms is coupled with a Provençal tale of Peire Vidal, who disguised himself as a wolf in the excess of his passion for La Louve of Pennautier.[5] Vidal is chased by dogs, but, unhappily, is only wounded and is nursed back to health by La Louve herself. He does not seem to have attained his desire.

These four tales are 'told' in an extraordinarily condensed and interlayered manner which Pound was later to call 'candied'. He was sufficiently pleased with the canto to have had it privately printed as a pamphlet in 1919 for free distribution to his friends, and most readers have found it to be an impressive *tour de force*, although not especially communicative. Indeed, one study of the *Cantos* devotes fifty pages to canto 4 in an effort to unravel its complexities.[6] No such massive explication will be attempted here. It will be sufficient if the main thrust of the canto can be established.

Disregarding the mythic or symbolic possibilities of the two Ovidian tales of violation and metamorphosis crossed with two Provençal tales of adultery and murder, there is a clear—even coarse—parallel between Clytemnestra's murder of her cuckolded husband in *Agamemnon* and these sexually inspired murders. These scenes of violence are private images of the organized violence of war, such as that which reduced the towers of Ilium to 'a heap of smouldering boundary stones'. They are further images of the disorder and moral perversion which follows the destruction wrought by war. The sexual character of the tales is appropriate because Pound, following Aeschylus, remembers that the Trojan war was caused by an adulterous affair, and bred more adultery and family strife.

Canto 5, in fact, introduces a Provençal Troy complete with a Paris, Helen, and Menelaus:

> And Pieire won the singing, Pieire de Maensac,
> Song or land on the throw, and was *dreitz hom*
> And had De Tierci's wife and with the war they made:
> Troy in Auvergnat
> While Menelaus piled up the church at port
> He kept Tyndarida. Dauphin stood with de Maensac.

Pound has condensed to six lines an already very brief *vida* here given in full:

> Peire de Maensac was from Auvergne, a poor knight of the country of the Dauphin. He had a brother named Austor de Maensac—both of them were troubadours. They agreed between themselves that one should have the castle, and the other the poetry. It was Austor who won the castle, and the other the poetry; and he wrote his verses for the wife of sire Bernart de Tierci.
>
> He sang, praised, and served her so well that the lady allowed herself to be carried off by him. He brought her to a castle of the Dauphin d'Auvergne. And the husband made a great fuss with the support of the Church, and made a great war for his wife. But the Dauphin protected the troubadour so well that he never gave her up.
>
> He was a talented man and good company; he made songs, graceful in music and words, and good, entertaining lyrics (*coblas*).[7]

Even with the *vida* before one, Pound's very condensed retelling of the story requires a gloss. *Dreitz hom* is a standard laudatory characterization in the Provençal *vidae*. It translates as 'straight man', but means something more like 'good fellow'. Menelaus is, of course, Helen's husband, the pattern for Bernart de Tierci. Tyndarida is an interesting invention of Pound's as a name for the anonymous wife of de Tierci. The name is presumably formed on an analogy with Tyndaridae, meaning the sons of Tyndareus: Castor and Pollux. Tyndareus was Leda's husband; therefore Helen could also be described as the daughter of Tyndareus even though Zeus was her natural father. Pound thus makes de Tierci's wife, Tyndarida, a namesake of Helen of Troy. But Troy in Auvergnat is not an exact parallel of the Trojan war, for the cuckolded husband is not successful in regaining his wife, and moreover, there is no ruined city or castle. Pound 'corrects' this discrepancy much later in canto 23.

Canto 6 as published in the *Dial* is a rather Browningesque biography of Eleanor of Aquitaine, queen to Louis of France and then to Henry of England, complete with a war and marital infidelity. As it now stands the canto is considerably condensed but not essentially altered. Obviously Eleanor (who is given Helen's epithets) and her story are another analogue of the Trojan war with its ruined city and sexual complications. At least one dimension, then, of cantos 4, 5, and 6 is that they employ that 'repeat in history' which Pound later identified as one of the elements of the *Cantos*. What is repeated is a paradigmatic version of the Trojan cycle in which war would seem to be regarded as just one form of violence rather than an heroic enterprise, and which concentrates on the roles of the two sisters, daughters of Tyndareus, Helen, the temptress, and Clytemnestra the adulterous murderess. Pound, furthermore, highlights the ruinous fate of the city of Troy, reflecting a greater interest in the victims of violence than in the perpetrators of it. The tone, however, particularly of canto 6, is far from sentimental:

> For the fourth family time Plantagenet
> Faces his dam and whelps, . . . and holds Gisors,
> Now Alix' dowry, against Philippe-Auguste
> (Louis' by Adelaide, wood-lost, then crowned at Etampe)
> And never two years sans war.
>   And Zion Still
> Bleating away to Eastward, the lost lamb
> Damned city . . . . .[8]

Canto 7, the last of the 1919 cantos, describes the contemporary world in terms of urban sterility and decay—in some respects anticipating *The Waste Land*—without touching upon the Trojan theme in any way that would have been apparent when it was published in 1921 together with cantos 5 and 6. However, when read together with the 'Eighth Canto' which appeared in the May 1922 number of the *Dial*, it is apparent that this portrait of modernity depends upon the general allusion to the Trojan cycle. The 'Eighth Canto' is now canto 2—virtually unchanged except for the deletion of a transitional 12 lines. There Pound repeats the lines describing Eleanor and Homer quoted above from canto 6, and then paraphrases some fifteen lines from the *Iliad* (III. 146–60):

'Eleanor, ἑλέναυς and ἑλέπτολις!'
            And poor old Homer blind, blind, as a bat,
Ear, ear for the sea-surge, murmur of old men's voices:
'Let her go back to the ships,
Back among Grecian faces, lest evil come on our own,
Evil and further evil, and a curse cursed on our children,
Moves, yes she moves like a goddess
And has the face of a god
            and the voice of Schoeney's daughters,
And doom goes with her in walking,
Let her go back to the ships,
            back among Grecian voices.'

The old men speaking are the Trojan elders watching Helen take the air on the wall of Troy near the Scaean Gate.

The elders are not immune to Helen's beauty, but recognize and fear its power for evil. They are unable to do any more than mumble under their breath being, Homer tells us, old and infirm, although still eloquent speakers. These old men are echoed in canto 7:

The old men's voices, beneath the columns of false marble,
The modish and darkish walls,
Discreeter gilding, and the panelled wood
Suggested, for the leasehold is
Touched with an imprecision . . . about three squares;
The house too thick, the paintings
a shade too oiled.
And the great domed head, *con gli occhi onesti e tardi*
Moves before me, phantom with weighted motion,
Grave incessu, drinking the tone of things,
And the old voice lifts itself
            weaving an endless sentence.

The 'great domed head "with eyes honest and slow"' is Henry James,[9] a man of whom it might be said that he wrote of two cities and, like Homer, of the violence (even if only moral violence) wrought in the sexual relations between them. In any event the contemporary world would appear to be in a threatened position, as Troy was—although it is not clear that the old men recognize it. Of course, the threat in 1919 is moral and cultural decay, not military defeat. Subsequent events in Europe only reinforced the parallel.

The old men in canto 7 do not see Helen or anything like her, but the poet sees a vision of beauty, and responds more in the manner of Actaeon than that of the elders of Troy:

> And all that day
> Nicea moved before me
> And the cold grey air troubled her not
> For all her naked beauty, bit not the tropic skin,
> And the long slender feet lit on the curb's marge
> And her moving height went before me,
> We alone having being.
> And all that day, another day:
> Thin husks I had known as men,
> Dry casques of departed locusts
> speaking a shell of speech . . .
> Propped between chairs and table . . .
> Words like the locust-shells, moved by no inner being;
> A dryness calling for death.

The speaker of these lines does not fear beauty, and is contemptuous of those who do. The implied statement would seem to be that it is better to suffer the fate of Actaeon than to be either insensitive to, or afraid of, the beauty of woman. This canto honours the 'passion to breed a form in shimmer of rain-blur', and not the prudent fear of the Trojan elders or the timid remorse of 'Dido choked up with sobs, for her Sicheus'.

Thus, although Pound uses Aeschylus' *Agamemnon* as a point of reference from which he can plot his own reading of the relationship between society and war, he fundamentally alters Aeschylus' treatment of the roles of Helen and Clytemnestra. The motifs of rape, adultery, and murder, which Pound takes from Aeschylus, are not for him instruments of a tragic destiny, but images of energy perverted and gone wrong; they are domestic images of the communal violence of war. These four 1919 cantos depict the chaotic state of society in the wake of war, the state of society in the fallen, destroyed city. This view is most succinctly conveyed in 'Hugh Selwyn Mauberly' written at the same time:

There died a myriad,
And of the best, among them,
For an old bitch gone in the teeth,
For a botched civilization,

Charm, smiling at the good mouth,
Quick eyes gone under earth's lid,

For two gross of broken statues,
For a few thousand battered books.

Here the focus is on those who died in an unworthy cause, but it is worth noticing that the unworthiness of the *ancien régime* is expressed in terms of sexual ugliness and infertility.

That these stories of rape, murder, and adultery are to be read as images or indices of a general social disorder is made clear later in canto 13, the Confucian canto:

And Kung said, and wrote on the bo leaves:
        If a man have not order within him
He can not spread order about him;
And if a man have not order within him
His family will not act with due order;
        And if the prince have not order within him
He can not put order in his dominions.

Pound wanted violence and disorder in these early cantos because he was depicting *his* post-war world, although he looked primarily to other times and other wars. When beginning research for the Malatesta cantos in 1922 he wrote, for example, 'If I find he [Malatesta] was TOO bloody quiet and orderly it will ruin the canto. Which needs a certain boisterousness and disorder to contrast with his own constructive work.'[10] The reader of the 1919 cantos, then, must be alert to the references to Homer and Aeschylus as a *point d'appui* on which he can raise the apparently random instances of violence and sexual strife into a coherent comment on the contemporary world and the flow of history; just as the Chinese reader of 'The Jewel Stairs' Grievance' may be supposed to interpret the apparently random selection of detail in that poem as a comment on the lover's tardiness or lack of ardour.

3. 'TROY IN AUVERGNAT'

Although he had not, with the 1919 cantos, 'got a form', Pound would appear to have had some fairly clear ideas about his theme and how to handle it. We find the traditional epic theme of love and war, but with an unusual emphasis on love gone wrong—turning to rape and murder. And he uses the Trojan story to provide a loose context for a bewildering array of historical, legendary, and mythical instances of sexual violence. An inspiration for this manner of formulating a great variety of stories from different places and periods may be found in two books Pound reviewed in 1906: *Origine et esthétique de la tragédie* and *Le Secret des Troubadours* by Joséphin Péladan.[11]

Sar Péladan (1858–1918), as he styled himself, was a French Rosicrucian of prodigious literary output, but rather minor fame. As well as *Le Secret des troubadours*, he published *Le Secret des corporations* (1905), *Le Secret de la renaissance de l'humanisme* (1909), and *Le Doctrine de Dante* (1907) all of which are designed to demonstrate the existence of a neo-Platonic form of Christianity of which his Ordre de la Rose Croix du Temple et du Sanct Graal is the modern inheritor. Péladan was neither an original scholar, nor a man of great literary talent. There is very little in Péladan's vast output that, judging from a rather cursory perusal of those works available, Pound could not have found better expressed and more cogently argued in other sources.[12]

His review of Péladan's works was not very favourable. He certainly recognized the kind of crankish mind he was dealing with:

> Peladan usually sees things from the point of view of the day after to-morrow. Unfortunately the day after to-morrow does not always arrive, and the scholar looks upon M. Peladan as the litterateur upon Conan Doyle.[13]

He was, however, rather impressed with the first of the two books:

> Peladan's 'Origine et Esthetique de la Tragedie' (1905) is, however, a contradiction to this being apparently sound, and brim full of clear views on the drama from its Greek beginnings in the Mysteries of Eleusis to the point in literature where Sancho Panza takes unto himself the functions of the chorus of Euripides.

There is no more said of this work in the review. Pound turns to a lengthy dismissal of *Le Secret* whose argument he summarizes:

In 'Le Secret' the derivation of Don Quixote, and the distinctions between that bedraggled hero of La Mancha and Parsifal, are sound and brilliant. Parsifal is the idealist triumphant, the seeker of the Sanc-Graal in enthusiasm. Don Quixote—Cervantes's self in many ways—is the idealist vanquished, the seeker in disappointment. But Peladan invades the realm of uncertainty when he fills in the gap between these two with four centuries of troubadours singing allegories in praise of a mystic extra-church philosophy or religion, practised by the Albigenses, and the cause of the Church's crusade against them.

Pound is impressed by the pairing of Parsifal and Don Quixote in which both are seen as seekers of the ideal—one triumphant, and the other failed. Péladan makes it clear that Quixote's failure is a consequence of the prevailing forces of the period of history in which Cervantes lives. He is the hero who lacks the power to attain the ideal and whose action is therefore limited to the state of dream. This notion of the failed hero, of the man who has some part of the vision, but who cannot bring that vision into reality is fundamental to the *Cantos*, and is most clearly exemplified in the Malatesta cantos. Browning's Sordello was himself such a figure. Of course, neither Malatesta nor Sordello is a comic figure, but there is an unstressed pathos in their situation. Indeed, the whole enterprise of the *Cantos* has a dimension of Quixotic pathos which becomes apparent only in the *Pisan Cantos*, where Pound himself emerges as a failed hero, as the 'idealist vanquished'.

The second aspect of Péladan's argument is of more immediate interest in connection with the 1919 cantos, even though Pound's review expresses an ironic scepticism about the hypothesis 'of a mystic extra-church philosophy or religion' practised by the troubadours and Albigenses. Péladan's argument is that the legend of Parsifal, his search for the Grail, and final rest in triumph and security at Monsalvat is a disguised sacred text of this hypothetical religion. Cervantes is a late *fidèle d'amour*, as one styles adherents to this faith, and he preserves its doctrines in the ironic form of *Don Quixote*. Péladan informs us (accurately) that the Inquisition was established by Innocent III expressly to stamp out the Albigensian heresy, and further that as a consequence of ecclesiastical persecution all the documents relative to this religion are either hidden away or so deviously expressed that only initiates can understand them. The young Pound is not seduced by such arguments. He expresses his scepticism in heavy irony:

Peladan being unable to clinch his *quod erat demonstrandum* declares that the documents proving his point are hidden in the library of the Vatican, because Mother Church does not want the evidence of her crime against the Albigenses brought to light. Considering the present attitude of France toward the monastic orders, this is utterly convincing. And the author proudly proclaims that 'there lies the secret'.

But the scepticism of 1906 seems to have developed into cautious agreement only a few years later in *The Spirit of Romance*:

We must, however, take into our account a number of related things; consider, in following the clue of a visionary interpretation, whether it will throw light upon events and problems other than our own, and weigh the chances in favor of, or against, this interpretation. Allow for climate, consider the restless sensitive temper of our jongleur, and the quality of the minds which appreciated him. Consider what poetry was to become, within less than a century, at the hands of Guinicelli, or of 'il nostro Guido' in such a poem as the *ballata*, ending: 'Vedrai la sua virtù nel ciel salita,' and consider the whole temper of Dante's verse. In none of these things singly is there any specific *proof.* Consider the history of the time, the Albigensian Crusade, nominally against a sect tinged with Manichean heresy, and remember how Provençal song is never disjunct from pagan rites of May Day. Provence was less disturbed than the rest of Europe by invasion from the North in the darker ages; if paganism survived anywhere it would have been, unofficially, in the Langue d'Oc. That the spirit was, in Provence, Hellenic is seen readily enough by anyone who will compare the *Greek Anthology* with the work of the troubadours. They have, in some way, lost the names of the gods and remembered the names of lovers. Ovid and *The Eclogues* of Virgil would seem to have been their chief documents.[14]

Pound has altered Péladan's argument by placing the emphasis on an aesthetic and imaginative continuity rather than a doctrinal one, but there can be no mistaking the outlines of Péladan's hypothesis.

By the 1930s Pound has become much less cautious and devious about this particular reading of history, and now identifies Albigensianism with Eleusis:

One cult that it [the Church] had failed to include was that of Eleusis.

. . . . .

It is equally discernible upon study that some non christian and inextinguishable source of beauty persisted throughout the Middle Ages maintaining song in Provence, maintaining an enthusiasm, maintaining the grace of Kalenda Maya.

And this force was the strongest counter force to the cult of Atys and asceticism. A great deal of obscurity has been made to encircle it. . . . The usual accusation against the Albigeois is that they were Manicheans. This I believe after long search to be pure bunkumb. The slanderers feared the truth. . . .

The best scholars do not believe there were any Manicheans left in Europe at the time of the Albigensian Crusade. If there were any in Provence they have at any rate left no trace in troubadour art.

On the other hand the cult of Eleusis will explain not only general phenomena but particular beauties in Arnaut Daniel or Guido Cavalcanti.[15]

The point to be taken from this is not that Pound relies on Péladan—because he does not—but that Péladan planted a seed in his mind over which he obviously mulled for many years until it took on the aspect of a belief, not only in the existence of an underground mystery cult, but also in the truth of that cult's doctrine in a form which he had himself reconstituted. 'Given the material means,' he wrote in reply to T. S. Eliot's query as to what he believed, 'I would replace the statue of Venus on the cliffs of Terracina. I would erect a temple to Artemis in Park Lane. I believe that a light from Eleusis persisted throughout the middle ages and set beauty in the song of Provence and of Italy.'[16]

Péladan is less talented, but little more eccentric than many another sage or poet of the late Victorian and Edwardian periods in England. He fits well enough into the 'Nineties' beloved of Pound and peopled by aesthetic mystics like Lionel Johnson, George Russell, and W. B. Yeats himself. Pound's enthusiasms seem always to be singular, but he might have found equally wild interests in the more familiar works of Edward Carpenter or Havelock Ellis.[17] He must have been encouraged to entertain Péladan's ideas by his contact with the unusual interests in religious backwaters of G. R. S. Mead, Allen Upward, A. R. Orage, and Yeats.

What Pound takes from Péladan is the conception of this mystery cult—although not the details of its belief—and the idea of formulating history in terms of such a secret cult. In *Le Secret* Péladan identifies the Italian Renaissance as the period of the greatest flowering of 'old Albigensianism':

If one were to study the hidden meaning of Medieval literature, the Renaissance would no longer appear to be a sudden resurrection of antiquity.

Neo-platonism had already penetrated profoundly our novels of adventure, and when it showed itself openly under the Medicis, it was because they assured it of effective protection against the Roman inquisition.

Gemisto Plethon and Marsilio Ficino are the official teachers of old Albigensianism, as Dante is the prodigious Homer.

Fiction and history correspond on this subject with singular parallelism: is not the order of Templars a realization of the order of Templars a realization of the order of the Grail, and does not Monsalvat have a real name, Monségur.[18]

Pound's interest in the Medicis, Renaissance neo-Platonists, and Dante corresponds to Péladan's, although it hardly needs such a model to explain it. But the idea of fiction and history corresponding is one that Pound most probably did borrow from him. We have seen Pound using the Trojan story, and other legends or 'fictions' in the 1919 cantos to establish a paradigmatic story to which history can be made to conform—as he subsequently does with the history of Malatesta. In canto 5 he told the story of the war which developed between Peire de Maensac and Bernart de Tierci as an analogue of the Trojan war. In canto 23 he repeats that tale at greater length, this time interweaving it with bona fide history:

And my brother De Maensac,
Bet with me for the castle,
And we put it on the toss of a coin,
And I, Austors, won the coin-toss and kept it,
And he went out to Tierci, a jongleur
And on the road for his living,
And twice he went down to Tierci,
And took off the girl there that was just married to Bernart.

And went to Auvergne, to the Dauphin,
And Tierci came with a posse to Auvergnat,
And went back for an army
And came to Auvergne with the army
But never got Pierre nor the woman.
And he went down past Chaise Dieu,
And went after it all to Mount Segur,
    after the end of all things,
And they hadn't left even the stair,
And Simone was dead by that time,
And they called us the Manicheans
Wotever the hellsarse that is.

In this expanded version Pound sticks to the *vida* quoted above (except that he makes Austors de Maensac the speaker), until we are told that Pierre 'went down past Chaise Dieu,/And went after it all to Mount Segur'. Montségur (as it is more usually written) was the fortress temple of the Albigenses. It was destroyed in 1244 in the last great battle of the crusade against the Albigenses, begun in 1209 and officially concluded in 1249 with the heresy efficiently suppressed. The crusade virtually destroyed the brilliant culture of Provence, whose most precious flower was the song of the troubadours. Pound is here unmistakably adopting Péladan's hypothesis that the singers of *gay savoir*, like de Maensac, were themselves Albigenses. Certainly there is no justification either in history or legend for supposing that de Maensac was at Montségur—either at its fall or afterwards. But de Maensac's story corresponds to the crusade itself in that with the support of the Dauphin he fought a great war against the husband, de Tierci, who had the support of the Church. And this correspondence is not entirely in the wilds of the minds of Pound and Péladan, for a modern, scholarly edition of Provençal *vidae* also draws attention to the peculiarity of de Maensac's *vida*:

We have collected this life of Peire de Maensac—partly because it is succinctly related—because it offers us an example—real or imaginary—of that which might be the brotherhood among the 'fidèles d'amour' (connected to the literary brotherhood) of which the entire century has postulated the existence. Is it not curious to see a great lord, Dauphin d'Auvergne, taken with courtly love and a poet himself, take up arms to defend the 'right' of an adulterous love of a troubadour against the rights of the husband . . . and of the Church?[19]

III · A Light from Eleusis

I. 'THE STONE PLACE'

POUND'S stated belief 'that a light from Eleusis persisted throughout the middle ages and set beauty in the song of Provence and of Italy', goes beyond anything he found in *Le Secret des troubadours* in that it links the cult of *amor* with the ancient Athenian mysteries. The notion of some connection between the Provençal singers of *gay savoir* and the Albigenses is, as we have seen, a persistent if minority view. And, of course, it is undisputed that Dante and the Italian *dolce stil nuovo* are heavily indebted to their Provençal predecessors. But the further identification of this late-medieval complex of associations with the Mysteries is, so far as I can determine, peculiar to Pound.[1]

It seems likely that he was led to make this further link by the other book of Péladan's he reviewed in 1906, *Origine et esthétique de la tragédie*. In his review Pound tells us that Péladan traces Greek drama from its beginnings in the mysteries of Eleusis, but he has little to say about the book beyond that it is 'sound and brim full of clear views'. Since, in fact, the book is brim full of misinformation and tendentious views, it seems safe to assume that Pound was at the time not very well informed on the subjects of Greek drama and the Mysteries. He accepts without cavil Péladan's assertion that Greek drama originated in the Eleusinian festival when all authorities agreed that the drama was associated with the Dionysian festival, which took place in the spring, and not the very different festival of Eleusis, which took place in the autumn. Péladan appears to confuse the two festivals—perhaps because Dionysus also had a role in the Mysteries.

From the book Pound would have learned that the two principal divinities of the Mysteries were Demeter and Dionysus. The former Péladan identifies with the Christian *Mater Dolorosa*—not a wild association since her role in the Mysteries is that of the grieving mother of Persephone, who has been carried off by Pluto, god of the

Underworld. He identifies Dionysus with joy and exaltation. The essence of the Mysteries, according to Péladan, is a ritual encounter with death (personified by Persephone who has eaten of a pomegranate seed in the Underworld) by the worshippers, who are in a psychological state compounded of both joy and sorrow. All of this is accurate enough in a general sort of way, although he overemphasizes the role of Dionysus, and virtually ignores Persephone, who would seem to be the most important divinity in the rites.

Pound's failure to detect the errors and tendentious views in *Origine et esthétique de la tragédie* would tend to support the opinion that he was introduced to the Greek Mysteries by this book. And, even though Péladan scarcely mentions *gay savoir*, Pound could hardly have missed noticing the similarity between the beliefs ascribed to the worshippers at Eleusis and those attributed to the Albigenses in *Le Secret des troubadours*. Nonetheless, in adopting the outlines of *Le Secret* in 'Psychology and Troubadours', Pound associates Provençal song with 'the pagan rites of May Day', and not with Eleusis. It is not until his statement in 'Credo' (1930) that he mentions Eleusis in this connection—or, indeed, in any other connection.

Just where Pound got the idea of associating Eleusis with the Albigenses and the cult of *amor* is of no particular importance in itself. But the association is so unusual that one is almost compelled to look for some source. And if Péladan is indeed the source for it, then we can be confident that the idea of a continuity of belief reaching from Eleusis through Provence and Dante himself had been planted in Pound's mind long before his first mention of it, and even several years before he began composition of the *Cantos*.

Since he would have learned from Péladan that some kind of encounter with the dead was at the very centre of the Eleusinian rites, it is at least possible that he had Eleusis in mind when he incorporated a translation of the *nekuia* from the *Odyssey* in 'Three Cantos'. Indeed, we have seen that in 'Three Cantos' Pound was trying various models for his poem, each of which permitted him to walk with the dead. Of course, we may regard the *nekuia* as simply a metaphorical means of entering the past. But even in 'Canto One', he writes of gods and goddesses in a manner alien to a primarily historical bias:

> . . . *O Virgilio mio*, and gray gradual steps
> Lead up beneath flat sprays of heavy cedars,

Temple of teak wood, and the gilt-brown arches
Triple in tier, banners woven by wall,
Fine screens depicted, sea waves curled high,
Small boats with gods upon them,
Bright flame above the river! Kwannon
Footing a boat that's but one lotus petal,
With some proud four-spread genius
Leading along, one hand upraised for gladness,
Saying, 'Tis she, his friend, the mighty goddess!'
Paean![2]

Indeed, this passage from 'Canto One' has much more to do with some sort of paradisal vision than with history. It is not retained in *A Draft of XVI Cantos*, but is replaced by the similarly visionary and aquatic second canto (originally eighth in the sequence), and the gray steps and cedars are incorporated into the first part of canto 3: 'Or, the gray steps lead up under the cedars',[3] These stone steps are of some interest because when they next appear they are clearly identified as leading into (and presumably also out of) the Underworld:

Then light air, under saplings,
the blue banded lake under aether,
an oasis, the stones, the calm field,
the grass quiet,
and passing the tree of the bough
The grey stone posts,
and the stair of grey stone,
the passage clean-squared in granite:
descending,
and I through this, and into the earth,
patet terra,
entered the quiet air
the new sky,
the light as after a sun-set.
(16/69:73)

In this account he would appear to be borrowing from both Dante and Virgil; although he is faithful to neither.[4] Pound has described canto 16 as a Purgatorio: 'You have had a hell in Canti XIV, XV; purgatorio in XVI etc.'[5] But the passage cited conforms more easily to a simple descent into the underworld than it does to a movement from Hell to Purgatory.

One of the problems of interpretation facing readers of the *Cantos* is that of the function of the *nekuia* of canto 1. Clearly it establishes the retrospective or historical aspect of the poem, but at the same time it introduces the reader immediately into the divine metamorphic world of canto 2. Moreover, in *A Draft of XVI Cantos* Pound concludes canto 1 with the phrase 'So that' followed by a full colon, suggesting that the balance of the poem is somehow a consequence of this initial descent. That 'So that' is picked up in the first line of *A Draft of Cantos 17–27*, introducing a canto which Pound himself has described as 'a sort of paradiso terrestre'.[6] Neither Homer nor Dante provide a model for a descent which leads directly to a 'paradiso terrestre'. Dante's Earthly Paradise is not encountered until he reaches the top of the Mount of Purgatory in the twenty-eighth canto of the *Purgatorio*—although the first circle of Hell has some of the characteristics of an earthly paradise. There is nothing paradisal about Homer's Underworld. Only Aeneas *descends* into a paradisal world, and even he first encounters places of punishment.

It is well known that Virgil is not placed high in the Poundian canon of great writers. His attitude to the great Latin poet is perhaps most succinctly expressed in an anecdote he attributes to Yeats:

> A plain sailor man took a notion to study Latin, and his teacher tried him with Virgil; after many lessons he asked something about the hero.
> Said the sailor: 'What hero?'
> Said the teacher: 'What hero, why, Aeneas, the hero.'
> Said the sailor: 'Ach, a hero, him a hero? Bigob, I t'ought he waz a priest.'[7]

Still, Book VI of the *Aeneid* has long been regarded as the literary description of a descent into the Underworld most closely conforming to the Eleusinian rites, and Pound most assuredly would have been aware of this. Thus the phrase '*O Virgilio mio*' which begins the passage from 'Canto One' cited above—even though it is in Italian—may well be taken as a reference to the *Aeneid* as much as to the *Commedia*.

In 'Canto One' the gray steps lead upward between walls depicting sea waves and boats with gods upon them until the concluding announcement, 'Tis she, his friend, the mighty goddess'. In canto 17 we appear to be moving downward, and there are no gray steps. There are, however, gods and boats, and, most importantly, the wondrous appearance of a goddess:

Cave of Nerea,
she like a great shell curved,
And the boat drawn without sound,
Without odour of ship-work,
Nor bird-cry, nor any noise of wave moving,
Nor splash of porpoise, nor any noise of wave moving,
Within her cave, Nerea,
she like a great shell curved.
(17/76:80)

This 'Nerea' of canto 17 appears nowhere else in the poem, and would appear to be an invention of Pound's—some kind of marine goddess. Her shell, however, is reminiscent of Aphrodite's in the famous Botticelli painting, *La Nascita*, a painting Pound invokes in 'Canto One'.

If Botticelli
Brings her ashore on that great cockle-shell—
His Venus (Simonetta?),
And Spring and Aufidus fill all the air
With their clear-outlined blossoms?[8]

This manifestation of a goddess (whether Aphrodite or some other) is surely the 'bust thru from quotidien into "divine or permanent world"' identified by Pound as the third 'subject' of the *Cantos*. It is clear that such a theophany was not a later development in Pound's plans because we find it already in the earliest available draft. The status and function of this theophany is, however, less clear. If we accept it as a *paradiso terrestre*, we wonder why it comes so early in the poem and in such a form.

Some of these questions can be answered once it is recognized that Pound has the Eleusinian Mysteries in mind. At Eleusis the candidates descended a few steps into the Telesterion or inner temple in order to take part in the nocturnal celebration of the sacred mysteries. In the temple the hierophant would preside over the *epopteia*, or 'showing forth', which must have been some kind of theophany, accompanied by a great fire. The Mysteries are based upon the myth of the rape of Persephone by Pluto—or, perhaps more accurately, the myth serves to explain in a veiled manner the nature of the Mysteries.[9] The principal divinities are Demeter, her daughter, Persephone, whose mystic name is Koré (daughter), and Pluto or chthonic Dionysus (or father Zagreus and son Zagreus, husband and reading of canto 17

child of Persephone). Hermes, as psychopomp and messenger, also has a role in the ritual. Aphrodite, Athena, and Semele were added to the list by graphic artists in Hellenic times.

In canto 17 Pound inserts the chant, in capitals 'ZAGREUS! IO ZAGREUS!' at line six. Lines nine and ten introduce Artemis as 'the goddess of the fair knees'. Line twenty informs us either that it is night or that we are in the Underworld: 'The light now, not of the sun'. On the next page (line 48) Hermes and Athene are mentioned. On the bottom of the third page of the canto Athene, Aletha, and Koré appear in the company of dancers (there is a dancing-floor around a fountain just outside the Telesterion at Eleusis):

> Now supine in burrow, half over-arched bramble,
> One eye for the sea, through that peek-hole,
> Gray light, with Athene.
> Zothar and her elephants, the gold loin-cloth,
> The sistrum, shaken, shaken,
> the cohorts of her dancers.
> And Aletha, by bend of the shore,
> with her eyes seaward,
> and in her hands sea-wrack
> Salt-bright with the foam.
> Koré through the bright meadow,
> with green-gray dust in the grass:
> (17/78:82)

Nerea, Zothar, and Aletha are probably inventions of Pound's; at any rate, they have nothing to do with Eleusis. All of the other divinities, however, do belong in the Mysteries, and Zagreus and Koré are designations peculiar to Eleusis. The *mise en scène* of the canto is also of interest. The scene appears to be a meadow or grove near 'cities set in their hills' at the edge of the sea, and we seem to move through this landscape toward a cave in a sea-cliff:

> cliff green-gray in the far,
> In the near, the gate-cliffs of amber,
> And the wave
> green clear, and blue clear,
> And the cave salt-white, and glare-purple,
> cool, porphyry smooth,
> the rock sea-worn.

But this is no ordinary seaboard landscape, for we are told that there is 'No gull-cry, no sound of porpoise,/Sand as of malachite, and no cold there,/the light not of the sun'.

It is not possible to identify either the ceremony or the scene in canto 17 with what is known of the Eleusinian rites, despite the presence of divinities associated with Eleusis (who are only mentioned and not given any specific roles). Another passage, at the end of canto 21, suggests an Eleusinian context for itself more clearly:

> Yellow wing, pale in the moon shaft,
> Green wing, pale in the moon shaft,
> Pomegranate, pale in the moon shaft,
> White horn, pale in the moon shaft, and Titania
> By the drinking hole,
>   steps, cut in the basalt.
> Danced there Athame, danced, and there Phaethusa
> With colour in the vein,
> Strong as with blood-drink, once,
> With colour in the vein,
> Red in the smoke-faint throat. Dis caught her up.
>
> (21/100:104)

The pomegranate is the fruit Persephone eats in the Underworld making it impossible for her to return to the world of the living. The repetition of 'pale in the moon shaft' identifies the scene as nocturnal. The stone steps from cantos 3 and 16 recur here. The final line alludes to the rape of Persephone by Dis or Pluto, which is, of course, the core of the myth associated with Eleusis. There is dancing, also appropriate to Eleusis. And, finally, Pound alludes to the blood drink of Odysseus which enabled him to communicate with the dead.

The 'white horn' is the 'turris eburnea' (tower of ivory) of Phoibos invoked on the previous page and elaborated in canto 29:

>   Let us consider the osmosis of persons
> nondum orto jubare;[a]
> The tower, ivory, the clear sky
> Ivory rigid in sunlight
> And the pale clear of the heaven
> Phoibos of narrow thighs,
> The cut cool of the air,
> Blossom cut on the wind, by Helios
> Lord of the Light's edge, and April
> Blown round the feet of the God, . . .
>
> (29/145:150)

[a] before sunrise.

Here, the tower of ivory is clearly a phallic emblem, and is identified with Phoibos, the sun in its fructifying aspect. It is manifest as a shaft of light visible just before the sun's appearance at dawn. It may be that Pound interprets the burst of light manifest in the *epopteia* at Eleusis as the sunrise itself. In any event, he combines this phallic dimension of the sun's light with Odysseus' initiation into the world of the dead in canto 39. (Titania is Circe, a goddess who has no role at Eleusis, but who is, as it were, the psychopomp for Odysseus' visit to the Underworld.)

It is possible to identify the scene from canto 17 with that of canto 39:

> From star up to the half-dark
> From half-dark to half-dark
>   Unceasing the measure
> Flank by flank on the headland
>   with the Goddess' eyes to seaward
> By Circeo, by Terracina, with the stone eyes
>   white toward the sea
> With one measure, unceasing:
>   'Fac deum!' 'Est factus.'
> Ver novum!
>   ver novum!
> Thus made the spring,
> Can see but their eyes in the dark
>   not the bough that he walked on.
>
> (39/195:203–4)

The crucial signature which associates this passage with that from canto 17 is the line, 'with the Goddess' eyes to seaward'. In canto 17 it is simply 'with her eyes seaward', but this echo, taken together with the repetition of characteristics of the *mise en scène* of canto 17 such as the headland, the dance, and the 'half-dark', establishes beyond much doubt that we are encountering the same event in canto 39 as in canto 17.

It may seem excessively zealous to insist upon the identity of the events described or evoked in these two cantos, but it must be remembered that Pound is leaving the reader to infer a great deal after the manner of traditional Chinese poetry. In such poetry the information from which one draws inferences should be unobtrusive, but precise. A verbal signature such as 'with eyes seaward' is one such precise repetition, and, slender reed that it is, great weight may be placed upon it.

The signature, in fact, is a little more complex involving all the elements of the three lines: 'with the Goddess' eyes to seaward/By Circeo, by Terracina, with the stone eyes/white toward the sea.' Circeo is a promontory forming the north-western headland of the gulf of Gaeta in Italy. From the sea it appears to be an island, and is traditionally identified with Circe's island, Aeaea. Victor Bérard follows this traditional identification in *Les Phéniciens et l'Odyssée*—the work Joyce used in working out many of the Homeric parallels in *Ulysses*. Terracina is a town a few miles to the east along the coast of the gulf. Hence the topography suggests that the goddess in question is Circe.

However, elsewhere it is clear that the goddess at Terracina is Aphrodite (or her Roman equivalent, Venus): 'Given the material means I would replace the statue of Venus on the cliffs of Terracina', Pound declared in 'Credo'. There has never been a statue to Venus on the cliffs of Terracina. The ruins of two temples are still to be found in the region—a temple dedicated to Jove on the cliffs, and one dedicated to a pre-Roman goddess, Feronia, on the rock of Circeo. Bérard identifies Feronia as the prototype of Circe, and cites one de Blanchère to the effect that she was assimilated to Prosperine and identified with Koré, the virgin daughter of Demeter—that is to say, Proserpine before her rape by Pluto.[10] About all that is known for certain about Feronia is that slaves were brought to her temple for the performance of a rite of manumission—a rite Bérard sees mimed in Odysseus' freeing of his men from Circe's enchantment.

Within the *Cantos* the goddess whose eyes face seaward at Terracina is not clearly identified until canto 74:

> as by Terracina rose from the sea Zephyr behind her
> and from her manner of walking
> as had Anchises[11]
> till the shrine be again white with marble
> till the stone eyes look again seaward.
> (74/435:461–2)

It is, of course, Aphrodite—or, rather, Venus—that Anchises, the father of Aeneas, identified by her walking. In the *Pisan Cantos* Aphrodite draws all the goddesses to herself. She becomes *Dea, the* Goddess, and it is her theophany that is celebrated at Eleusis. To put it another way, the Goddess appears in various aspects. Aphrodite is her most sublime aspect, and Circe is a more threatening and chthonic aspect.

From this long chain of inference, then, we can conclude that canto 17 celebrates the theophany of Aphrodite—either in her real presence, or as a statue—and further that Pound is conflating Odysseus' encounter with Circe and the Eleusinian nights. The seaboard landscapes of both cantos 17 and 39 are probably to be identified with the shore line between Circeo and Terracina. Pound doubtless knew the area, and in any case could have found photographs of sea caves and cliffs in Bérard.

The best authorities agree that a theophany of Aphrodite did not form part of the *epopteia*,[12] but Foucart mentions the opinion of Ch. Lenormant, shared by several others, that the manifestation of Aphrodite did form the climax of the *epopteia*.[13] It is impossible to determine just how much Pound knew about Eleusis when he wrote canto 17 (about 1924)—or, indeed, at any other time. And, of course, he was at liberty to adapt what he did know to suit his own purposes, since he did not acknowledge any relationship between the Mysteries and his poem until 1930. In fact, he seems to have made no distinction, as late as 'Terra Italica' (1931), between May Day celebrations sacred to Aphrodite, and Eleusis. He quotes the *Pervigilium Veneris* in canto 39, but speaks of 'Spring overborne into summer/late spring in the leafy autumn' in an apparent attempt to fuse the spring rites of May Day with the autumn rites of Eleusis.

The strongest link between the theophanies of cantos 17 and 39, and Eleusis is in the fact that they are both associated with Odysseus' encounter with Circe, an encounter that leads to the Underworld. The last lines of canto 17 lead us to the Underworld where we have been preceded by the three dead men, Borso, Carmagnola, and Malatesta:

> 'For this hour, brother of Circe.'
> Arm laid over my shoulder,
> Saw the sun for three days, the sun fulvid,
> As a lion lift over sand-plain;
>   and that day,
> And for three days, and none after,
> Splendour, as the splendour of Hermes,
> And shipped thence
>   to the stone place,

Pale white, over water,
known water,
And the white forest of marble, bent bough over bough,
The pleached arbour of stone,
Thither Borso, when they shot the barbed arrow at him,
And Carmagnola, between the two columns,
Sigismundo, after that wreck in Dalmatia.
Sunset like the grasshopper flying.

Such a visit to the Underworld is the touchstone for Eleusis. All authorities agree on the preoccupation of the Mysteries with the life after death, and on the chthonic character of its rites—although Farnell argues against there being some kind of enactment of a visit to the dead in the Telesterion.

Foucart, whom Pound may well have consulted, argues forcefully that central to the rites is exactly an encounter with the dead, and perhaps with Persephone, Queen of the Underworld herself. And he is supported in this contention by Kerenyi's recent book on Eleusis. Foucart cites a number of classical texts to support his argument, including Heracles' claim that he was able to visit the Underworld and return unharmed because he had been initiated into the Mysteries. But the most interesting text for a reader of the *Cantos* is from Plutarch, who is comparing the sensations and experiences of the soul at the moment of death to those of the Eleusinian novice:

[There are at first] chance directions, difficult detours, disquieting and endless walks through the darkness. Then, before the end, complete terror; one is overcome by shivering, trembling and breaks out into a cold sweat. But then a marvellous light bursts before one's eyes, and one walks in pure meadows where voices echo and figures dance. Sacred words and divine apparitions inspire a religious respect. At that time, the man, from then perfect and initiated, becomes free and holy and moving about without restraint celebrates the Mysteries, a crown on his head. He lives with pure and holy men, and sees on earth the crowd of those who are not initiated and purified, crush and jostle themselves in the mud and darkness, and because of fear of death, remain among evils from failure to believe in the joy of the beyond.[14]

I have no evidence that Pound read this passage, but since it is cited by both Foucart and Farnell, and is characterized as well known by Foucart, it is likely that he did come across it or at least that whatever commentaries he did read would have drawn upon it. From Plutarch's description one sees the Eleusinian experience as a difficult and aimless journey concluded by a marvellous revelation, which in turn transports one into a paradisal landscape and transforms one's personality so that those ordinary mortals around one appear to be mired in darkness. Had Pound read this account of the Eleusinian experience, could he have resisted reading it as the germ of Dante's *Commedia*? Did not Péladan tell him that Dante was the prodigious Homer of old Albigensianism, a cult Pound himself identified with Eleusis?

In any case, the whole matter of Odysseus' descent is altered by cantos 17, 39 and 47 into something quite remote from anything to be found in the *Odyssey*—an alteration already foreshadowed in canto 1 by the evocation of Aphrodite as a psychopomp, 'bearing the golden bough of Argicida'.[15] Pound transforms Aphrodite into a psychopomp because in his version of Eleusis it is by means of the rites of the goddess of love that one procures entry into the Underworld. It is after Odysseus, protected by Hermes' *moly*, couples with Circe that he is able to visit the Underworld and return. In canto 39 Odysseus' conquest of Circe is seen as a triumph over sexuality itself —not by the chaste restraint of the Red Cross Knight or other questing heroes, but by withstanding her enchantments and exacting a promise from her that she will not unman him if he goes to bed with her.

Canto 39 begins with the song of Circe and then the voice of Elpenor speaking with a coarseness unique in the poem:

> When I lay in the ingle of Circe
> I heard a song of that kind.
>   Fat panther lay by me
> Girls talked there of fucking, beasts talked there of eating,
> All heavy with sleep, fucked girls and fat leopards,
> Lions loggy with Circe's tisane,
> Girls leery with Circe's tisane.

Obviously the swinishness of Odysseus' men, as seen by one of those transformed, is a kind of Hugh Hefner paradise of sensual fatigue. Even though her dreadful drugs do not work on Odysseus, Circe offers him the delights already afforded to his men: 'Nay, come, put up thy sword in its sheath, and let us two then go up into my bed, that couched together in love we may put trust in each other.'[16] Pound cites a fragment from Circe's offer, 'Euné kai philoteti ephata Kirkh' ('couched together in love'), and from Odysseus' cautious reply, 'es thalamon' ('into the bedroom'), and paraphrases her offer: 'Discuss this in bed said the lady'.

Pound indicates nothing of Odysseus' caution, but telescopes two hundred and sixty of Homer's lines into six of his own:

> 'I think you must be Odysseus . . .
> feel better when you have eaten . . .
> Always with your mind on the past . . .
> Ad Orcum autem quisquam?
> nondum nave nigra pervenit . . .
> Been to hell in a boat yet?'[17]

Thus he brings very close together the offer of bed and the voyage to the Underworld. Indeed, what would appear to be a descent, combined with elements of May Day celebrations, immediately follows Circe's question:

> Sumus in fide
> Puellaeque canamus
> sub nocte. . . .
> there in the glade
> To Flora's night, with hyacinthus,
> With the crocus (spring
> sharp in the grass,)
> Fifty and forty together[18].

However, this dance/descent, which incorporates the manifestation of a goddess, rather surprisingly modulates into a symbolical evocation of the act of copulation, as if Odysseus' visit to Circe's bed were not so much the prelude to a descent as the descent itself:[19]

> Beaten from flesh into light
> Hath swallowed the fire-ball
> A traverso le foglie
> His rod hath made god in my belly
> Sic loquitur nupta
> Cantat sic nupta
>
> Dark shoulders have stirred the lightning
> A girl's arms have nested the fire,
> Not I but the handmaid kindled
> Cantat sic nupta
> I have eaten the flame.

Taking cantos 17 and 39 together, then, we find a close association between the Odyssean descent and the theophany or 'bust thru from quotidien into "divine or permanent world"'. This dimension can be fairly identified as Eleusinian so long as one remembers that the connection with Eleusis is allusive and not accurate in detail. Since the descent leads to a kind of *visio beatifica* as in the Eleusinian rites, the Eleusinian allusion provides a bridge between the *Commedia* and the *Odyssey* so far as their relevance to the *Cantos* is concerned. For, in the *Commedia* as in the *Cantos*, a 'live man goes down into the world of the dead', sees the 'repeat in history' of crimes, sins, errors, failures and triumphs, and is finally rewarded with the beatific vision. Dante's vision concludes his poem; the reader does not accompany him on his return to the world of men.

In the *Cantos* the vision is frequently foretasted—as it is not in the *Commedia*—because the *Cantos* is not processional like the *Commedia*, but convoluted and reflexive. Once we have made the descent with Odysseus in canto 1, we are in a fluid and Protean world. We are, of course, in the Underworld where 'chance directions, difficult detours, disquieting and endless walks through the darkness' confuse and frighten us. And it is Odysseus' *periplus*, or tortuous sea-coasting journey, that is the metaphor for these Underworld wanderings. The *nostos*, or homeward journey which Forrest Read sees as the relevant Odyssean parallel does not, I think, apply to the *Cantos*.[20] Penelope and Ithaca have no roles in Pound's epic.

Pound announced early in the poem that it would not move processionally, like the *Commedia*, toward a concluding and all-encompassing vision, but would be more fragmentary and indirect with the vision omnipresent but fugitive:

> Measureless seas and stars,
> Iamblichus' light,
>   the souls ascending,
> Sparks like a partridge covey,
>   Like the 'ciocco', brand struck in the game.
> 'Et omniformis': Air, fire, the pale soft light.
> Topaz I manage, and three sorts of blue;
>   but on the barb of time.
> The fire? always, and the vision always,
> Ear dull, perhaps, with the vision, flitting
> And fading at will.
>
> (5/17:21)

Hence Aphrodite appears already in the first canto, and the second canto moves immediately to a pantheist aquatic landscape and theophany of Dionysus as told by Ovid. The early appearance of Dionysus, and the nature of his appearance does not fit neatly into the notion that it was the Eleusinian descent which Pound had in mind as his informing model. However, Dionysus has his role at Eleusis, in the procession from the Agrai to Eleusis where one of his names, Iacchos, is shouted by the procession. He probably also had a role in the Telesterion as both the adult husband (Zagreus) of Persephone and her infant son (Dionysus). However, it must be admitted that Ovid's story has nothing to do with Eleusis, but it is a mythical account of the establishment of the worship of Dionysus in his own right in Greece.

A very early poem from *A Lume Spento*, 'Salve O Pontifex', lends credence to the supposition that Pound was aware of Dionysus' association with Eleusis, or, at least, that he thought of him in connection with Persephone's story, central to Eleusis. Much of the seaboard imagery of the *Cantos* is already present in this poem published in 1908:

> O High Priest of Iacchus,
> Being now near to the border of the sands
> Where the sapphire girdle of the sea
> Encinctureth the maiden
> Prosephone, released for the spring.
> Look! Breathe upon us
> The wonder of the thrice-encinctured mystery
> Whereby thou being full of years art young
> Loving even this lithe Prosephone
> That is free for the seasons of plenty;
>
> Whereby thou being young art old
> And shalt stand before this Prosephone
> Whom thou lovest,
> In darkness, even at that time
> That she being returned to her husband
> Shall be queen and a maiden no longer,
>
> Wherein thou, being neither old nor young,
> Standing on the verge of the sea
> Shalt pass from being sand,
> O High Priest of Iacchus,
> And becoming wave
> Shalt encircle all sands,

Being transmuted through all
The girdling of the sea.
            O High Priest of Iacchus,
Breathe thou upon us.[21]

Although 'Salve O Pontifex' mentions neither Aphrodite nor Eleusis and does not suggest any actual descent into the Underworld, it does celebrate, as the central ritual function of the High Priest of *Iacchos*, a sexual coupling with Persephone, who is returned to her husband (Pluto) 'queen and maiden no longer'. As in canto 39 the sexual coupling is described as a sacred act associated with the spring and the 'seasons of plenty'. The priest himself is transformed from age to youth and then back to age, enacting the double role of Dionysus/Zagreus, and finally, 'being neither old nor young', is transformed from sand to wave encircling all sands.

More will be said on the subject of this sexual theme in the next chapter. The conclusion one can draw from these Eleusinian references is that Pound's decision to begin the *Cantos* with a translation of Homer's *nekuia* involves the adoption of the Eleusinian ritual of spiritual death and rebirth in the form of a *journey* to the Underworld. In other words, the *Cantos* require of the reader a reinterpretation of the *Odyssey* if the parallel between the two works is to be properly understood. For in the *Cantos* Odysseus is a *spiritual* voyager whose principal acts are the conquest of Circe and the visit to the Underworld. These acts parallel the central ritual acts of the hierophant at Eleusis, but are by no means Odysseus' most important actions in Homer's *Odyssey*.

There are no extended references in the *Cantos* to Odysseus' fabulous adventures apart from his encounter with Circe and his visit to the Underworld. Nor does Pound ever allude to his return to Ithaca and reunion with Penelope. The latest incident within the Odyssean narrative to which he refers is Odysseus' shipwreck, during which he is saved by the interposition of the sea-nymph, Leucothea, and thrown up on the Phaecian shore. Although the whole of Odysseus' *periplus* or wanderings are certainly implied, those wanderings are in fact ignored except for two cardinal journeys: one to the Underworld, the other back to the ordinary world of Alcinous' court. The first journey opens the poem, the second comes towards its close in *Rock-Drill*—particularly the last lines of canto 95.

We have seen that Pound introduced the dream vision of John

Heydon in 'Three Cantos' of 1917 as a possible model for his own communication with the past, but subsequently dropped that idea, along with *Sordello*, in favour of the Odyssean frame, emphasizing the retrospective nature of the *Cantos*. It should now be clear that the Odyssean frame, viewed in the light of Pound's understanding of Eleusis, also functions as an enclosing spiritual or psychological action, conforming in considerable degree to the action of the *Commedia*. In short, the adoption of the *Odyssey* as his principal model did not involve the rejection of the lyrical and visionary dimensions of *Sordello* and John Heydon's dream vision.

At the same time, the Odyssean frame as understood here is not in conflict with Pound's persistent habit of speaking of the *Cantos* in terms appropriate to the *Commedia*—even though the explicit, large-scale allusions are to the *Odyssey*, a poem which would seem to have very little in common with Dante's epic. An early description of the *Commedia* is useful in attempting to determine just what Pound's understanding of that poem was:

> . . . the *Commedia* is, in the literal sense, a description of Dante's vision of a journey through the realms inhabited by the spirits of men after death; in a further sense it is the journey of Dante's intelligence through the states of mind wherein dwell all sorts and conditions of men before death; beyond this, Dante or Dante's intelligence may come to mean 'Everyman' or 'Mankind', whereat his journey becomes a symbol of mankind's struggle upward out of ignorance into the clear light of philosophy. In the second sense I give here, the journey is Dante's own mental and spiritual development. In a fourth sense, the *Commedia* is an expression of the laws of eternal justice.[22]

In the *Cantos* Odysseus is the prototypical figure embodying the third sense of Dante's poem, 'the struggle upward out of ignorance into the clear light of philosophy'. And, by beginning with the *nekuia*, or descent, from the *Odyssey*, Pound adapts his Odyssean frame to make it correspond to the second sense of the *Commedia* as a journey 'through the states of mind wherein dwell all sorts and conditions of men before death'. This is the literal sense of the *Cantos*, the history which they contain. The first, or literal, sense of the *Commedia* is not imitated in the *Cantos*. The fourth sense, 'an expression of the laws of eternal justice', is certainly something Pound hoped his poem would achieve, and is tentatively incorporated at an early stage in the thirteenth or 'Confucian' canto.

2. 'DISCUSS THIS IN BED SAID THE LADY'

Even if Pound began the *Cantos* without any clear plan, he had, from the very beginning, at least the elements of a mythology that he could expect to provide him with a thematic core. That mythology was constructed out of his understanding of Eleusis and his knowledge of the twelfth-century love cult, or religion of *amor*. Indeed, after the conclusion of 'Dona mi Prega' in canto 36, (a poem which serves as a 'gospel' of Eleusis) he reminds us of the Albigenses:

> 'Called thrones, balascio or topaze'
> Eriugina was not understood in his time
> 'which explains, perhaps, the delay in condemning him'
> And they went looking for Manicheans
> And found, so far as I can make out, no Manicheans
> So they dug for, and damned Scotus Eriugina
> 'Authority comes from right reason
> never the other way on'
> Hence the delay in condemning him
> Aquinas head down in a vacuum,
> Aristotle which way in a vacuum?
> Sacrum, sacrum, inluminatio coitu.[a]

'Eriugina' is Johannes Scotus Erigena, a ninth-century Irish theologian and neo-Platonist whose major work, *De Divisione Naturae*, was condemned by the Church in 1225 more than three and a half centuries after its publication. Apparently, it was so belatedly condemned because it had become popular with the Albigenses. Following Péladan, Pound sees the Albigenses as adepts of a pagan love cult, but they were accused at the time of Manichaeanism.[23] The belief attributed to Erigena, that authority comes from right reason, is one he actually held, and it may have played a part in his belated condemnation, but can hardly have been what the Albigenses found appealing in him. In fact, Pound is guessing, from his scant knowledge of Erigena, at what it was in his philosophy which would have connected him with the Albigenses. It is not until somewhat later that he gets around to reading Erigena, and finds something that fits his needs better:

> I have now the text of Erigena, and *if* I could get hold of the recent publications about him. I could write quite a chunk. Not that I am letch-

[a] A sacred thing, a sacred thing, the illumination of coition.

ing to. Lot to connect wiff Cavalcanti's poem, if any more is wanted on them lines. Or allusions to Dant.

I shd. start rev. of mod. esp. of Erig, with Schleuter's Latin comment dated Westphalia 1838. A bit special but *non*-political. Johnny Scot. 'Pietate insignia atque hilaritate.' Johnny had a nice mind. Omnia quae sunt lumina sunt. I haven't yet found anything that fits what I had read about what he thought, but it may be in the 600 pages double col. Migne, vol. 122.[24]

There is little evidence that Pound actually waded his way through the 600 closely printed pages of Erigena's Latin, but he did adopt as his own the phrase, 'omnia quae sunt, lumina sunt' ('all things which are, are lights'). When he discovered the phrase, the first seventy-one cantos were already in print. The next section published was the *Pisan Cantos*, and the phrase is alluded to in the first of them, canto 74, facing the Chinese ideogram for 'bright': 'in the light of light is the *virtu*/"sunt lumina" said Erigena' (74/429: 455). Lower down on the same page he expands the allusion:

> Light tensile immaculata
> the sun's cord unspotted
> 'sunt lumina' said the Oirishman to King Carolus,
> 'OMNIA,
> all things that are are lights'
> and they dug him up out of sepulture
> soi disantly looking for Manicheans
> Les Albigeois, a problem of history.

And it is repeated on the next page in conjunction with Pound's own image of the creative power of *amor*:

> Sunt lumina
> that the drama is wholly subjective
> stone knowing the form which the carver imparts it
> the stone knows the form[25].

The complete formula is cited in the last of the *Pisan Cantos* (83/528: 563) in conjunction with a reference to Erigena's supposed disinterment during the Albigensian crusade (led by Simon de Montfort): 'omnia, quae sunt, lumina sunt, or whatever/so they dug up his bones in the time of De Montfort/(Simon)'. And, to complete the list, the phrase occurs one further time in canto 87 of *Rock-Drill*, this time in English.

In glossing the reference to Erigena in canto 36 it has been necessary to look ahead in the poem as far as *Rock-Drill*, published in 1955. Such a digression may have been avoidable, but it is instructive in that it shows the dynamic character of the *Cantos*' mythology. When Pound mentioned Erigena in canto 36, he knew of his historical association with the Albigenses, but very little of the man's thought. When he does learn more, he is able to incorporate it into his own understanding of the Albigenses and of history. He makes history serve his own poetic purposes, and is even able to salvage uninformed guesses. For Erigena's notion that 'all things which are, are lights' fits perfectly into Pound's reading of 'Dona mi Prega' as 'a sort of metaphor on the generation of light'.

He shows the same resourcefulness in the mythologizing of history. We have examined above his use in canto 5 of the war which developed between Peire de Maensac and Bernart de Tierci, as an analogue of the Trojan war, and his return to the same story in canto 23, this time expanding the account and interleaving the *vida* of de Maensac with the Albigensian crusade itself. By bringing them together as he does, Pound accomplishes two things at once. On the one hand, he perfects the parallel between Troy in Auvergnat and the classical Troy, by having his Provençal story end with the destruction of a temple and of a whole culture—for the crusade did indeed destroy the brilliant culture of twelfth-century Provence. And on the other hand, he brings Péladan's secret history into the poem, thereby clarifying his reading of the Trojan cycle as itself a story of the consequences of withstaying the power of *amor*.

He underlines this point by following Austors' monologue with an account of the departure of Aeneas and Anchises from burning Troy:

> And that was when Troy was down, all right,
>   superbo Ilion . . .
> And they were sailing along
> Sitting in the stern-sheets,
> Under the lee of an island
> And the wind drifting off from the island.
> 'Tet, tet . . .
>   what is it?' said Anchises.
> 'Tethnéké', said the helmsman, 'I think they
> 'Are howling because Adonis died virgin.'
> Huh! tet . . .' said Anchises,
>   'well, they've made a bloody mess of that city.'

Canto 23 thus takes us well beyond anything that could have been borrowed from either Aeschylus or Homer, who wrote of sexual relations either in terms of honour, duty, and legal contract, or as an appetite. Although they must have been familiar with the liturgical function of sexuality in the rites of their own popular religions, they paid scant attention to it. Even Péladan does not think of interpreting the Trojan war as a disguised account of a *lutte d'amour* despite the obvious susceptibility it has to such a reading when viewed in outline.

There is a note dated 1916 appended to the discussion of the mystery cult in *The Spirit of Romance* which throws some new light on Pound's conception of Helen, and which is certainly foreign to anything he could have found in classical sources:

> Let me admit at once that a recent lecture by Mr. Mead on Simon Magus has opened my mind to a number of new possibilities. There would seem to be in the legend of Simon Magus and Helen of Tyre a clearer prototype of 'chivalric love' than in anything hereinafter discussed. I recognize that all this matter of mine may have to be reconstructed or at least re-oriented about that tradition. Such rearrangement would not, however, enable us to dispense with a discussion of the parallels here collected, nor would it materially affect the manner in which they are treated.[26]

Pound never did reconstruct 'all this matter' contained in chapter 5 of *The Spirit of Romance*. Nor does he have much to say of Simon Magus and Helen of Tyre—although the lady turns up mysteriously in canto 91 for the first time.

I have no way of knowing what the 'recent lecture' by Mr. Mead was, but Mr. Mead is G. R. S. Mead, editor of *The Quest* (in which periodical chapter 5 of *The Spirit of Romance* first appeared), and an energetic student of Gnosticism. Although the 'recent lecture' is probably unprocurable, it seems likely that it contained much the same information and opinion that Mead recorded in *Simon Magus: An Essay* published in 1892. In that work he traces all that was known about this obscure sage who gave his name to the ecclesiastical vice of simony. The most important of the many sources he cites is from the *Philosophumena* of Hippolytus which includes the following passages from the *Revelation* of Simon:

> Of the universal Aeons there are two shoots, without beginning or end, springing from one Root, which is the Power invisible, inapprehensible

Silence. Of these shoots one is manifested from above, which is the Great Power, the Universal Mind ordering all things, male, and the other (is manifested) from below, the Great Thought, female producing all things.

Hence pairing with each other, they unite and manifest the Middle Distance, incomprehensible Air, without beginning or end. In this is the Father who sustains all things, and nourishes those things which have a beginning and end.

This is He who has stood, stands and will stand, a male-female power like the preexisting Boundless Power, which has neither beginning nor end, existing in oneness. For it is from this that the Thought in the oneness proceeded and became two.

. . . . .

Hence they pair with each other being one, for there is no difference between Power and Thought. From the things above is discovered Power, and from those below Thought.

In the same manner also that which was manifested from them, although being one is yet found as two, the male–female having the female in itself. Thus Mind is in Thought—things inseparable from one another—which although being one are yet found as two.[27]

The Gnostic myth, conceiving the two great principles of the universe, Mind (potentiality) and Thought (incarnation) as male and female, would surely have appealed to the author of the 'Postscript' to *The Natural Philosophy of Love*, had he been exposed to it. But it is the legend of Helen of Tyre and Simon Magus that Pound mentions rather than any Gnostic theology. Mead collects many forms of that legend in *Simon Magus*; the most elaborate one he also finds in Hippolytus:

. . . he [Simon Magus] gives an allegorical interpretation of the wooden horse, and Helen with the torch, and a number of other things, which he metamorphoses and weaves into fictions concerning himself and his Thought.

And he said that the latter was the 'lost sheep', who again and again abiding in women throws the Powers in the world into confusion, on account of her unsurpassable beauty; on account of which the Trojan War came to pass through her. For this Thought took up its abode in the Helen that was born just at that time, and thus when all the Powers laid claim to her, there arose faction and war among those nations to whom she was manifested.

. . . . .

And subsequently, when her body was changed by the Angels and lower Powers—which also, he says, made the world—she lived in a brothel in Tyre, a city of Phoenicia, where he found her on his arrival. For he professes that he had come there for the purpose of finding her for the first time, that he might deliver her from bondage. And after he had purchased her freedom, he took her about with him, pretending that she was the 'lost sheep', and that he himself was the Power which is over all. Whereas the impostor having fallen in love with this strumpet, called Helen, purchased and kept her, and being ashamed to have it known by his disciples, invented this story.[28]

It may well be, however, that Mead did not include these documents in the lecture Pound attended. They would, after all, be rather difficult to absorb at a single hearing. What Pound heard may have been closer to the summary comment Mead gives in *Fragments of a Faith Forgotten*, a large work collecting the principal documents relevant to Gnosticism:

The main symbolism, which the evolvers of the Simon-legend parodied into the myth of Simon and Helen, appears to have been sidereal; thus the Logos and his Thought, the World-Soul, were symbolized as the Sun (Simon) and the Moon (Selene, Helen); so with the microcosm, Helen was the human soul fallen into matter and Simon the mind which brings about her redemption. Moreover one of the systems appears to have attempted to interpret the Trojan legend and myth of Helen in a spiritual and psychological fashion.[29]

In the 1916 note Pound found the legend of Simon Magus and Helen of Tyre to be 'a clearer prototype of "chivalric love"' than anything he himself had unearthed in 'Psychology and Troubadours'. One can safely assume from this comment that Mead had conveyed both the sexual and theological dimensions of the legend in his lecture. However, it should be noted that Mead himself was quite prudish about the sexual symbolism inherent in the legend, and warns the readers of *Simon Magus* against the error of any lewd interpretation:

This is the mystery of the Helen, the 'lost sheep'. Then follows the mystical marriage of the Lamb, the union of the Human and Spiritual Soul in man, referred to so often in the Gospels and other mystical scriptures.

Naturally the language used is symbolical, and has naught to do with sex, in any sense. Woe unto him or her who takes these allegories of the Soul as literal histories, for nothing but sorrow will follow such materialization of divine mysteries. If Simon or his followers fell into this error, they worked their own downfall, under the Great Law, as surely do all who forge such bonds or matter for their own enslavement.[30]

Pound did not share that prudishness. Indeed he is quite explicit about the role of sexuality in his highly syncretic version of Eleusis. The following is Pound's gloss on a line near the end of canto 45, 'They have brought whores for Eleusis':

'Eleusis' is *very* elliptical. It means that in place of the sacramental —— —— —— —— in the Mysteries, you 'ave the 4 and six-penny 'ore. As you see, the moral bearing is very high, and the degradation of the sacrament (which is the coition and *not* the going to a fat-buttocked priest or registry office) has been completely debased largely *by* Xtianity, or misunderstanding of that Ersatz religion.[31]

There is only a passing reference to Helen in 'Three Cantos' of 1917,[32] but she is given a prominent place in the 1919 cantos (4, 5, 6, and 7). We know that the 1917 cantos were already well under way by 5 June 1916, because Pound threatened Harriet Monroe with a '40 page fragment from a more important opus' on that date.[33] They were probably not influenced by the Mead lecture.[34] The 1919 cantos, on the other hand, not only introduce Helen of Troy and her analogue, Eleanor of Aquitaine, but are absorbed throughout with the theme of sexuality. Of course, such a theme is not new to Pound, nor to poetry. We have found it in a quite explicit form as early as 'Salve O Pontifex'. But in that poem as well as in canto 39, the act of love is liberating and sacred. In the 1919 cantos it leads to strife, sorrow, and death. One tale in canto 5 would seem to be a 'repeat' with variations of Simon's discovery of Helen in a brothel in Tyre:

And from Mauleon, fresh with a new earned grade,
In maze of approaching rain-steps, Poicebot—
The air was full of women,
        And Savairic Mauleon
Gave him his land and knight's fee, and he wed the woman.
Came lust of travel on him, of *romerya*;
And out of England a knight with slow-lifting eyelids
Lei fassa furar a del, put glamour upon her . . .
And left her an eight months gone.
        'Came lust of woman upon him,'
Poicebot, now on North road from Spain
(Sea-change, a grey in the water)
        And in small house by town's edge
Found a woman, changed and familiar face;
Hard night, and parting at morning.[35]

According to the Gnostic texts Helen of Tyre was an embodiment of the '"lost sheep", who again and again abiding in women throws the Powers in the world into confusion, on account of her unsurpassable beauty'. Helen of Troy was another such embodiment, but Helen of Tyre is found by Simon in a house of ill repute, just as Poicebot found his wife. By linking a divine manifestation of beauty (which Helen is in the legend) with the raw commercial sexuality of a brothel, the legend provides a bridge between Aphrodite and Circe, a bridge that Pound most certainly uses in cantos 39 and 47. Both Circe and Aphrodite stand at the gateway to the Underworld, both hold the keys to revelation. They are in the *Cantos* a pair rather like Persephone and Koré in the Eleusinian rites. Circe is the fearsome aspect of the goddess (*Kuthera deina*) which must somehow be conquered (just as the Mysteries enable the initiate to conquer death, personified by Persephone, Queen of the Underworld); Aphrodite is the radiant aspect of the goddess, imagined always as at her birth taking form from the sea foam (as in the Mysteries, Koré is the daughter of Demeter, reborn into the light, and appears to the faithful in a blaze of light).

In effect Pound has used the Simon legend to metamorphose the familiar neo-Platonic ladder of *eros* into a bridge. Rather than ascending from a carnal to an intellectual or spiritual love, one remains always with carnal love, but it may lead either to death or to the conquest of death. For Cabestan, Tereus, Vidal, and Actaeon (in canto 4), it leads to death; for Anchises in canto 23, it leads to revelation. Hence the many references to Adonis and Tammuz. They too met death in the service of *eros*. Their stories express the paradox of *eros*, for their deaths lead to resurrection, a resurrection that is retained ironically in the Ovidian tales of Tereus and Actaeon as a metamorphosis.

Odysseus does not die, but he must undergo a ritual death by journeying to Hades. Circe tells him three times that he must go—in canto 17, in canto 39 (in Greek), and in canto 47:

> First must thou go the road
>   to hell
> And to the bower of Ceres' daughter Proserpine,
> Through overhanging dark, to see Tiresias,
> Eyeless that was, a shade, that is in hell
> So full of knowing that the beefy men know less than he,

Ere thou come to thy road's end.
                    Knowledge the shade of a shade,
Yet must thou sail after knowledge
Knowing less than drugged beasts.

And on each of these three occasions the poem celebrates a theophany of a goddess whom we have identified as Aphrodite. In cantos 39 and 47, it is not just a theophany, but a *hieros gamos*, a divine marriage, apparently between a sky god and an earth goddess:

The light has entered the cave. Io! Io!
The light has gone down into the cave,
Splendour on splendour!
By prong have I entered these hills:
That the grass grow from my body,
That I hear the roots speaking together,
The air is new on my leaf,
The forked boughs shake with the wind.[36]
(47/238:248)

Odysseus is thus in the *Cantos* a sacred hero, a priest, like Virgil's Aeneas. In his 'marriage' with Circe, he plays the part of the hierophant who acts out the marriage of Pluto and Persephone with a priestess in the Eleusinian rites as practised at Alexandria.[37]

Odysseus' conquest of a cunning and dangerous opponent leads to the acquisition of knowledge and escape from his wanderings. His adventure is the model or paradigm for the adventure of the *Cantos* as a whole, and for each of the several adventures contained within them. The essential modalities of Odysseus' adventure are: war guilt, fruitless wandering (or the *selva oscura*), the recognition of beauty (for in the *Cantos*, Circe's beauty is emphasized), the attempt to conquer beauty (in both an intellectual and a sexual manner), and finally the attainment of knowledge through this conquest of beauty, a knowledge which Pound calls a 'full *Eidous* in canto 81. Of course, the metaphor for the attainment of this *Eidous* ('seeing') is the descent, but a descent carefully interfused with a *hieros gamos* and a theophany of Aphrodite.

If this pattern were successfully worked out in the *Cantos*, its own descent into the past would conclude with some revelations of the historical and political processes, with the embodiment in itself of beauty, and perhaps also with a religious revelation. Instead it concludes still lost in the *selva oscura*:

I have brought the great ball of crystal;
        who can lift it?
Can you enter the great acorn of light?
        But the beauty is not the madness
Tho' my errors and wrecks lie about me.
And I am not a demigod,
I cannot make it cohere.
If love be not in the house there is nothing.
The voice of famine unheard.
How came beauty against this blackness,
Twice beauty under the elms—
        To be saved by squirrels and bluejays?
                'plus j'aime le chien'
Ariadne.[38]

IV · Amor and Usura

I. CAVALCANTI'S 'DONA MI PREGA'

IN discussing Pound's synoptic Eleusis we are dealing with the imaginative heart of his poem, with the metaphorical structure which has prevented it from flying apart. It must be admitted, however, that an understanding of Eleusis by no means removes all the poem's obscurities and vagaries. Nor, of course, does it account for all of its content—much of which is political and economic history. Still less does the Eleusinian action—the conquest of beauty leading to revelation—guarantee the success of a poem which mimes it. Indeed, it would appear that Pound himself finally lost faith in his own work. When Daniel Cory offered him several attractive hypotheses to account for the obscurity of the *Cantos*, he reports Pound as replying, 'It's a botch.' Asked if he meant that it didn't come off, Pound replied, 'Of course it didn't. That's what I mean when I say I botched it.' And he continues a little later: 'I picked out this and that thing that interested me, and then jumbled them into a bag. But that's not the way to make . . . *a work of art*.'[1]

There is no reason to doubt Cory's good faith or the accuracy of his transmission of what Pound said. Indeed, the *Cantos* do constitute a failure in some very obvious ways. They are incomplete; they are hopelessly obscure; and they are all too frequently no more than undistinguished patchwork. Pound had good reason to feel that he had botched his epic. However, he was less vicious with himself in canto 116 (first published in 1962)—although admitting that the poem had collapsed on him. In fact after admitting that he cannot make it cohere, he shortly regains confidence in his vision if not in his poem:

> but about that terzo
> Third heaven,
>   that Venere,
> again 'is all paradiso'
>   a nice quiet paradise
>   over the shambles,

and some climbing,
                    before the take-off,
to 'see again'.
                    the verb is 'see' not 'walk on'
i.e. it coheres all right
                    even if my notes do not cohere,
Many errors,
                    a little rightness
to excuse his hell and my paradiso
            and as to why they wrong,
                    thinking of rightness
And as to who will copy this palimpsest?[2]

The point to be taken here is that even after Pound has lost all confidence in the poem he laboured over for so many years, he retains his faith in 'that terzo/Third heaven,/that Venere', that is, in Aphrodite. To see her again 'is all paradiso', and 'the verb is "see" not "walk on"', Pound insists. Canto 116 in effect brings us full circle to the closing lines of 'Canto One' where 'Botticelli brings her ashore on the great cockle shell'. The entire poem is a hymn to beauty. In a sense, the *Cantos* are a vast Edwardian epic spawned in the hell of modern warfare and hatched in the purgatory of the European collapse into Fascism. With his mind always on the past like Odysseus, Pound never really understood what was happening around him. He mistook Italian Fascism for a return to Latin roots, and apparently chose to remain ignorant of what the Nazis stood for, and what they did. Although he purged his poetry of the vague prettiness he had affected in his early verse, he never lost the Edwardian 'inner belief . . . that the transcendent is immanent in the earthy',[3] and built his poem around his sense of the transcendent power of earthly beauty.

Eleusis is a machine designed to give flesh and ligature to Pound's worship of beauty; its touchstone is Propertius' line, 'Ingenium nobis ipsa puella facit', 'My genius is no more than a girl'. In that line, he says,

> is the whole of the XIIth century love cult, and Dante's metaphysics a little to one side, and Gourmont's Latin Mystique; and for image-making both Fenollosa on 'The Chinese Written Character', and the paragraphs in 'Le Problème du Style'.[4]

Despite the obvious irony of Propertius' line in context—an irony certainly not missed in 'Homage to Sextus Propertius'—it is this sentiment that inspires Pound's epic, not his reading of Péladan or Mead, of Frazer or Foucart. In the familiar lyric impulse of sexual love Pound pretends to find the source of the beauties of Provence, of the *dolce stil nuovo*, and even of Dante. It seems to me not to matter very much whether we find this supposition plausible or bizarre. If Pound thinks it true of the poets he most admires, it is probably true of himself. The beautiful Envoi in *Hugh Selwyn Mauberly* might well be printed at the end of the *Cantos*:

Go, dumb-born book,
Tell her that sang me once that song of Lawes:
Hadst thou but song
As thou hast subjects known,
Then were there cause in thee that should condone
Even my faults that heavy upon me lie,
And build her glories their longevity.

Tell her that sheds
Such treasure in the air,
Recking naught else but that her graces give
Life to the moment,
I would bid them live
As roses might, in magic amber laid,
Red overwrought with orange and all made
One substance and one colour
Braving time.

Tell her that goes
With song upon her lips
But sings not out the song, nor knows
The maker of it, some other mouth,
May be as fair as hers,
Might, in new ages, gain her worshippers,
When our two dusts with Waller's shall be laid,
Sifting on siftings in oblivion,
Till change hath broken down
All things save Beauty alone.

Of course, the *Cantos* preserve as many flies in amber as roses, and one might well protest that it would be difficult to imagine a more wrong-headed hymn to beauty than the *Cantos*. It is, admittedly, 'a tangle of works unfinished' dominated in bulk by fragmentary historical notes and buttressed by shrill and tendentious prose essays on history and economics. But within that tangle can be found poetry of great beauty, and a vision that is neither shrill nor wildly eccentric. The argument put forth in these pages is that the vision and the beauty lie at the heart of the poem and give it force and motion.

As late as 1944 Pound was still able to think of his poem as a new *Commedia*, an imitation of 'the tremendous lyric of the subjective Dante'. Maintaining 1904 as the year in which he began the *Cantos*, he wrote: 'For forty years I have schooled myself, not to write the economic history of the U.S. or any other country, but to write an epic poem which begins "In the Dark Forest", crosses the Purgatory of human error, and ends in the light, "fra i maestri di color che sanno".'[5] One can hardly accept this as an accurate description of the seventy-one cantos then in print, but it is no doubt a fair account of what Pound wished his poem to be. Of course, his journey among 'all sorts and conditions of men' is modelled upon the Odyssean descent and *periplus* rather than Dante's ambulatory dream vision.[6]

Dante manages to incorporate a good deal of politics, and even private feuds, into the *Commedia* without doing any violence to the integrity of his vision. Pound hoped to do the same, but lacked the universally accepted and copiously articulated moral framework Dante possessed. To fill this gap Pound tried to create such a framework by building on the Propertian–Provençal cult of sexual love. For this purpose he chose the impenetrable Cavalcanti canzone, 'Dona mi Prega'. Pound devoted a great deal of time to Cavalcanti, even publishing an edition of his poetry, *Guido Cavalcanti Rime*, in 1932 complete with translations and commentary,[7] and later made a new translation for inclusion in canto 36. Despite his efforts, canto 36 has not fared well with the critics. George Dekker recognizes its status as an integral element in the *Cantos*, but concludes that it is deliberately impenetrable.[8] Noel Stock also sees this canto 'as a possible key to the underlying nature of the whole work', but does not pursue the matter.[9] There is a critical consensus on the centrality of the Cavalcanti translation, and its identification with sanity or light, but there the matter rests.

The critical tradition on canto 36 could fairly be described as prudent, beginning with W. B. Yeats who was to have written something on it for 'A Packet for Ezra Pound', and did write something, but destroyed it, finding it impossible to make it clear or even read able.[10] The only really forthright statement on Pound's translation to be found (although an earlier version than that contained in canto 36) is that of J. E. Shaw who has devoted an entire book to the study of 'Dona mi Prega':

> The translation in English verse [in *Guido Cavalcanti Rime*] is more obscure than the original in any version, and the 'Partial Explanation' contributes no light on the meaning; nor do the desultory remarks entitled 'The Vocabulary' and 'Further Notes'.[11]

Shaw's forthrightness, unhappily, is of little assistance in coming to an understanding of canto 36.

I am not competent to quarrel with Shaw's assessment of Pound's understanding of Cavalcanti, but it is impossible to dismiss canto 36 in the face of the importance Pound obviously attaches to it. We have seen that he links Cavalcanti in canto 36 to the whole matter of Eleusis, and he alludes to the canzone more than ten times in later sections of the poem. As early as 'Psychology and Troubadours' he mentions Cavalcanti as the *doctor* of the religion of Amor:

> The rise of Mariolatry, its pagan lineage, the romance of it, find modes of expression which verge over-easily into the speech and casuistry of Our Lady of Cyprus, as we may see in Arnaut, as we see so splendidly in Guido's 'Una figura della donna miae'. And there is the consummation of it all in Dante's glorification of Beatrice. There is the inexplicable address to the lady in the masculine. There is the final evolution of Amor by Guido and Dante, a new and paganish god, neither Erôs nor an angel of the Talmud.[12]

There can be little doubt that 'Dona mi Prega' is a crucial text for the *Cantos*, and particularly for an understanding of Eleusis.

Pound was fortunate enough to have his edition of Cavalcanti reviewed by Étienne Gilson, a most eminent medieval scholar. Gilson's review is extraordinarily gentle, but leaves no doubt that Pound's translation is quite incorrect in places, and tends to create obscurities where none exist.[13] Although Pound called it a 'dull review', he in fact accepted two of Gilson's corrections for the translation in canto 36. Of particular interest is the third correction offered by Gilson which Pound failed to accept. Gilson points out that Pound's translation of

E l antenzione
            per ragione
                        vale

Discerne male
in chui é vizio amicho

as

Maintains intention reason's peer and mate;
Poor in discernment, being thus weakness' friend

is quite wrong. The lines mean, he says, 'For intention's value rests on reason/And it sees but little in whom has vice for friend.' Gilson's translation is obviously correct, and Pound can hardly have failed to recognize that it was correct. None the less, he retains the erroneous translation in canto 36: 'Deeming intention to be reason's peer and mate,/Poor in discernment, being thus weakness' friend'. One must assume that he persisted in the error ot his ways because he wanted Amor to be weakness' friend even though Cavalcanti's meaning is that Amor will have nothing to do with the vicious.

This example of Pound's refusal to accept learned advice suggests that his meaning is not necessarily Cavalcanti's, and that we would do well to examine canto 36 as an independent work rather than as a translation. Of course, one must recognize that it *is* a translation or it would lack the historical *quidditas* essential to the epic recovery of the past. We must recognize in the translation the oracular voice of lost wisdom. But at the same time, we must accept what the oracle says without checking his references too closely. As the gospel of Eleusis according to Cavalcanti, the poem cannot be an original work by Ezra Pound, but neither can any misunderstandings of Eleusis by Cavalcanti be permitted to survive.[14]

The poem, then, is a definition of Amor addressed to 'present knowers/Having no hope that low-hearted/Can bring sight to such reason'. Cavalcanti/Pound puts his readers on notice immediately that what follows is for the initiated only—a qualification that offends Dekker, but it is entirely in keeping with a sacred text. The exposition begins: 'Where memory liveth, it takes its state'. Gilson explains, in terms of the epistemology of the time, why it is that Amor dwells in the memory, but for Pound the line, 'In quella parte/ dove sta memoria', has more to do with his own understanding of memory:

... by naming over all the most beautiful things we know we may draw back upon the mind some vestige of the heavenly splendour.

I suggest that the troubadour, either more indolent or more logical, progresses from correlating all these details for purpose of comparison, and lumps the matter. The Lady contains the catalogue, is more complete. She serves as a sort of *mantram*.[15]

'The whole break of Provence with this world', he tells us in the Cavalcanti essay, speaking of the Greek world of 'plastic plus immediate satisfaction', 'and indeed the central theme of the troubadours, is the dogma that there is some proportion between the fine thing held in the mind, and the inferior thing ready for instant consumption.'[16] But it is perhaps in the *Pisan Cantos*, themselves a 'naming over of all the most beautiful things' Pound knows, that the meaning of this line for him becomes clear:

> nothing matters but the quality
> of the affection—
> in the end—that has carved the trace in the mind
> dove sta memoria.
>
> (76/457:485)

For Pound, then, Amor lives in the memory because it is the remembered that he most loves: 'What thou lovest well remains,/ the rest is dross/What thou lov'st well shall not be reft from thee/ What thou lov'st well is thy true heritage.' Surely such a sentiment is not hopelessly obscure, nor alien to normal sensibility. It may be remote from anything Cavalcanti had in mind, but to put the sentiment into Cavalcanti's mouth is itself an instance of the sanctity of the remembered.

The poem continues:

> Formed like a diafan from light on shade
> Which shadow cometh of Mars and remaineth
> Created, having a name sensate,
> Custom of the soul,
> will from the heart;
> Cometh of a seen form which being understood
> Taketh locus and remaining in the intellect possible.

For 'diafan' Pound refers us to *Paradiso*, x. 69 where we read, 'quando l'aere è pregno', 'where the air is charged' (or 'pregnant'). He also cites Albertus, asserting the god-like power of the intellect: 'Ex possibili et agente compositus est intellectus adeptus, et divinus dicitur, et tunc homo perfectus est. Et fit per hunc intellectum homo

Deo quodam modo similis, eo quod potest sic operari divina . . .' In canto 51 Pound follows instructions for the tying of the trout fly, 'Blue dun', with the comment:

> That hath the light of the doer, as it were
> a form cleaving to it.
> Deo similis quodam modo
> hic intellectus adeptus[a].

And in canto 76:

> Cythera potens, *Κύθηρα δεινά*
> no cloud, but the crystal body
> the tangent formed in the hand's cup
> as live wind in the beech grove
> as strong air amid cypress.
> (76/456–7:485)

Aphrodite is the 'seen form' *par excellence* in the *Cantos*: she is the beatific vision toward which the poem moves. Cavalcanti provides Pound with scriptural support for the validity of visionary experience, but his understanding of that experience is grafted on to Cavalcanti rather than derived from him.[17]

However, Pound has long identified with Cavalcanti the idea that divinity is manifest in the beauty of woman. The earliest expression of the idea as derived from Cavalcanti is in his introduction to *The Sonnets and Ballate of Guido Cavalcanti*, dated November 1910. In his correction of Rossetti's translation of Sonnet VII, he propounds the essential substance of the phrase, 'cometh of a seen form'. Pound translates the line, 'E la beltate per sua Dea la mostra', as 'Beauty displays her for her goddess'. And he comments: 'That is to say, as the spirit of God became incarnate in the Christ, so is the spirit of the eternal beauty made flesh dwelling amongst us in her' (p. xv). As we shall see, he later refines this notion, advancing to an even more ineffable manifestation of divinity in vision, beyond incarnation. But the essential notion Pound reads into 'Ingenium nobis ipsa puella facit' is certainly present in this early comment on Cavalcanti.[18]

Taking advantage of any opening allowed him by Cavalcanti, Pound in his commentary recreates the poem as 'a sort of metaphor on the generation of light'. It is not too much to say that the key to the canzone for Pound is found in a summary of Grosseteste's

[a] Godlike, in a way, this intellect which grasps.

theory of the propagation of light by Étienne Gilson, judged by Pound to be 'far more suggestive of the canzone, "Dona mi Prega", than the original Latin of Grosseteste'. He cites an entire paragraph from Gilson's *La Philosophie au moyen âge*:

Light is an extremely subtle corporeal substance, which is almost incorporeal. Its characteristic properties are those of reproducing itself perpetually and of diffusing itself spherically and instantaneously about a point. Let us take a point as the centre of an immense luminous sphere. The diffusion of the light can be arrested in only two ways; either it reaches an opacity which stops it, or it ends by reaching the extreme limit of its rarefication, and the propagation of light ends in the same way. This extremely tenuous substance is also the stuff of which all things are made; it is the primary corporeal form and some call it corporeality itself.[19]

It is this paragraph as much as Cavalcanti's poem which stands behind the lines:

Cometh from a seen form which being understood
Taketh locus and remaining in the intellect possible
Wherein hath he neither weight nor still-standing,
Descendeth not by quality but shineth out
Himself his own effect unendingly
Not in delight but in the being aware
Nor can he leave his true likeness otherwhere.

Obviously a poem which defines love in terms of the propagation of light belongs at the heart of an epic moving toward a beatific vision attained through the agency of sexual love. Paradise, we recall, is—at least in canto 116—something seen, not a place, not even a sustained state, but the vision unattended. Amor, quite simply, dwells with beauty, with Aphrodite, and with the clear, sharp song of Circe. He visits only those who can perceive beauty, but is independent of morality and even—surprisingly—of talent:

He is not vertu but cometh of that perfection
Which is so postulate not by the reason
But 'tis felt, I say.
Beyond salvation, holdeth his judging force
Deeming intention to be reason's peer and mate,
Poor in discernment, being thus weakness' friend
Often his power cometh on death in the end,
Be it withstayed
                and so swinging counterweight.

Amor certainly 'cometh on death in the end' with sufficient frequency in the *Cantos*. The fates of Actaeon, Cabestan, and Tereus are merely private instances of the fate of Troy and other civilizations embroiled in the potent net of Amor. But, of course, it is also through the power of Amor that death is conquered as with Odysseus and Circe, or Persephone and Zagreus. Amor represents, above all, life, but he is capable of perversion—of which more later.

But Amor is no *logos* shining in the darkness which comprehendeth it not. He is an attribute of—or perhaps a response to—awakened human perceptivity, an attribute of Dante's *directio voluntatis*:

> Cometh he to be
>   when the will
> From overplus
> Twisteth out of natural measure,
> Never adorned with rest Moveth he changing colour
> Either to laugh or weep
> Contorting the face with fear
>   resteth but a little
> Yet shall ye see of him That he is most often
> With folk who deserve him
> And his strange quality sets sighs to move
> Willing man look into that forméd trace in his mind
> And with such uneasiness as rouseth the flame.

It is precisely this will twisted out of natural measure that Mauberly lacks:

> He had passed, inconscient, full gaze,
> The wide-banded irides
> And botticellian sprays implied
> In their diastasis;
>
> Which anaesthesis, noted a year late,
> And weighed, revealed his great affect,
> (Orchid), mandate
> Of Eros, a retrospect.

The lotophagoi who decline to follow Odysseus on his perilous journey to Circe's bed and the Underworld also lack it:

>   Reclining,
> With the silver spilla,
> The ball as of melted amber, coiled, caught up, and turned.

Lotophagoi of the suave nails, quiet, scornful,
Voce-profondo:
  'Feared neither death nor pain for this beauty;
If harm, harm to ourselves.'
And beneath: the clear bones, far down,
Thousand on thousand.
  'What gain with Odysseus,
'They that died in the whirlpool
'And after many vain labours,
'Living by stolen meat, chained to the rowingbench,
'That he should have a great fame
  'And lie by night with the goddess?
(20/93–4:97–8)

But even though he 'cometh to be' in response to human perceptivity, he is nonetheless an ineffable divinity:

Nor is he known from his face
But taken in the white light that is allness
Toucheth his aim
Who heareth, seeth not form
But is led by its emanation.
Being divided, set out from colour,
Disjunct in mid darkness
Grazeth the light, one moving by other,
Being divided, divided from all falsity
Worthy of trust
From him alone mercy proceedeth.

From this, canto 36 proceeds to Erigena, the Albigenses, and 'Sacrum, sacrum, inluminatio coitu'. Are these perhaps the puzzling 'mestiers ecoutes' of canto 7?

The translation of 'Dona mi Prega', then, incorporates into the *Cantos* a philosophical expression of Pound's Eleusis. The ritual expression of the Eleusinian religion as Pound has formulated it, is the sacred marriage of man and goddess, as between Odysseus and Circe, or Anchises and Aphrodite; that it to say, a union of perceiving intellect and perceived beauty in epistemological terms, or of mind (male) and Thought (female) in the Gnostic terminology of G. R. S. Mead. Amor is a vital force rather like Bergson's *élan vital* or the 'something within' of the Hermetics:

The ancient teachers of evolution, though less exact in detail, were more accurate in fact, in postulating a 'something within' which alone could make the external evolution of form of any intelligible purpose. The

Spiritual Soul—the Life, Consciousness, Spirit, Intelligence, whatever we may choose to call it—was formless in itself, but ever assuming new forms by a process called metempsychosis. . . .[20]

It is Amor that reveals the rose in the steel dust, and conveys the god-like power of grasping to the human intellect. Amor is manifest in the Divine Mind, described in canto 92 as 'abundant/unceasing/*improvisatore*/Omniformis/unstill', and echoed in the human mind, seen in canto 113 to be 'as Ixion, unstill, ever turning'.

The vital and creatively metamorphic power of Amor is most perfectly manifested in the drive toward the creation of beauty as in Sigismund Malatesta's construction of the Tempio. It is most perfectly known in the beatific vision, which in the *Cantos* takes the form of the theophany of Aphrodite. But often the creative and metamorphic power of Amor 'cometh on death in the end,/Be it withstayed/and so swinging counterweight'. Amor, conceived as an emanating and immaterial force like light, can be arrested or subverted, as light is, by opaque or tinted objects. Light can be replaced, through the obstructive power of opaque objects, with its opposite, darkness, which is a nullity, merely the absence of light. Similarly Amor, the vital, creative force, can be replaced by its opposite, death, the absence of life. Mythically the vital force of Amor is represented by the corn goddess, Demeter, and its opposite by Pluto, the god of the Underworld. But the abstract conception of the opposite to Amor in the *Cantos* is Usura:

> With *Usura*
> With usura hath no man a house of good stone
> each block cut smooth and well fitting
> that design might cover their face,
> with usura
> hath no man a painted paradise on his church wall
>
> . . . .
>
> with usura, sin against nature,
> is thy bread ever more of stale rags
> is thy bread dry as paper,
> with no mountain wheat, no strong flour
> with usura the line grows thick
> with usura is no clear demarcation
> and no man can find site for his dwelling.
> Stonecutter is kept from his stone
> weaver is kept from his loom.
>
> (45/229:239)

It should be obvious that Usura is not simply usury, the economic sin of renting money at excessive rates, but is, within the imaginative world of the *Cantos*, evil itself. It is the darkness which does not know the light. Evil is traditionally a negative, an absence, and is therefore faceless and imperceptible. Milton, whose divinity was a personification of omniscience and charity, presented evil as a personification of cunning and malevolence. Pound's divinity is an immaterial vital force. His evil is an immaterial fatal force which subverts the power of Amor.

Of course, Usura is a materialization of evil in economic terms, just as Amor is a conception of divinity in sexual terms. It was a bold step to attempt to portray evil in terms of the dismal science, but not a foolish one. Pound thought that the economic theories of Major Douglas provided him with an understanding of modern economics. He could see around him, as everyone else could during the Great Depression, that a great deal of human suffering was being caused by some grave malfunction of the economic system. The munitions industry, it seemed to Pound, fostered wars for its own economic benefit, and the banks fostered both unemployment and wars for their benefit.

Pound's economics are fully integrated into the imaginative structure of the *Cantos*. Usura is the antitype of Amor; the prostitute replaces the priestess: 'They have brought whores for Eleusis'. Amor lives in the memory, but Usura denies the past and dwells in the immediate satisfaction to be derived from the present exchange in money or in kind:

> Usura rusteth the chisel
> It rusteth the craft and the craftsman
> It gnaweth the thread in the loom
> None learneth to weave gold in her pattern;
> Azure hath a canker by usura; cramoisi is unbroidered
> Emerald findeth no Memling
> Usura slayeth the child in the womb
> It stayeth the young man's courting
> It hath brought palsey to bed, lyeth
> between the young bride and her bridegroom
>   CONTRA NATURAM
> They have brought whores for Eleusis
> Corpses are set to banquet
> at behest of usura.
>
> (45/230:240)

The corpses set to banquet are those of Itys, Tereus' son and Cabestan, Sérémonde's lover—as in canto 4 where the essentially contractual and economic marriage vows interfere with the overweening power of Amor.

2. POUND, DOUGLAS, AND J. M. KEYNES

Although Usura appears in the *Cantos* as an immaterial fatal force opposed to the vitality of Amor, Pound does hold specific views on economics, and incorporates them into the poem. They are derived from Major Clifford Hugh Douglas, the founder of Social Credit. Since Pound's economic views led him to oppose the Allies and support the Fascist powers in the Second World War, their importance to Pound's life and career can hardly be exaggerated. They also led him into anti-Semitism—which, coupled with his Fascist sympathies, has put him beyond the limits of tolerance for many who might otherwise admire his literary achievement.

The precise nature of Pound's economic opinions lies outside the ordinary scope of a literary study, but our final opinion of Pound as a man and as an intellectual cannot be separated from those opinions. Therefore it will be necessary to consider—with as much brevity and clarity as possible—the nature and origin of Pound's economics.

Douglas was an industrial engineer who believed he had discovered a basic error in the system of industrial accounting and price setting while reorganizing the Royal Aircraft works at Farnborough during the First World War. He very soon set about to let the world know of his discovery, and by February of 1919 had the attention of A. R. Orage, editor of the *New Age*, and was appearing in that Guild Socialist weekly—Pound's principal source of financial support since 1911. Douglas soon converted Orage and Pound to his views. Pound remembered Douglas's impact:

> Sometime in 1918 or thereabouts an ex-engineer, ex-head of Westinghouse's Indian branch, then managing an airplane factory noticed that his factory was creating prices faster than it emitted the power to buy.
>
> . . . . .
>
> The Major's first observation is on a par with the observation of the falling apple or of the kettle lid lifted by steam: a point of departure.
>
> . . . . .
>
> Douglas's perception was that under the present accounting system the actual money available can never buy all the available goods.[21]

Douglas shared Pound's assessment of the importance of his perceptions:

I had the idea that I had got hold of some specific technical information and I had only to get it accepted; I had the idea that I was like a clever little boy and that I had only to run to father and he would be very pleased about it.[22]

As the tone of Douglas's remark suggests, his ideas were not to be so readily welcomed by either economists or governments. But he could not complain that his ideas were refused a hearing. Besides his easy access to the pages of the *New Age*, and the publication of four books in as many years, he was called as an expert witness to a Canadian Parliamentary Committee on Banking and Commerce in 1922, and the Labour Party established a high-power committee to consider his theories in the same year. Its conclusions indicate the kind of reception his ideas ultimately received. Having made recommendations of its own, the committee concludes:

In the meantime we re-affirm our conviction that proposals constructed upon the lines we have indicated are very much more likely to lead to a genuine control of the financial mechanism in the interests of the workers and of the nation than are the sovereign remedies of the Douglas theory, whose illusory character we have endeavoured to expose in the first part of this Report.[23]

Interest in Douglas subsided as the post-war slump passed away. It revived somewhat in 1925 when Winston Churchill put England back on the gold standard, in an act described as 'perhaps the most decisively damaging action involving money in modern times'.[24] The truly devastating consequences of this action for Britain's export industries—especially the coal industry—did nothing to strengthen confidence in the economic wisdom of the government. But it was not until the Depression that everyone became interested in such abstruse matters as economics. Then Douglas attracted a good deal of support—but not always of the right kind. John Hargreaves adopted Social Credit for his Fascist Greenshirts—with Douglas's approval. Douglas himself became politicized in the 1930s —exactly as Pound did. He became profoundly anti-democratic, and adopted a paranoid belief in the existence of an international conspiracy of Jews and Freemasons who controlled the banks of the world.[25]

There is little doubt that Pound's political and racial extremism stems primarily from his economic views, even though, as we shall see, they are buttressed by cultural and religious views. It is not uncommonly assumed that the economics which have led to such abhorrent political and racial opinions are equally abhorrent, or, at best, stupid. Earle Davis has devoted an entire book to the study of Pound's economics and concludes that Douglas's views had some virtue even if essentially incorrect, and were, moreover, designed to serve socially valuable ends. Davis's book, however, is flawed by his failure to consider chronology—either in the development of Pound's own views or in the changing climate of economic opinion between 1920 and the present.[26]

It should also be remembered that the Communist revolution in Russia was only three years old in 1920. No one was yet sure if it would be permanent, but everyone feared the possibility of its spread over Europe—especially those who recognized the futility of the 1914–18 war and thought that the leadership of the Western democracies was morally and intellectually bankrupt. Douglas and Pound both feared the anti-individual and anti-intellectual cast of Communism. At the same time, they were aware that a large proportion of the population of Europe suffered economic hardship. Douglas's economics promised a means of preserving individual freedoms from state supervision while, at the same time, removing economic hardship. A revolution in economic thought would render a political and social revolution unnecessary. The political aims of Social Credit, then, were conservative—but not, in 1920, Fascist. Douglas opposed all forms of state control of individual freedoms whether Fascist or Communist.

The extremism of Douglas and Pound arose from their failure to convince any significant element of the community of the justice and truth of their views. Pound tells us that 'Douglas's perception was that under the present accounting system the actual money available can never buy all the available goods.' He incorporates the theoretical statement of this perception (called the A plus B theorem) into canto 38:

> A factory
> has also another aspect, which we call the financial aspect
> It gives people the power to buy (wages, dividends
> which are power to buy) but it is also the cause of prices
> or values, financial, I mean financial values

It pays workers, and pays *for* material.
What it pays in wages and dividends
stays fluid, as power to buy, and this power is less,
per forza, damn blast your intellex, is less
than the total payments made by the factory
(as wages, dividends AND payments for raw material
bank charges etcetera)
and all, that is the whole, that is the total
of these is added into the total of prices
caused by that factory, any damn factory
and there is and must be therefore a clog
and the power to purchase can never
(under the present system) catch up with
prices at large,

and the light became so bright and so blindin'
in this layer of paradise
that the mind of man was bewildered.
(38/190:197–8)

The A plus B theorem is a causal analysis designed to explain the occurrence of under-consumption in industrial economies. As such, it flies in the face of Say's Law, the rock-bed foundation of classical economics. Say's Law states that 'the whole of the costs of production must necessarily be spent in the aggregate, directly or indirectly, on purchasing the product'.[27] No matter how he might twist and turn, Douglas could not alter his theorem so that it would conform with Say's Law. For this reason it was rejected by all competent economists:

[Say's Law] ruled in economics for more than a century. And the rule was no casual thing; to a remarkable degree acceptance of Say was the test by which reputable economists were distinguished from the crackpots. Until late in the '30s no candidate for a Ph.D. at a major American university who spoke seriously of a shortage of purchasing power as a cause of depression could be passed. He was a man who saw only the surface of things, was unworthy of the company of scholars. Say's Law stands as the most distinguished example of the stability of economic ideas, including when they are wrong.[28]

Say's Law was revoked by Keynes with the publication of his *General Theory* in 1936, although general acceptance of his argument was not achieved until after 1945. 'Say's Law sank without trace. There could, it was henceforth agreed, be oversaving.'[29] Keynes himself had been educated in an economics dominated by Say's Law, and his discovery of its error came with something of the force of a revelation. He is hard put to account for its long dominance over men's minds, and in doing so is scarcely more complimentary toward the motives of its adherents than Pound and Douglas were wont to be:

> The completeness of the Ricardian victory [Ricardian economics is built upon Say's Law and a commodity theory of money] is something of a curiosity and a mystery. It must have been due to a complex of suitabilities in the doctrine to the environment into which it was projected. That it reached conclusions quite different from what the ordinary uninstructed person would expect, added, I suppose, to its intellectual prestige. That its teaching, translated into practice, was austere and often unpalatable, lent it virtue. That it was adapted to carry a vast and consistent logical super-structure, gave it beauty. That it could explain much social injustice and apparent cruelty as an inevitable incident in the scheme of progress, and the attempt to change such things as likely on the whole to do more harm than good, commended it to authority. That it afforded a measure of justification to the free activities of the individual capitalist, attracted to it the support of the dominant social force behind authority.[30]

It was in such a climate of opinion as Keynes describes that Douglas and Pound sought to preach their economic theory of underconsumption. Small wonder that their voices grew shrill.

Douglas's perception that underconsumption was a cause of depression in modern industrial economies was, then, correct. The A plus B theorem as an analysis of the *causes* of that underconsumption seems to have been incorrect or at least over-simplified, but Pound's acceptance of that analysis was not unreasonable once the possibility of underconsumption is granted. However, Douglas's understanding of the specific nature of the causes of underconsumption led him to certain conclusions about the role of banks in modern industrial economies. In economic terms underconsumption and oversaving are the obverse and reverse of the same coin. Therefore, if there is underconsumption, there must be oversaving. Banks are the principal repository of savings. Banks, therefore, benefit from the chronic condition of underconsumption of modern industrial economies.

Douglas is quite forthright on this issue:

> There is no doubt whatever, and I do not suppose that anyone at all

familiar with the subject would dispute the statement for a moment, that the present trade depression is directly and consciously caused by the concerted action of the banks in restricting credit facilities, and that such credit facilities as are granted have very little relation to public need; that, whatever else might have happened had this policy not been pursued, there would have been no trade depression at this time, any more than there was during the war; and that the banks, through their control of credit facilities, hold the volume of production at all times in the hollow of their hands. You will, of course, understand that no personal accusation is involved in this statement; the banks act quite automatically according to the rules of the game, and if the public is so foolish as to sanction these rules I do not see why it should complain.[31]

The disclaimer of personal accusation in the last sentence does not ring true, and, indeed, does not represent Douglas's true feelings on the matter. But, if one accepts the disclaimer, the statement is substantially correct and is in agreement with Keynesian analysis of trade cycles. The principal difference between Douglas's analysis and that of Keynes is in Douglas's belief that the depression of 1920 and 1921 was 'directly and consciously caused by the concerted action of the banks'. In that difference lie the seeds of his extremism. His failure to convince economists of the plain truth of his opinions served to strengthen his belief that the banks controlled economic opinion as well as the economy of the nation.

Pound incorporates a little anecdote demonstrating the wilful stupidity of economists into canto 22 (C.H. is Douglas, and H.C.L. is 'High Cost of Living'):

> And C.H. said to the renowned Mr. Bukos:
> 'What is the cause of the H.C.L.?' and Mr. Bukos,
> The economist consulted of nations, said:
> 'Lack of labour.'
> And there were two millions of men out of work.
> And C.H. shut up, he said
> He would save his breath to cool his own porridge,
> But I didn't, and I went on plaguing Mr. Bukos
> Who said finally: 'I am an orthodox
> 'Economist.'
>
> (22/101–2:105–6)

Mr. Bukos is said to be J. M. Keynes, and Earle Davis is puzzled that Pound should be so opposed to Keynesian economics, since he believes Keynes's proposals to have some common ground with

Douglas's. But Davis forgets that canto 22 was published in 1928, eight years before Keynes became a Keynesian. As Keynes wrote, 'I myself held with conviction for many years the theories which I now attack.'[32] The conversation is probably apocryphal, but the response assigned to Mr. Bukos is not a great deal more irrational than many of the economic pronouncements of the day.

Keynes himself was aware of Douglas's theories and pays them measured tribute in *The General Theory*:

> Since the war there has been a spate of heretical theories of under-consumption, of which those of Major Douglas are the most famous. The strength of Major Douglas's advocacy has, of course, largely depended on orthodoxy having no valid reply to much of his destructive criticism. On the other hand, the detail of his diagnosis, in particular the so-called A+B theorem, includes much mere mystification. . . . Major Douglas is entitled to claim, as against some of his orthodox adversaries, that he at least has not been wholly oblivious of the outstanding problem of our economic system. Yet he has scarcely established an equal claim to rank—a private, perhaps, but not a major in the brave army of heretics—with Mandeville, Malthus, Gesell and Hobson, who, following their intuitions, have preferred to see the truth obscurely and imperfectly rather than to maintain error, reached indeed with clearness and consistency and by easy logic but on hypotheses inappropriate to the facts.[33]

However, Keynes is more impressed with the theories of Silvio Gesell than those of Douglas. Gesell's idea was to create carrying cost for money artificially, by requiring bills to have stamps affixed to them at intervals. Since the holder of the bills would have to purchase the stamps, it would be in his interest to spend the money rather than hoard it—thus creating employment for others.[34] Pound also discovered Gesell and his stamp-scrip money, and knew of an experiment with Gesellist money in the Tyrolean town of Wörgl in the 1930s:

> the state need not borrow
> as was shown by the mayor of Wörgl
> who had a milk route
> and whose wife sold shirts and short breeches
> and on whose book-shelf was the Life of Henry Ford
> and also a copy of the Divina Commedia
> and of the Gedichte of Heine
> a nice little town in the Tyrol in a wide flat-lying valley

near Innsbruck and when a note of the
small town of Wörgl went over
a counter in Innsbruck
and the banker saw it go over
all the slobs in Europe were terrified
'no one' said the Frau Burgomeister
'in this village who cd/ write a newspaper article.
Knew it was money but pretended it was not
in order to be on the safe side of the law.'[35]
(74/441:468–9)

Gesell's solution to the economic problems of industrial nations was very different from Douglas's, focusing as it did on the instrument of currency rather than on the institutions that manage the currency, the banks. But Gesell's programme was based on the same foundation as Douglas's. They both held a quantity theory of money, and they both implicitly denied the validity of Say's Law in their belief that the fundamental modern economic problem was underconsumption. The quantity theory of money is now universally accepted by Western economists. Its prophets were Irving Fisher and J. M. Keynes.[36]

It was from Fisher himself that Pound learned of Gesell and the Wörgl experiment. He enthusiastically reviewed Fisher's *Stamp Script* in the 26 October 1933 number of Orage's new journal, the *New English Weekly*. Fisher was still a voice in the wilderness in 1933, but Pound immediately recognized him as a monetary ally. It is not true, however, that he abandoned Douglas for Fisher and Gesell. Stamp scrip remains a stop-gap measure on the road to a Douglasite utopia with a national dividend. Pound reviewed Fisher's *Inflation* less enthusiastically on 5 April 1934, and Gesell's own *The Natural Economic Order* on 31 January 1935 (all in the *New English Weekly*). In both these later reviews he remains faithful to Social Credit theory, but berates Social Creditors for ignoring the valuable ideas in Gesell.

The quantity theory of money, in its simplest expression, amounts to the proposition that the price of goods and services is a function of their costs, the supply, the demand for them, *and* the supply of money. Given a constant supply of and demand for goods and services, their price will rise and fall with the supply of money. The theory seems self-evident, but in the 1930s it had to overcome the massive influence of Ricardo, who held a commodity theory of money, based on a labour theory of value. In effect, this theory stated that money was a commodity like any other. Therefore the value of money was a function of its supply and of the costs of its production, that is, the amount of labour necessary to produce a given quantity of money. Paper money was only a certificate of claim on true commodity money—gold. Karl Marx built his critique of capitalism on these Ricardian principles of commodity money and the labour theory of value.

Against the pre-eminent influence of Ricardo, Douglas offered unsophisticated common sense:

> Money is only a mechanism by means of which we deal with things—it has no properties except those we choose to give to it. A phrase such as 'There is no money in the country with which to do such and so' means simply nothing, unless we are also saying 'The goods and services required to do this thing do not exist and cannot be produced, therefore it is useless to create the money equivalent of them.' For instance, it is simply childish to say that a country has no money for social betterment, or for any other purpose, when it has the skill, the men and the material and plant to create that betterment. The banks or the Treasury can create the money in five minutes, and are doing it every day, and have been doing it for centuries.[37]

And Pound put it even more simply:

> Money is a title, quantitatively determined, exchangeable at will against any kind of commodities offered on the market. In this respect it differs from a railway ticket, which is a specific title without any general application.[38]

It cannot be too strongly emphasized—given Pound's reputation for dottiness on economic matters—that the understanding of the nature of money expressed in these statements has prevailed among economists. However, both Douglas and Pound remained economic mavericks even after the Keynesian revolution—preferring to see all professional economists as apologists for the status quo. As late as 1945 Douglas attacked the Keynesian policy of a managed money supply. It is, he wrote, 'simply a vicious form of managed inflation, ultimately accompanied of necessity by cumulative industrial waste. Assuming that it is understood by its sponsors, it is an attempt to perpetuate government by finance.[39]

Pound is uncharacteristically eloquent and clear-headed on the subject of commodity money:

Fascinated by the lustre of a metal, man made it into chains. Then he invented something against nature, a false representation in the mineral world of laws which apply only to animals and vegetables.

The nineteenth century, the infamous century of usury, went even further, creating a species of monetary Black Mass. Marx and Mill, in spite of their superficial differences, agreed in endowing money with properties of a quasi-religious nature. There was even the concept of energy being 'concentrated in money', as if one were speaking of the divine quality of consecrated bread. But a half-lira piece has never created the cigarette or the piece of chocolate that used, in pre-war days, to issue from the slot-machine.[40]

He should have written Ricardo and Marx, rather than Marx and Mill, but otherwise Pound's complaint that Marx endowed gold with quasi-mystical properties is essentially correct. For Marx, gold is 'congealed labour'. Into it is transubstantiated the value of the human labour required to produce it:

The commodity that functions as a measure of value, and, either in its own person or by a representative, as the medium of circulation, is money. Gold (or silver) is therefore money. It functions as money, on the one hand, when it has to be present in its own golden person. It is then the money-commodity, neither merely ideal, as in its function of a measure of value, nor capable of being represented, as in its function of circulating medium. On the other hand, it also functions as money, when by virtue of its function, whether that function be performed in person or by representative, it congeals into the sole form of value, the only adequate form of existence of exchange-value, in opposition to use-value, represented by all other commodities.[41]

It was this commodity theory of money (and perhaps also its extraordinarily convoluted expression) that enabled Pound to resist the Marxist temptation.

The belief that money possesses intrinsic value is the first article of faith of usury. Its foundation is the labour theory of value—that the value of a thing is a function of the amount of labour required to produce it. Although Pound never isolated and attacked the labour theory of value, he recognized the philistinism of its fruits. The aesthetic equivalent of the labour theory of value is the grandiose. No artist can accept the quantity of effort expended in the creation of a thing as a measure of value. For the artist, value must be a matter of quality, not quantity; that is, it must rest on human needs and desires. The atom bomb probably embodies more human labour than Notre-Dame Cathedral, but its value to humanity is not therefore greater. But the most vicious implication of a labour theory of value is that the abundance of nature is thought to be without value, because it does not embody human labour:

> Usury is against Nature's increase
> Whores for Eleusis;
> Under usury no stone is cut smooth
> Peasant has no gain from his sheep herd.
> (51/250–1:261–2)

The monetary heresy of Douglas and Pound, then, consists in their belief that money is a fiction, an artificial creation of human ingenuity. Money, like the city itself, is a work of art. To speak of money as a thing, a natural object, possessing an inherent value such as that possessed by soil, air, and water, is, for Pound, a species of idolatry. Both the arch-capitalist, Ricardo, and the arch-socialist, Marx, were in Pound's view, idolatrous worshippers at the shrine of usury because they both attributed intrinsic value to money. Ironically, even though the artificial character of money is now universally recognized outside the Communist world, Pound's monetary views are still thought to be crazy. Perhaps his decision to personify usury as the object of idolatrous worship was not as far-fetched as it might at first appear.

However, the conversion of the world from a commodity to a quantity theory of money has failed to bring about the earthly paradise, as Pound permitted himself to believe it might. His simple faith in ideas, in the power of the human mind, was misplaced. He was right, I think, in his perception of the capacity of ideology to produce evil, but he woefully overestimated its capacity to produce good. He also overestimated the capacity of his own mind to see clearly where others were muddled. He could recognize the face of evil in the idolatry of gold, but could not recognize it in the human faces of Mussolini and Hitler. Nor did he have the patience to learn how correct economic principles could be applied to reorganize society.

Douglas's solution for the chronic underconsumption which afflicted industrial economies was simply to create enough money to purchase all the goods and services the nation was capable of delivering, and give to every citizen of the nation whatever was left over when the costs of production had been covered. It was his belief that with modern technology the costs of production of goods (in raw material and wages at current levels) would be far below their demand value. With technological improvements in productivity, an ever decreasing number of workers would be required to produce the same volume of goods. Fewer workers meant less money available to purchase the goods produced. Therefore it was necessary to give money to those displaced from work. The money they would receive was called a national dividend, and they were entitled to it because the tremendous wealth created by technological development was the property of all. He called this wealth the 'increment of association'. The scheme is highly attractive in outline, although its social organization, as Douglas describes it, is distressingly like Orwell's *Nineteen Eighty Four*. I have no idea if it is practicable; it certainly sounds too good to be true.

Pound does not demonstrate much interest in Douglas's actual schemes of economic and social reorganization. It is his theoretical analysis of industrial economies that attracted Pound. However, he does adopt one dimension of Douglas's criticism of industrial democracies which is technical rather than theoretical. Douglas believed, as a deduction from his A plus B theorem, that a very considerable proportion of industrial production had to be wasted or exported in order to prevent the supply of goods from outrunning the supply of money by too great a margin. The resultant competition for export markets was, he believed, a principal cause of war. But, the most important evil of all, in his view, was the only socialized form of consumption known in the 1920s—the market for military hardware. Arms and munitions did not have to be paid for out of wages, salaries, and profits. They were financed, at least in time of war, by government borrowing. Douglas thought this borrowing benefited the banks as well as those involved in the munitions industry. He therefore perceived an unholy alliance between bankers and manufacturers of munitions—a more sinister version of what President Eisenhower much later called the 'military–industrial complex'. Waste—such as that represented by the manufacture of armaments—was necessary to keep industrial economies going with their present structure. War was therefore an almost inevitable consequence of the economic structures of Western nations—hence, Pound's fulminations against Britain and the United States throughout the 1930s and during the war. The governments of these nations had to be the tool of the bankers or they would change the structure of their economies so as to make war unprofitable.

The belief that banks, through their control of the money supply (bank deposits and bank credit represent the greater part of a modern nation's money supply), exercised a very considerable degree of control over the economies of nations was substantially correct. The notion that the profitability of manufacturing armaments is an incentive to war is plausible. The conclusion from these premises, that bankers and armaments manufacturers deliberately and consciously conspire to create unemployment and war, attributes far greater understanding, intelligence, and unity of purpose to these postulated groups than they are likely to have possessed—not to speak of a truly unbelievable quantity of purposeless malevolence. The conclusion is the result of paranoia, not logic.

Given the further irrational deduction that banks were controlled by Jews, it was an easy matter to mistake the racism of the Fascists for opposition to the conspiracy of bankers. The fact that neither Hitler nor Mussolini shared Pound's economics counted for little when they shared his hatred of banks and of the Western democracies controlled by bankers.[42]

The 'logic' of Pound's political and racial opinions as I have described them took many years to develop. He was by 1920 a convert to Douglasite economics, but he was not a Fascist sympathizer until 1931. And he was not wholly given over to a belief in an international conspiracy of Jewish bankers until the 1940s. That these extreme views arose out of the frustration caused by the failure to shake men's faith in the socially harmful principles of Ricardian economics, even in the face of widespread human suffering, does not excuse them. By the same token, the abhorrent nature of Pound's political and racial views cannot be seen to invalidate his economic views.

The exposés of industrial waste, sabotage, and activities of munitions salesmen in cantos 18 and 19, then, reflect Douglas's understanding of the inevitable consequences of the capitalist system of price setting—organized waste and war:

> And old Biers was out there, a greenhorn,
> To sell cannon, and Metevsky found the back door;
> And old Biers sold the munitions,
> And Metevsky died and was buried, *i.e.* officially,
> And sat in the Yeiner Kafé watching the funeral.
> About ten years after this incident,
> He owned a fair chunk of Humbers.

'Peace! Pieyce!!' said Mr. Giddings,
'Uni-ver-sal? Not while yew got tew billions ov money,'
Said Mr. Giddings, 'invested in the man-u-facture
'Of war machinery.'

(18/81:85)

The heavy-handed frivolity of Pound's exposure of the perfidious Sir Zenos Metevsky and other businessmen is neither very amusing nor very objectionable. He does a little better with Baldy Bacon in canto 12, but the story of the 'pore honest sailor' in that canto has elicited more groans than laughter. The Hell cantos (14 and 15) stand as a singularly apt example of the triumph of feeling over art.

In all, Pound devotes 13 of the first 71 cantos to exposure or ridicule of business men, bankers, economists, etc. They are 12, 14, 15, 16, 18, 19, 22, 27, 28, 35, 38, 41, and 46. These cantos are designed to apprise the reader of the way the world is run—as revealed to those equipped with the Douglas economic analysis. As poetry they are almost entirely without interest or distinction. As satire they are too specific, or insufficiently pointed. As exposé they are far too obscure. As a didactic element in the poem explaining the nature of Western economic organization they have suffered from the failure of anyone to understand clearly what Pound was getting at. One can get the point much better from Douglas:

the policy of more and yet more production at prices fixed on a basis of cost and profit is a mere aggravation of the prevailing difficulty. Because the available purchasing power would absorb a decreasing proportion of this production it must either be exported or wasted, and both of these lead straight to war, the supreme waster.[43]

Scattered about in these cantos one occasionally meets a praiseworthy individual of a constructive bent such as Pa Stadtvolk and 'that man [who] sweat blood to put through that railway' in canto 28. 'That man' is also invoked in canto 21 (97:101) and 22 (101:105). His role was for a long time a little mystifying to me. What Pound means by him is much clearer in 'The Revolt of Intelligence' than it is in the *Cantos*. Pound is reporting one relative's account of the exploits of a shared, deceased relative:

'That man! He sweated blood to build that line of railroad. I dropped money on it. What he ever got out of it I don't know.' Apart from the titillation of vanity that might have come to a man from having his name in large brass letters on the front of a locomotive—for the early Western enthusiasm for transport named the individual machines as seamen have named ships through the ages—I must conclude that the reward must have been very largely in the sensation of accomplishment. The typical Capitalist, Warenhauser, received, I believe, the cash benefits. I am disinclined to believe that the railroad builder was led on by the hope of riches. The hope of riches could not have moved him to the greater and later labour of getting measures for the irrigation of the American desert through Congress.[44]

The didactic point is clear from this account: some men work out of the love of creation—others ('the typical capitalists') are moved by the desire for money. He who desires money is a usurer. He who creates is an artist. The two types are in eternal opposition, for the capitalist or usurer can get money only by taking it from those who create things. The usurer most frequently wins, but 'that man' has a victory to his credit:

> And that man sweat blood to put through that railway,
> And what he ever got out of it?
> And one day he drove down to the whorehouse
> Cause all the farmers had consented
> and granted the right of way,
> But the pornoboskos wdn't. have it at any price
> And said he'd shoot the surveyors,
> But he didn't shoot ole pop in the buckboard,
> He giv him the right of way.
> And they thought they had him flummox'd,
> Nobody'd sell any rails;
> Till he went up to the north of New York state
> And found some there on the ground
> And he had 'em pried loose and shipped 'em
> And had 'em laid here through the forest.
> (28/138:143)

The thirteen cantos devoted to the exposure of contemporary economic chicanery are, then, not very successful. They are mildly amusing, mildly confusing, occasionally a little rude, and seldom very instructive. But they are not a very serious weakness in the poem. They represent an effort to achieve a didactic purpose by means of anecdote—in line with Pound's principles of ideogrammic composition. Their rather moderate degree of success is still greater than that achieved in later attempts to apply the same technique for similar didactic purposes to the past—as we shall see. The usura cantos, by contrast, are a very effective poetic statement of the same economic perceptions.

Economics undeniably became an obsession for Pound, and he devoted increasingly larger proportions of his effort to the exposure of financial chicanery as the economic situation in the West deteriorated between the wars, adding Silvio Gesell, Brooks Adams, and Alexander Del Mar to his list of economic sages. Much of his historical research—which was meant to serve different purposes—was deflected toward economics. As economics came to dominate Pound's interest, it inevitably dominated the *Cantos*. But this was a gradual development, and it was far from the original impetus of the *Cantos*. By 1941 he thought he had finished with economics, and could turn to 'matters of belief'—matters closer to his real competence. As it happened he never finished with economics. It persists as a major concern to his death. On the whole his efforts to deal directly with economic theory and economic history in the *Cantos* are damaging to the poem, as they were damaging to his life.

That Pound should have been so absorbed by economics attests to his social conscience and his desire to incorporate all important aspects of modern thought into his epic. That he was so grievously misled into abhorrent political and racial views attests to his impatience and overweening self confidence. Economics, as Keynes suggests, is a moral discipline and hence a proper subject for the poet. Pound was unwise to think he had all the answers. But was he unwise to seek for answers to human suffering caused by war and deprivation? He was unwise to follow Major Douglas into paranoid racism. But he was not unwise to accept the Major's contention that underconsumption and mismanagement of money were the principal causes of unemployment and waste in the period between the wars.

Canto 46 contains a general summing-up of the economic lesson taught by the *Cantos*:

> with great difficulty got back to Patersons'
> The bank makes it *ex nihil*
> Denied by five thousand professors, will any
> Jury convict 'um? This case, and with it
> the first part, draws to a conclusion,
> of the first phase of this opus, Mr Marx, Karl, did not
> foresee this conclusion, you have seen a good deal of
> the evidence, not knowing it evidence. . . .
>
> (46/233–4:244)

The impassioned outburst of this canto sounds like a guide to the preceding cantos, withheld from the reader until now for rhetorical reasons. In fact, it is a record of Pound's reaction to the revelations contained in a book he had just read, Christopher Hollis's *The Two Nations*.[45] It is from Hollis that Pound gets the remark attributed to Paterson, the original proposer of the Bank of England, 'The bank hath benefit of the interest on all moneys which it creates out of nothing.'[46] Here was finally exposed with crystal clarity the organized robbery of banks. Hollis dates the birth of usurocracy from the foundation of the Bank of England in 1694. It was established, according to Hollis, in order to finance Charles II's war needs. Charles had been circulating promissory notes which performed every function of paper money, but he was persuaded to withdraw them in favour of paper issued by the new Bank:

> By a strange anomaly private persons were to be permitted to invent that money and put it into circulation in the form of loans. Nor is it any paradox to say that that anomaly is the cause of the greater part of the evils that have since afflicted mankind. Had Charles' experiment [of the promissory notes] succeeded, had it come to be recognized that, when new money was required, it was the business of the King to issue it, the whole history . . . of the world must necessarily have been changed.[47]

Here was something much more clear and more damning than anything Pound had managed to unearth himself. Not even Douglas had been able to catch the bankers off their guard so completely as Hollis had done. Moreover, Hollis explained how it was that the bankers got away with it:

> The elements of monetary theory had been perfectly understood since the time of the Greeks. As Macaulay records, Gresham's Law is found noted in Aristophanes. In the Middle Ages the quantitative theory was familiar to every educated person, nor was it, as will be later shown, until in the eighteenth century the educational machine deliberately imposed confusion on men's minds, that there was any misunderstanding of the ABC of these problems. Both Elizabeth and all other educated people were then well aware that if silver 'poured' into England it would cause a rise in prices.[48]

Hollis's book was published the year before Keynes's *General Theory* yet recommends fiscal policies almost identical to those followed by governments today on Keynesian principles. Hollis has praise for Major Douglas, for Keynes's *Treatise on Money*, and for

President Roosevelt's New Deal. Like Keynes, he praises the monetary policies of the medieval world and of the mercantilists. And, like Keynes, he adopts the quantitative theory of money, then recently formulated by Irving Fisher. He is unlike Keynes in labelling the eighteenth and nineteenth centuries as the Age of Usury, and in postulating a conspiracy of bankers and educators to mislead the world with 'Whig' history.

The Two Nations is a remarkable and intelligent work, and it is too bad that Pound chose to take only the exposure of the alleged banking fraud and not the admiration for Keynes and Roosevelt. It is strange that the book is not better known, for even though Hollis is rather harsh on banks, it is an absorbing study of financial history. But, although the hero of his book is Benjamin Disraeli, Hollis does betray a degree of anti-Semitism:

> It is clear then that the battle between capitalism and communism, so far from being the eternal struggle of our race, was in reality little more than a family quarrel between two Jews for the divine right to deceive mankind —between the Dutch Jew Ricardo and the German Jew Marx. And before the menace of a real challenge to the system—the challenge that has come in our day from President Roosevelt—even the family quarrel is forgotten. . . .[49]

Pound held Hollis's view of Marx's economics, but not his view of Roosevelt.

Despite the radical views expressed in this book, Hollis went on to a distinguished career as an educator. His account of his relationship with Pound reveals the degree to which Pound had isolated himself from the intellectual community which he hoped to influence:

> I made at that time through my writings another strange friend [F. D. Roosevelt is the previous one], Ezra Pound. Ezra Pound was of course an enthusiastic supporter of Mussolini and imagined—I think with little evidence—that Mussolini's attack on the Money Power was of the same kind as that which I had exposed in *The Breakdown of Money* [this is not the book Pound read]. I soon found the enthusiasm of his argument embarrassing. During the war I had at the Air Ministry the duty of monitoring foreign broadcasts and was a little dismayed to read one day in an extract from an Italian talk by Ezra Pound, 'Who today in England dares speak of Christopher Hollis?' He obviously took it for granted that I had been suppressed in the reign of terror that ruled war-time England —probably shot under 18B. I concealed the extract from my superiors at

the Air Ministry and have never, I think, till this day, mentioned it to anyone.[50]

To Hollis, Pound was nothing more than a mad voice whose unaccountable enthusiasms threatened embarrassment. This was late in the development of Pound's extremism. But Pound was never able to escape the crankiness which is always a risk for those isolated from their own intellectual home. His self-exile in Italy had many different causes—some of them personal—but its effect was to intensify the intellectual isolation he had already imposed on himself by accepting Major Douglas's economic theories; eventually destroying the man, the poet, and damaging the poem: 'But the beauty is not the madness/Tho' my errors and wrecks lie about me.'

Before we can look for that beauty again—in the *Pisan Cantos* and after—we shall have to examine Pound's massive effort to incorporate history into the *Cantos*—an effort which becomes increasingly futile and counter-productive with each new section. Nonetheless it is an effort he could not avoid if he were to be true to his own conception of his role as an epic poet. Whatever else Pound was, he was honest to himself and to others. Having set himself the impossible task of writing a truly epic poem, he did not seek ways of evading its insurmountable difficulties. If Pound is a martyr as many would have him be, he is a martyr to his own conception of the serious artist. His effort was a noble one. We should not be too quick to condemn him for his errors.

3. 'HOMOLOGIES, SYMPATHIES, IDENTITIES'

If we turn back to the 'Postscript' to *The Natural Philosophy of Love* where Pound placed so much weight on Propertius' line, 'Ingenium nobis ipsa puella facit', we will find a more modern, quasi-scientific theory bringing together Mead's Gnostic sexual metaphor, Péladan's fabricated religious history, Cavalcanti's canzone, and Eleusis:

> . . . man has for centuries nibbled at this idea of connection, intimate connection between his sperm and his cerebration, the ascetic has tried to withhold all his sperm, the lure, the ignis fatuus perhaps, of wanting to super-think; the dope-fiend has tried opium and every inferior to Bacchus, to get an extra kick out of the organ, the mystics have sought the gleam in the tavern, Helen of Tyre, Priestesses in the temple of Venus, in Indian temples, stray priestesses in the streets, unuprootable custom, and probably with a basis of sanity.[51]

De Gourmont's book proposes a theory of animal evolution in which the principal role is played by an entelechy or *élan vital* manifesting itself through the infinite variety of techniques for sexual reproduction in the animal world. Pound later developed an enthusiasm for Louis Agassiz, an eminent American biologist who also opposed Darwin's theory of animal evolution through the natural selection of the most adaptive chance mutations. Agassiz maintained a faith in spontaneous mutation, again on the Aristotelian model of some force, entelechy, or *directio voluntatis* within the organism.[52] Obviously such a theory, finding its most graphic illustration in insect metamorphosis, comports well with the Cavalcanti/Pound conception of the nature and function of Amor:

> The spermatozoide is, I take it, regarded as a sort of quintessence; the brain is also a quintessence, or at least 'in rapport with' all parts of the body; the single spermatozoide demands simply that the ovule shall construct a human being, the suspended spermatozoide (if my wild shot rings the bell) is ready to dispense with, in the literal sense, incarnation, en-fleshment. . . .
>
> Three channels, hell, purgatory, heaven, if one wants to follow yet another terminology: digestive excretion, incarnation, freedom in the imagination, i.e., cast into an exterior formlessness, or into form material, or merely imaginative visually or perhaps musically or perhaps *fixed* in some other sensuous dimension, even of taste or odour.[53]

The last notion, of heaven fixed in the sensuous dimension of taste or odour, finds its poetic expression in the *Pisan Cantos*:

Le Paradis n'est pas artificiel
but spezzato apparently
it exists only in fragments unexpected excellent sausage,
the smell of mint, for example,
Ladro the night cat.
(74/438:465)

De Gourmont's theory of spontaneous metamorphosis of animal form through some kind of connection between the animal's will and imagination, and his sperm, struck a responsive chord in Pound. But, fortunately, he confines himself in the *Cantos* to the more traditional imagery of light and of metamorphosis on an Ovidian model. De Gourmont's idea is, then, not important to the *Cantos* as a source of imagery or form. Its interest for us is that it leads Pound to bring together in the 'Postscript' the various threads of his imaginative world, and he brings them together under the rubric of sexuality. When Pound tells us that 'a great treasure of verity exists for mankind in Ovid and in the subject matter of Ovid's long poem',[54] he is thinking of metamorphosis, not as a poetic fiction, but as a metaphor for the relationship between the human and the divine, the third subject of the *Cantos*, 'the magic moment or moment of metamorphosis, bust thru from quotidien into "divine or permanent world"'. In Ovid, metamorphosis is always akin to death as well as a means of escape—often an escape from sexual violation. It is the same in canto 4, but the image of apotheosis in the *Cantos* is to lie with the goddess and live to tell the tale, rather than an escape from sexual violation.

Although the linking of love and death is an ancient motif, and, moreover, is intimately connected with the Eleusinian myth, de Gourmont does provide a perspective on it rather different from those found in literary sources. He makes much of the pre-eminence of the female in the more primitive forms of life such as the spider and the moth, where the adult male frequently lives only long enough to impregnate the female and then dies or is eaten by her. This perspective lies behind the rather unexpected lines in canto 47 where Odysseus' conquest of Circe is once again celebrated:

> Two span, two span to a woman,
> Beyond that she believes not. Nothing is of any importance.
> To that is she bent, her intention
> To that art thou called ever turning intention,
> Whether by night the owl-call, whether by sap in shoot,
> Never idle, by no means by no wiles intermittent
> Moth is called over mountain
> The bull runs blind on the sword, *naturans*
> To the cave art thou called, Odysseus,
> By Molü hast thou respite for a little,
> By Molü art thou freed from the one bed
> that thou may'st return to another.
>
> (47/237:247)

And it also informs canto 29, one of the three cantos added to the first two sections in order to create *A Draft of XXX Cantos*:

> She is submarine, she is an octopus, she is
> A biological process,
>
> . . . . .

. . . 'But this beats me,
'Beats me, I mean that I do not understand it;
'This love of death that is in them.'
(29/145:150)

De Gourmont's theory is thoroughly sexist, giving the evolutionary power of the entelechy entirely to the male sperm, 'the insect representing the female'. Pound attempts in the 'Postscript' to avoid the charge of anti-feminism, but without much success, giving to man 'the inventions; the new gestures, the extravagance, the wild shots, the impractical', and to woman utility and extreme economy. In canto 29 he is uncompromisingly anti-feminist: 'Nel ventre tuo, o nella mente mia,/"Yes, Milady, precisely, if you wd./ have anything properly made."'[55] De Gourmont's ideas on evolution are embarrassingly crude, particularly when compared to the similar, but much more subtle theories later developed by Teilhard de Chardin.[56] They have, however, little effect on the *Cantos*, and attract Pound primarily as a 'scientific' corroboration of his basic notion that the relationship between men and women, as between men and gods, is one of subject and object. Women, in their beauty, represent—or, indeed, embody—the principal attribute of divinity, while men perceive that beauty and (because the act of perception is itself a creative act)[57] also create it.

It is a perilous undertaking to conceive of the sexual relationship in terms of male subject and female object—however flattering it may be to female beauty, it dehumanizes women. But the problem is not Pound's; it belongs to the tradition of courtly love from which he derives his aesthetic and his religion. In that tradition women lose their humanity in order to take on the aspect of a divinity. Fenollosa, on the other hand, expressed the subject–object relationship for Pound in terms free of sexism:

The whole delicate substance of speech is built upon substrata of metaphor. Abstract terms, pressed by etymology, reveal their ancient roots still embedded in direct action. But the primitive metaphors do not spring from arbitrary *subjective* processes. They are possible only because they follow objective lines of relations in nature herself. Relations are more real and more important than the things which they relate. The forces which produce the branch-angles of an oak lay potent in the acorn. Similar lines of resistance, half-curbing the out-pressing vitalities, govern the branching of rivers and of nations. Thus a nerve, a wire, a roadway, and a clearing-house are only varying channels which communication forces for itself. This is more than analogy, it is identity of structure. Nature furnishes her own clues. Had the world not been full of homologies sympathies, and identities, thought would have been starved and language chained to the obvious. There would have been no bridge whereby to cross from the minor truth of the seen to the major truth of the unseen.[58]

Fenollosa is the American sinologist from whose notes Pound produced *The Chinese Written Character as a Medium for Poetry*. The notes were given to him by Fenollosa's widow late in 1913. She had met Pound at a literary party in London earlier in the year, and had been sufficiently impressed to entrust him with the task of editing and publishing her husband's notes.[59] Fenollosa is included in the passage from the 'Postscript' to *The Natural Philosophy of Love*, quoted above, as one of those whose ideas can be derived from 'ingenium nobis ipsa puella facit'.

It was through these notes that Pound became interested in Chinese culture, and particularly the Chinese ideogram and the manner of its operation as Fenollosa understood it. Like Agassiz and de Gourmont, Fenollosa obviously believed in the vitality of the objective or perceived world. For him metaphor was the basis of all language because metaphor mimes 'the objective lines of relation in nature herself'. The Chinese ideogram, because it is frequently a composite picture of things in nature simply placed in conjunction with one another, is the most perfect linguistic mimesis of these lines of relation in nature. Pound gives an example of this mimesis in *The ABC of Reading* with an analysis of the Chinese character for 'red':

He puts (or his ancestor put) together the abbreviated pictures of

ROSE CHERRY
IRON RUST FLAMINGO

That, you see, is very much the kind of thing a biologist does (in a very much more complicated way) when he gets together a few hundred or thousand slides, and picks out what is necessary for his general statement. Something that fits the case, that applies in all of the cases.

The Chinese 'word' or ideogram for red is based on something everyone KNOWS.[60]

This is a perfect example of Pound's understanding of the creativity of the act of perception—however imperfect it may be as an example of the processes of the Chinese language. The perceiving subject observes objects entirely independent of himself, but creates out of them a new thing which is neither object nor subject but the 'seen form' which arises from the interaction of object and subject—presumably acting in accordance with homologies which embrace both subject and object.

Pound anticipated Fenollosa's 'objective lines of relation in nature' in 'Psychology and Troubadours' where he speaks of those who have a 'germinal' consciousness. 'Their thoughts', he says, 'are in them as the thought of the tree is in the seed, or in the grass, or the grain, or the blossom. And these minds are the more poetic, and they affect mind about them, and transmute it as the seed the earth. And this sort of mind is close on the vital universe.'[61] The terms 'subject' and 'object' can have only a functional meaning in a vitalist universe of 'wood alive, or stone alive', because all existing things are themselves subjects, as in the Erigenian tag, 'All things which are, are lights':

Sunt lumina
that the drama is wholly subjective
stone knowing the form which the carver imparts it
the stone knows the form
sia Cythera, sia Ixotta, sia in Santa Maria dei Miracoli[62].
(74/430:457).

Fenollosa's understanding of the function of the Chinese ideogram obviously owes a great deal to a conception of the universe as a kind of vital organism—a conception he had probably brought with him to Japan from Harvard. In any event, whatever the origin of his vitalism, it dovetailed admirably with ideas Pound had already absorbed. To Fenollosa, the basic unit of Chinese written language, the ideogram, was pure poetry because it was pure metaphor:

Metaphor, the revealer of nature, is the very substance of poetry. The known interprets the obscure, the universe is alive with myth. The beauty and freedom of the observed world furnish a model, and life is pregnant with art. It is a mistake to suppose, with some philosophers of aesthetics, that art and poetry aim to deal with the general and the abstract. This misconception has been foisted upon us by mediaeval logic. Art and poetry deal with the concrete of nature, not with rows of separate 'particulars', for such rows do not exist. Poetry is finer than prose because it gives us more concrete truth in the same compass of words. Metaphor, its chief device, is at once the substance of nature and of language. Poetry only does consciously what the primitive races did unconsciously. The chief work of literary men in dealing with language, and of poets especially, lies in feeling back along the ancient lines of advance.[63]

This paragraph provides an admirable rationale for the kind of poem the *Cantos* were to become.

For some reason Pound did not publish Fenollosa's essay until 1920, in *Instigations*. Instead he used Fenollosa's cribs on some Chinese poems to produce *Cathay* (1915), learning in the process of translation how to write what I have called poetry of inference. He would like to think of the *Cantos* as a poem exemplifying the principles of the ideogram, dealing with the 'concrete of nature', and 'the beauty and freedom of the observed world', and 'feeling back along the ancient lines of advance'; a poem which, perhaps, like Fenollosa's primitive metaphors follows 'objective lines of relations in nature herself'. But these notions are epistemological, and not rhetorical. Poetry must be written on rhetorical principles whether acknowledged as such or not. And the rhetoric of the *Cantos* is akin to that of the Chinese poetry in *Cathay*, a rhetoric of inference or implicit allusion.

One might argue that in the *Cantos* Pound assembles the concrete of man instead of the 'concrete of nature'. As the character for 'red' juxtaposes abbreviated pictures of a rose, a cherry, a flamingo, and iron rust, the *Cantos* juxtapose abbreviated pictures of Chinese, classical, medieval, Renaissance, and modern culture. And as the concept red arises from the abbreviated pictures in the Chinese character, so the concepts of love, beauty, and justice may be expected to arise from the abbreviated portraits in the *Cantos*. As Pound himself has said, 'I picked out this and that thing that interested me, and then jumbled them into a bag.' Somehow out of the jumble would arise a coherent unity greater than the parts, as the rose emerges from the steel dust under the influence of a magnetic field. Such a method relies either on the coherence implicit, but unseen, in the material collected, or on some coherence in the mind of the collector. In either case, it's not the way to make a work of art—at least, Pound told Cory it was not.

Pound describes the ideogrammic method as 'the examination and juxtaposition of particular specimens—e.g. particular works, passages of literature, as an implement for acquisition and transmission of knowledge.'[64] This method becomes dominant in the *Cantos* as early as *A Draft of Cantos 17–27* (1928), and the technique for applying it was devised in the composition of the Malatesta group (1922–3). As a method of acquiring and transmitting knowledge, it obviously relates to the poem's content and its didactic purpose rather than to its aesthetic or rhetoric. The didactic purpose of the poem, as Pound stated it in 1962, is 'to resist the view that Europe and civilisation is going to Hell'. And he expands on the remark leaving no doubt of the centrality of this didactic purpose in the *Cantos*:

If I am being 'crucified for an idea'—that is, the coherent idea around which my muddles accumulated—it is probably the idea that European culture ought to survive . . . along with whatever other cultures, in whatever universality. Against the propaganda of terror and the propaganda of luxury, have you a nice simple answer? One has worked on certain materials trying to establish bases and axes of reference.[65]

Much earlier, in response to Ivor Winter's comments on the *Cantos*, he also described his poem as essentially didactic:

The poem is not a dualism of past against present. Monism is pretty bad, but dualism (Miltonic puritanism, etc.) is just plain lousy.

The poem should establish an hierarchy of values, not simply: past is good, present is bad, which I certainly do not believe and have never believed.

If the reader wants three categories he can find them rather better in: permanent, recurrent and merely haphazard or casual.[66]

This didactic purpose of the *Cantos* becomes, for Pound, central to its claim of epic status. '*Epic*', he told Harriet Monroe on her refusal to print canto 37, 'includes history and history ain't all slush and babies' pink toes. I admit that economics are *in themselves* uninteresting, but heroism *is* poetic, I mean it is fit subject for poesy.'[67] But he did not always think of his poem as an epic. In 1924 he told the printer of *A Draft of XVI Cantos* that 'it ain't epic. It's part of a long poem.'[68] The 1924 remark may have been prompted by modesty, but I think it more likely that at that time Pound still preferred to think of his poem in terms of the *Commedia* which he believed to be lyric rather than epic.

There can be no question but that Pound intended from the very beginning to incorporate the past into his poem. But his early use of history conformed to the traditional motifs of love and violence, crime and heroism—all appropriate to a lyric modelled on the *Commedia*—or, indeed, to one modelled on *Sordello*. The Malatesta group itself is essentially the record of the struggle of the failed hero like Péladan's Quixote—or, again, like Browning's Sordello. Malatesta's story conforms to the framing Odyssean adventure as transformed by Pound into an Eleusinian revelation achieved by the conquest of beauty incarnate in woman—except that Malatesta fails.

Sigismund Malatesta is a fifteenth-century Italian *condottiere* of particularly unsavoury reputation, who engaged on several sides in the profusion of wars, alliances, betrayals, and pillagings that enliven Italian history of the period.[69] Eventually he got himself excommunicated:

> So that in the end that pot-scraping little runt Andreas
> Benzi, da Siena
> Got up to spout out the bunkum
> That that monstrous swollen, swelling s.o.b.
> Papa Pio Secundo
> Aeneas Silvius Piccolomini
> da Siena
> Has told him to spout, in their best bear's-greased latinity;
>
> *Stupro*, *caede*, *adulter*,
> *homocidia*, *parricidia ac periurus*,
> *presbitericidia*, *audax*, *libidinosus*,
> wives, jew-girls, nuns, necrophiliast, *fornicarium ac sicarium*,
> *proditor*, *raptor*, *incestuosus*, *incendiarius*, *ac*
> *concubinarius*. . . .
>
> (10/44:48)

The reasons for Malatesta's excommunication were doubtless complex—having at least as much to do with the tangled political struggles of the peninsula as with religion. Pound does not enlighten his readers on the Pope's reasons, but leaves little doubt that *his* sympathies are with Malatesta. The bulk of the Malatesta group is made up of the transcription of documents which reveal his activities to be the conduct of military campaigns, finding employment as a *condottiere*, writing love poems to Isotta degli Atti, supervising construction of the Tempio Malatestiano, and tending to the affairs of his family, progeny of two wives and at least two mistresses. One of the mistresses, Isotta degli Atti, he eventually married (1456). Their love (dating from Malatesta's twentieth year) was a celebrated affair of the day. Pound cites a contemporary opinion of Isotta:

'et, amava perdutamente Ixotta degli Atti'
e 'ne fu degna'
'constans in proposito
'Placuit oculis principis
'pulchra aspectu'
'populo grata (Italiaeque decus)

'and he loved Isotta degli Atti to distraction' and 'she was worthy of him' 'constant in purpose, she was pleasing to the eyes of the prince, beautiful to look at, she was liked by the people' (and the honour of Italy).

(9/41:45)

He follows this praise of Isotta with mention of Sigismund's most singular achievement, the rebuilding of the church of San Francesco at Rimini. The much enlarged church became known as the Tempio Malatestiano because it was thought to be more a pagan temple than a Christian church:

'and built a temple so full of pagan works'
i.e. Sigismund
and in the style 'Past ruin'd Latium'
The filagree hiding the gothic,
with a touch of rhetoric in the whole
And the old sarcophagi,
such as lie, smothered in grass, by San Vitale.

As an excommunicated poet, lover, and builder of a paganish church, Malatesta is obviously a man who conforms to the pattern established by Peire de Maensac. He is another *fidele d'amour* whose great passion, Pound implies, leads him to create a great work of art (the Tempio), and brings him into opposition with the Church. Sigismund is, however, an 'idealist vanquished' like Don Quixote because he never completes the Tempio, and his fortunes go from bad to worse:

And he with his luck gone out of him
64 lances in his company, and his pay 8,000 a *year*,
64 and no more, and he not to try to get any more
And all of it down on paper
sexaginta quatuor nec tentatur habere plures
But leave to keep 'em in Rimini
i.e. to watch the Venetians.

(11/51:55)

Although Pound does not so inform us, these are the terms of the contract Malatesta managed to get with the Pope in 1567, a year before his death. The Latin is from the terms of the contract, 'sixty-four and not to try to get more', for the Pope still feared Malatesta.

Any notions that Pound might have been attempting with Malatesta to incorporate bona fide history into the *Cantos* on ideogrammic principles are undermined by a letter he wrote when he was still doing research for what was then to be a single Malatesta canto:

> Am reading historical background for Canto IX don't know that it will in any way improve the draft of the canto as it stands; shall probably only get more bewildered; but may avoid a few historic idiocies, or impossibilities.
>
> Authorities differ as to whether Sigismund Malatesta raped a german girl in Verona, with such vigour that she 'passed on', or whether it was an Italian in Pesaro, and the pope says he killed her first and raped her afterwards; also some authorities say it was Farnese and not Malatesta who raped the bishop of Fano, and in fact all the *minor* points that might aid one in forming an historic rather than a fanciful idea of his character seem 'shrouded in mystery' or rather lies.
>
> I suppose one has to 'select'. If I find he was TOO bloody quiet and orderly it will ruin the canto. Which needs a certain boisterousness and disorder to contrast with his constructive work.
>
> Francesco Sforza whom I had first cast for the villain seems also to have had good reason for etc. etc. At any rate I have had some interesting hours of research or at least reading; which are probably of no paractical [sic] use.[70]

Clearly Pound wanted in Malatesta a figure who would conform to some preconceived pattern. He was anxious to achieve historical accuracy if possible, but had poetic or fictional requirements which took precedence over history. Nor, indeed, could it have been otherwise.

The point to be taken here is not that the history contained in the *Cantos* is inaccurate, but that it conforms to a fictional pattern established by the poem. The fabric of history is composed of recurrences or repeats of a permanent pattern. Malatesta is another Odysseus, *Poliorcetes*, and 'a bit too *polumetis*', struggling alone in a hostile and impercipient world toward some perception of beauty. Isotta degli Atti is his *puella*, his Circe/Aphrodite; the German girl he raped in Verona, his Circe/whore:

And there was the row about that German-Burgundian female
And it was his messianic year, Poliorcetes,
but he was being a bit too POLUMETIS
And the Venetians wouldn't give him six months vacation.
(9/36:40)

Unlike Odysseus, he does not lie with the goddess, and does not achieve the revelation, but he does build the Tempio, which Pound tells us 'is both an apex and in verbal sense a monumental failure. It is perhaps the apex of what one man has embodied in the last 1000 years of the occident. A cultural "high" is marked.'[71] The Tempio is a failure because it had no effect, no progeny. It remained an incomplete, but beautiful monument to one man's struggle. While it may, in Browning's terms, loose a truth, it fails to hurl 'the world's course right'. Malatesta, then, is Odysseus as Quixote. He managed, Pound claims, 'all that a single man could . . . *against* the current of power'.[72]

Against the ideogram as the model for the organization of the *Cantos*—a model which rules out of court any consideration of architectonics—we can place the following paragraph:

Thus we learn that the equation $(x-a)^2+(y-b)^2=r^2$ governs the circle. It is the circle. It is not a particular circle, it is any circle and all circles. It is nothing that is not a circle. It is the circle free of space and time limits. It is the universal, existing in perfection, in freedom from space and time. Mathematics is dull ditchwater until one reaches analytics. But in analytics we come upon a new way of dealing with form. It is in this way that art handles life. The difference between art and analytical geometry is the difference of subject-matter only. Art is more interesting in proportion as life and the human consciousness are more complex and more interesting than forms and numbers.[73]

It is because the equation for human life and consciousness does not emerge from the *Cantos* with any clarity that Pound has judged it to be a botch. Still, the equation is there in the poem—even if obscurely and imperfectly expressed. The foregoing chapters have been an effort to expose the parameters of this equation through an examination of isolated portions of the *Cantos* and what Pound was reading and writing as he was composing early portions of the poem. It cannot be pretended that the Odysseus–Eleusis equation expresses the 'meaning' of the *Cantos*. But it does embrace the entire poem, even the most uncompromisingly political and economic didacticism of *The Fifth Decad of Cantos* or the Chinese and Adams cantos.

V · An Epic Includes History

I. 'THE PROCESS NOW GOING ON'

A MOST troubling dimension of the *Cantos* is the 'history' they contain or purport to contain. Pound has been criticized for falsifying history,[1] for embracing an erroneous analysis of history,[2] for fantasizing history,[3] and for idealizing history.[4] This last criticism by Roy Harvey Pearce is closest to the mark, and, in effect, includes all of the others. Pearce describes Pound's idealization of history with great intelligence and sanity:

> History, in the broadest and most inclusive sense, becomes for the poet the only authentic language. But even that language has become corrupt; and the poet's obligation is to cleanse it by tearing it—but with loving care—out of its matrix in sheer factuality and by getting to the roots of its moments of truth. For him facts are true to the degree that, as we know them, they lead us to classify things in organic categories, so to attain in turn verbal precision, self-discipline, and social and political equilibrium. Such a criterion for truth not only directs Pound's choice of materials for the *Cantos* but his way of presenting them.[5]

Pearce in no way questions Pound's right to treat history in this manner, but does stress his belief that one must distinguish between the actual historical personage and the 'true' or conceptualized personage found in the *Cantos*.

There is very little in Pearce's account with which one would wish to disagree. Pound lays no claims to be a disinterested historian. On the contrary, he counts his interestedness as an advantage:

> I am not satisfied with my own journalism. I suspect it of being coloured by my own convictions. The indifferent or 'cold' historian may leave a more accurate account of what happens, but he will never understand WHY it happens.[6]

Pound would seem to deny the very possibility of knowing the actuality of the past:

We do NOT know the past in chronological sequence. It may be convenient to lay it out anesthetized on the table with dates pasted on here and there, but what we know we know by ripples and spirals eddying out from us and from our own time.[7]

The implication of this assertion is that there is a bias or interestedness entailed by the very nature of historical knowledge in that our knowledge of, and interest in, the past is determined by the actuality of the present. However, Pound does not press this argument. Instead he claims that mere knowledge of past actualities cannot be put to use:

it does not matter a two-penny damn whether you load up your memory with the chronological sequence of what has happened, or the names of protagonists, or authors of books, or generals and leading political spouters, so long as you understand the process now going on, or the process biological, social, economic now going on, enveloping you as an individual, in a social order, and quite unlikely to be very 'new' in themselves however fresh or stale to the participant.[8]

Obviously no self-respecting historian could accept Pound's historiographical principles because they are not, strictly speaking, historical at all. Pound is not interested in the actuality of the past; he is interested only in its instrumentality. For him, the past is a window on the present: 'As the present is unknowable we roust amid known fragments of the past "to get light on it", to get an inkling of the process which produced what we encounter.'[9] Such an approach to the past denies the most sacred principles of historiography, designed to transcend the incompleteness and bias inherent in our knowledge of the past, to sift out, as near as may be, the actuality of the past from the dross of tradition, prejudice, hearsay, wishful thinking, and outright lies. Once one admits Pound's notion that the past should be a window on the present, then tradition, prejudice, hearsay, wishful thinking, and outright lies are just as admissible as hard evidence. The aim of historical writing is to create as complete and accurate a picture of the past as is possible. Therefore the historian must take great care to ascertain the authenticity of his evidence, and be careful to examine all pieces of evidence. And he must transcend the bias of his own time, race, and nationality in his effort to reconstruct an event which can be known only through testimony and the silent witness of surviving artefacts.

It must be granted, then, that the *Cantos* are not respectable as history because they do not meet the three principal criteria of historical writing: validation of evidence, examination of all the evidence, and the careful exclusion of authorial bias. It is true, of course, that bona fide historical writing never meets these criteria absolutely either, but one can apply them to assess the relative validity of different examples of historical writing. Pound does not pretend to meet them; indeed, he argues that such criteria must inevitably result in either mental paralysis or irremediable ignorance:

About thirty years ago [that would be about 1908 when the eager young Pound first arrived in London], seated on one of the very hard, very slippery, thoroughly uncomfortable chairs of the British Museum main reading room, with a pile of large books at my right hand and a pile of somewhat smaller ones at my left hand, I lifted my eyes to the tiers of volumes and false doors covered with imitation book-backs which surround that focus of learning. Calculating the eye-strain and the number of pages per day that a man could read, with deduction for say at least 5 per cent of one man's time for reflection, I decided against it.[10]

We might see in this picture of the young Pound, appalled at the immeasurable sweep of his ignorance, the arrogant and ignorant young American despairing in the effort to recover the cultural heritage his emigrant forefathers had abandoned. Surely only an American would imagine that he could or should single-handedly *learn* his cultural heritage. But we can also discern the modern Western man—whether of Europe or America—set adrift from his cultural heritage by a condition known in computerese as information overload. Flaubert first studied this specifically modern state in *Bouvard et Pécuchet*, but James Joyce portrayed it even more cogently in the mind of Leopold Bloom, and created a paralyzing mimesis of information overload in *Finnegans Wake*. It may be that Pound has not entirely escaped the fate of Bouvard and Pécuchet, two Parisian clerks who set out to expand human knowledge when one of them comes into an inheritance. They restlessly engage in various research projects in every discipline imaginable, dropping each one in turn as they prove to lack the necessary skills, and fail to achieve immediate results. Their problem was that knowledge was fragmented into a multiplicity of specialties, each one of which required a great deal of time and discipline to master. Leopold Bloom, on the other hand, allowed his mind to range freely over all disciplines (like the *polumetis*—or many-minded—Odysseus), but was therefore imprisoned in the superficial and the trite.

Faced with the unassimilable bulk of the British Museum's collection, Pound 'decided against it'. 'There must be some other way', he thought, 'for a human being to make use of that vast cultural heritage.' Once again, his problem is not how to write history, but how to *make use* of the past while avoiding the fate of Leopold Bloom or of Bouvard and Pécuchet. Since knowledge of the past is unattainable, Pound must seek to understand it without knowledge:

> Knowledge is or may be necessary to understanding, but it weighs as nothing against understanding, and there is not the least use or need of retaining it in the form of dead catalogues once you understand process.
>
> Yet, once the process is understood it is quite likely that the knowledge will stay by a man, weightless, held without effort.[11]

It is statements like this that divide Pound's readers into enthusiasts and detractors, for it is possible to read this remark as an invitation to biased and prejudiced interpretation of history—and Pound's 'history of the world' unhappily succumbs on occasion to both of these faults. On the other hand, it cannot be denied that all interpretation of the past requires some general principles whose function is explanatory. Pound's interest is in those general explanatory principles and the historical process which they reveal.

Professional historians are, quite properly, deeply suspicious of general explanatory principles because it is thought that the events which such principles purport to explain are much too complex to be caught in any preformed conceptual net. One can point apprehensively to the relationship between the historical theories of Hegel and those of Hitler, or the impact of Marx's theories in this century.[12] Oswald Spengler's *Decline of the West* (a work contemporaneous with the early *Cantos*) followed Hegel and Leo Frobenius to reveal a historical process which the Nazis found very much to their taste—although Spengler did not find the Nazis to his taste. Both Spengler and Marx, by revealing the dynamic of history, relieved the actors in history of much of the responsibility for their actions, and—more importantly—gave their actions a sanction greater than that possessed by any rulers other than anointed kings. Arnold Toynbee's *History of the World* is another 'historicist' work (to use Karl Popper's term) roughly contemporaneous with the *Cantos* (1934–54) which seeks to explain the past through general principles accounting for human behaviour in the mass. Toynbee synthesizes the spiritual and organic conceptions of Hegel and Spengler with the determinist and economic–technological conceptions of Marx. Toynbee's explanatory principles are much more palatable to those in the humanist–liberal tradition, but they, too, relieve the actors in the historical drama of much of the responsibility for the success or failure of their actions.

Pound's principle of historical explanation is neither Spenglerian nor Marxist; it is Douglasite. One understands the process of history when one understands the place and function of money and credit in society. Douglas's economic theories were not devised to explain the past. His interest was in the present and the immediate future. Moreover, the notion that great historical events can be explained by the touchstone of sound monetary principles is so simplistic that one can account for wars and economic or political collapse only by crediting the leaders of nations with incredible stupidity or boundless malice. Pound does not shrink from this necessity.

He tells us, for example, that Alexander Hamilton was a 'prime s.o.b.', and that John Adams was *pater patriae*; that the Bank of England robbed the British people, and that the Monte dei Paschi of Siena was the foundation of Sienese prosperity. Pound, in short, expresses judgements on real people and real institutions—judgements which may be true or false. As readers of a poem, we are not obliged to assess the validity of these judgements. The present writer does not know if all the people Dante put in Hell deserve to be there. If one were to discover that all of them were damned on false evidence, or on the basis of Dante's personal dislike for them, or on the basis of his religious and political prejudices, it would not, I think, greatly damage one's admiration for the poem—although it might make one think less of Dante. Dante belonged to a political faction and expressed the views and prejudices of that faction. Pound in his London years, also had a political faction with which he identified himself—although it was neither very coherent nor very political. The *New Age* office did provide him with a reasonably coherent, politically-aware, intellectual community. But Pound was never the spokesman of that community, and when he left London in 1920, he left behind all hope of an audience sympathetic to his political and economic views. The *Cantos* are probably the first epic which had no audience, that is, which did not express the opinions and prejudices of *some* group, however few, however fit. Great poetry, we are told, creates its own audience, but it rarely creates it *ex nihilo*. The *Cantos*' failure is in part a failure to create an audience for itself. Pound recognized—at least late in life—the audacity of the task he had set himself.

The difficulty with the history contained in the *Cantos*, then, is not that it is false, prejudiced, distorted, or wrong-headed, but that it is a history which few if any of Pound's potential audience want. It *is*, of course, occasionally false, always prejudiced, habitually distorted, and often wrong-headed—or perhaps one should say, always wrong-headed—but none of these shortcomings would stop people from reading the poem if Pound's prejudices and distortions reflected their own. T. S. Eliot put his finger delicately on this problem in a late essay on Pound:

> In the *Cantos* there is an increasing defect of communication, not apparent when he is concerned with Sigismondo Malatesta, or with Chinese dynasties, but, for instance, whenever he mentions Martin Van Buren. Such passages are very opaque: they read as if the author was so irritated with his readers for not knowing all about anybody so important as Van Buren, that he refused to enlighten them.[13]

Cryptic references to George Washington or Abraham Lincoln would be acceptable—at least to an American audience—but similarly cryptic references to the eighth president of the United States of America are merely puzzling and irritating.

Of course, there are difficulties of comprehension of the history in the *Cantos* which have nothing to do with the quality of the historical information they contain, but depend rather on the manner in which that information has been incorporated into the poem. That difficulty is associated with the ideogrammic method and inferential rhetoric. At the same time, the fragmentary nature of historical information in the *Cantos* is a mimesis of the true nature of historical knowledge. That is to say, Pound presents to readers an artificial equivalent of the raw data upon which the historian constructs his coherent and explanatory narrative. Thus, although Pound selects the 'data' according to his own interests and biases (just as the historian must do), he does not rationalize the data with explanatory hypotheses, and he does not disguise its fragmentary nature by enclosing it in a narrative or discursive frame.

Pound *has* an explanatory hypothesis which guides his selection of data and areas of interest, but it is implicit rather than explicit in the *Cantos*. His major hypothesis is simply that the social, cultural, and economic health of a society depends upon the clarity and honesty of its means of communication; the most important of which in a functional sense is money, followed by language, and the arts. In terms of causal sequence, however, it is the quality of the arts which determines the quality of the other modes of communication. He has no hypothesis to explain either a decline or an amelioration in the quality of the arts, language, and money other than truisms about human nature such as that many or most people are ignorant, lazy, and greedy. A corollary of this truism is that social amelioration depends upon those rare individuals who are knowledgeable, energetic, and altruistic; and this agrees very well with the conception of the heroic role Pound borrowed from Browning's *Sordello* and from Péladan.

I think it could be said without fear of contradiction that Pound's explanatory hypothesis is inadequate to account for the enormous complexity of historical action. It is clearly less adequate than the hypotheses of Hegel, Marx, Spengler, or Toynbee. Pound's case is certainly less well argued than theirs, and the historical data he collects to support his argument are meagre in scope and careless in detail compared to the latter three theoretical historians. Nonetheless, Pound's adaptation of Douglas is neither stupid, incoherent, nor insane. His reading of history is perfectly sensible and coherent within the context of the poem, and, moreover, conforms to the patterns of human action elaborated in the poem's mythology.

Hegel, Marx, Spengler, and Toynbee all have as their primary aim the reduction of collective human action to intelligibility. They rely on others for their historical data just as Pound does. Invariably their data is inferior in detail and accuracy to that of the specialist professional historian. However, the professional historian's primary interest is to discover explanations for specific events, that is, to render specific and unique events intelligible. The 'historicist' professes to render *all* past (and, by implication, present and future) events intelligible by some few universal explanatory principles. The task he sets himself is the traditional task of the epic poet, to make of the past an intelligible story.

One might say of Marx and Toynbee as of Virgil and Spenser that they mythologize and rationalize history in order to justify a social organization which already exists or may be brought into existence. Or one could say of Hegel and Spengler as of Dante and

Milton that they mythologize history in order to explain the failure of some desired form of social organization to come into existence, or to persist. In both cases history is rendered intelligible by revealing its *telos* or fulfilment, by making of it a *mythos* or story with a beginning, middle, and end. Marx and Virgil explain history by providing a secular conclusion to the tale: the withering away of the state, and the foundation of the eternal city, respectively. Hegel and Milton provide a transcendent conclusion to their stories in the realization of spirit for Hegel, and the 'new heav'ns, new earth, ages of endless date' Michael promises Adam at the end of time.

It is, of course, secondary epic which is primarily concerned to explain the past. Primary epic *chronicles* the past. Its function is to preserve the past, to record the deeds of men as a model for the guidance of men. Primary epic need not explain history because it is innocent of any knowledge of history as a transforming process. The Homeric epics dominated Greek civilization for a thousand years, holding it to the past as the repository of models for human conduct, of the Greek *paideia*. For the Greeks the present and future could be justified only by their congruence with the past. Virgil turned the Homeric *epos* inside out by beginning the story of Rome with the fall of Troy. He thus introduced into the understanding of history a dynamic element absent from Homer. In the *Aeneid* Augustan Rome is justified by the principle of *renovation*: Rome is New Troy, which, if destroyed, could presumably be built again. Virgil still legitimizes the present by its congruence with the past, but that congruence is now merely symbolic: Rome is not Troy, it is the spiritual heir of Troy. Moreover, the legend of Aeneas is known by Virgil and his audience to be a legend. In short, the Virgilian epic is fiction, not history.

In so far as the *Cantos* address themselves to the historical function of epic, they are Virgilian in that they adopt the Virgilian principle of renovation. The idea of renovation was for Virgil merely a means of legitimizing the Roman civilization by establishing a continuity with the Homeric past. The modern historical imagination attaches no special reverence to the past. Indeed, through the influence of providential Christian thinking, we are more inclined to look toward the future with reverence as Hegel and Marx do. But for Pound the past is a repository of human achievement which can be recovered and renewed. As early as 'Patria Mia' (1912) he described his understanding of the uses of the past:

Despite Sismondi's remark in the preface to his 'Italian Republics', I can never get any of my more progressive friends to believe that I have any better reason for studying the Middle Ages than is found in a crotchety humour and pedanticism. Sismondi said that one studied the past so as to learn how to deal with the present or something of that sort, I forget his exact phrasing.

One wants to find out what sort of things endure, and what sort of things are transient; what sort of things recur; what propagandas profit a man or his race; to learn upon what the forces, constructive and dispersive, of social order, move; to learn what rules and axioms hold firm, and what sort fade, and what sort are durable but permutable, what sort hold in letter, and what sort by analogy only, what sort by close analogy, and what sort by rough parallel alone.[14]

These paragraphs predate the earliest efforts on the *Cantos*, but describe a rationale for historical study that it persistent throughout composition of the *Cantos*. In fact, in 1932 Pound told John Drummond that the best division for the matter of his epic was probably 'the permanent, the recurrent, the casual'.[15]

Pound takes renovation from Confucius as one of his basic principles. In *The Great Digest* the Emperor Tching Tang writes the phrase MAKE IT NEW on his bath-tub in letters of gold:

AS THE SUN MAKES IT NEW
DAY BY DAY MAKE IT NEW
YET AGAIN MAKE IT NEW.[16]

Pound quotes the phrase in English and Chinese characters in *Guide to Kulchur* without comment, and paraphrases *The Great Digest* in canto 53:

Tching prayed on the mountain and
    wrote MAKE IT NEW
on his bathtub
    Day by day make it new
cut underbrush
pile the logs
keep it growing.

(53/264–5:274–5)

The historical underbrush is chronology and the 'names of protagonists, or authors of books, or generals and leading political spouters' that overload the mind. History is made new by cutting all of that out and piling up only the logs: the permanent and the recurrent, with a little of the casual for colour.

We have already seen that Troy has considerable importance in the *Cantos* through the *Agamemnon*. Troy's destruction and the working out of Greek war guilt provide Pound with a miniature paradigm of historical action applicable to medieval and Renaissance wars and political intrigue. But neither Troy in Auvergnat, nor Eleanor of Aquitaine, nor the story of Niccolo d'Este and the infidelity of his wife, Parisina and son Ugo (told in cantos 8, 20, and 24) are examples of renovation on the Virgilian model. They are, rather, depressing recurrences of similar failures. The only permanence in this dreary round is the persistence of the Odyssean figure (whether de Maensac or Malatesta or Ugo Aldovrandino) always striving, always attempting to break through the prison of recurrence. Like Péladan's Quixote, they are always defeated by an inhospitable cultural environment.

Virgil celebrates the success of Aeneas in his task of making Troy new. But what is Pound's new Troy? Guy Davenport records a rather puzzling comment Pound made to him while still at St. Elizabeth's: 'My *Paradiso* will have no St Dominic or Augustine, but it will be a *Paradiso* just the same, moving toward final coherence. I'm getting at the building of the City, that whole tradition. Augustine, he don't amount to a great deal.'[17] If Davenport has quoted him accurately, Pound would appear to equate his *Paradiso* with the building of a city, to render the *Commedia* and the *Aeneid* equivalent as comedies rising to a recognition of a perfected human community. Virgil's city is secular and actual; Dante's is transcendent. Pound's city is neither actual nor transcendent; it is 'the city in the mind indestructible', an ideal city constructed out of the actualities of past human achievement and wisdom, made new for contemporary use.

2. 'THE CITY IN THE MIND INDESTRUCTIBLE'

Although epic is most commonly defined in terms of some hero, some representative of public virtues, or some heroic action, it would be more accurate to define it in terms of its concern with the fate of cities, of human communities. The heroic action, after all, is not so much one that is peculiarly arduous, or that requires rare qualities and skills, as it is an action affecting all men. The fate of Troy depended upon the military prowess of Hector and Achilles; the fate of Rome, upon the devotion to duty of Aeneas; the fate of Hrothgar's hall, upon Beowulf's thirst for glory; the fate of mankind, in *Paradise Lost*, upon Christ's compassion. Pound, writing 'to resist the view that Europe and civilisation is [*sic*] going to Hell', asks in 'Mauberly', 'What god, man, or hero/Shall I place a tin wreath upon?' Upon what does the fate of Europe and civilization depend? This is a question Pound must answer if he is to write his epic. It is a question about the process of history, and its answer is seldom sought in large-scale studies. Clearly it cannot depend upon some simple heroic action such as Achilles' triumph over Hector or Roland's stand against the Saracen.

If one must have a hero, the hero who might rescue Europe cannot be a warrior. The time for such fables is past. He might be a political leader if a suitable one could be found—and Pound comes perilously close to adopting Benito Mussolini for such a role (on the evidence of *Jefferson and/or Mussolini*). He might be an economist like Major Douglas, a scientist like Louis Agassiz, a historian like Leo Frobenius, a sage like Confucius, or a poet like Ezra Pound. Wordsworth had inadvertently solved the problem of writing epic in his own heteroclite age by making himself the hero of *The Prelude*—'inadvertently' because *The Prelude* was not conceived as an epic, but rather as the preparation for the writing of a philosophical epic, *The Recluse*. His example has led readers to presume that Pound is, or ought to be, doing the same thing.[18]

But, of course, the *Cantos* do not have *a* hero. They are built around a heroic action, the 'struggle upward out of ignorance', typified by the Odyssean adventure interpreted in an Eleusinian light. That heroic action has many manifestations and many protagonists both serious and comic. The poet himself is engaged in the heroic action, and occasionally places himself at centre stage (most notably in the *Pisan Cantos*), but critical focus on the nature of the Poundian hero misses the point; what matters is what the hero does, not who he is. Critical exegesis can provide a grammar of heroic action, the 'rose in the steel dust', that emerges only too obscurely from the poem. Any attempt to isolate a particular figure, whether it be Malatesta, John Adams, or Yong Tching, as *the* Poundian hero can only lead to serious misrepresentation. Whatever else they are, the *Cantos* are an extraordinarily supple creation, not to be understood by means of vigorous simplification.

From 'Patria Mia' on, Pound has consistently maintained his faith in the civic ideal, and it is that faith which inspires the history in the *Cantos*, providing a public and factual counterpoint to the private and mythical 'struggle upward out of ignorance' of Odysseus. 'In studying the course of Europe,' he writes in 'Patria Mia',

one finds that in the past certain things have worked and certain things have not.

All the fine dreams of empire, of a universal empire, Rome, the imperium restored, and so on, came to little. The dream, nevertheless, had its value, it set a model for emulation, a model of orderly procedure, and it was used as a spur through every awakening from the eighth century to the sixteenth. Yet it came to no sort of civic reality, either in the high sheriffage of Charles the Great, or in its atavistic parody under Napoleon.[19]

'Patria Mia' is designed to spur his fellow countrymen to an awareness of their own virtues, and a belief in the imminence of an 'American Risorgimento'. It draws on the impressions he retained from a six months visit to New York in the autumn and winter of 1910–11 (in fact, June to February). He adopts New York city as a symbol of the vigour of the American awakening:

I see . . . a sign in the surging crowd on Seventh Avenue (New York). A crowd pagan as ever imperial Rome was, eager, careless, with an animal vigour unlike that of any European crowd that I have ever looked at. There is none of the melancholy, the sullenness, the unhealth of the London mass, none of the worn vivacity of Paris. I do not believe it is the temper of Venice.

One returns from Europe and one takes note of the size and vigour of this new strange people. They are not Anglo-Saxon; their gods are not the gods whom one was reared to reverence. And one wonders what they have to do with lyric measures and the nature of 'quantity'.

One knows that they are the dominant people and that they are against all delicate things.[20]

And he sees the architecture of the city as 'the first sign of the "alba" of America, the nation, in the embryo of New York'.

Twelve years after he wrote 'Patria Mia' Pound began to seek out ways to incorporate American history into the *Cantos*. We are fortunate in having a series of letters between Pound and his father written during 1924 which reveal some of the stages of his adaptation of American history for the poem. At the time the letters were written, *A Draft of XVI Cantos* had not yet been published, although the manuscript was in the hands of William Bird of Three Mountains

Press.[21] The first letter enlists Homer Pound in a search for usable material on American presidents:

This note mainly to ask if you know anything about American Presidents. I have what I need on Wash. and Jefferson, but that's about all. I don't care a damn about their public eye-wash. I want facts indicative of personality.[22]

Clearly Pound's interest is in the quality of man engaged in the American experience rather than public event. As always, he wants to get behind official history and its clutter of factual impedimenta to the 'true' history of the private man. But he does not seem to have been well informed in the spring of 1924, for he tells his father in the same letter that he has read Jefferson's letters, but of other presidents admits that he 'can't remember the names of a lot of 'em. There was a Johnny named Polk and two bums called Adams.'

The disparaging reference to the Adams family reveals that Pound's attitude to American presidents was to undergo considerable revision as his knowledge increased. Indeed, at this point it would seem he intended to reveal the intellectual and cultural poverty of America. For in a later letter, apparently in reply to his father's objection that American presidents were not very interesting men, Pound replies, 'THAT (i.e. the uninterestingness of U.S. presidents) is PREcisely the point. I hope, with a few well chosen phrases, to rub it in. Only I want an almost infinite number of facts to select from.'[23] Obviously Pound's historical research—at least in this instance—begins with a strong bias. The research is designed to discover facts suitable to illustrate already formed opinions.

In the same letter he told his father that he had already found 'one or two plums':

George W's death; Jefferson trying to get a gardener who cd. play the french horn in quartette after dinner (wanted to import one along with a clavicord). Shd. like something of the Lincoln family that hadn't been worn to death & that didn't feature J. Christ too heavily. Also Grant. The row of duds begins early with Mr. Adams.

Neither Washington, Grant, nor the Lincoln family ever find their way into the *Cantos* as figures of principal interest. But Mr. Adams and his son both emerge as major American heroes. Thus, one can conclude that, although Pound begins his American research with little knowledge and strong biases, he is sufficiently flexible to permit the facts as he discovers them to alter his bias. It would also appear that he did not at this time intend to make extensive use of American history, but would perhaps use it as a minor refrain counterpointing the main historical burden, which was to be European.

Possibly he hoped to devote a number of cantos to an American president on the model of the Malatesta cantos published in the previous year. At least he mentions the Malatesta group in a letter to his father written late in 1924, announcing the abandonment of his American plans:

> must start on another LONG hunk of Canti, like the Sigismundo, having used up the chop-shop in the five now drafted . . .
>
> As you say U.S. presidents do not present ALL the features required for the full mind. Am using a bit of Jefferson in the XX or thereabouts.[24]

A later letter to his mother indicates that Pound is now looking elsewhere for a suitable historical personage to follow Malatesta:

> trying to find some bhloomin [*sic*] historic character who can be used as illustration of intelligent constructivity. Private life being another requisite. S[igismundo] M[alatesta] amply possessed of both; but other figures being often fatally deficient.[25]

Here, for the first time, he indicates the kind of man he seeks—someone who 'can be used as an illustration of intelligent constructivity'. He wants a builder, a creator, someone who plays the role of artist in the affairs of men.

The historical characters he in fact uses for the new section, *A Draft of Cantos 17–27* (published 1928), are once again Italian Renaissance figures, Niccolo d'Este and the Medicis. The 'bit of Jefferson' which Pound said he was using 'in the XX or thereabouts' is to be found in canto 21. It is the same bit about the gardener that he mentioned in the May letter to his father, and to which he had referred approvingly four years earlier in 'Indiscretions'. The context in which he places the Jeffersonian detail reminds one of the remark that 'the uninterestingness of U.S. presidents is PREcisely the point'. Cosimo Medici is heard complaining about financial difficulties in the passage preceding Jefferson's letter. In the midst of these difficulties we are told that Cosimo 'caught the young boy Ficino/And had him taught the Greek language'. Jefferson, in similarly straitened circumstances, also wishes to foster cultural activity, but his efforts are rather less impressive than Cosimo's patronage of the young Marsilio Ficino:

> 'Could you,' wrote Mr. Jefferson,
> 'Find me a gardener
> Who can play the french horn?
> The bounds of American fortune
> Will not admit the indulgence of a domestic band of
> Musicians, yet I have thought that a passion for music
> Might be reconciled with that economy which we are
> Obliged to observe. I retain among my domestic servants
> A gardener, a weaver, a cabinet-maker, and a stone-cutter,
> To which I would add a vigneron. In a country like yours
> (id est Burgundy) where music is cultivated and
> Practised by every class of men, I suppose there might
> Be found persons of these trades who could perform on
> The french horn, clarionet, or hautboy and bassoon, so
> That one might have a band of two french horns, two
> Clarionets, two hautboys and a bassoon, without enlarging
> Their domestic expenses.
>
> (21/97:101)

The letter is undoubtedly from the hand of a highly cultivated man—'one of perhaps half-a-dozen Presidents with whom one would have cared to hold a second or third conversation', as he is described in 'Indiscretions'. There can be no doubt that Pound had a great deal of respect for Jefferson at this time, and wished to convey that respect in canto 21. But, nonetheless, the respect is mixed with a clear awareness of the limitations both of Jefferson and of eighteenth-century America, in comparison with Renaissance Italy. However admirable Jefferson's efforts to create a domestic ensemble of brasses and reeds may be, it cannot stand comparison with the Medici patronage of Ficino. By juxtaposing Jefferson's thrifty scheme to import music into backwoods America with Cosimo's rather more impressive efforts to support culture in Florence, Pound forces his readers to make that unflattering comparison. Ultimately one is more impressed by Jefferson's parsimony than by his cultivation.

There are other American references in *A Draft of Cantos 17–27*, but they are anecdotes of modern American enterprise such as had already appeared in the first section. For 'historic characters of intelligent constructivity' Pound had once again turned to Europe and Italy, permitting Jefferson only a brief and equivocal appearance. Pound had not been able to find an American figure to fit the type of Sigismund Malatesta, his historical Odysseus, an artist, lover, warrior, and builder. The 'animal vigour' of the New York crowd might be expected to throw up some such vigorous hero, but the closest Pound had been able to come to him was the shady Baldy Bacon of canto 12, an entrepreneur and insurance agent:

> Baldy's interest
> Was in money business.
> 'No interest in any other kind uv bisnis,'
> Said Baldy.
>
> . . . . .
>
> . . . when I met him,
> Doing job printing, i.e., agent,
> going to his old acquaintances,
> His office in Nassau St., distributing jobs to the printers,
> Commercial stationery,
> and later, insurance,
> Employers' liability,
> odd sorts of insurance,
> Fire on brothels, etc., commission,
> Rising from 15 dollars a week,
> *Pollon d'anthropon iden*,
> Knew which shipping companies were most careless;
> where a man was most likely
> To lose a leg in bad hoisting machinery;
> Also fire, as when passing a whore-house,
> Arrived, miraculous Hermes, by accident,
> Two minutes after the proprietor's *angelos*
> Had been sent for him.
>
> (12/53–4:57–8)

But Baldy is a parody of the Odysseus/Malatesta type, intended as a vehicle of satirical humour at the expense of contemporary America.

Pound had some difficulty finishing *Cantos 17–27*. In October of 1924 Homer Pound already had cantos 18 and 19 in his possession, and in October of the following year Pound reported that cantos 17 to 23 were 'about finished'. But it was April of 1927 before he had enough to send to his printer, and then only the first nine cantos of the eleven canto section. Canto 26 was finished in July, and canto 27 in September of 1927 under pressure to complete the volume for publication.[26] Cantos 25 and 26 deal with the history of Venice, but lack any central historical figure. Canto 27 is made up largely of personal reminiscences and a mythologized account of the Russian Revolution. From the point of view of history, *Cantos 17–27* are much more disjointed and obscure than the Malatesta section. Pound's slowness to finish may well reflect a dissatisfaction with the way the section had developed. Certainly the explanatory letters to his father do not reveal a strong sense of structural order. The principle of organization he cites for cantos 18 and 19 seems to operate throughout the section:

> As to Cantos 18–19; there aint no key/ Simplest parallel I can give is radio where you tell who is talking by the noise they make. If your copies are properly punctuated they shd. show where each voice begins and ends.
>
> You hear various people letting cats out of bags at maximum speed. Armaments, finance, etc. A 'great editor', at lest edt. of the woilds best known news sheet, a president of a new nation, or one then in the making, a salesman of battleships, etc. with bits of biography of a distinguished financier, etc.
>
> Mostly things you 'oughtn't to know', not if you are to be a good quiet citizen. That's all. Who made the bhloody war? The cantos belong rather to the hell section of the poem; though I am not sorting it out in the Dantescan manner, cantos 1–34 hell, next 33 purgatory, and next 33 paradiso.
>
> Am leaving the reader, in most cases to infer what he is getting. Though re two cantos there will be a very narrow margin for error.[27]

A later letter describes cantos 17 and 20, again alluding to Dante, but without at all clarifying where it is all heading:

> Canto XVII deals with a sort of paradiso terrestre. XVIII and XIX, I think you have. Geryone, fraude [*sic*]. You can look it up in yr. Dante. The minor hell of rascality. XX lotophagoi; further sort of paradiso. Or something in that direction. Then some narrative. Medici and Este.[28]

The three years it took Pound to complete *Cantos 17–27* is certainly not an unusually long time, but the character of the section itself and the tone of his letters suggest that he was uncertain. Supporting this contention is the peculiarity that he entirely omitted this section in the selection of cantos he made in 1966. At the time he sent canto 27 to the printers he had cantos 28 to 30 already blocked out, but withheld them. They were used less than two years later to round out the first two sections to an even 30 cantos for *A Draft of XXX Cantos*, published in 1930. There is no record in the correspondence of the reason for this collection. It may have been no more than a trade move designed to encourage sales which could not have been brisk, but only 212 copies were printed. At the same time, *XXX Cantos* marks a long pause in progress on the poem, for *Eleven New Cantos* was not finished until 1933, six years after completion of the preceding section.

3. PAIDEUMA: 'THE TANGLE OR COMPLEX OF INROOTED IDEAS OF ANY PERIOD'

The notion of the city or community as an unrealized, but approachable ideal is, as it were, endemic in Pound's thought. However, it received a powerful impetus from his encounter with the work of the German anthropologist Leo Frobenius in 1925 or 1926.[29] Frobenius is constantly invoked by Pound in the essays of the 1930s: especially *Jefferson and/or Mussolini*, 'Date Line', 'A Visiting Card', 'The Jefferson–Adams Letters as a Shrine and a Monument', and *Guide to Kulchur*. In the latter work Pound defines the term 'paideuma':

> To escape a word or a set of words loaded up with dead association Frobenius uses the term Paideuma for the tangle or complex of the inrooted ideas of any period.
>
> . . . . .
>
> The Paideuma is not the Zeitgeist . . .
>
> As I understand it, Frobenius has seized a word not current for the express purpose of scraping off the barnacles and 'atmosphere' of a long-used term.
>
> When I said I wanted a new civilization, I think I cd. have used Frobenius' term.
>
> At any rate for my own use and for the duration of this treatise I shall use Paideuma for the gristly roots of ideas that are in action.
>
> I shall leave 'Zeitgeist' as including also the atmospheres, the tints of mental air and the idées reçues, the notions that a great mass of people still hold or half hold from habit, from waning custom.[30]

Pound seems not to have recognized the Greek word for 'teaching', *paideia*, in Frobenius's Germanized form. Frobenius may have excluded the Greek meaning in favour of the sense of an untaught wisdom—a kind of folk-knowledge, or perhaps a cast of mind prior to knowledge, but which shapes and moulds that knowledge in its application. Spengler's notion of a 'culture soul' is an adaptation of

Frobenius's 'paideuma', but Frobenius distinguished three paideumas:

... the first level (P_1) embraced a generalized world culture; the second (P_2) the culture of single populations (nation-states, linguistic spheres, breeding populations, etc.); and the third (P) the course of spiritual development of the individual person as viewed within the contexts of the preceding.

Each paideuma level participates in what we call an organic cycle of birth, growth, zenith, decay, and death. As expressed for P_1, but probably applicable to the other two levels, the original growth impulse reaches its high point in mythology, especially the solar and lunar cults, and reaches senility with materialism, world economics, specialization and 'the machine age'.[31]

The familiar argument of Spengler's *Decline of the West* is readily discernible in Welke's account of Frobenius's ideas. But Pound did not share Yeats's enthusiasm for Spengler. Pound wrote to his father after dismissing some other sage:

... Spengler, who is also tripe, but of a larger order.

At least Spengler does recall a lot of things one had forgotten. Was interested in opening chapters and even thought of doing a refutation ...

However, guess I'd better stick to me-yown jawb. As S. seems to mean by 'The West' a lot of things I dislike, I shd' like to accept his infantine belief that they are 'declining', but still ... [These last Pound's own suspension points.][32]

Pound is attracted to Frobenius by his argument for a persistence in cultural values, but rejects the correlative notion, stressed by Spengler, that those values have a natural term and eventually die out.

Pound does not seem to have read a great deal of Frobenius—no doubt because he did not read German easily—but he did meet him, and is constantly complaining that *Erlebte Erdteile*[33] has not been translated, and he did own the German work. Although he does not refer to it, he might well have read *The Voice of Africa*, published in an English translation in 1913. There he would have encountered an early form of Frobenius's *Kulturmorphologie* very much in line with his own interests and needs. In that work Frobenius describes the persistence of the culture or paideuma of the Yoruba:

And Yoruban culture belongs to antiquity by virtue of its inherent 'style'. The slave traffic of Medievalism, modern industrial conditions, and the foreign rule of to-day have, beyond question, distorted, transformed and ruined it. Yet we need not first delve a few yards beneath the soil and dig up terra-cottas to see from their features after such long concealment that these have an austere severity, a 'beautiful' style, which is a certain index of the Templum, and compare it with other religions we wot of, to find that this philosophic idea corresponds to that ancient style and method of thought, the profoundest essence of which is still stirring the life of this nation to-day.[34]

Frobenius's argument in *The Voice of Africa* is that the Yoruban culture is, in effect, a survivor, collateral with European culture, of an ancient Atlantic-worshipping culture, and he bases this hypothesis on a stylistic comparison of Yoruban artefacts with ancient artefacts. Frobenius's conclusions were rather more startling than Frazer's, but the general tendency of his work was similar in that both men demonstrated a persistence into modern times of ancient cultural forms and practices which had been thought to be barbarisms long discarded. Frazer's study is presented as a protracted effort to explain the peculiar habits of the Priest of Diana at Nemi, and propounds no particular hypothesis of cultural development—although it implicitly undercuts the whole historical foundation of Christianity. Frobenius, on the other hand, was consciously seeking to explain cultural development. In order to do so he had to be able to distinguish one culture from another on descriptive grounds. The distinctive characteristics of a culture are its 'paideuma'. Once a culture's paideuma has been isolated, one can study the development and alteration of that culture through time and space.

Perhaps inevitably, Frobenius found that culture was linked to race, and developed a stable of racially labelled cultures competing with one another in the Mediterranean basin. Such an idea is at least as old as Gibbon's *Decline and Fall of the Roman Empire*, but it was one that the Nazis found particularly compatible with their notions of purity of race. Frobenius and Spengler were not Nazis, and had no sympathy with them, but Pound was not so wise or so clear-headed. Much of his anti-Semitism stems from the notion of cultural purity. Of course, one cannot excuse Pound's anti-Semitism by arguing that it was based on cultural rather than racial considerations, but it will help to explain how he fell into this particularly virulent intellectual trap.

He placed his faith in a 'Mediterranean paideuma' which lasted down to Leo the Tenth and whose clearest formulation is Dante's 'in una parte piu e meno altrove', a phrase which he translates as 'a sense of gradations'. And Pound claims that this Mediterranean paideuma

> fell before, or coincident with, the onslaught of brute disorder of taboo. The grossness of incult thought came into Europe simultaneously with manifestations called 'renaissance', 'restoration' and muddled in our time with a good deal of newspaper yawp about puritans.
>
> Certain things were 'forbidden'. Specifically, on parchment, they were forbidden to hebrews. The bible emerged and broke the Church Fathers, who had for centuries quoted the bible. All sense of fine assay seemed to decline in Europe.[35]

He sees the Protestant Reformation as the triumph of Hebrew over Mediterranean values in European culture, and these former values are seen to be ones of taboo and restriction. Mediterranean values are identified with the more positive virtues of Amor:

> By 1934 Frazer is sufficiently digested for us to know that opposing systems of European morality go back to the opposed temperaments of those who thought copulation was good for the crops, and the opposed faction who thought it was bad for the crops (the scarcity economists of pre-history). That ought to simplify a good deal of argument. The Christian might at least decide whether he is for Adonis or Atys, or whether he is Mediterranean. The exact use of dyeing Europe with a mythology elucubrated to explain the thoroughly undesirable climate of Arabia Petraea is in some reaches obscure.[36]

The Hebrew paideuma, in Pound's *kulturmorphologie*, is expressed in Judaism, which he sees as a religion of prohibition and restriction, appropriate to the inhospitable Semitic environment. He further identifies it with the Atys cult, or religion of emasculation, not suited, he says, 'to the pleasanter parts of the Mediterranean basin'.

One hardly needs to observe that Pound's capsule history of religion is over-simplified and tendentious. It is the kind of imaginative simplification which the poet traditionally applies to historical events, but which has become less tolerable in our empirical age. The general distaste for imaginative simplification is further intensified in Pound's case by his entanglement in the rather similar historical simplification of the Nazis. It is impossible to defend Pound in the face of his truly vicious stupidities about the Nazis and the Jews. It can only be observed that the simplification of history in which he indulges is common to all epic poets, and is virtually unavoidable for anyone who would wish to reduce great historical movements to intelligibility within a poem. Pound differs from other epic poets in that he attempted to explain a great historical movement *while it was still in progress*. Historical epic traditionally justifies the present by its patterning of the past. Pound, by contrast, wishes to formulate the immediate *future* by his patterning of the past. His future has not come to pass, and therefore his imaginative oversimplifications are perceived as lies, or at best vicious errors, rather than as the metaphors they are.

To return to Pound's religious history, we learn in another essay, earlier than those already cited, that the Mediterranean paideuma is Eleusinian. In speaking of the medieval Church he writes:

> One cult that it had failed to include was that of Eleusis.
>
> It may be arguable that Eleusinian elements persisted in the very early church, and are responsible for some of the scandals . . .
>
> It is equally discernable upon study that some non christian and inextinguishable source of beauty persisted throughout the Middle Ages maintaining song in Provence, maintaining an enthusiasm, maintaining the grace of Kalenda Maya.[37]

Still later, after he has read Claudius Salmasius' *De Modo Usurarum* and learned something of the Roman Church's deep opposition to usury and Imperial Rome's organization of maritime commerce, he is inclined to be even more well disposed toward the Latin paideuma, which, therefore, becomes more fully an inheritor of the Eleusinian tradition:

> Latin is sacred, grain is sacred. Who destroyed the mystery of fecundity, bringing in the cult of sterility? Who set the Church against the Empire? Who destroyed the unity of the Catholic Church with this mud-wallow that serves the Protestants in the place of contemplation? Who decided to destroy the mysteries within the Church so as to be able to destroy the Church itself by schism? Who has wiped the consciousness of the greatest mystery out of the mind of Europe, to arrive at an atheism proclaimed by Bolshevism?
>
> Who has received honours by putting argumentation where had before been faith?[38]

Pound's answers to these questions are, of course, Judaism and the usurers, but he was not always careful to distinguish Judaism from Jews, or Jews from usurers.

Like Frobenius, Pound can identify the Eleusinian paideuma on stylistic grounds, as an 'inextinguishable source of beauty'. But Frobenius's theory has undergone a peculiar transmogrification in Pound's hands. For Frobenius means by 'paideuma' the shared culture of a people. It must be isolated from ephemeral and alien encrustations, but there is nothing underground or secret about it. Pound's Eleusis, by contrast, is a hidden and even mysterious cultural heritage:

> Shallow minds have been in a measure right in their lust for 'secret history'. I mean they have been dead right to want it, but shallow in their conception of what it was. Secret history is at least twofold. One part consists in the secret corruptions, the personal lusts, avarices, etc. that scoundrels keep hidden, another part is the 'plus', the constructive urges, a *secretum* because it passes unnoticed or because no human effort can force it on public attention.[39]

Both of these secret histories find their way into the *Cantos*, the first under the general rubric of usury, the second more varied but always related somehow to natural increase, the sacredness of grain, the awareness that copulation is good for the crops, that is to say, related to Eleusis.

Pound is not unaware that he has strayed from Frobenius, but he sees his departure in terms of a different focus of interest. He told Eliot that he claimed 'to get on from where Frobenius left off, in that his Morphology was applied to savages and my interest is in civilizations at their *most*'.[40] But the difference is not merely one of focus, for Frobenius's technique is a descriptive one and Pound's is evaluative. For Pound civilization is 'a conspiracy of intelligence', the phalanx of particulars upon which he erects his generalities are carefully selected on *a priori* principles. Moreover, distorting the basic sense of 'paideuma' for Frobenius, Pound believes that a paideuma can be inculcated, and repeatedly outlines programmes for doing just that. *Guide to Kulchur* purports to discover the Mediterranean paideuma, but other essays, like 'For a New Paideuma', outline programmes of study to create a paideuma:

> Frobenius has left the term with major implications in the unconscious (if I understand him rightly). I don't assert that he would necessarily

limit it to the unconscious or claim that the conscious *individual* can have no effect in shaping the paideuma, or at least the next paideuma.

I take it that the 'indifferent have never made history', and that the paideuma makes history. There are in our time certain demands, demands, that is, of the awakened intellect, and these demands are specific. It is useless to discuss them 'at large' and in the vague if one can't bring them down to particulars.[41]

This is followed by a curriculum somewhat different in detail, but very similar in spirit to the one he had outlined twenty-six years earlier in the *New Age* 'Patria Mia'.

Pound, then, twists Frobenius to bring his ideas into line with his own conception of civilization as the precious and embattled possession of a conspiracy of intelligence. The paideuma is transformed from the inescapable expression of a people's cultural awareness to the rare and unrecognized insights of exceptional men. Indeed, he has twisted Frobenius sufficiently to make him conform to the theme of Browning's *Sordello*, and the notion of the failed hero found in Péladan. Pound's paideuma is equivalent to Browning's 'casual truth, elicited/In sparks so mean, at intervals dispread/So rarely'. And the possessor of this paideuma is the outsider, the defeated, the betrayed. This unrealized paideuma is Pound's city of Dioce, labelled the *Pisan Cantos*, 'the city in the mind indestructible' in a phrase he borrowed from a Sonninke legend via Frobenius.

Frobenius provides Pound with some new vocabulary, with a theoretical basis to justify what he was doing anyway, and, unhappily, with the perception that culture is based on race. The notion of a culture existing as a potential in the mind, except in the collective sense of a racial predisposition toward certain cultural forms, is entirely alien to Frobenius. Similarly the notion that 'the history of a culture is the history of ideas going into action'[42] is an inversion of Frobenius's theoretical approach. Because he based his *Kulturmorphologie* on the study of artefacts, there could be no question of ideas or concepts that had not been made manifest. Pound inverts this to claim that only those actions which reveal their conceptual origin are worthy of interest.

VI · America, Italy, and China

1. 'OUT OF WHICH THINGS SEEKING AN EXIT'

WE have seen that Pound paused after completion of *Cantos 17–27* (still labelled 'draft') to collect the first two sections plus three new cantos into *A Draft of XXX Cantos*, published in 1930. *Eleven New Cantos* (the first section not labelled 'draft') was completed in 1933 and published the following year. It is difficult to read any clear purpose into Pound's division of the *Cantos*, but the collection of the first thirty into a single volume seems to mark a shift of emphasis in the poem. He had begun in the midst of the 1914–18 war, and had concerned himself with the question of war and war guilt. Now, the shadow of the Great Depression of the 1930s had fallen between the first thirty cantos and the new section. By 1931 Pound was dating his letters Fascist style, from the 1922 March on Rome, and his attitude to political revolution had changed from the contempt expressed for the Russian revolution in canto 27:

> These are the labours of tovarisch,
> That tovarisch wrecked the house of the tyrants,
> And rose, and talked folly on folly,
> And walked forth and lay in the earth
>
> . . . . .
>
> Saying:
> 'Me Cadmus sowed in the earth
> And with the thirtieth autumn
> I return to the earth that made me.
> Let the five last build the wall;
>
> . . . . .
>
> 'Baked and eaten tovarisch!
> 'Baked and eaten, tovarisch, my boy,
> 'That is your story. And up again,
> 'Up and at 'em. Laid never stone upon stone.'
>
> (27/131–2:136–7)

Pound had failed to find an American hero on the model of Malatesta for *Cantos 17–27*, and had been unable to adapt the American paideuma to either the heroic or historical paradigms of his poem. But he had taught himself a good deal of American history. He had read W. E. Woodward's debunking biography of Washington,[1] and had been much influenced by his analysis of the revolution as two distinct movements: (1) an imperial civil war in which propertied men and merchants—such as John Hancock and George Washington—sought to foster their own economic interests without British interference, and (2) a people's revolution of inarticulate, disorganized violence such as the mob assault on Captain Preston, and the eager enlistment in Washington's army—followed by wholesale desertion when there was no fighting. Inspired by this revelation of economic chicanery at the birth of his own nation Pound acquired and read Charles Francis Adams's *The Life and Works of John Adams* (in ten volumes), Paul Willstach's selection, *The Correspondence of John Adams and Thomas Jefferson*, *The Writings of Thomas Jefferson*, *The Autobiography of Martin Van Buren*, and the *Diary of John Quincy Adams*.

With these works at his elbow he produced five new American cantos (31, 32, 33, 34, and 37) entirely through quotation. The first three are based on the correspondence of Jefferson and Adams. Pound wrote no part of these cantos, and provided no explanatory notes or comment except for a few parenthetical remarks such as: '(*parts of this letter in cypher*)' following the otherwise inexplicable line, 'This country is really supposed to be on the eve of XTZBK-49HT' (31/154:158)

The three cantos are very difficult to understand in even the most rudimentary degree without some considerable knowledge of the American revolutionary period, and particularly of the roles played in the revolution by Adams and Jefferson. Doubtless, the American revolution was an important enough event in the history of the English speaking world that we all ought to know something about it, but it is difficult to forget that Pound knew next to nothing about it in 1924, just seven years before the publication of cantos 31–3 in *Pagany*. Their subject is revolution, now viewed with approval and a Fascist colouring:

> The heritage of Jefferson, Quincy Adams, old John Adams, Jackson, Van Buren is HERE, NOW *in the Italian peninsula* at the beginning of fascist second decennio, not in Massachusetts or Delaware.
>
> To understand this we must have at least a rudimentary knowledge of the first fifty years of United States history AND some first-hand

knowledge of Italy 1922–33 or 1915–33, or still better some knowledge of 160 years of American democracy and of Italy for as long as you like.[2]

In effect, Pound is dumping newly acquired and undigested information on to his readers' heads as if irritated with them (as Eliot remarked)—and, indeed with himself—for not having known about it long since.

Cantos 31 to 33 are designed to evoke the paideuma of the American revolutionary period. We learn that the French (and some Americans) were woefully ignorant of government and history:

'When Lafayette harangued you and me and John Quincy Adams
'through a whole evening in your hotel in the Cul de Sac . . .
'. . . silent as you were. I was, in plain truth as astonished
'at the grossness of his ignorance of government and history,
'as I had been for years before at that of Turgot,
'La Rochefoucauld, of Condorcet and of Franklin.'
To Mr Jefferson, Mr John Adams.[3]
(31/155:159)

Jefferson, too, is scathing on the merits of the Europeans:

I can further say with safety there is not a crowned head
in Europe whose talents or merits would entitle him
to be elected a vestryman by any American parish.
T.J. to General Washington, May 2, '88.
(31/154–5:158–9)

There is much more in this vein—intemperate criticism of European knowledge, European royalty, European commercial organization, political organization, and economic management—all of it very much more confident, not to say strident, than the hesitant juxtaposition of Jefferson and the Medicis in canto 21.

The Jeffersonian and Adamite judgements are intended to demonstrate that America had 'a national mind, . . . the mental formation, the inherited habits of thought, the conditionings, aptitudes of a given race or time'.[4] But, quite apart from the difficulty of extracting any clear sense from the fragments of letters Pound collects, the national mind which emerges is one of arrogant self-satisfaction, and a parochial, intemperate dismissal of foreigners—an impression much less strong in the letters themselves than in Pound's redaction from them. The Jefferson of these cantos is not the same man as the modest author of the letter in canto 21. And John Adams has ceased to be the first of a 'row of duds' in the presidential office.

Just as the focus of the *Cantos* altered in the 1930s, so Pound's understanding of American history underwent a radical transformation. In 1912 Pound had thought that one could not consider America as older than 1870, and his opinion remained the same in 1924. But in 1938 he wrote:

> A national American culture existed from 1770 till at least 1861. Jefferson could not imagine an American going voluntarily to inhabit Europe. After the debacle of American culture individuals had to emigrate in order to conserve such fragments of American culture as had survived.[5]

In 1912 America was, for Pound, a nation *in potentia* and he looked forward with some pride, as well as some misgiving, toward its dominance. He declared his belief in the imminence of an American renaissance, and devised a programme to hasten and consolidate that renaissance. But in the 1930s it had become for him a nation betrayed, a civilization fully exemplified only in the correspondence of two old men who had once played a prominent role in the affairs of the young nation:

> 'As monument' or I should prefer to say as a still workable dynamo, left us from the real period, nothing surpasses the Jefferson correspondence. Or to reduce it to convenient bulk concentrating on the best of it, and its fullest implications, nothing surpasses the evidence that CIVILIZATION WAS in America, than the series of letters exchanged between Jefferson and John Adams, during the decade of reconciliation after their disagreements.[6]

The notion of betrayal, of a malevolent force consciously working against the benefit of mankind, is an unfortunate feature of Pound's mental furniture in the 1930s—and for a very long period thereafter. But a more interesting aspect of his portrayal of the American paideuma is that it is so much a matter of words and ideas rather than one of actions and achievements.

His American heroes are Jefferson, John Adams, John Quincy Adams, and Martin Van Buren, the last, president from 1837 to 1841 and Vice President to Andrew Jackson in his second term (1833–7). All of them are presented to the reader through their own words. They reveal their opinions of others engaged in the government of the nation or of other nations. We garner an impression of their learning, of their sense of humour, of their honesty, and of their wisdom. They are all made to look, as near as may be, as resourceful as Odysseus, and to know men's minds and their various cities as well as he. William Vasse's description of Quincy Adams would serve very nicely for all four men as they are portrayed in *Eleven New Cantos*: 'Quincy Adams is important not so much for what he did as for what he thought, for his moral judgments upon men and their actions.'[7]

The role of these American heroes ought, one would think, to be parallel to the role of Odysseus who is journeying up out of darkness into the light. On the secular level that journey is manifested by the building of the city, that is, the creation of institutions, the erection of buildings, the enunciation of ideas, or the fabrication of works of art. Malatesta has been established as the type of the secular hero, struggling against a hostile and impercipient environment, and, like Quixote, ultimately failing although leaving behind a monument to his struggle in the Tempio and a few poems. But the monuments of the struggles of the American heroes shown to us are their letters, diaries, and autobiographies. Canto 37, for example, is drawn from Van Buren's autobiography dated 'Sorrento, June 21st. Villa Falongola', as Pound duly records it (37/185:191). 'At the age of seventy one, and in a foreign land,' Van Buren tells his readers, 'I commence a sketch of the principal events of my life.'[8] The principal motive of his autobiography would seem to be to place credit and blame where it belongs in the bank war between Andrew Jackson and Nicholas Biddle, president of the second Bank of the United States. The Jackson administration emerged victorious, but the impression conveyed by this singularly uncommunicative canto is one of corruption, deceit, and betrayal:

> 'employing means at the bank's disposal
> in deranging the country's credits, obtaining by panic
> control over public mind' said Van Buren
> 'from the real committee of Bank's directors
> the government's directors have been excluded.[9]
>
> (37/184:190)

There is a good deal of round moral condemnation in the Malatesta cantos as well, but there it is offset by the boisterous and morally ambivalent figure of Malatesta who gave as good as he got. Our American heroes are crotchety old men who fight with the pen, not the sword. Pound's admiration for Mussolini by contrast is based on 'his passion for construction'. 'Treat him as *artifex*', Pound tells us, 'and all the details fall into place. Treat him as anything save the artist and you will get muddled with contradictions.'[10] However inflating this may be as a characterization of Mussolini, it is appropriate for a hero of the *Cantos*. But the American heroes do not appear as artists. They are, rather, scholars, observers of men and their minds (like Odysseus), but not builders, not creators.

The American hero emerges from these cantos not as the man who acts, but as the man who knows. As an actor, he remains a pale imitation of the European. The American Revolution itself is seen as a pedagogical rather than a military or political achievement. Pound twice has Adams remark that 'the revolution took place in the minds of the people', and it is only a partial distortion of what Adams actually wrote:

> From 1760 to 1766, was the purest period of patriotism; from 1766 to 1776 was the period of corruption; from 1775 to 1783 was the period of war. Not a revolutionary war, for the revolution was complete, in the minds of the people, and the union of the colonies, before the war commenced in the skirmishes of Concord and Lexington on the 19th of April, 1775.[11]

Adams does not say that the 'revolution *took place* in the minds of the people', but that it '*was complete* in the minds of the people', and he adds the political necessity of the union of the colonies. Pound's emendation and omission have the effect of changing the American revolution from a political and military event to a purely intellectual and cultural one.

In 'Patria Mia' Pound had declared that America needed an Abelard and a University of Paris. Contemporary America is given only intermittent and satirical attention in the *Cantos*. But the American heroes before 1870, despite the fact that they are all politicians and presidents, turn out to be pedagogues like Abelard—although with a different lesson to teach. Even the revolution is seen as a lesson learned. America in the *Cantos* is not so much the 'laboratory experiment' that William Vasse says it is[12] as a classroom where the art of government is taught.

All of the real action in the *Cantos* is located in Europe. It is there that wars are fought, cities burned, assassinations perpetrated, and crimes of passion committed. It is also in Europe that paintings are commissioned, poems composed, great passions consummated, temples built, and cities erected. America is, by contrast, a classroom where nothing happens but everything is understood. Or it is like Dioce's city of plotted streets, a fine dream which never was completely realized in bricks and mortar. America is one of the four things to which Pound defiantly clings in the *Pisan Cantos*: 'I surrender neither the empire nor the temples/plural/nor the constitution nor yet the city of Dioce'. The America Pound refuses to surrender is neither the nation, its people, nor its achievements, but the ideal expression of the American polity, the constitution. All four terms of this list are ideas or possibilities rather than actual historical realities. The temples are pointedly plural, and Ecbatan (Dioce's city) was never more an actual community than the site of a World Fair. The empire, too, is an idea rather than some historical empire. It is an idea or dream he described as early as 'Patria Mia':

> All the fine dreams of empire, of a universal empire, Rome,the imperium restored, and so on, came to little. The dream, nevertheless, had its value, it set a model for emulation, a model of orderly procedure, and it was used as a spur through every awakening from the eighth century to the sixteenth. Yet it came to no sort of civic reality, either in the high sheriffage of Charles the Great, or in its atavistic parody under Napoleon.[13]

America, too, is a dream. Initially, it was a dream of the future, of an American *risorgimento* in which the vigour of the New York crowd would express itself in the creation of an entire new culture foreshadowed by the soaring architecture of New York city. In the *Cantos* themselves, it becomes a dream from the past, a recollection of a revolution which took place in the minds of the people, but which came 'to no sort of civic reality'. America lives, like the city of Dioce, 'in the mind indestructible'.

Of course, it is not Pound's intention to make the American paideuma appear to be only *in potentia*, so much as to show it as having been betrayed. He sees himself to be recovering the true tradition. The criticism of Europe transcribed from Jefferson and Adams prepares his readers for the portrayal of contemporary Europe in cantos 35, 38, and 41 where Machiavellian munitions salesmen, bankers, and politicians rob, cheat, and murder the people. The implication would appear to be that the American paideuma of Jefferson, Adams, John Quincy Adams, and Martin Van Buren might have prevented all of this had it prevailed.

Canto 40 brings together modern tales of commercial chicanery with a condensation of Hanno's *Periplus*—a collocation worthy of the *Cantos*. Both the modern tales and Hanno's account are followed by the line, 'Out of which things seeking an exit'. The 'things' are the brutality, dishonesty, and violence of commercial exploitation, as old as Carthage, and as new as tomorrow.[14] The exit is to be found in Italy, in its paideuma now to be represented by the Monte dei Paschi and Benito Mussolini. Il Duce is heard at the beginning of canto 41 remarking of the *Cantos*, 'But this is amusing' to its author's unbounded delight:

> 'Ma questo,'
> said the Boss, 'è divertente.'
> catching the point before the aesthetes had got there:
> Having drained off the muck by Vada
> From the marshes, by Circeo, where no one else wd. have
> drained it.
>
> (41/202:210)

It is sadly typical of Pound's tunnel vision during this period that he should take Mussolini's non-committal, and doubtless uncomprehending remark as an instance of penetrating insight.

Canto 41 provides a transition to the following section, *The Fifth Decad of Cantos*, through the reference to Mussolini, and one to the Monte dei Paschi of Siena; for the *Fifth Decad* reveals the Italian paideuma of which Mussolini is seen to be the inheritor and reviver. It is a different Italy from that encountered in the earlier cantos. The focus of interest is now financial and political where before it had been aesthetic and philosophic. Of course Pound maintains his original aesthetic and religious interests simultaneously with the newer economic and political ones. The one does not displace the other, but the history is more sharply isolated from the mythical and aesthetic interests (found in cantos 36, 39, 45, 47, and 51) than in earlier sections.

The *Fifth Decad* was published in 1937, only three years after *Eleven New Cantos*. There is a continuity between the two sections not found between earlier ones, and a rapidity of composition exceeded only by the twenty cantos of the Chinese and Adams section which follow a further three years later (1940). Pound thought them 'clearer than the preceding ones',[15] and they do avoid the more impenetrable obscurities of his jottings from American sages. Nonetheless, the reader still finds himself confronted with notations from

Pound's reading, from which he must reconstruct the gristly roots of ideas going into action.

The first two cantos of the new section (42 and 43) introduce the Monte dei Paschi of Siena through Pound's translations from the Italian documents concerned with the foundation of the bank.[16] The bank was established in 1623 with its capitalization based on the rents from the pastures of Maremma, and operated by the Council (Bailey) of Siena. Hence: 'there first was the fruit of nature/there was the whole will of the people' (43/218:227–8). Moreover, as Galigani points out, 'the specie trade was in fact a purchase of "Loca Montis", i.e. lots of pasture land, for still in the 17th century, as in Dante's time, lending for interest was considered immoral.'[17] And finally the bank was to lend only to those who could make good use of the money, and was to distribute its surplus profit among the poorer citizens of Siena:

> and 6thly that the Magistrate
> give his chief care that the specie
> be lent to whomso can best use it USE IT
> (*id est, piú utilmente*)
> to the good of their houses, to benefit of their business
> as of weaving, the wool trade, the silk trade
> And that (7thly) the overabundance every five years shall the Bailey
> distribute to workers of the contrade (the wards) . . .
> (42/209–10:217–18)

Clearly this is a bank based on the fecundity of nature, and hence part of the Eleusinian paideuma holding that copulation is good for the crops, while all other banks belong to the Hebrew paideuma believing that copulation is bad for the crops.

> Two kinds of banks have existed: the Monte dei Paschi and the devils. Banks differ in their intention. Two kinds of bank stand in history: banks built for beneficence, for reconstruction; and banks created to prey on the people.[18]

The other kind of bank is represented by the second Bank of the United States of America under Nicholas Biddle—of which Van Buren has so much to say in canto 37—and the Bank of England, cryptically represented by a couple of lines from its prospectus of 1694:

Said Paterson:
Hath benefit of interest on all
the moneys which it, the bank, creates out of nothing.
(46/233:243)

Pound seizes upon these lines as an admission of theft and deception:

'Will any jury convict on this evidence?
1694 anno domini, on through the ages of usury
On, right on, into hair-cloth, right on into rotten building,
Right on into London houses, ground rents, foetid brick work,
Will any jury convict 'um? The Foundation of Regius Professors
Was made to spread lies and teach Whiggery, will any
JURY convict 'um?
The Macmillan Commission about two hundred and forty years
years LATE
with great difficulty got back to Paterson's
The bank makes it *ex nihil*[19].
(46/233:243–4)

The history of Tuscany contained in cantos 44 and 50[20] is less clear in its implications. It brings us into contact with Napoleon Bonaparte through his sister Marie Anne Elisa, Grand Duchess of Tuscany, and to a period contemporaneous with that lived through by Jefferson, Adams, and John Quincy Adams. Pound's attitude to Napoleon in these cantos would seem to be approving, although neither he nor his American presidents had had much good to say of him in earlier cantos:

And 'Semiramis' 1814 departed from Lucca
but her brother's law code remains.
monumento di civile sapienza
dried swamps, grew cotton, brought in merinos
mortgage system improved[21].
(44/227:237)

Napoleon's improved status in Pound's eyes is no doubt due to his opposition to the British, and hence to financial and commercial interests as in canto 78:

'and the economic war has begun'
Napoleon wath a goodth man, it took uth
20 yearth to crwuth him
it will not take uth 20 years to crwuth Mussolini'[22].
(78/477:508).

Although the precise nature of the Italian paideuma, apart from the bank of Siena, remains rather unclear in the *Fifth Decad*, the general movement of the nineteenth century, throughout Europe, is unambiguous:

> in their soul was usura
> and in their hand bloody oppression
> and that son of a dog, Rospigliosi,
> came into Tuscany to make serfs of old Tuscans.
> S . . t on the throne of England, s . . t on the Austrian sofa
> In their soul was usura and in their minds darkness
> and blankness, ...
>
> (50/248:259)

This vituperation directed at rulers and statesmen echoes that of Jefferson and Adams in *Eleven New Cantos*, but it is Pound speaking in his own person. There is no authority from without the poem for these ill-tempered remarks. As the poem moves toward the contemporary world, Pound himself becomes one of 'those who know'. He takes on the role of Jefferson or Adams in the absence of any alternative candidate who can be quoted:

> And if you will say that this tale teaches . . .
> a lesson, or that the Reverend Eliot
> has found a more natural language . . . you who think you will
> get through hell in a hurry . . .
> . . . . . Seventeen
> Years on this case, nineteen years, ninety years
> on this case
> An' the fuzzy bloke sez (legs no pants ever wd. fit) 'IF
> that is so, any government worth a damn can
> pay dividends?'
> The major chewed it a bit and sez: 'Y—es, eh . . .
> You mean instead of collectin' taxes?'
> 'Instead of collecting taxes.' That office?
>
> (46/231:241)

The 'fuzzy bloke' is Pound himself speaking to Major Douglas in the *New Age* office seventeen years earlier than this record of it (that is, 1918). He had just become aware of the implications of Douglas's economic theories for the redistribution of wealth, and is heard going beyond even Douglas's awareness.[23]

The *Fifth Decad* brings Pound's historical summary up to the present, and therefore would seem to complete it. Canto 47 juxtaposes the death of Adonis (whence 'Wheat shoots rise new by the altar./flower from the swift seed') with Odysseus' conquest of Circe, perceived as an Eleusinian revelation. This *hieros gamos* is a repetition of that in canto 39, and is the mythical equivalent of the revelation of history and economics now achieved in the poem—a reading rather cryptically authorized by the lines in canto 38 following an account of Douglasite economics:

> and the light became so bright and so blindin'
> in this layer of paradise
> that the mind of man was bewildered.
> (38/190:198)

Even the Albigenses are invoked in an apparent reminiscence of a visit to Montségur by Pound himself:

> Velvet, yellow, unwinged
> clambers, a ball, into its orchis
> and the stair there still broken
> the flat stones of the road, Mt Segur.
> From Val Cabrere, were two miles of roofs to San Bertrand
> so that a cat need not set foot in the road
> where now is an inn, and bare rafters,
> where they scratch six feet deep to reach pavement
> where now is wheat field, and a milestone
> an altar to Terminus, with arms crossed
> back of the stone
> Where sun cuts light against evening;
> where light shaves grass into emerald
> Savairic; hither Gaubertz;
> Said they wd. not be under Paris.
> (48/243:253)

Gaubertz de Poicebot is a troubadour, and Savairic de Mauleon is his patron. Their story is told in canto 5, and in 'Troubadours: Their Sorts and Conditions'. Here they are assigned parts in the resistance to the conquest of Provence by Simon de Montfort on behalf of the Pope and the King of France.

And usury is identified in cantos 45 and 51 as against Nature's increase, as the canker which has blighted the flower of civilization. Set over against Usura are the Monte dei Paschi and Odysseus' *hieros gamos*. In alliance with Usura are the rulers of Europe and betrayers of America; the bankers, munitions dealers, professors, men of commerce, and even men of letters who either openly or tacitly serve Usura.

The *Fifth Decad*, then, completes the historical survey begun with Odysseus' descent into the Underworld in canto 1. But within the Odyssean narrative, the poem has progressed crab-like backward from the descent to the encounter with Circe, the necessary prelude to the descent. This inverted order fits Pound's Eleusinian reading of the *Odyssey*, for at Eleusis the descent precedes the revelation. In effect, Pound has, like Odysseus, descended into the Underworld, lain with the goddess, and heard the Fates weep for Adonis. That is to say, he has discovered the infamy of usury, and the glory of wealth and money based on nature's increase and the increment of association, and has seen the betrayal of those who had some part of the vision. Having brought the poem through its *nekuia* to the moment of revelation, he must now turn in a new direction.

Tiresias' prophecy for Odysseus was to become true for Pound as well:

> And he strong with the blood, said then: 'Odysseus
> 'Shalt return through spiteful Neptune, over dark seas,
> 'Lose all companions.'
>
> (1/4–5:9)

But Pound did not know that in 1937. The perils Odysseus encountered after his visit to the Underworld—the sirens, Scylla and Charybdis, the oxen of the Sun, and the tender trap of Calypso's isle—are only too appropriate to Pound's career over the next ten years. But that ironic parallel must wait upon the *Pisan Cantos* for its expression. Instead Pound sets out on new journeys, to China, and, once again, to America.

2. CHINA

The Chinese and Adams sections were written together, and at great speed. Pound had the *Fifth Decad* off his hands by March 1937. In July of that year he claims not to have any cantos to give to Ronald Duncan for the *Townsman*. In June of 1938 he is 'in the middle of de Mailla's *Histoire Générale de la Chine*', and by March of 1939 Faber have in their hands the typescript of *Cantos 52–71*.[24]

Pound told F. V. Morley of Faber that 'you are gittin something NEW in the Cantos; not merely more of the same. Trust at least two advances in mode will be perceptible by you and the PSM [Eliot].'[25] The novelty of these twenty cantos can scarcely be denied. Never before had Pound simply transcribed from a single work for a whole section as he does for both the Chinese and Adams sections (with some trifling exceptions). Never before had an entire section been bare of any substantial reference to the Odyssean and Eleusinian themes. Never before had he put together twenty cantos with only half a dozen lines of original composition.

I can think of no possible defence for the rhetoric and organization of these sections. They are essentially marginal notes to multi-volume works without any alteration in the order of presentation adopted by his sources. In the case of the Adams cantos this means that Pound traces Adams's career first via Charles Francis Adams's biography of his grandfather, next via John Adams's own diary, then from his published writings, and, finally, as it is reflected in Adams's correspondence. Pound's contribution is merely to select those portions of the story he deems important or relevant to his purposes. As histories, the Chinese and Adams sections are scarcely intelligible without some considerable knowledge of Chinese and American history.

One can defend the fragmented and grasshopper-like progression of these cantos on the grounds that it creates for the reader a mimesis of the manner in which we actually apprehend the past, 'in ripples and spirals eddying out from us and our time'. However, such a defence is seriously compromised, in the case of the Chinese section, by the fact that Pound merely condenses a perfectly coherent and consecutive narrative. But even if one accepts the appropriateness of the manner of presentation of these cantos, one is left with the problem of the matter. What has China to do with this epic of the West? and why need we explore America yet again?

Pound's interest in Chinese culture was already long established before he came to write the Chinese section. He had incorporated (or, rather, interpolated) Chinese wisdom into the *Cantos* in canto 13 with excerpts from the *Analects* of Confucius, and had paid tribute to the beauty of Chinese poetry in canto 49, the 'Seven Lakes' canto 26.[26] But these were mere digressions, asides to remind the reader that not all beauty or wisdom is to be found in the West. His decision to incorporate Chinese history into the poem *en gros* is a new departure prompted by factors other than the internal dynamics of the poem, as Hugh Kenner explains. (He is speaking of Moyriac de Mailla's *Histoire Générale de la Chine*, Pound's source for almost all of the section.)

And no volumes could have come more patly than did these to Ezra Pound in Rapallo, 1938, to reactivate the Enlightenment rationalism he had secreted during the first war and was drawing on once more as war clouds darkened. To know clear simple principles in a time of confusion, this is a great resource; to know that statecraft has principles not beyond grasping, that action can be taken and men (Mussolini) found capable of taking it, that history affords paradigm after paradigm. In 1914 he had used China as a mirror for the Great War. Now he could use China again as a mirror of Modern Europe, and of eternal principles of government. . .[27]

Cantos 1 to 51 trace in a 'candied' manner the history of the West from Troy to the present. That history is rendered intelligible by a paridigmatic structure derived from Browning, Aeschylus, and Péladan. Wars are the result of the withstaying of the light of Amor—of the ignorance or suppression of a few simple basic truths so profound they can be expressed only metaphorically:

The truth having been Eleusis? and a modern Eleusis being possible in the wilds of a man's mind only?

. . . I mean or imply that certain truth exists. Certain colours exist in nature though great painters have striven vainly, and though the colour film is not yet perfected. Truth is not untrue'd by reason of our failing to fix it on paper. Certain objects are communicable to a man or woman only 'with proper lighting', they are perceptible in our own minds only with proper 'lighting', fitfully and by instants.[28]

The Chinese cantos trace a past separate and independent from that of the West, and a past that has been shaped by two and a half millenia of Confucian history.

The Adams cantos are a different matter. American history had already been incorporated into the poem in *Eleven New Cantos*, and it is not obvious that more needed to be said on that subject. Perhaps Pound was aware that his American heroes still looked rather pale beside the Europeans, and sought with Adams to create an American hero as resourceful as Odysseus and with some of the vigour of Malatesta. Certainly we are shown Adams in this new section as a man who has travelled and seen the world. Moreover, with the Chinese example before us, Adams can be better appreciated as an ideal ruler to whom Americans should look for guidance as the

Chinese do to Yao, Chun, and Yu, their ideal emperors. In other words, Pound must have come to see his treatment of America in *Eleven New Cantos* as inadequate, just as his treatment of Jefferson in *Cantos 17–27* had earlier proved to be unsatisfactory. Instead of revising or suppressing these earlier treatments of the subject, Pound merely appends a new one reflecting his deeper understanding. Thus the Adams cantos are part of the record of Pound's education, now, he believed, at the stage of revelation symbolized by Odysseus lying with the goddess. But, of course, Pound will return again in the *Pisan Cantos*, and again in *Rock-Drill*, and again in *Thrones*, and again, finally, in *Drafts & Fragments* to the same subjects with ever new, and increasingly gnomic revelations.

No commentary on the Chinese cantos could possibly reduce them to ready intelligibility, since they are nothing less than a severely condensed history of China from its mythical beginnings to 1780. Unless we know a great deal of that history, we will necessarily encounter a good measure of blank confusion in reading through them. The sheer unintelligibility of these cantos is a fault no amount of argument can get around. The only practical approach for the critic is to reveal the manner in which they were composed, and to show their relationship to the embracing patterns of the poem.

The entire section is essentially marginalia on the twelve-volume French history of China by the Jesuit missionary, Moyriac de Mailla. De Mailla spent more than forty years in China, dying there in 1748. He had brought his manuscript to France in 1737, but the Jesuits were unable to get it into print for another forty years, edited, revised, and brought up to date by M. le Roux des Hauterayes.[29] The history continues right up to 1780, the date of publication of the eleventh volume (the twelfth consists of appendices and index), which would suggest that M. le Roux des Hauterayes wrote the later portions of the history himself.

Pound begins with a few transitional lines as if he thought it necessary to remind his readers that this new section is indeed related to earlier ones:

> And I have told you of how things were under Duke
>   Leopold in Siena
> And of the true base of credit, that is
>   the abundance of nature
> with the whole folk behind it.
>
> (52/257:267)

And after thirty-two lines of denunciatory vituperation (marred by several black lines thought necessary by his publishers) he invokes earlier interests of the poem even back to El Cid in Burgos of canto 3:

> Between KUNG and ELEUSIS
> Under the Golden Roof, la Dorata
> her baldacchino
> Riccio on his horse rides still to Montepulciano
> the groggy church is gone toothless
> No longer holds against *neschek*
> the fat has covered their croziers
> The high fans and the mitre mean nothing
> Once only in Burgos, once in Cortona
> was the song firm and well given
> old buffers keeping the stiffness,
> Gregory damned, always was damned, obscurantist.
> Know then: . . .
>
> (52/258:268)

The 'know then' is followed by a translation from the *Li Ki* or Confucian Book of Rites, which informs a man of the proper employments for each season much in the manner of Hesiod's *Works and Days*, a portion of which was translated in canto 47. Pound is cryptically telling his readers: 'You have heard the history of the West wherein Eleusis has been neglected leading to the loss of antique beauty, reverence, and prosperity. Hear then how Confucian wisdom has persisted throughout the vicissitudes of China's long history.' His readers are then treated to seventy-nine pages of redaction from de Mailla's twelve volumes.[30]

Canto 53 provides a very illuminating insight into the manner in which Pound composed this section. He has worked his way into Volume II of de Mailla, and is just beginning his account of the reign of Siuen-ouang:

> . . . Siuen went against the west tartars
> His praise lasts to this day: Siuen-ouang contra barbaros
> legat belli ducem Chaoumoukong,
> Hoailand, fed by Hoai river
> dark millet, Tchang wine for the sacrifice.
>
> (53/270:281)

The innocent reader is bound to be a little startled at the sudden appearance of Latin in this Chinese history. The serious reader will turn to the *Annotated Index* and learn from this remarkable work that Pound is quoting Alexandre Lacharme, *Confucii Chi-King*, page 308. But the *Index* will not tell him that the entire passage is from Lacharme, nor how it got there.

Of course, Pound possessed a copy of Lacharme's Latin translation of the Confucian Odes, and he learned from de Mailla's notes, or was reminded by them, that Siuen-ouang was celebrated in the Odes. De Mailla's notes mention five specific Odes, none of which are cited in the passage. Instead Pound begins with Lacharme's note to the eighth Ode of the third part of Book III (Ode 262 in Pound's translation, published in 1954):

> Siuen-ouang imperator contra barbaros australes belli ducem Chao-mou-king legat. Anno a. Chr. 826 ['Siuen went against the west tartars . . . Siuen-ouang contra barbaros/legat belli ducem Chaomoukong'.]
>
> Hoai regio qual alluit fluvius Hoai in provincia King-nan. ['Hoailand, fed by Hoai river'.]
>
> Princeps Chao-hou est princeps Chao-mou-kong.
>
> Kouei erat prosceptro, erat etiam in caerimontiis pro lance, vel potius pro hypopatera.
>
> Kiu, Milium nigrum ['dark millet'] quo in sacrificiis utebantur; et vinum Tchang ['Tchang wine for the sacrifice'] vinum odorum in sacrificiis.[31]

In a manner characteristic of his late style, Pound paraphrases Lacharme and cites bits of Latin, rearranged presumably for easier intelligibility for English-speaking readers. The comment, 'his praise lasts to this day' is a paraphrase of de Mailla's comment which sent him to the Odes. And he has mistranslated 'australes' as 'western'.

The next bit of Latin begins a paraphrase of the next Ode from the same section (Ode 9):

> Juxta fluvium Hoai acies ordinatur nec mora
> Swift men as if flyers, like Yangtse
>   Strong as the Yangtse,
>   they stand rooted as mountains
>   they move as a torrent of waters
> Emperor not rash in council: agit considerate.
>   (53/270–1:281)

Once again the *Annotated Index* identifies the Latin as from Lacharme. (It gives the correct Ode, but the wrong page—263 instead of the correct 188.) The Latin is from stanza 4, 'juxta fluvium Houai dictum ordinatur acies, nec mora' ['by the river Hoai the battle line is drawn up without delay']. The next four lines paraphrase the first part of stanza 5:

> Imperatoris milites quanto sunt numero! hos volare diceres; quasi si alas gererent ['swift men as if flyers'] similes sunt fluvii Kiang, similes fluvii Han ['like Yangtse/Strong as the Yangtse'], montis radices imitantur illa ['they stand rooted as mountains']; aquam torrentum repraesentant ['they move as a torrent of waters'] . . .[32]

The last line of the passage cited is still from the ninth Ode, but from stanza 3:

> Clarrissimus, splendissimus imperator coeli filius, quanta oris dignitate, majestate quanta! Non consilio praeceps, sed mature et considerate agit; non praepropere, nec tamen lente se gerit . . .[33]

Pound should have written, 'Emperor not rash in counsel' rather than 'council', but the error is not significant. The next fifteen lines return to de Mailla's account of Siuen's reign—which was neither prosperous nor peaceful.

Pound concludes the Siuen portion of this canto with a return to the Odes:

> Siuen established this people hac loca fluvius alluit
> He heard the wild goose crying sorrow
> Campestribus locis.
>
> (53/271 : 282)

The first Latin phrase, 'the river washes these places' is not from Lacharme, nor from de Mailla, but serves as an appropriate description of the landscape described in the Ode alluded to in the following lines:

> Cantat ciconia in novem insulis, quae in medio lacu positae sunt; ejus vox in campestribus locis longe lateque auditur. ['The storks sing in the new island placed in the middle of the lake; their voices are heard far and wide in the countryside.'][34]

It may be that Pound invented 'hac loca fluvius alluit'—although it would be uncharacteristic of him to do so. As to why he changed Lacharme's storks to geese, I cannot guess. They are cranes in the Confucian Odes.

From all of this the reader is left with an impression of Siuen as an energetic and careful ruler who is well memorialized in the Odes, for all his carelessness in having neglected the performance of the spring sowing rites—the result of which was four years of drought. It is a somewhat more favourable portrait than that of de Mailla, but not essentially different. There is a certain pleasure in deciphering these lines for the scholar who has ample time and financial support to take him to a great research library. The reward of his labours is an understanding of how Pound came to create such a puzzling pastiche. Once possessed of this knowledge, the whole passage makes sense. The poetic record of Siuen's exploits in the Odes is briefer, more pointed, and has a greater claim upon our attention than de Mailla's prose account. This sense, however, is accessible only to Pound himself, and to the occasional reader who has the time and inclination to trace Pound's footsteps. In other words, the historical verse of the Chinese cantos is private in a peculiarly musty and bookwormish manner. And this extreme privacy is not alleviated by any local felicity of expression.

Of course the bulk of the Chinese cantos is straight from de Mailla without much alteration except that Pound evinces a hostility toward eunuchs, Taoists, and Buddhists (whom he calls 'hochangs') rather greater than that manifested in de Mailla's account. For example, in canto 54 Pound writes:

> The Prince of Ouei put out hochangs
> put out the shamen and Taotssé
> a. d. 444, putt 'em OUT
> in the time of OUEN TI
> 'Let artisans teach their sons crafts'
> Found great store of arms in a temple
> Then To-pa-tao went after the shave-heads, the hochang.
> (54/283:294–5)

These lines are based on pages 49 to 54, and 57 to 58 of Volume V of de Mailla. The Prince of Ouei (To-pa-tao) initially expelled the Buddhists in A.D. 444 after learning something of their teachings from a famous Chinese Buddhist. Two years later they appear to be still in China and are discovered to be arming themselves:

To-pa-tao surpris que des religieux eussent fait un arsenal de leur temple, ... [He sent imperial judges and soldiers to look into the matter.] ... il leur commanda d'aller se saisir des *Ho-chang* de ce temple, de les faire tous mourir sans attendre de nouvel ordre et se s'emparer de tous leur effets. On y trouva, entre autres choses, quantité de vin, dont l'usage étoit défendu par leur secte, et plusieurs femmes dans un appartement reculé. [And the Prince issues an even sterner edict than that of 444, driving them underground.] . . . leurs temples et leurs tours furent détruits de fond en comble, et il n'en resta aucune sur pieds.[35]

Although de Mailla makes no comment, in his account it appears to be a sorry and sordid affair, smelling strongly of rampant prejudice and brutal religious persecution. Pound's account (and this is only one of many outbursts against eunuchs, Taoists, and Buddhists) is clearly partisan. He is cheering the home team on to rout the opposition. And the opposition is represented by the triple threat of eunuchs, Taoists, and Buddhists; whereas, in fact, de Mailla's account is concerned only with Buddhists. It is true, however, that de Mailla's history reflects the Confucian antipathy of his Chinese source toward both Taoists and Buddhists. The eunuchs are also frequently attacked for wielding excessive and improper influence. Their role was to guard and oversee the Emperor's harem, but they would seem to have frequently wielded great political influence at court. What, in effect, happens is that the alien Buddhists and native Chinese Taoists catch all of the virulence Pound was later to direct at the Jews and money conspirators in his radio broadcasts. They represent the 'secret corruptions, the personal lusts, avarices, etc., that', Pound tells us in *Guide to Kulchur*, 'scoundrels keep hidden.'

The style of Confucian history is well suited to Pound's taste for private and anecdotal history whose *parti pris* and immediate character clarifies and simplifies grand and complex issues. The classic of Confucian history, the *Chou King*, is a series of colloquies between ministers and emperors interspersed with harangues addressed by emperors or generals to their troops. De Mailla's history follows this pattern, quoting long conversations between ministers, and reports directed to the emperor. It adds straight narrative accounts of battles which are not to be found in the *Chou King*. Obviously most, if not all, of the conversations must be inventions of one historian or another. They are, in fact, a device whereby the historian can present and debate the political, social, economic, or whatever issues raised by the historical events. But the net effect is to achieve a feeling of immediacy very similar to that sought after in Pound's own treatment of history—based as it is upon first-hand documents or reminiscences.

These debates, both in the *Chou King* and in de Mailla, are highly stylized in their structure, and repetitive in their content. Essentially the object is to demonstrate that whatever course of action one seeks to justify is in accord with the ancient practices approved by Confucius. And these practices are most eminently exemplified by the first three emperors of China (Yao, Chun, and Yu) celebrated by Pound in canto 53. Hence, we find the names of these three emperors recurring repeatedly throughout the Chinese cantos. We also find emperors and ministers speaking directly. Neither of these features of the section originate with Pound. They merely echo de Mailla's history.

One such debate to which Pound devotes a good deal of space is that involving Ouang-ngan-ché, first minister to the emperor Chin-Tsong. This is found in the middle of canto 55 (296–9:309–11). Ngan (as Pound calls him) was a highly controversial minister whom the history characterizes as opinionated and self-serving. Indeed it goes so far as to mention Chin-Tsong's long support of Ngan against strong criticism as his only important failing, in the paragraph of eulogy announcing the emperor's death. However, Pound's treatment of Ngan is highly sympathetic. The cause of his troubles was a series of regulations he established to control agriculture and commerce. He re-established the market tribunals to set the prices of merchandise and collect a tax on it, established public grain storage houses whence the farmers could buy grain in the spring for sowing, made the taxes proportionate to the amount of commercial exchange rather than fixed, and regulated the supply (and, therefore the value) of money. 'All of these changes annoyed, greatly, the bureaucrats,' Pound tells us, quoting directly from de Mailla.

Despite strong opposition from other ministers, virtually the whole mandarin class, and from provincial governors, Ngan held his position from 1069 to 1076, and even after his fall, his regulations remained in effect until 1086 when Ssé-ma kouang revoked them:

> and merchants in Caïfong put up their shutters in mourning
> for Ssé-kouang
> anti-tao, anti-bhud, anti-Ngan
> whose rules had worked 20 years
> till Ssé-kouang reversed 'em.
>
> (55/298:311)

In the history[36] Ngan's regulations are seen as a ruinous burden that lay on the nation for almost twenty years until Ssé-ma-kouang finally removed it. Moreover, the history quite plainly states that Ngan was corrupted by Buddhist and Taoist philosophy as, it says, can be clearly seen in his commentaries on the *Chou King*, the *Chi King* and the *Li Ki* (the history classic, the Book of Odes, and the Book of Rites), and from his dictionary. Ngan's commentaries were made mandatory for those sitting the civil service examinations, resulting, according to the history, in the virtual abandonment of the Confucian classics and adoption of Buddhist doctrine. Pound dutifully records this (with some distortion): 'Students went Bhud rather than take Kung via Ngan.'

The charge that he had replaced Confucian doctrine with Buddhist and Taoist doctrine, is probably the most damaging the history can bring against Ngan. And, as we have seen, it is the kind of accusation that Pound gleefully echoes and even exaggerates elsewhere in the Chinese section. One wonders why Pound has inverted in this instance the bias of the history which otherwise he so enthusiastically follows. It is true that M. des Hauterayes appends a note on page 305 disagreeing with the history's estimate of Ngan. (A note which Pound echoes in the line, 'Mandarins oppressing peasants to get back their grain loan'.) But Pound quite happily ignored the editor's cautionary notes to Martin Van Buren's account of the Bank War. However, des Hauterayes does mention that Ngan's regulations 'must have been odious to the usurers who exist only on the blood of the unfortunate', and this mention of usurers would certainly have struck a responsive chord in Pound. But perhaps most important of all is the fact that Ngan's regulations as recorded by the history do correspond to Pound's own economic principles, based as they are upon management of nature's increase, and control of money and prices.

By choosing to reverse the bias of the history towards Ngan, Pound has created yet another maligned and misunderstood hero on the model of Malatesta, and yet another example of historical obfuscation and deceit. Ngan fits very nicely into the historical line of the Albigenses, Malatesta, and Martin Van Buren—all losers buried under a mound of historians' lies. But Chinese history must demonstrate—if it is to have any meaning at all in the *Cantos*—a history which does not lie because it is inspired throughout by the breath of Confucian wisdom. Pound's treatment of Ngan undercuts this view of Chinese history, and would seem to very nearly vitiate the entire section, given that its *raison d'etre* is feeble at best.

The clearest expression of the significance of Chinese history for Pound is found in the note (dated 1945) to his second translation of the *Ta Hsio* (his first was published in 1928):

> Starting at the bottom as market inspector, having risen to be Prime Minister, Confucius is more concerned with the necessities of government, and of governmental administration than any other philosopher. He had two thousand years of documented history behind him which he condensed so as to render it useful to men in high official position, not making a mere collection of anecdotes as did Herodotus.
>
> His analysis of why the earlier great emperors had been able to govern greatly was so sound that every durable dynasty, since his time, has risen on a Confucian design and been initiated by a group of Confucians. China was tranquil when her rulers understood these few pages. When the principles here defined were neglected, dynasties waned and chaos ensued. The proponents of a world order will neglect at their peril the study of the only process that has repeatedly proved its efficiency as social coordinate.[37]

And certainly the history translated by de Mailla is based on this principle of historiography. If only Pound can establish, once and for all, the Western paideuma as Confucius established the Chinese paideuma, Western history could be similarly codified. What Pound fails to see in his determined search for a clear and stable code, is that even if such a code were established, there will remain honest disagreement about whether a particular individual is following the code or abusing it. The case of Ngan illustrates this sufficiently obvious point very clearly. Ngan cites Confucian principles, and practices praised by Confucius, to justify his course of action. Nonetheless, the history damns him for having corrupted Confucius with Buddhist and Taoist doctrine. In this one instance Pound chooses to disbelieve the history and believe Ngan. Where then is the certainty of the Confucian design? If the history lies here, who is to say it does not lie elsewhere?

Oddly enough the history records another instance of agricultural policies almost identical to those of Ngan without condemning them. In this case the policy is instituted by Lieu-uy-y, minister to Yong Tching. It is recorded in canto 61 (335:351), and Pound appends to it a note referring the reader to canto 35 where he reads of a *fontego* established in Mantua in 1401 to lend money on cloth. He also alludes to the 'Ammassi' or grain pools of Fascist Italy, apparently as a feature of an equivalent policy. Because of this agricultural policy Yong Tching is highly praised by Pound. The history also praises him highly, but not especially for his agricultural policy. Yong Tching was considerate enough to die on 7 October 1735, the month and year of John Adams's birth, and was succeeded by his son, Kien Long, '40 years before "our revolution"', who was still the reigning emperor when the history concluded its narrative in 1780. He is the 'literary kuss' with whom the Chinese cantos conclude.

It seems odd that Pound did not conclude his account of Chinese history with the death of Yong Tching since that provided him with such a fortuitous and neat transition to the following Adams cantos. There is nothing in the few pages devoted to the reign of Kien Long (whose dynastic title is Cai Tsong Hien Hoang Ti) of any great interest for the *Cantos*. The bit on page 339 (356) about melting down cannon for cash 'to keep commerce moving' is good grist for Pound's mill, but hardly worth the price of trailing off to a dying fall as canto 61 does with Kien Long. One suspects darkly that Pound was simply not paying very close attention to his work at this time. It is difficult to find any other explanation for his persistence in following de Mailla to the very last page of his history.

Much more could be said about the Chinese section, but it would only be further demonstration of the points already made, or explication, perhaps interesting in itself, but contributing little to one's understanding of the *Cantos*. There remains only the matter of the few allusions to the Eleusinian theme in the Chinese section.

The Eleusinian references are, to say the least, scattered. The first occurs in canto 52, already cited, and the second in canto 53 on the introduction of Confucius (Kung-fu-tseu), and it is extremely uncommunicative: 'Kung and Eleusis/to catechumen alone' (272: 283). Just what this means beyond suggesting a compatibility between Confucius and Eleusis, I cannot say. Later in the section Pound seizes upon a very slender reed to imply an equivalence between his own synoptic Eleusis and at least one Confucian's teaching:

> Lux enim per se omnem in partem
> Reason from heaven, said Tcheou Tun-y
>   enlighteneth all things
> seipsum seipsum diffundit, risplende
>   Is the beginning of all things, et effectu, . . .
>
> (55/298:311)

This occurs in the midst of his treatment of Ngan. De Mailla has mentioned the scholar, Tcheou Tun-y who resigned his mandarin rank and post over an unjust condemnation of an accused murderer. He then goes on:

Tcheou-tun-y aimoit passionément l'étude; c'est à lui qu'on doit la figure du *Tai-ki* de l'*Y-king*; dans l'explication qu'il en donne, il prétend fair voire que la raison émane du ciel, et éclaircit le commencement et la fin de toutes choses.[38]

Tcheou Tun-y's belief reminds Pound of the statements of Grosseteste from *De Luce* which he had found illuminating in his edition of Cavalcanti, and particularly for the interpretation of 'Dona mi Prega'. In the Cavalcanti essay he cites several phrases, among them: 'Lux enim per se in omnem partem se ipsam diffundit . . . a puncto lucis quamvis magna . . . generatur. . . . Lux prima forma in materia creata, seipsam seipsam . . . multiplicans.' ('For light of itself into every region diffuses itself . . . from a point of light, a sphere of light of any size is generated. . . . Light [is] the primary form in created matter, itself, it multiplies itself.') Pound presents the passage as a possible source for Cavalcanti's line, 'risplende in perpetuale effecto', which he translates, 'shineth out/Himself his own effect unendingly'. Thus Tcheou Tun-y shares at least some part of the mystery of Eleusis with Cavalcanti.[39]

The next reference to Eleusinian matters is also via Cavalcanti. It is at the beginning of canto 59 where Pound has come to the reign of the emperor Chun Tchi. He opens the canto by quoting and paraphrasing Chun Tchi's preface to the Book of Odes as Lacharme printed it in his Latin translation of the Odes. The relevant passage is as follows:

> Ut animum nostrum purget, Confucius ait, dirigatque
> ad lumen rationis
>   perpetuale effecto/
>
>   (59/324:339)

Pound has Chun Tchi write, 'To purge our minds, Confucius said, and to guide them to the light of reason', and adds from Cavalcanti, 'with perpetual effect'. This remark tends to align Confucius with Pound's Eleusinian philosophers of light, however feebly. One may doubt that Pound had any such intention on the grounds that if he did, he could surely have made himself at least as clear as he did in canto 55. However, his distortion of Chun Tchi's actual remarks serves to focus attention on the phrase 'ad lumen rationis'. What Pound read in Lacharme was a good deal less concentrated and pointed, although not really different in import:

Liber Chi-King, ait Confucius, in eo positus est ut animum nostrum purget dirigatque: [The Chi-King is placed there in order to purge our minds and direct them;] . . . nos ad lumen rationis nobis inditum fixos habere jubet oculos. [(it) orders us to have our eyes fixed on the light of reason.][40]

This kind of cryptic allusion is typical of the much later *Rock-Drill* and *Thrones* sections where Pound's poetry of inference loses all discipline. It is still rare in the Chinese section where it would seem merely to assert a comparability between the Confucian and Eleusinian paideumas—a comparability which is hardly demonstrable. The often quoted lines which follow Chun Tchi's preface, 'periplum, not as land looks on a map/but as sea bord seen by men sailing' are doubtless intended to justify the seat-of-the-pants scholarship in which Pound is engaging. The reader sees the world in the storm-tossed vision of Pound in his cockpit 'between NEKUIA . . . and the Charybdis of action', as he puts it in the *Pisan Cantos*. He is our guide, like Dante's Virgil, but he has not Virgil's perspective on what we encounter.

3. ADAMS

Although the Chinese and Adams sections were written consecutively, and in exactly the same manner—by redaction from multi-volume works—the Adams section has fared rather better with the critics. The reason for its greater acceptability is simply that most of Pound's readers know something of American history and are willing to learn a little more. In other words, the relative success of the Adams cantos compared to the Chinese cantos is dependent upon readers' attitudes to, and knowledge of, its subject rather than upon any greater artistry in Pound's treatment of the subject.

Pound's own estimate of the value of the Chinese and Adams sections was high. In 1939 he thought *Cantos 52–71* his 'best book'[41] and he devoted sixteen pages of the *Selected Cantos* to them when he made that selection in 1966.[42] Despite Pound's high opinion, very little has been written about the section even by those who assert its success and importance.[43] The reason for this is that it does not yield anything to literary analysis. One can appreciate Pound's admiration for his achievement only by working through the section with the *Life and Works*, a process that can scarcely be translated into a commentary of acceptable length.

The career of John Adams is itself a fascinating one, and it fits very neatly into Pound's new conception of the historical process, and of American history in particular. Born in Braintree, Massachusetts in 1735, John Adams came of Puritan stock. His ancestors emigrated to America in 1628. He abandoned the Puritanism of his forefathers, but transferred their religious fervour to politics and the law:

> 'Passion of orthodoxy in fear, Calvinism has no other agent
> study of theology
>   wd/ involve me in endless altercation
> to no purpose, of no design and do no good to
>   any man whatsoever . . .
> not less of order than liberty . . .
>   Burke, Gibbon, beautifiers of figures . . .
>
> (62/341:357)

Although much less well known in the pre-revolutionary period than his cousin Samuel Adams, John Adams entered the debate on the legal relationship between the colony and the British parliament in 1765 with the 'Dissertation on the Canon and Feudal Law' published in the *Boston Gazette*, and shortly after reprinted in the *London Chronicle*:

> WHERE TOWARD THE ARGUMENTS HAD BEEN
> as renouncing the transactions of Runing Mede?
> Prince of Orange, King William by the people
> that their rights be inviolable
> which drove out James Second . . . IS still active.
> Nothing less than this seems to have been meditated for us
> by somebody or other in Britain
>   reprinted by Thos. Hollis
>   seventeen sixty-five.
>
> (66/381–2:402)

So runs Pound's summary of that composition.

He was selected as a delegate from Massachusetts to the first Continental Congress of 1774 in recognition of his political pamphleteering, despite his defence of Captain Preston, charged with the killing of a barber's apprentice in the 'Boston Massacre' of 1770. This incident is rather obscurely noted in canto 62:

> so about 9 o'c in the morning Lard Narf wuz bein' impassible
> was a light fall of snow in Bastun, in King St.
> and the 29th Styschire in Brattle St
> Murray's barracks, and in this case was a
>   barber's boy ragging the sentinel
> So Capn Preston etc/[44].
>
> (62/342:358)

He helped frame the Declaration of Independence[45] and was named head of the Board of War, responsible for the provisioning of the revolutionary army.[46]

On 15 February 1778, he sailed for France as delegate to France and Holland to negotiate financial and military assistance from the French, and the Dutch bankers:

> Sunday 15th came under sail before breakfast
>   hauled my wind to southward
>   found they did chase me
>   Log book, Sl. Tucker 19 Feb.
>
> (65/368:387)

He was back in America from June to November 1799 during which period he framed a constitution for the state of Massachusetts, which is said to have formed the basis for the constitution of the United States. However, the Diary is silent on this activity and therefore Pound jumps from Adams's impression of John Paul Jones, whom he met while preparing to sail from France in May of 1779, to his landing in Spain in November of 1779:

> His voice (P. Jones's)
> is still, and soft, and small
> Laws of the Visigoths and Justinian still in use in Galicia[47].
>
> (65/373:392)

Adams then remained in Europe throughout the period of the revolutionary wars, signing the peace treaty in 1783, and becoming the first American ambassador to England in 1785. He did not return to America until 1788; became Vice President to George Washington the next year, and President in 1796 when he was chosen by Congress over Jefferson. He was defeated in the election of 1800, and retired to Braintree.

It is a fascinating experience to read through the *Life and Works*, for one first gets a good sense of Adams's career from the biography, then a first-hand account from 1758 to 1796 from John Adams's Diary (punctuated by various contemporary documents), followed by the published works of Adams, and the whole concluded by four volumes of letters beginning with Adams's commission to France in 1777 and ending in 1815. Adams emerges from all of this as intelligent, observant, industrious, stubborn, patriotic, and querulous. He was not only a principal actor in the birth of the American nation, but a knowledgeable observer of the French Revolution, and of the birth of the modern militarist nation under Napoleon. And, not least important for Pound's interest in him, he was engaged from 1779 to 1785 in negotiating the financing of the American war effort in the money markets of Holland, and at the court of France. Despite his great services to the Revolution and to his country, Adams was, in his old age, forgotten by his compatriots, or remembered with unjust ingratitude as the man who would have established an aristocracy—and even a monarchy—in America.

There should be no need to explain Pound's decision to devote eighty-one pages of his epic to such a man. It is odd that it should have taken Pound so long to discover Adams, and distressing that the Adams cantos represent the third revised version of American history in the *Cantos*, but these are hazards of the life work published as it is in progress. There is, however, a need to explain the Adams cantos because the sense of Adams described above is derived from the *Life and Works*, not from the *Cantos*.

I noted at the beginning of the chapter that Pound follows the order of presentation that he finds in his sources for both the Chinese and Adams cantos. Charles Francis Adams's edition of the *Works* begins with a biography, followed by a Diary (interrupted by excerpts from debates in the Continental Congress of 1775), then by Adams's published works, and finally concludes with correspondence.[48]

Pound slavishly follows the organization despite the absence of any logic or rationale other than editorial convenience. He has printed marginalia, and called it poetry. For *him*, the marginalia convey, in an abbreviated and intensified form, the image of Adams that emerges from the *Life and Works*. When approached by a puzzled, but admiring, reader, he could only retreat into a rather aggressive appeal to the reader's faith in his own competence and good faith:

> There is *no intentional* obscurity. There is condensation to maximum attainable. It is impossible to make the deep as quickly comprehensible as the shallow.[49]

But the difficulty with the Adams cantos, as with the Chinese cantos, is that they are far too prolix, rather than too condensed.

A small example of this proloxity is to be found on the last page of canto 64. Pound is working his way through the Diary and reads (II, p. 318):

> This afternoon received a collection of seventeen letters written from this Province, Rhode Island, Connecticut, and New York by Hutchinson, Oliver, Moffat, Paxton, and Rome in the years 1767, 1768, 1769.

At the bottom of the page he finds an editorial note informing him that 'These are the celebrated letters transmitted by Dr. Franklin . . . the publication of which caused a duel between Messrs. Temple and Whately, in England.' And Adams returns again and again to these letters over the next five pages of Diary entries. Hutchinson was the native-born Governor of Massachusetts, and these letters revealed him to be opposed to the agitation against imperial taxation. They were published, to Hutchinson's embarrassment. Pound tells us nothing of this, but transcribes from pages 318 and 319 as follows:

> 22; Monday (this was 1773)
>   Hutchinson's letters received
> Oliver, Moffat, Paxton and Rome
>   for 1767, '8, '9
> avaricious, ambitious, vindictive
> these were the letters that Franklin got hold of
> Bone of our bone, educated among us,
> serpent and deputy serpent
>   that Sir John Temple procured them
>   God knows how or from whom.
>   (64/362:379–80)

He then skips to pages 322 and 323, picking up only an observation on the weather from the intervening pages:

> Gentle rain last night and this morning
> Hutchinson sucking up to George IIIrd.
> falsehood in Rome's letters quite flagrant
> Col. Haworth
> attracted no attention until
> he discovered his antipathy to a cat.
> (64/362:380)

All of this is direct quotation from the Diary or from editorial notes. Colonel Haworth was merely a fellow dinner guest, and has no importance either in Adams's Diary or in the *Cantos*. His correct name is Howarth.

The next two lines are a recognizable reference to the Boston Tea Party from the Diary entry for 17 December 1773, still on page 323: 'Three cargoes Bohea/were emptied, this is but an attack upon property.' This is followed by three lines taken from an entry on page 329 referring to the possibility of impeaching the judges of the Superior Court of Massachusetts. The selection is neither self-explanatory nor grammatical:

> I apprehend it was necessary, absolute, indispensable
> irregular recourse to original power
> IMpeachment by House before Council.
> (64/362:380)

The next two lines refer to the same difficulties with the judges of the Superior Court, whose pay was now coming directly from the Crown in contravention of the Royal Charter of the Massachusetts colony: 'Said shd/be glad if constitution cd/carry on/without recourse to higher powers unwritten . . .'. These lines are quoted from page 331 as are the last lines of the canto: 'Says Gridley: You keep very late hours!' Adams had been holding meetings in his house running into the small hours of the morning. He records meeting the Loyalist, Ben Gridley, one morning, who said to him: 'Brother Adams, you keep late hours at your house.'

In 24 lines Pound has referred to four distinct pre-revolutionary issues: the Hutchinson letters, the Boston Tea Party, the issue of the Superior Court judges, and Colonel Howarth's dislike of cats. One might call this condensation—certainly one has to expand it a good deal to make it intelligible. But even when we know what it is all about, we still do not know why it need be mentioned at all. There is nothing in these lines vitally important to Adams's career or to the American Revolution. Nothing would be lost if they were blue pencilled—no important information, no dimension of characterization of Adams or America, no humour, beauty, or satire. These lines represent nothing more nor less than Pound's marginalia on fourteen pages of Adams's Diary. They are perfunctory and self-indulgent.

In the Chinese and Adams cantos Pound seems to have forgotten what he was doing. It was his task to condense history so as to fit it into his poem. But the Adams cantos are not a condensation of the American Revolution, nor of the career or life of John Adams. They are simply a condensation of the *Life and Works of John Adams*. The revolution and the man can indeed be found in these ten cantos, but they are not the true subject of the section as they ought to be. The true subject is that ten volume edition which massively interposes itself between the reader of the *Cantos* and John Adams.

It is particularly surprising that the Adams cantos are not more pointed because Pound had read W. E. Woodward's *A New American History* as well as his *Washington: Image and Man* before he wrote the section. In those works he found a perfectly coherent view of the economic causes of the American Revolution. He is echoing Woodward (whose analysis is supported by Christopher Hollis's *Two Nations*) when he writes:

> The cardinal fact of the American Revolution of 1776 was the suppression, in 1750, of the paper money issue in Pennsylvania and other colonies but history as taught in the U.S.A. speaks of more picturesque matters, such as the Boston Tea Party.[50]

John Adams, involved as he was in negotiating loans to finance the War of Independence, has a great deal to say about money and banking, and his views are not so very remote from Woodward's.

But we encounter Adams's economic views only randomly as Pound proceeds through the *Life and Works*. It is true that Pound stresses some of Adams's economic observations, but he does not use them to focus or structure his treatment of Adams, as, for example, he uses the Tempio to focus and structure his treatment of Malatesta. In canto 66 he picks up a Latin tag from the charter of the bank of Siena, already quoted in large capitals in cantos 42 and 43:

> OB PECUNIAE SCARSITATEM
> this act, the Stamp Act, wd/ drain cash out of the country
> and is, further UNconstitutional.
>
> (66/382:402)

These two lines are excerpted from 'Instructions of the Town of Braintree to their Representative', which was written by John Adams in 1765. The implication is that the agitation of the patriots against the British had the same root cause as the foundation of the Bank of Siena—that is, the scarcity of currency. It is a problem that was also recurrent in Chinese history. But the issue is not pursued. Pound simply moves on to

> yr/ humanity counterfeit
> yr/ liberty cankered with simulation

excerpted from 'The Earl of Clarendon to William Pym', a series of polemical imaginary letters Adams began publishing in the *London Evening Post* in 1765. Pound gives the origin of his lines as the *Boston Gazette*, 17 January 1768, three years later than the remark on the Stamp Act, and unrelated to it.

We do not encounter economic matters again until Pound has worked his way through Adams's published works and into the correspondence, which he reaches in the middle of page 396 (417), marked by the line, 'Commission to France '77'. Soon we hear Adams defending the ruinous inflation in America in an effort to reassure the European money lenders:

> 'The depreciation of paper, a tax (T, A, X, tax)
> the Americans have laid on themselves . . .
>
> (68/399:420)

Pound refers to Adams's argument approvingly in 'An Introduction to the Economic Nature of the United States'[51] and returns to it in canto 69. Of course, inflation is the Achilles' heel of Social Credit monetary theory. In that theory, economic distress in the modern world is caused by a breakdown in distribution rather than by an absolute shortage of commodities. Hence, Social Creditors argue, one need only give people sufficient money to buy the commodities society has the capacity to produce, and all will be well. The source of this money is bank credit from a nationalized banking system. Their detractors claim that such money would soon become worthless through inflation. Pound's answer to this criticism is not very detailed:

The term 'inflation' is used as a bogey to scare people away from any expansion of money at all.

Real inflation only begins when you issue money (measured claims) against goods or services that are undeliverable (assignats of the French Revolution issued against the state lands) or issue them in excess of those wanted.

That amounts to saying: two or more tickets for the same seat at the same time, or tickets in London for theatre performance tonight in Bombay, or for a dud show.

Money can be expended as long as each measured claim can be honoured by the producers and distributors of the nation in goods and service required by the public, when and where they want them.[52]

The one issue which neither Pound nor the Social Credit monetary theory ever faces squarely is that of the control of the issue of money. They are quite clear on the flagrant robbery of giving that right to private banks, but are less clear on the problem of controlling the state's manipulation of money. The American Revolution provides an example of how state-issued paper money can go wrong. Pound would have read the following paragraph shortly before he had written the Adams cantos:

The crumpled finances of the Continental Congress had reached the wastepaper stage at the beginning of 1780. When a man went to get his hair cut he carried about a pound of paper money to the barber's, and men in the tobacco shops ostentatiously lighted their pipes with Continental bills. You may have heard the expression, 'Not worth a continental'. It originated in that period and has come down through the generations as a definition of pure worthlessness.[53]

Faced with this situation at home—aggravated by military reverses—Adams found himself exercising some ingenuity in reassuring the Dutch money men. Pound quotes generously from his letter to Baron Van der Capellen of 21 January 1781, where Adams develops the argument that inflation is a tax:

The depreciation of paper money is the most difficult to be answered, because it is the most difficult to explain to a gentleman who has not been in the country and seen its operation. The *depreciation of* the *money* has been a real advantage, because it is *a tax* upon *the people*, *paid as it advances*, *and*, *therefore prevents the public from being found in debt*. It is *true it is an unequal tax, and* therefore *causes* what your friend, G. Livingston, justly calls *perplexity, but by no means disables* or weakens *the people from carrying on the war.* The body of the people lose nothing by it. The *merchant*, the *farmer*, the *tradesman*, the *laborer* lose nothing by it. *They are the moneyed men, the capitalists, those who have money at interest* and live upon *fixed salaries*,—that is, the officers of government,—who *lose* by it, and who have borne this tax.[54]

I have italicized those portions cited by Pound. For the most part he quotes verbatim, with elisions, but occasionally alters the expression: for example, 'paid in advance' for 'paid as it advances'.

> depreciation of money a TAX on the people
> paid in advance and
> therefore prevents the public from being found in debt, true
> it is an unequal tax and causes perplexity
> but by no means disables the people from carrying on the war
> Merchants, farmers, tradesmen and labourers gain
> they are the moneyed men,
> The capitalists those who have money at interest
> or those on fixed salaries
> lose.[55]
>
> (69/403:425)

That this letter does not represent Adams's true views on inflation is clear from a letter he wrote late in life (which Pound also quotes, in canto 71, marking it by a heavy black line in the margin):

Funds and banks I never approved, or was satisfied with our funding system; it was founded in no consistent principle; it was contrived to enrich particular individuals at the public expense. *Our whole banking system I ever abhorred*, I continue to abhor, and shall die abhorring.

But I am not an enemy to *funding systems.* They are absolutely and indispensibly necessary in the present state of the world. *An attempt to annihilate* or prevent them *would be as romantic an adventure as any in Don Quixote or in Oberon.* A national bank of deposit I believe to be wise, just, prudent, economical and necessary. But *every bank of discount*, every bank by which interest is to be paid or profit of any kind made by the deponent, *is downright corruption.* It is *taxing the public for the benefit and profit of individuals*; it is worse than old terror, continental currency, or any other paper money.

Now, Sir, *if I should talk in this strain, after I am dead*, you know the *people of America would pronounce that I had died mad.*[56]

I have italicized those portions of the letter cited in canto 71:

> Funds and Banks I
> never approved I abhorred ever our whole banking system
> but an attempt to abolish all funding in the
> present state of the world wd/ be as romantic
> as any adventure in Oberon or Don Quixote.
> Every bank of discount is downright corruption
> taxing the public for private individuals' gain.
> and if I say this in my will
> the American people wd/ pronounce I died crazy.
> (71/416:438)

Adams's distrust of banks echoes Pound's distrust, but it is based on a distrust of paper money, and the whole system of currency creation—whether by the state or by private banks. The bank of discount is 'worse' than 'continental currency, or any other paper money', but only because the bank enriches private individuals at public expense. Both systems, he believes, operate at public expense. His views become clear only in the concluding portion of the letter, not quoted in canto 71:

> My opinion is, that a circulating medium of gold and silver only ought to be introduced and established; that a national bank of deposit only, . . . should be allowed; that every bank in the Union ought to be annihilated, and every bank of discount prohibited to all eternity. Not one farthing of profit should ever be allowed on any money deposited in the bank.

Adams is, then, a commodity money man, and as such is at the opposite end of the spectrum of monetary theory from Major Douglas and Ezra Pound:

> A single commodity (even gold) base for money is not satisfactory.
> State authority behind the printed note is the best means of establishing a just and honest currency.
> The Chinese grasped that over 1,000 years ago, as we can see from the Tang state (not bank) note.
> Sovereignty inheres in the power to issue money and to determine the value thereof.[57]

It is a measure of the failure of the Adams cantos that it is not possible to know whether Pound deliberately distorted Adams's views, or simply did not understand them. He quotes Adams again toward the end of the canto, stating his commodity view of money as if Pound did not recognize its total opposition to Social Credit theory:

> ... Gold, silver are but commodities
> Pity, says Tracy, they ever were stamped save by weight
> They are commodities as is wheat or is lumber.
> (71/420:443)

Social Crediters also make this observation, but use it as the basis for the demonetization of gold. Adams, by contrast, wishes to have only gold and silver as media of exchange.

It is worth quoting at length from the letter to John Taylor of Caroline that is Pound's source here. It scarcely seems possible that Pound could have misunderstood Adams's position if he had read this letter through:

> I have never had but one opinion concerning banking, from the institution of the first, in Philadelphia, by Mr. Robert Morris and Mr. Gouverneur Morris, and that opinion has uniformly been that the banks have done more injury to the religion, morality, tranquillity, prosperity, and even wealth of the nation, than they can have done or ever will do good. ... Silver and gold are but commodities, as much as wheat and lumber; the merchants who study the necessity, and feel out the wants of the community, can always import enough to supply the necessary circulating currency, as they can broadcloth or sugar, ... I am old enough to have seen a paper currency annihilated at a blow in Massachusetts, in 1750, and a silver currency taking its place immediately, and supplying every necessity and every convenience. [Adams then refers to a work in manuscript by Count Destutt Tracy, which had been translated from the French by Thomas Jefferson. He quotes:]
>
> 'It is to be desired, that coins had never borne other names than those of their weight, and that the arbitrary denominations, called moneys of account, as £, *s.*, *d.*, etc. had never been used. But when these denominations are admitted and employed in transactions, to diminish the quantity of metal to which they answer, by an alteration of the real coins, is to steal; ... A theft of greater magnitude and still more ruinous, is the making of paper money; ... All these iniquities are founded on the false idea, that money is but a sign.'[58]

If Pound, who believed that 'the cardinal fact of the American Revolution of 1776 was the suppression, in 1750, of the paper money issue in Pennsylvania and other colonies', and who believed that shortage of currency was the worst evil a nation could suffer, could read this letter and agree with it: if Pound can have done that—as he seems to have done—he cannot have understood anything at all of the monetary theory he proselytizes. If he had wished to misrepresent Adams, he would surely not have quoted from this letter at all. He must have misunderstood Adams—either through careless reading of the letter, or through simple lack of comprehension of the issues. He sees clearly enough the parallel error of Brooks Adams on monetary matters: 'he slides into the concept, shared by Mill and Marx, of money as an accumulator of energy'.[59]

Not only do these cantos give a scant and random representation of Adams's economic views, they also misrepresent those views. One knows more of the importance of Adams in Pound's scheme of things from his prose than from the poem, which presents us only with shards and fragments, dug, not from the multi-layered bed of the half-forgotten past, but from a single published work. The early cantos had created a rather implausible, but metaphorically rich romance of history dominated by religious, martial, and amorous zeal set over against the fearful voices of the old men on the wall of Troy or in the suburbs of London. Gradually the romance of history, and its attendant legend of Odysseus, the hierophant of Eleusis, was pushed aside by the true stuff of history, until in the Chinese and Adams cantos it was entirely displaced—no longer by the true stuff of history perceived in a fragmented and obscure manner, but by history books *transcribed* in a fragmentary and obscure manner.

VII · Pisa

1. 'AS A LONE ANT FROM A BROKEN ANT-HILL'

WHAT seems to have happened in the sections following *A Draft of XXX Cantos* is that Pound progressively abandoned the search for historical characters, of 'sufficient constructivity' to fit the Odysseus/Malatesta heroic type. The American heroes of *Eleven New Cantos* scarcely fit the pattern, and the *Fifth Decad* has no heroes at all except for Odysseus himself—outside the historical subject. The Malatestan hero is increasingly replaced by the sage or wise man, and the most central wise man in the *Cantos* is the poet himself. As the poem becomes increasingly burdened with historical content, the focus of interest moves away from the actors in history—potential candidates for heroic roles—to the significance of historical actions. The Malatesta cantos are validated by the character and role of Malatesta. The Sienese cantos are validated by the author's belief that the Monte dei Paschi is the kind of bank on which economic prosperity could be founded. Not only is this latter treatment of history much more unabashedly didactic, it also makes of the author, who has discovered this solution to our ills, the hero of the poem. It is by this process that Pound comes to produce the dreary *longueurs* of the Chinese and Adams cantos. In those sections the poet leads the reader by the hand through voluminous works he is too lazy or too misguided to read for himself. Whereas, before, Pound himself had been the journeyer through the past, like Dante in the other world, now he becomes Virgil, and the reader must perforce adopt the arduous role of Dante, being led, bewildered, toward some bright revelation.

Only the most charitable reader could find that bright revelation in the Chinese and Adams cantos. The only real virtue of these sections is that they are removed from the contemporary scene of the late 1930s. As a consequence, Pound is able to keep out of the poem much of the stridency of the prose of this period. They represent a peculiarly Poundian retreat from the world, and are, despite his continued admiration for them, not much more than a parody of the technique of writing historical poetry developed in the Malatesta sequence. The marvel is that the poem can absorb them at all, for with all their length and perfunctory composition, they do bear upon the issues joined by the poem, and the Adams section, at least, has found readers.

We must seek the explanation for the nature of these cantos in biography rather than in literary form or technique. Unfortunately the biographical information which might account for Pound's failure of judgement is not available. Certainly his increasing isolation from the literary world in which the poem took birth must have been a factor. The *Cantos* are a product of the London of 1908 to 1920, where modernism in literature was born. He had left London for Paris in 1920, and Paris for Rapallo in 1924. While in London and in Paris, he was in daily contact with men whose literary judgement he valued. Although the record is scanty, we know that he sought the opinion of Joyce and Ford on his poetry and he surely must have discussed the *Cantos* with Eliot, as we know he did with Yeats. It is true that both Yeats and Eliot published comments on the *Cantos* after Pound had moved to Rapallo, but that is not the same thing as discussion of it while still in draft.

Of course, one cannot assert that criticism by his peers before publication would have been received with any more graciousness than it was when given in print, after publication. Pound was obstinately going his own way, and was no longer interested in, or even polite to, his old London friends. Joyce sent him the Shaun episode of *Finnegans Wake* for comment, and Pound was unable to generate even the semblance of polite interest:

> I will have another go at it, but up to present I make nothing of it whatever. Nothing so far as I make out, nothing short of divine vision or a new cure for the clapp can possibly be worth all the circumambient peripherization.
>
> Doubtless there are patient souls, who will wade through anything for the sake of the possible joke . . . but . . . having no inkling whether the purpose of the author is to amuse or to instruct . . .[1]

I am confident that Pound's lack of interest in Joyce's new work—equalled only by his lack of interest in Eliot's—was not prompted by envy of reputation and accomplishment, but reflected a real parting of the ways.

Wyndham Lewis, another of the London men (with whom Pound had collaborated in the Vorticist periodical, *Blast*), attacked Pound and Joyce as benighted adherents of 'time philosophy' in *Time and Western Man* (1927). Ford Madox Ford, to whom Pound owed a great deal of his literary education, was received rather rudely when he visited Rapallo in 1932, and Pound no longer sought his opinion of the *Cantos* as he had done when in Paris. T. E. Hulme and Gaudier-Brzeska had been killed in the war. Pound kept in touch with his old college friends, William Carlos Williams and Hilda Doolittle, but there had never been much agreement on literary matters there.

If literary modernism had ever been a coherent movement, it was so only for a short period in London before the First World War. And whatever coherence it had can scarcely be separated from the person of Ezra Pound, disciple of W. B. Yeats, Henry James, and Ford Madox Ford; literary patron of James Joyce, T. S. Eliot, and even Robert Frost; co-founder of Imagism and Vorticism; and general propagandist of new art. That world, and that movement spawned the *Cantos*, but both had ceased to exist by the 1930s. The *Pisan Cantos* memorialize Pound's London years, and derive much of their power and energy from their return to that period.

The *Pisan Cantos* are a most startling sequel to the Chinese and Adams sections, and it is natural to assume that the accident of Pound's arrest by the American army and his imprisonment at Pisa (accident, that is, with respect to the *Cantos*) forced a shift from history to autobiography in the poem. However, there is evidence that at least the contemplative character of the *Pisan Cantos* was not the fortuitous result of Pound's arrest, but part of his programme for the poem. In November of 1939 he told Douglas Macpherson: 'My economic work is done (in the main). I shall have to go on condensing and restating, but am now definitely onto questions of BELIEF.'[2] And he set to work studying Johannes Scotus Erigena.

On the evidence of the letters, it is plain that the next section of the *Cantos* would have been concerned with religious and ethical matters rather than economics and history—and these are the concerns of the *Pisan Cantos*. We can get some inkling of what the new section might have been had the accidents of current history been different or postponed, for Pound published one fragment of a canto beyond the Adams section before the débâcle, and another has been preserved in a letter. They were both intended for canto 72, and were both written in 1941. They have been reprinted in *Drafts & Fragments* as 'Addendum for Canto C', made up of 'Canto Proceeding (72 circa)', *Vice Versa*, (January 1942), and the untitled 'Now sun rises in Ram sign' (originally appearing in *Letters* as an enclosure in a March 1941 letter to Katute Kitasono as 'Lines to go into Canto 72 or somewhere').

The first fragment is still concerned with economics: 'The Evil is Usury, *neschek*/the serpent/ *neschek* whose name is known, the defiler.' But economics are now seen *sub specie aeternitatis*, and the verse takes on that magical incantatory quality that one associates with the *Pisan* section and with Pound's poetry at its best:

> All other sins are open,
> Usura alone not understood.
> Opium Shanghai, opium Singapore
> 'with the silver spilla . . .
>   amber, caught up and turned . . .'
>   Lotophagoi.[3]

The quotation is from canto 20, described by Pound as a 'general paradiso' although concerned with murder and drug addiction. Thus the retrospective allusion to earlier sections of the *Cantos*, so characteristic of the *Pisan* section, is present in this 1941 fragment.

The second, shorter fragment, which Pound offered to Kitasono as evidence that he was 'not wholly absorbed in saving Europe by economics', is a landscape which would not be out of place in the *Pisan* section:

> Now sun rises in Ram sign.
> With clack of bamboo against olive stock
> We have heard the birds praising Jannequin
> and the black cat's tail is exalted.

But, for some reason, Pound would not appear to have written anything more than these fragments between 1941 and his arrest in 1945.[4] The reason is perhaps sufficiently obvious—it was surely the war. But the enormity of the second great holocaust in Pound's adult life was slow to divert him from questions of belief. The fragments for canto 72 were written after he had begun broadcasting for Rome radio in January of 1941, and he had been actively engaged in pressing his economic views on the Italian people from as early as 1939. All we know of Pound's reaction to the war, outside the *Pisan Cantos* themselves, is contained in his polemical prose and broadcasts of the period. They reveal his endorsement of the Fascist cause and implacable hatred of Roosevelt and Churchill. But the stridency of those utterances surely reveals intolerable personal strains of which we know nothing.

In effect, the war caught Pound in the impossible position of being intellectually committed to the Axis powers because of his economic interpretation of Western history, while his emotional commitment, through ties of nationality, upbringing, culture and friendship, was to the Allies. In these circumstances he could not write poetry. The device employed in the Chinese and Adams sections permitted him to maintain the illusion of advancing his poem, but he knew that he had exhausted whatever traces of gold might have lain in that vein. The new subject of belief could not be addressed in the midst of carnage.

The partisan's knock on Pound's door, leading to his detention at the Pisan 'Disciplinary Training Centre' brought an abrupt end to his pamphleteering and propagandizing. Suddenly he was without books, without audience, and without friends or family. He was held at Pisa for six months, and in that relatively short period he composed eleven new cantos, published in 1948 as the *Pisan Cantos.* At one hundred and eighteen pages, it is the longest section of the poem,[5] and is certainly also the richest and most complex. These cantos represent a remarkable outburst of poetic energy, after five years of unproductiveness. Indeed, taking into consideration the perfunctory character of the writing in the Chinese and Adams sections, Pound had written almost no original poetry since 1937 when he completed the *Fifth Decad of Cantos.*

The contrast in character and quality between the *Pisan Cantos* and earlier sections is so marked that it has led Noel Stock to a most peculiar judgement. Having praised, albeit reservedly, the *Pisan Cantos*, Stock feels he

> must draw attention to weaknesses on account of which we cannot place them among the highest poetry. The first and most obvious is the disjointed surface. And then there is this difficulty. Although it is a separate poem quite unrelated as poetry to the preceding seventy cantos, it cannot be understood without our knowing the earlier sections, much of Pound's prose, and of course the books he has read.[6]

Of course, the *Pisan Cantos* are not a separate poem, and their dependence on the rest of the *Cantos* can hardly be accounted a weakness. The scholar's task is surely to elucidate that relationship, rather than to assert that such a relationship ought not to exist and then complain that, none the less, it does.

Still, the *Pisan Cantos* do not relate to preceding sections of the poem in an obvious way. They are private and memorious in character for the most part, rather than public and historical, and dominated by the persona of the author in the detention camp at Pisa. Only in canto 46 had Pound previously spoken in his own voice rather than in the voice of the impersonal chronicler ,'ego scriptor cantilenae'. There, as we have seen, he speaks of his personal struggle to educate his contemporaries in the truths of economics. The *Pisan Cantos* adopt this personal tone, but the focus of attention is on the man, Pound, rather than the message of his poem.

In *The Spirit of Romance* Pound asserted that the *Divine Comedy* 'must not be considered as an epic'. 'It is', he wrote, 'in a sense lyric, the tremendous lyric of the subjective Dante.' He added, 'an epic cannot be written against the grain of its time: the prophet or the satirist may hold himself aloof from his time, or run counter to it, but the writer of epos must voice the general heart.'[7] If one bears in mind that Pound moved to Rapallo in October of 1924, two years after Mussolini's march on Rome, and that all the collections of the *Cantos* were published after that date, one can understand that he may well have believed that he was voicing the general heart of a corporate, Fascist, European future. The fall of Italy and his own arrest forced upon him the long delayed awareness that he was indeed writing against the grain of his time, and was very far from voicing the general heart—even of Italians. He must also have become aware at Pisa that the broadcasts of 'Old Ez' had not spoken, and had not reached, the hearts of the American soldiers.

It was this revelation that he was a voice in the wilderness, more than physical discomforts or the lack of his library, that led to the very particular character of the *Pisan Cantos*. For they turn from history, the proper subject of epic, to autobiography, the proper subject of lyric. Pound structures his own biography in terms of the *Cantos*' Odysseus, groom to the Goddess and hierophant of the sacred mysteries:

> *ΟΥ̓ ΤΙΣ, ΟΥ̓ ΤΙΣ?* Odysseus
> the name of my family.
> (74/425:451)

In turning from epic back to lyric, Pound brings once more into the foreground of the poem those mythical dimensions which had dominated the first thirty cantos, and had not been displaced until the Chinese and Adams sections. The parallel with Dante's 'tremendous lyric' becomes operative once again.

2. 'THE CITY OF DIOCE'

The *Pisan Cantos* begin with a lament for the death of Benito Mussolini and Clara Petaci, introducing the elegiac and *ubi sunt* tone of the section:

> The enormous tragedy of the dream in the peasant's bent shoulders
> Manes! Manes was tanned and stuffed,
> Thus Ben and la Clara *a Milano*
> by the heels at Milano
> That maggots shd/ eat the dead bullock
> DIGONOS, Διγονος, but the twice crucified
> where in history will you find it?
> yet say this to the Possum: a bang, not a whimper,
> with a bang not with a whimper,
> To build the city of Dioce whose terraces are the colour of stars.
>
> (74/425:451)

Here the death of a vain and foolish leader is lifted to the level of myth by associating him with Dionysus, the twice-born, and Manes, the martyred founder of Manichaeanism. But, more importantly, Pound announces that the end of *his* world has come 'with a bang not with a whimper', parodying the conclusion of Eliot's 'Hollow Men':

> This is the way the world ends
> This is the way the world ends
> This is the way the world ends
> Not with a bang but a whimper.[8]

'To build the city of Dioce' alludes to canto 5, for the city of Dioce is Ecbatan:

> Great bulk, huge mass, thesaurus;
> Ecbatan, the clock ticks and fades out
> The bride awaiting the god's touch; Ecbatan,
> City of patterned streets.
>
> (5/17:21)

The bride awaiting the god's touch is Danaë, mother of Perseus, who was visited by Zeus in a shower of gold despite having been imprisoned in a bronze tower by her father. In canto 4 Pound placed her 'upon the gilded tower in Ecbatan' where 'lay the god's bride, lay ever, waiting the golden rain'. Danaë does not properly belong in Ecbatan, but Pound placed her there (with the licence he has borrowed from Joyce and Eliot to transform myths) because he wants this bright image of a *hieros gamos*, or divine marriage, in the ideal city of Ecbatan.

Ecbatan was a new capital city built by Deioces (or Dioce, as Pound spells it), a Median king. It is an ideal city, not because it can serve as a model for other cities, but because it had the balance and perfection of a work of art. It was a planned city 'of patterned streets', but never became an important centre. It represents the city as a work of art, the city in the mind, in contradistinction to the actual cities and nations chronicled in the history which the *Cantos* contain. It is, if one likes, the city out of history, a dream city.

We have encountered an early version of this particular conception of the ideal city—in 'Patria Mia'—although imperial Rome is there both a dream and a model. One of the tasks of the *Cantos* had been the adumbration of some such dream of an ideal polity appropriate for the twentieth century. Pound ransacked European, American, and finally Chinese history in search of the materials for the paideuma of a new polity. The *Pisan Cantos* abandon the historical dimensions of this civic dream in the face of the catastrophe of the Axis defeat, but maintain faith in the ideal, now a dream only.

In the midst of his despair Pound turns to an African myth never before mentioned in the *Cantos*: 'and with one day's reading a man may have the key in his hands/Lute of Gassir. Hooo Fasa' (74/427: 454). The myth is of Sonninke origin and is collected as *Gassire's Lute* by Frobenius and Fox in *African Genesis*.[9] It tells the story of Gassire, a prince of the kingdom of Wagadu, who loses his inheritance and the lives of all but one of his sons in wars he waged as a means of giving his lute heart so that it would 'sing' the *Dausi*. Pound does not make use of the legend proper, but rather of the description of Wagadu which brackets the legend:

> Four times Wagadu stood there in all her splendour. Four times Wagadu disappeared and was lost to human sight: once through vanity, once through falsehood, once through greed and once through dissension. Four times Wagadu changed her name. First she was called Dierra, then

Agada, then Ganna, then Silla. Four times she turned her face. Once to the north, once to the west, once to the east and once to the south. For Wagadu, whenever men have seen her, has always had four gates; one to the north, one to the west, one to the east and one to the south. Those are the directions whence the strength of Wagadu comes, the strength in which she endures no matter whether she be built of stone, wood and earth or lives but as a shadow in the mind and longing of her children. For really, Wagadu is not of stone, not of wood, not of earth. Wagadu is the strength which lives in the hearts of men and is sometimes visible because eyes see her and ears hear the clash of swords and ring of shields, and is sometimes invisible because the indomitability of men has over tired her, so that she sleeps. Sleep came to Wagadu for the first time through vanity, for the second time through falsehood, for the third time through greed and for the fourth time through dissension. Should Wagadu ever be found for the fourth time, then she will live so forcefully in the minds of men that she will never be lost again, so forcefully that vanity, falsehood, greed and dissension will never be able to harm her.

Hoooh! Dierra, Agada, Ganna, Silla! Hooh! Fasa![10]

Pound could scarcely have written a legend more suited to his own formulation of the theme of the city, and his present needs in 1945. Wagadu is the city represented as an ideal or dream which persists 'in the hearts of men' and 'in the minds of men' quite independently of the vicissitudes of history. Although the city, Wagadu, is repeatedly destroyed by vanity, falsehood, greed, and dissension, the dream cannot be destroyed. Wagadu can be seen to be equivalent to 'the Truth' in *Sordello*. Although he does not press the parallel, Pound finds himself at Pisa in much the same dilemma that Browning had created for Sordello—caught between poetic vision and effective action:

> between NEKUIA where are Alcmene and Tyro
> and the Charybdis of action.
> (74/431:457)

Pound's 'truth' had spectacularly failed to 'hurl the world's course right', and, as we shall see, he must remain content with 'some mean spark/Of some chance-blow, the solitary hint/Of buried fire'.

Pound can only acknowledge his 'failure' and assert his faith in the dream:

> a man on whom the sun has gone down
> nor shall diamond die in the avalanche
> be it torn from its setting

first must destroy himself ere others destroy him.
4 times was the city rebuilded, Hooo Fasa
Gassir, Hooo Fasa dell' Italia tradita
now in the mind indestructible, Gassir, Hoooo Fasa,
With the four giants at the four corners
and four gates mid-wall Hooo Fasa
and a terrace the colour of stars.
(74/430:457)

Wagadu, Italy, and Ecbatan are here all images of the dream which is out of history although constantly striving to enter it. The paradox of a civic ideal which is *in* but not *of* history is expressed a few pages later:

'I believe in the resurrection of Italy quia impossibile est
4 times to the song of Gassir
now in the mind indestructible.
(74/442:470)

According to the legend, the strength of Wagadu comes from the four compass points, and 'she endures no matter whether she be built of stone, wood and earth or lives but as a shadow in the mind and longing of her children'. Pound's dream is similarly four-fold and enduring:

300 years culture at the mercy of a tack hammer
thrown thru the roof
Cloud over mountain, mountain over the cloud
I surrender neither the empire nor the temples
plural
nor the constitution nor yet the city of Dioce.
(74/434:461)

The empire stands for European cultural unity, the temples for variety of religious faith, the constitution for government sanctioned by law, and the city of Dioce for the community as artefact, of which Venice is the dominant image:

free then, therein the difference
in the great ghetto, left standing
with the new bridge of the Era where was the old eyesore
Vendramin, Contrarini, Fonda, Fondecho
and Tullio Romano carved the sirenes
as the old custode says: so that since

then no one has been able to carve them
    for the jewel box, Santa Maria Dei Miracoli,
Dei Greci, San Giorgio, the place of skulls
        in the Carpaccio
and in the font to the right as you enter
    are all the gold domes of San Marco.
(76/460–1:489)

Wagadu has a different name in each of her manifestations: Dierra, Agada, Ganna, and Silla. Each disappearance, then, is followed not only by a reappearance, but also by a transformation—out of evil issues good:

Every time that the guilt of man caused Wagadu to disappear she won a new beauty which made the splendor of her next appearance still more glorious. Vanity brought the song of the bards which all peoples (of the Sudan) imitate and value today. Falsehood brought a rain of gold and pearls. Greed brought writing as the Burdama still practice it today and which in Wagadu was the business of the women. Dissension will enable the fifth Wagadu to be as enduring as the rain of the south and as the rocks of the Sahara, for every man will then have Wagadu in his heart and every woman a Wagadu in her womb.[11]

It will be noticed that each new manifestation of Wagadu is brought about by the vice corresponding to the fruits of the preceding manifestation's virtue. Dierra is destroyed by vanity, which in turn creates the song of the bards proper to Agada.[12] Agada's ruin, and Ganna's creation are brought about by falsehood, a consequence of the bards' songs. Falsehood brings gold which generates greed, destroying Ganna and bringing Silla to birth. But gold or wealth generates writing, the virtue proper to Silla, the fourth Wagadu. Writing, in its turn, generates dissension, destroying Silla and creating the fifth and final Wagadu, which is enduring, but at the cost of being private. The point would seem to be that writing destroys the tribal world of communality and collective awareness, replacing it with the modern world of individuality and private awareness.

Gassire's Lute, then—or at least its framing myth—describes the process of history as a series of four cataclysms, which accomplishes a progression wherein each cataclysm creates 'a new beauty which made the splendor of her [Wagadu's] next appearance still more glorious'. Each new splendour contains within itself the seed of its own destruction. The series is brought to a conclusion only by the final idealization of Wagadu in a form independent of history. The final form is not, however, parallel to the New Jerusalem, for one issues from the ceaseless round of progression by internalizing the ideal rather than by projecting it into another realm.

This modest Sonninke myth addresses itself to the problem that occupied Milton in *Paradise Lost*: how to explain or justify the human misery so amply witnessed by history. A partial solution is to discover that out of suffering and misery issues a new beauty; that without the Fall there would be no Redemption. But as the African bard and Milton both recognized, a new beauty, even Redemption, only brings more suffering and misery. Milton, too, internalizes his ideal, granting to Adam and Eve 'A paradise within . . . happier far'. The Sonninke myth, because its focus is on the salvation of the community rather than the individual, is more interested in permanence than happiness.

Pound had not set out in his epic to justify history, but to reveal it. Wordsworth's *Prelude* was a journey into his private past, a kind of descent and mental journey designed to reveal the genesis of the adult poet, and provide the means of prognosis of his poetic future. Pound had set out upon his journey into the public past (history) in precisely the same spirit—to reveal the genesis of the contemporary cultural mix and provide a prognosis of the future of the Western 'city'. Wordsworth's prognosis of a philosophical epic proved to be no more accurate than Pound's prognosis of a renaissance of the West under the banner of the corporate state. Faced with the defeat of his 'side', he suddenly had need of historical justification in order to 'save' his epic. Hence Pound adopts from *Gassire's Lute* specifically the internalization of the civic ideal as a means of achieving its permanence. Already we have seen the occurrence of the phrase, 'now in the mind indestructible', twice in canto 74. In canto 76 he once again alludes to the legend, adopting this time the locus of heart as in the second paragraph quoted above from *Gassire's Lute*: 'Faasa ! 4 times was the city remade,/now in the heart indestructible/4 gates, the 4 towers' (76/465:494).[13]

Gassire's Lute, then, is used as a means of internalizing the historical thrust of the *Cantos* toward the building of the city, that is, the total human community. The city of Dioce, although it represents the city as an artefact (as the city's physical body of stone and mortar), is essentially the internalized city. It is an image of the city in the mind indestructible. In short, the *Pisan Cantos* concern themselves with private vision, whereas the earlier cantos had increasingly concerned themselves with public, historical event. Their task is 'to build the city of Dioce whose terraces are the colour of stars'. But this is far from Stock's notion that the *Pisan Cantos* are a separate poem. What they do rather (here and in other dimensions, as will be apparent shortly), is to transform the thematic concerns of preceding sections of the poem. Those concerns are transformed from a public and historical form to a private and memorious one. But they are transformed, not abandoned.

The coherence of the *Pisan Cantos* with earlier sections is maintained largely through those religious and mythical dimensions which had become less and less evident as the poem advanced. Pound made no use of the Albigensian Crusade and the destruction of the Albigensian stronghold as an analogue of the Trojan war between canto 23 and the *Pisan Cantos*, and alluded to it only once.[14] However, this motif returns strongly in the *Pisan Cantos*. There, as we have already seen, Pound draws a strong link between Johannes Scotus Erigena and the Albigenses, using as a touchstone Erigena's dictum, 'omnia quae sunt, lumina sunt'. He develops the Erigenian role in canto 74 (429–30:455–7) between the two major allusions to *Gassire's Lute*. Erigena's dictum is interpreted by Pound as another means of internalizing events: 'Sunt lumina/that the drama is wholly subjective'. (74/430:457)

But it is the Albigensian stronghold of Montségur which most strongly unites the city in the mind with Troy in Auvergnat. Montségur has 'disappeared' like Wagadu: 'and in Mt Ségur there is wind space and rain space/no more an altar to Mithras' (76/452: 480). Still later Pound invokes cryptically 'Mt Ségur and the city of Dioce' (80/510:544). Montségur and Dioce's city both differ from Wagadu in that they possess a topological endurance as sacred places. Wagadu is entirely internalized, but Pound maintains an intimate, if fictionalized, association between the city in the mind and historical actuality.

Pound thinks of the relationship between outward and inward as a kind of dialogue, and therefore cannot rest content with that which is entirely internalized. In describing the composition of 'In a Station of the Metro', Pound wrote that 'in a poem of this sort one is trying to record the precise instant when a thing outward and objective transforms itself, or darts into a thing inward and subjective'. On the same page he describes 'two opposed ways of thinking of a man: . . . as the toy of circumstance, as the plastic substance *receiving* impressions; . . . [or] as directing a certain fluid force against circumstance, as *conceiving* instead of merely reflecting and observing'.[15] Pound clearly favours the second hypothesis, and incorporates it into his translation of 'Dona mi Prega', where it is said that Amor 'Cometh from a seen form which being understood/ Taketh locus and remaining in the intellect possible.' Ecbatan and Montségur are instances of the 'seen form', the external reality which gives rise to Wagadu, which in turn is equivalent to 'that formèd trace' in the mind:

> and that certain images be formed in the mind
> to remain there
> *formato locho*
> Arachne mi porta fortuna[a]
> to remain there, resurgent EIKONE[b]
> and still in Trastevere
> for the deification of emperors
> and the medallions
> to forge Achaia[16].
> (74/446–7:474)

Thus, while history is internalized in the *Pisan Cantos*, Pound maintains a link between the city in the mind and the historical city, between 'that formèd trace' and 'the seen form'. Even though the link is to the secret or fictionalized history of Eleusis, a dialogue between internal and external is clearly maintained. In other words, Pound does not abandon the second of his beliefs listed under 'Credo' in 'A Retrospect':

> *Symbols.*—I believe that the proper and perfect symbol is the natural object, that if a man use 'symbols' he must so use them that their symbolic function does not obtrude; so that *a* sense, and the poetic quality of the passage is not lost to those who do not understand the symbol as such, to whom, for instance, a hawk is a hawk.[17]

In the *Cantos* history is the 'natural object', and the city in the mind is what it symbolizes.

The relationship of object to conception, of 'seen form' to

[a] Arachne brings me luck.
[b] pictures, ikons.

'formèd trace' is rather light-heartedly explored at the beginning of canto 83:

> the queen stitched King Carolus' shirts or whatever
> while Erigena put greek tags in his excellent verses
> in fact an excellent poet, Paris
> toujours Pari'
> (Charles le Chauve)
>
> and you might find a bit of enamel
> a bit of true blue enamel
> on a metal pyx or whatever
> omnia, quae sunt, lumina sunt, or whatever
>
> so they dug up his bones in the time of De Montfort
> (Simon)
>
> Le Paradis n'est pas artificiel
> and Uncle William dawdling around Notre Dame
> In search of whatever
> paused to admire the symbol
> with Notre Dame standing inside it.
> (83/528:563)

Passages like this have a tendency to corroborate for some readers the allegations that Pound was of unsound mind. It certainly appears to be an aimless hodge-podge—even though I have not cited the first ten lines of the canto where Gemisto Plethon, Yeats, and Grosseteste are cited. However, the passage makes clear enough sense if one is sufficiently alive to the dynamics of the poem to draw the appropriate inferences.

'Le Paradis n'est pas artificiel' is a remark repeated some four times in the *Pisan Cantos*. It states the corollary of the belief that the ideal has somehow its manifestation in the world, as in the passage from canto 74 locating paradise in sausages (cited above).

In the *Cantos* paradise is, of course, not a place, but a psychic state, 'the bust thru from quotidien into "divine or permanent world"'. Sausage, King Carolus' shirts, Erigena's greek tags, a bit of enamel, and Notre-Dame are all, in a manner, quotidien. They are not symbols of paradise, but manifestations of paradisal forces. Paradise is therefore as real as the things which manifest it. Yeats's error in this anecdote is to regard the sensory manifestation of

Notre-Dame as accidental and without primary interest. To him the reality is the ineffable which the church merely symbolizes. Erigena's dictum, 'all things which are, are lights', expresses the radical integrity of the universe in opposition to alleged Yeatsian dualism. Because the Church rested its faith on a dualism of matter and spirit, Erigena's bones were dug up 'in the time of De Montfort' (the military leader of the Papal forces in the Albigensian Crusade) and he was condemned.[18]

Something should be said at this point about Erigena's thought because it seems to have been seized upon by Pound as at least sympathetic with his own 'religious' views. Pound probably owned, and certainly made constant use of Étienne Gilson's *La Philosophie au moyen age*, for he cites it in the Cavalcanti essay, and refers to it elsewhere. In his section on Erigena, Gilson does not mention the Albigenses, but he does say that Erigena's works were repeatedly condemned during the Middle Ages usually on the grounds that they supported pantheism. Gilson does not think he was a pantheist, but describes his doctrine of creation in terms that could easily be taken for pantheism:

> The God of Erigena is like unto a principle which, incomprehensible in its simplicity, reveals itself at a stroke in the multiplicity of its consequences. This self-manifestation of God is the true meaning of creation in Erigena's doctrine. This is why he often calls it a 'theophany', that is to say, an 'apparition of God'. For God to create is to reveal himself, and since to create is to reveal, to say that God reveals himself is tantamount to saying that he creates himself. In other words, just as revelation is creation, creation is revelation.[19]

This notion of creation as a theophany fits quite well with the vitalist cast of Pound's thought and that of his mentors such as Remy de Gourmont and Fenollosa. If creation is a theophany, paradise is to recognize thc quotidien or created world as revelation.

On the next page Gilson quotes Erigena's monistic doctrine, 'all things which are, are lights'. For some reason Pound had taken no notice of this doctrine when he first read Gilson, for he wrote of it to Eliot with a sense of discovery in 1940. Gilson explains the doctrine:

> The notion of creation conceived as a revelation introduces into the Erigenian universe another theme, that of 'illumination'. There were scriptural reasons to stress this notion. In a text of paramount importance

to medieval thinkers, and which Erigena himself has often quoted and commented, it is said that: 'Every best gift (*datum*), and every perfect present (*donum*), is from above, coming down from the Father of lights' (James, 1, 17). Moreover, Saint Paul has said: 'All that is made manifest is light' (Ephes., 5, 13). Thence comes, in many medieval doctrines, the two-fold illumination of grace (*donum*) and nature (*datum*). Thus conceived, nature is a light given by the Father of lights: *omnia quae sunt, lumina sunt*, and their very essence consists in being so many reflections of the divine light. Made up of that multitude of tiny lamps that things are, creation is only an illumination intended to show God.[20]

It is easy enough to pigeon-hole Erigena as a neo-Platonist, but it must be remembered that the stress of his Platonism—as Gilson summarizes it—is to sanctify the sensible universe in contradistinction to the transcendental stress of Italian neo-Platonism some six centuries later. And it is as sanctifiers of the sensible universe that Pound reads Cavalcanti and other singers of *gay savoir*. Pound's touchstone for all this is Propertius' line, 'My genius is no more than a girl'. It is above all in the beloved that paradise inheres:

What thou lovest well remains,
                              the rest is dross
What thou lov'st well shall not be reft from thee
What thou lov'st well is thy true heritage
Whose world, or mine or theirs
                        or is it of none?
First came the seen, then thus the palpable
    Elysium, though it were in the halls of hell,
What thou lovest well is thy true heritage.
                              (81/520–1:556)

'First came the seen, then thus the palpable.' 'The seen' is, if one likes, the ideal manifest as vision. It is Wagadu of the Sonninke legend, or Browning's 'truth' revealed. It is, finally, 'the city of Dioce'. But 'the palpable' is Dierra, Agada, Ganna, and Silla, the actual 'historical' cities of the Sonninke legend; it is history, and is represented in the *Pisan Cantos* on the one hand by the fortress at Montségur, and on the other by defeated Italy, and especially by Pound himself imprisoned in the Pisan D.T.C.

3. 'NOT THE PRIEST, BUT THE VICTIM'

As the history which the *Cantos* aspired to contain is internalized in the *Pisan Cantos*, so the quasi-historical paradigm of heroic enterprise, modelled on Odysseus' encounter with Circe and visit to the Underworld, is rendered personal and autobiographical. 'Odysseus', Pound tells us on the first page of the new section, is 'the name of my family'. He sees himself in the Pisan D.T.C. as Odysseus in Circe's pig sty:

> and the guards op/ of the . . .
> was lower than that of the prisoners
> 'all them g.d.m.f. generals c.s. all of 'em fascists'
> 'fer a bag o' Dukes'
> 'the things I saye an' dooo'
> ac ego in harum[a]
> so lay men in Circe's swine-sty;
> ivi in harum *ego* ac vidi cadaveres animae[b].
> (74/436:463–4)

The sense of Odysseus as a religious hero becomes insistent in the *Pisan Cantos*. Indeed Pound's self-identification with Odysseus as a religious hero widely exceeds the margins of modesty. Just before the passage quoted above we find

> I don't know how humanity stands it
> with a painted paradise at the end of it
> without a painted paradise at the end of it
> the dwarf morning-glory twines round the grass blade
> magna NUX animae with Barabbas and 2 thieves beside me.

At Pisa, Pound, the intellectual warrior, encounters his own dark night of the soul, and has the temerity to identify himself with Christ.

It is unlikely that Pound's medical examiners read canto 74, but had they done so, it would have served only to corroborate the judgement they reached:

> The defendant, now 60 years of age and in generally good physical condition, was a precocious student, specializing in literature. He has been a voluntary expatriate for nearly 40 years, living in England and France, and for the past 21 years in Italy, making an uncertain living by writing poetry and criticism. His poetry and literary criticism have achieved

[a] and I too in the pig sty.
[b] I went into the pig sty and I saw soul-corpses.

considerable recognition, but of recent years his preoccupation with monetary theories and economics has apparently obstructed his literary productivity. He has long been recognized as eccentric, querulous, and egocentric.

At the present time he exhibits extremely poor judgement as to his situation, its seriousness and the manner in which the charges are to be met. He insists that his broadcasts were not treasonable, but that all of his radio activities have stemmed from his self appointed mission to 'save the Constitution'. He is abnormally grandiose, is expansive and exuberant in manner, exhibiting pressure of speech, discursiveness, and distractibility.

In our opinion, with advancing years his personality, for many years abnormal, has undergone further distortion to the extent that he is now suffering from a paranoid state which renders him mentally unfit to advise properly with counsel or to participate intelligently and reasonably in his own defense. He is, in other words, insane and mentally unfit for trial, and is in need of care in a mental hospital.[21]

It is difficult to know whether Pound's precocity, voluntary expatriation, or uncertain living counted most in the doctors' judgement, but there can be little question that they were true to their own lights. One wonders what would have become of Milton, Coleridge, or Shelley in the hands of such a panel.

Pound's uncomfortable political opinions and paranoia are present in the *Pisan Cantos*. Circe's pig sty is not only the Pisan D.T.C.; it also encompasses the American government—and presumably any other which permits standard banking practice against, apparently, the best judgement of 'all the presidents':

> and all the presidents
> Washington Adams Monroe Polk Tyler
> plus Carrol (of Carrolton) Crawford
> Robbing the public for private individual's gain-*ΘΕΛΓΕΙΝ*
> every bank of discount is downright iniquity
> robbing the public for private individual's gain
> nec benecomata Kirkê, mah! κακὰ φάργακ' ἔδωκεν[a]
> neither with lions nor leopards attended
> but poison, veleno[b]
> in all the veins of the commonweal
> if on high, will flow downward all thru them
> if on the forge at Predappio? . . .
>
> (74/436–7:464)

[a] nor fair-tressed Circe, mah! she had given them powerful drugs.
[b] poison.

Those who meekly suffer the 'downright iniquity' of banks of discount are enchanted or bewitched (*thelgein*, to enchant or bewitch) as by Circe. The dreadful drug of the banks flows downward through the whole society to the 'a.h. of the Army', as the Pisan D.T.C. is described lower down on the page. A higher degree of moral rectitude and intellectual acuity 'on high' would perhaps result in greater virtue among the people: 'if on the forge at Predappio?' (Predappio is Mussolini's birthplace.) He later records a whimsical corroboration of his belief that the American army is protecting a government based on theft through banks of discount: '(O Mercury god of thieves, your caduceus/is now used by the american army/as witness this packing case)'. (77/471:501)

However, it is not the political thrust of the *Pisan Cantos* that gives them their peculiar power. That derives from a poetic realization of the congruence between the poet and Odysseus, the explorer of death's realm. A demonstration of this congruence requires the collection of scattered passages throughout the *Pisan Cantos*, and a consequent distortion of the normal experience of a reader. It may appear initially that too much weight is being placed upon fugitive allusions and references. Hopefully, if the reader bears with the demonstration, it will become clear that the poem mimes the quest of the religious hero for knowledge of the divine.

The passage just cited continues: 'sd/old Upward: "not the priest but the victim."'[22] Old Upward is Allen Upward (1863–1926), an English barrister, poet, amateur sinologist, and amateur religious historian. He was included in the first Imagist anthology, and was well known to Pound in his London years. The reference here is probably to Upward's book, *The Divine Mystery* reviewed by Pound in the November 1913 issue of *The New Freewoman.* The basic argument of the book is that religion has evolved from primitive earthly fertility rites through stellar worship to solar religions. Zarathustrian fire worship is seen as an important transitional stage between fertility religions and solar religions and as very influential in the genesis of Judaism and Christianity. (This latter notion may be the source of the rather puzzling comment on page 438 (465) of canto 74: 'Zarathustra now desuete.') In the early chapters Upward traces the evolution of the Divine Man, who is initially a Wizard, then a Priest, then a King (whose role is that of sacrificial victim either as a god himself or as a surrogate for the god), and finally as the Sacrificial Christ, that is, *christos*, the anointed one, wizard, priest, and king all at once.[23]

Pound's review begins with a long quotation from *The Divine Mystery*, worth citing for the illumination it may throw upon Pound's conception of his own role as artist:

> I was sitting like Abraham in my tent door in the heat of the day, outside a Pagan city of Africa, when the lord of the thunder appeared before me, going on his way into the town to call down thunder from heaven upon it.
>
> He had on his wizard's robe, hung round with magical shells that rattled as he moved; and there walked behind him a young man carrying a lute. I gave the musician a piece of silver, and he danced before me the dance that draws down the thunder. After which he went his way into the town; and the people were gathered together in the courtyard of the king's house; and he danced before them all. Then it thundered for the first time in many days; and the king gave the thunder-maker a black goat —the immemorial reward of the performing god.
>
> So begins the history of the Divine Man, and such is his rude nativity. The secret of genius is sensitiveness. The Genius of the Thunder who revealed himself to me could not call the thunder, but he could be called by it. He was more quick than other men to feel the changes of the atmosphere; perhaps he had rendered his nervous system more sensitive still by fasting or mental abstraction; and he had learned to read his own symptoms as we read a barometer. So, when he felt the storm gathering round his head, he put on his symbolical vestment, and marched forth to be its Word, the archetype of all Heroes in all Mysteries.[24]

Pound would seem to have adopted Upward's description of the wizard to apply to the artist in *The ABC of Reading* where he declares that 'artists are the antennae of the race', and continues:

> Before deciding whether a man is a fool or a good artist, it would be well to ask, not only: 'is he excited unduly,' but: 'does he see something we don't?'
>
> Is his curious behaviour due to his feeling an oncoming earthquake, or smelling a forest fire which we do not yet feel or smell?[25]

And in the much earlier 'Psychology and Troubadours'—published the year before *The Divine Mystery*, but not before his acquaintance with Upward—he expresses the theory that myth originates in an extraordinary psychic experience perhaps not dissimilar to that of the lord of the thunder:

> I believe in a sort of permanent basis in humanity, that is to say, I believe that Greek myth arose when someone having passed through delightful psychic experience tried to communicate it to others and found it necessary to screen himself from persecution. Speaking aesthetically, the myths are explications of mood: you may stop there, or you may probe deeper. Certain it is that these myths are only intelligible in a vivid and glittering sense to those people to whom they occur. I know, I mean, one man who understands Persephone and Demeter, and one who understands the Laurel, and another who has, I should say, met Artemis. These things are for them *real.*[26]

The *Pisan Cantos* are in essence just such an attempt to communicate to others an extraordinary psychic experience—although it is not entirely delightful.

Pound himself is the victim 'with Barabbas and 2 thieves beside me'. He has been chosen as victim because he has been recognized as alien and the possessor of dangerous knowledge—or so, at least, his daughter construes his situation.

> Now that I did not even know his whereabouts, he was no longer merely the Herr, il Signore, the Teacher, Tattile or il Babbo, but the hero, the victim, the righteous man who had tried to save the world and had fallen prey to evil powers.[27]

We shall see him developing the role of persecuted sage later in *Rock-Drill.* The remark attributed to Upward identifies the victim of sacrifice as the divine surrogate—perhaps the god himself—rather than the sacrificing priest. Pound may have had in mind a story, 'Karos, the God' published by Upward in *The New Freewoman* exactly one month after Pound's review in the same journal. Karos, a slave, runs away from his master and eventually finds himself in a strange village where he is greeted by a procession led by a priest behind whom came 'boys and girls with their hands full of flowers, and after them young men playing on reeds and wooden cymbals, and then a crowd of villagers. As they came along they kept up a joyous chant like the sacred chorus of Dionusos.'[28] Karos is treated royally, but constantly watched. When he asks to know the identity of the village's god, he is told, 'You are our god.' At this point Karos becomes more haughty and dignified until on the day of 'the great yearly festival of the seed' Karos finds himself on the altar with a stone axe descending on his neck.

Karos is neither wise nor beautiful. He is the god of the villagers merely because they have chosen him as the victim required by their religious practices. Pound would seem to adopt this notion of the sacred victim to his own situation, not out of egomania, but as a means of introducing his personal situation into the poem while maintaining the aesthetic distance appropriate for an epic poem. At Pisa Pound was, in fact, treated as a very special prisoner. He was isolated from the other prisoners in a wire cage, but allowed books and the use of a typewriter. To think of himself as a ritual victim, rather than as a victim of injustice or persecution, enormously dignifies the situation without regard to the worthiness or unworthiness of the victim.

But the allusion to Upward, although repeated, (78/479:511) is not of primary importance. It is merely one of several models of religious distress cited in canto 74. The priest of Diana at Nemi who awaited the arrival of his murderous successor in the sacred wood is another: 'at Nemi waited on the slope above the lake sunken in the pocket of hills' (74/438:465). The particular notion of victim is, however, important to the manner in which Pound makes use of Odysseus in the *Pisan Cantos*. For here Odysseus' encounter with Circe and his descent into the Underworld are transformed from the bright *inluminatio coitu* of cantos 39 and 47 into a dark, death-like *connubium terrae*. In canto 47 Odysseus' role was that of priest or hierophant. Although Adonis and Tammuz are both invoked, Odysseus would seem to have escaped their sacrificial roles. In the *Pisan Cantos*, Pound (now adopting the role of Odysseus) finds entry into the Underworld more terrifying.

Twice in canto 77 the reader encounters the query, 'How is it far, if you think of it?' It is once more repeated in canto 79, this time with some context:

> 'Prepare to go on a journey.'
> 'I . . .'
>
> 'Prepare to go on a journey.'
> or to count sheep in Phoenician
> How is it far if you think of it?
> (79/488:520)

The query is Pound's invention, but the allusion is clearly to Book X of the *Odyssey* where Circe instructs Odysseus to journey to the

Underworld, already cited in cantos 39 and 47. But this time the journey to the Underworld takes an Eleusinian form—departing from the *Odyssey*, but maintaining a link through (*a*) the allusions in canto 74, (*b*) this variation on Circe's instructions, and (*c*) a long passage in canto 80 which develops both Pound and Odysseus as failed heroes and sacrificial victims:

> as he had walked under the rain altars
>   or under the trees of their grove
>   or would it be under their parapets
> in his moving was stillness
> as grey stone in the Aliscans
>   or had been at Mt Segur
> and it was old Spencer (,H.) who first declaimed me the Odyssey
> with a head built like Bill Shepard's
> on the quais of what Siracusa?
>   or what tennis court
> near what pine trees?
>
> care and craft in forming leagues and alliances
>   that avail nothing against the decree
> the folly of attacking that island
>   and of the force ὑπὲρ μόρον[a]
>
> with a mind like that he is one of us
>   Favonus, vento benigno[b]
>   Je suis au bout des mes forces/[c]
> That from the gates of death,
>   that from the gates of death: Whitman or Lovelace
>   found on the jo-house seat at that
> in a cheap edition! [and thanks to Professor Speare]
> hast 'ou swum in a sea of air strip
>   through an aeon of nothingness,
> when the raft broke and the waters went over me.
>
> (80/512–13:547)

This passage, like much of the *Pisan Cantos*, has the character of a memorious reverie. The 'he' is unidentified, although it might be Abelard from the previous passage. Pound brings into his reverie the sacred stronghold of Montségur, his own first acquaintance with the *Odyssey*, Odysseus' war guilt consequent upon his attack upon the Cicones, his own suffering and despair, and the wreck of the

[a] beyond what is destined.
[c] I am at the end of my strength.
[b] West wind, with kindly breeze.

boat or raft Odysseus built for himself on Calypso's island. Pound will return to Odysseus' shipwreck in *Rock-Drill*, and play some new variations on it, but for the moment he is content with a simple allusion. Pound's makeshift raft, captained by Benito Mussolini, has broken up and he is left struggling in turbulent waters. It is in this context that he elaborates for the first time a descent into the Underworld in a form that is unmistakably Eleusinian.

4. 'LE PARADIS N'EST PAS ARTIFICIEL'

The concluding lyrical passage in canto 74 is designed to remind the reader of the *Commedia*, and to introduce the motif of ascension:

> Serenely in the crystal jet
>   as the bright ball that the fountain tosses
> (Verlaine) as diamond clearness
>   How soft the wind under Taishan
>   where the sea is remembered
>   out of hell, the pit
>   out of the dust and glare evil
>   Zephyrus/Apeliota
> This liquid is certainly a
>   property of the mind
> nec accidens est   but an element
>   in the mind's make-up
> est agens and functions   dust to a fountain pan otherwise
>   Hast 'ou seen the rose in the steel dust
>   (or swansdown ever?)
> so light is the urging, so ordered the dark petals of iron
> we who have passed over Lethe.
>
> (74/449:477)

'This liquid' is probably light itself imagined as a substance, and the whole second half of this passage (with the exception of the last line) should be read in the context of canto 36 where Amor is identified with light. But it is the balance of the passage that is of particular interest here. Taishan is a sacred Chinese mountain which Pound uses in the *Pisan Cantos* as a paradisal locus, and speaks of it as if he could see it from his cage at Pisa:

>   sinceritas
> from the death cells in sight of Mt. Taishan @ Pisa
> as Fujiyama at Gardone.
>
> (74/427:453)

Under Taishan would be, as it were, at the foot of Heaven. Pound both reinforces and confuses this supposition by the syntactically autonomous prepositional phrases, 'out of hell, the pit/out of the dust and glare evil', reminding the reader of Dante's processional ascent out of Hell, through Purgatory to Heaven. The final line is an unmistakable allusion to Dante's ascent, for the river of Lethe divides Purgatory from Hell, and Heaven from Purgatory in the *Commedia*, and Lethe is not among the four rivers of the Underworld named by Homer.

Although Lethe is traditionally the river of forgetfulness, Dante ascribes to it a primarily purgative function. He says little of his crossing of the river from Hell to Purgatory, but describes the second crossing in considerable detail. Just before he enters the river Beatrice was revealed to him in greater radiance than she had heretofore possessed. As frequently happens in the *Commedia*, Dante swooned momentarily.

> Then, when my heart restored my outward sense, the lady I had found alone [that is, Matilda] I saw above me, and she was saying: 'Hold me, hold me!' She had brought me into the river up to the throat and, drawing me after her, was passing over the water light as a shuttle. . . . The fair lady opened her arms, clasped my head, and plunged me under, where I must swallow the water; then she took me out and led me bathed into the dance of the four fair ones, and each covered me with her arms.[29]

'We who have passed over Lethe' would seem to mean those who have had some sort of visionary experience. Certainly, it can hardly mean those whose memories have been wiped clean when so much of the *Pisan Cantos* is devoted to the sanctity of the remembered: 'Quand vous serez bien vieille/remember that I have remembered.'[30] The *Cantos*, of course, are not processional like the *Commedia*, nor do they possess the topographical order with which Dante invested his three realms. Thus to cross the Lethe is not to move from one realm to another, but to undergo a specific kind of experience. The nature of the experience in the *Commedia* is purgative, but it is accompanied by a vision of Beatrice's increased radiance.

The words 'Zephyrus/Apeliota' in the passage cited, allude back to a similar visionary experience earlier in canto 74 where Aphrodite appears to Pound:

> enigma forgetting the times and seasons
> but this air brought her ashore a la marina

with the great shell borne on the seawaves
nautilis biancastra
By no means an orderly Dantescan rising
but as the winds veer
tira libeccio[a]
now Genji at Suma , tira libeccio
as the winds veer and the raft is driven
and the voices , Tiro, Alcmene
with you is Europa nec casta Pasiphaë
Eurus, Apeliota as the winds veer in periplum.
(74/443:471)

In the *Odyssey* when Odysseus' raft is being swamped by the storm, Homer names the four winds, Notus, Boreas, Eurus, and Zephyrus (*Odyssey*, V. 331–2). Pound is almost certainly recalling this passage although he substitutes Apeliota for Zephyrus. Odysseus is saved by the appearance to him of the water sprite, Ino or Leucothea (Homer uses both names) rather in the manner that Dante is taken over the Lethe by Matilda. But Odysseus' salvation is 'by no means an orderly Dantescan rising'. Indeed, he is thrown up on the shore of Phaecia half-drowned.

The *Cantos* make contextual use of both the *Commedia* and the *Odyssey* as a means of locating the reader in the poem's mythic action. The allusions can function only if one understands Pound's sense of the action of those poems and of his own as accounts of psychic experience. The theophany of Aphrodite is a 'delightful psychic experience' comparable to Dante's vision of Beatrice just before crossing the river Lethe. But Pound is at pains to remind his readers that in his world such visions cannot be read as milestones in some processional journey toward paradise. Aphrodite is born on her shell, as in Botticelli's *La Nascita*, but she is tossed by the winds, as is Odysseus on his raft. The *spezzato* nature of his visionary world was announced, as we have seen, in canto 5, in still another allusion to Dante:

'Et omniformis': Air, fire, the pale soft light.
Topaz I manage, and three sorts of blue;
but on the barb of time.
The fire? always, and the vision always,
Ear dull, perhaps, with the vision, flitting
And fading at will.
(5/17:21)

[a] the South wind blows.

Pound's vision is 'flitting and fading at will'. Dante's poem, in contrast, moves tortuously but surely toward a concluding beatific vision of the Supreme Light—of which he writes:

From that moment my vision was greater than our speech, which fails at such a sight, and memory too fails at such excess. Like him that sees in a dream and after the dream the passion wrought by it remains and the rest returns not to his mind, such am I: for my vision almost wholly fades, and still there drops within my heart the sweetness that was born of it.

(*Paradiso* xxxiii. 55–63)

Dante describes his vision as fading from his memory, but it is securely placed in the Empyrean beyond the ninth sphere of heaven.

But, of course, the whole of the *Commedia* is a vision, and it contains accounts or renderings of many 'delightful psychic experiences'. For Pound, they are all equally manifestations of 'the divine or permanent world'. The universe of the *Cantos* is without orderly topography—although it possesses specific 'places' (Venice, Montségur, Pisa)—and without orderly chronology—although it is replete with dates. The vision is 'on the barb of time', 'flitting and fading at will'. Aphrodite appears to Pound at Pisa as 'an enigma forgetting the times and seasons'.[31]

Dante's vision of Beatrice (a minor vision in the *Commedia*) precedes his purgative ordeal in the river Lethe, and is a kind of preparation for, or promise of, the beatific vision which is to be his ultimate reward. In the *Cantos* it is the vision which is an incident and the purgative ordeal is, as it were, the encompassing reality. Thus the vision of Aphrodite cannot be said to precede any particular ascending movement toward a final revelation. It does, however, itself represent an increasing awareness accompanying the purgative experience of Pisa. The revelation represented by Aphrodite is of beauty—*to kalon*, as Pound occasionally styles it—manifest in woman. To underline this point Pound invokes Tyro (spelt Tiro in this instance) and Alcmene, two of the beautiful women Odysseus encounters in the Underworld. 'With you is Europa nec casta Pasiphaë [nor chaste Pasiphaë]' is an inaccurate recollection of Propertius' line 'vobiscum Europe nec proba Pasiphae [with you is Europe nor proper Pasiphae]'[32] In 'Homage to Sextus Propertius' Pound translates the whole passage as follows:

Persephone and Dis, Dis, have mercy upon her,
There are enough women in hell,
            quite enough beautiful women,
Iope, and Tyro, and Pasiphae, and the formal girls of Achaia,
And out of Troad, and from the Campania,
Death has his tooth in the lot,
            Avernus lusts for the lot of them,
Beauty is not eternal, no man has perennial fortune,
Slow foot, or swift foot, death delays but for a season.[33]

Both the allusion to the Odyssean *nekuia* and the Propertian allusion remind us of the impermanence of beauty and the finality of death, balancing the transcendent tendency of the Dantean allusion.

This peculiar mixture of Dantean ascent and Homeric descent is explicable in terms of Eleusis, for at Eleusis the candidate *descends* into the Telesterion, into darkness and confusion, but is finally rewarded in the *epopteia* with a bright revelation—said by some to be a theophany of Aphrodite, by others, of Persephone, and by still others to be a *hieros gamos* or divine marriage enacted by a priest and priestess, adopting the roles of Pluto and Persephone or perhaps of Dionysus Zagreus and Aphrodite. In Chapter III we saw how Pound developed the encounter between Circe and Odysseus as a version of the Eleusinian descent and *epopteia* seen as a divine coupling—in that instance between Odysseus and Circe. The *Pisan Cantos* build upon that base, but Odysseus is now displaced by the imprisoned Pound, and the nature of the revelatory experience becomes elaborate.

Early in canto 74 Pound introduces Aphrodite in a little cryptogram: 'The suave eyes, quiet, not scornful.' Those eyes are Aphrodite's. They reappear shortly in a reminiscence of the 'marriage' of Anchises and Aphrodite rendered in canto 23:

as by Terracina rose from the sea Zephyr behind her
            and from her manner of walking
                                    as had Anchises
      till the shrine be again white with marble
      till the stone eyes look again seaward
                  The wind is part of the process
                  The rain is part of the process
and the Pleiades set in her mirror
Kuanon, this stone bringeth sleep;

offered the wine bowl
grass nowhere out of place
χθόνια γέα, Μήτηρ,[a]
by thy herbs menthe thyme and basilicum
(74/435:461–2)

The wine bowl in the tenth line of this passage is offered to Odysseus by Circe, the 'dreadful drug' which would have metamorphosed him into a pig were it not for Hermes' *moly*. The chthonic mother earth is to be the goddess in Pound's own *hieros gamos* enacted later in the Pisan section (canto 82). Kuanon is a Chinese goddess of mercy who is perhaps invoked to render aid in this perilous adventure, for Pound is at once Odysseus in Circe's boudoir, Odysseus encountering the dead, Odysseus tossed from his frail craft by the storm, and the Eleusinian initiand entering the darkness of the Telesterion in fear and trembling.

The vision returns in canto 76, this time with a transition from Pound's actual situation at Pisa:

l'ara sul rostro[b]
20 years of the dream
and the clouds near to Pisa
are as good an any in Italy
said the young Mozart; if you will take a *prise*
or following Ponce ('Ponthe')
to the fountain in Florida
de Leon alla fuente florida[c]
or Anchises that laid hold of her flanks of air
drawing her to him
Cythera potens, *Κύθηρα δεινά*[d]
no cloud, but the crystal body
the tangent formed in the hand's cup
as live wind in the beech grove
as strong air amid cypress

Κόρη, Δελιά δεινά/et libidinis expers[e]
the sphere moving crystal, fluid,
none therein carrying rancour

[a] nether earth, Mother.
[b] the altar on the rostrum.
[c] to the flowery fountain.
[d] powerful Cythera, dread Cythera.
[e] Daughter, dread Delia/to whom passion is unknown.

Death, insanity/suicide degeneration
that is, just getting stupider as they get older
πολλά παθεῖν[a]

(76/456–7:485)

Here, for the first time, Pound attaches the epithet *deina* or 'dread' to Aphrodite. She is now called dread because she adopts the role of the temptress, Circe, in addition to her primary role as the bright goddess born of sea-foam. Pound also invokes Koré, that is, Persephone, and Delia or Artemis. Artemis, too, is given the epithet *deina*. It is no surprise to find this epithet attached to the virgin goddess, for it is she who causes Actaeon's death in canto 4, and she is given a rather bloodthirsty monologue in canto 30.

Artemis is not very frequently invoked in the *Cantos*, but the contrast between her monologue in canto 30, and her appearance in the company of Aphrodite and Persephone in canto 76 is indicative of the difference in tone between the *Pisan Cantos* and earlier sections of the poem. For in canto 30 Artemis' dreadness is seen to be a beneficent cleansing through death of the weak and malformed. She is the weeder of life's garden. Pound there regrets that she is no longer permitted to perform her bloody but necessary function. The poet is entirely detached from the notion that the 'weeds' suffer pain and anxiety. Something of this unattractive spirit of brutal denunciation is retained in canto 76 in the list of ills that flesh is heir to: 'Death, insanity/suicide degeneration/that is, just getting stupider as they get older.' But now the speaker is not so clearly exempted from such frailties. The Greek tag, *polla pathein*, 'to suffer much', would appear to apply equally to the poet and to those 'getting stupider'. Indeed, Pound, too, is perhaps getting stupider as he gets older.

The following passage (already cited above in the discussion of canto 36) places true value in affection, in sharp contrast to the spirit of canto 30:

nothing matters but the quality
of the affection—
in the end—that has carved the trace in the mind
dove sta memoria.

(76/457:485)

Pound learned a certain humility at Pisa, and is no longer so stridently certain of his own virtue and others' viciousness. In the

[a] to suffer much.

midst of this uncertainty, his 'dark night of the soul', the mythical superstructure of his poem turns inward and becomes a religion. He sees himself, in a reminiscence of the procession in canto 20, as one of the lotophagoi:

> Lay in soft grass by the cliff's edge
> with the sea 30 metres below this
> and at hand's span, at cubit's reach moving,
> the crystalline, as inverse of water,
> clear over rock-bed
>
> ac ferae familiares[a]
> the gemmed field *a destra* with fawn, with panther,
> corn flower, thistle and sword-flower
> to a half metre grass growth,
> lay on the cliff's edge
> . . . nor is this yet *atasal*
> nor are here souls, nec personae
> neither here in hypostasis, this land is of Dione
> and under her planet
> to Helia the long meadow with poplars
> to *Κύπρις*
> the mountain and shut garden of pear trees in flower
> here rested.[34]
>
> (76/457–8:486)

It will be remembered that Pound described the latter portion of canto 20 as 'a general paradiso' in a letter to his father. A very puzzling paradiso it was, but now he modifies the vision: 'nor is this yet *atasal*'. This experience is not 'union with god'. He is, he says, in the land of Dione 'and under her planet'.

It is difficult to be confident of Pound's meaning here. Dione is the mother of Aphrodite, but according to G. R. S. Mead, she is the middle aspect of Venus:

> There are three main aspects of Venus, one connected with Uranus, the second with Saturn, and the third with Jupiter. The name of the middle Venus is Dione.[35]

Mead's source is Thomas Taylor, the eighteenth-century Platonist. Unfortunately, Mead tells us no more about Dione than that she is the middle Venus, and that her planet is Saturn. However, he later

[a] and domesticated wild animals.

cites Taylor on Hades, and Taylor's account of the nature of Hades would make sense of the lines 'nor is this yet *atasal*/nor are here souls, nec personae/neither here in hypostasis.'

The ancients by Hades signified nothing more than the profound union of the soul with the present body; and consequently, that till the soul separated herself by philosophy from such a ruinous conjunction, she subsisted in Hades even in the present life; her punishment hereafter being nothing more than a continuation of her state upon earth, and a transmigration, as it were, from sleep to sleep, and from dream to dream; and this, too, was occultly signified by the shows of the lesser mysteries.[36]

The soul in hypostasis would be completely separated from the body and, presumably, united with God. Pound's meaning would seem to be that his vision is earth-bound, but, none the less, vision:

> spiriti questi? personae?[a]
> tangibility by no means *atasal*
> but the crystal can be weighed in the hand
> formal and passing within the sphere: Thetis,
> Maya, Ἀφροδίτη.
>
> (76/459:487–8)

The image of this earth-bound middle Venus is, according to Taylor, the sea, which

signifies an expanded and circumscribed life; its profundity, the universally extended progression of such life; and its foam, the greatest purity of nature, that which is full of prolific light and power, and that which swims upon all life, and is as it were its highest flower.[37]

The sea, like the crystal, is translucent, but can be weighed in the hand. Pound turns, in the immediately following passage, to images of water and air, proper to the goddess born of sea-foam:

> no overstroke
> no dolphin faster in moving
> nor the flying azure of the wing'd fish under Zoagli
> when he comes out into the air, living arrow
> and the clouds over the Pisan meadows
> are indubitably as fine as any to be seen
> from the peninsula.
>
> (76/459:488)

[a] ghosts these? people?

It cannot be asserted that Pound is drawing on Mead, or directly on Taylor, but Taylor's views as cited by Mead provide a helpful gloss on the visionary experience recorded in canto 76.[38]

The secular sense of Pound's vision of Aphrodite is perhaps best conveyed on the next page:

Le Paradis n'est pas artifciel
States of mind are inexplicable to us
δακρύων δακρύων δακρύων[a]
L. P. gli onesti[b]
J'ai eu pitié des autres
probablement pas assez, and at moments that suited my own convenience
Le paradis n'est pas artificiel,
l'enfer non plus.
Came Eurus as comforter
and at sunset la pastorella dei suini
driving the pigs home, benecomata dea[39].

(76/460:488–9)

Paradise is not artificial, but it cannot be disentangled from 'mere' states of mind. The gloss I would offer for this passage is that paradise is perceived in suffering (which is also of this world). Heaven and Hell are as real or as illusory as the girl swine-herd ('la pastorella dei suini')—a real swine-herd to whom Pound speaks on the last page of the *Pisan Cantos*[40]—who is here described with Circe's epithet, *benecomata dea*, 'the fair-tressed goddess'. The 'reality' of Circe is the persistence of the beauty of women and its dangers for men. The 'divinity' of the girl is the reality of her (perhaps unconscious) power over the hearts and minds of men.

What must be understood if one is to make sense of the *Cantos* is that Pound is using myth and history as a language—a language which is sometimes too cryptic to be understood properly, but which has in general a discernible meaning so long as one recognizes that he is *speaking* in myth and not merely engaging in recondite allusiveness. 'When you don't understand it,' Pound cautions his readers, 'let it alone. This is the copy-book maxim whereagainst sin prose philosophers, though it is explicit in Kung on spirits. The mythological exposition permits this. It permits an expression of intuition without denting the edges or shaving off the nose and ears of a verity.'[41] In other words, Pound is using the classical myths to express his own intuitions. He does not guarantee fidelity to his

[a] weeping.
[b] the honest ones.

sources, and they are not always the best guide to his meaning—although his classical and modern sources are the correct places to *begin* the search for his meaning.

Thus, although Aphrodite, Circe, Maia, Persephone, Artemis, Thetis, and Gea may all have definite associations for Pound, it is not possible to isolate the particular significance and role of each goddess. It is least distorting to consider them all as aspects of the female in Pound's own mythological formulation of the encounter with the divine. And one must add to the list the mortal women brought into the context of these goddesses in the *Pisan Cantos*—most notably Sordello's wife, Cunizza da Romano and Malatesta's wife, Isotta degli Atti.[42] All of these female figures, except for Artemis,[43] are wives and lovers because Pound is exploring the encounter with the divine under the rubric of sexuality in accordance with his understanding of Eleusis as transmitted through the troubadours, Cavalcanti, and Dante.

5. 'CONNUBIUM TERRAE'

Aphrodite represents the bright aspect of the Goddess, certainly, but she is also associated with the dark Underworld aspect more properly belonging to Persephone:

> Le Paradis n'est pas artificiel
> *Κύθηρα,*   *Κύθηρα,*
> Moving ὑπὸ   χθονὸς   enters the hall of the records
> the forms of men rose out of γέα
> Le Paradis n'est pas artificiel
> nor does the martin against the tempest
> fly as in the calm air.
>
> (77/468:498)

Here Cythera, or Aphrodite, moves under the earth (*upo chthonos*), and apparently causes men to rise out of the earth (*gea*) much in the manner that Persephone returns from the Underworld through the earth in the form of grain. There is also a reminiscence of the soldiers who spring from the dragon's teeth sown by Cadmus, and who speak in canto 27. Cadmus is the archetypal city-builder, and soldiers are the destroyers of cities—a function with which Aphrodite has been associated in the earlier cantos through the role of Helen.

Indeed, these men rising out of the earth first occur a few pages earlier in conjunction with the Sonninke city myth:

> Faasa ! 4 times was the city remade,
> now in the heart indestructible
>   4 gates, the 4 towers
> (Il Scirocco è geloso)[a]
>   men rose out of χθόνος.
>   (77/465:494)

Hence we are forced to see Aphrodite as a dark and fearful goddess associated with death and destruction ,whatever her proper classical attributes may be.[44]

In canto 80 Pound ingeniously interfuses Aphrodite with Artemis. Firstly, he invokes Aphrodite while apparently speaking of Artemis:

> At Ephesus she had compassion on silversmiths
>   revealing the paraclete
> standing in the cusp
>   of the moon et in Monte Gioiosa
>   as the larks rise at Allegre
>   Cythera egoista
>   But for Actaeon
>   of the eternal moods has fallen away.
>   (80/500–01:534)

Although the passage remains somewhat obscure, the 'she' ought to be Artemis whose principal shrine was at Ephesus, and who caused the death of Actaeon. Yet 'she' is apparently called 'proud Cythera', that is, Aphrodite. That such an identification is intended is made apparent by the later parenthetical query, '(Cythera, in the moon's barge whither?/how hast thou the crescent for car?' (80/510:545). At this point Pound has become a little playful, for he answers his riddle on the next page:

> 'I am the torch' wrote Arthur 'she saith'
> in the moon barge βροδοδάκτυλος 'Ηώς
>
> with the veil of faint cloud before her
>   Κύθηρα δεινὰ as a leaf borne in the current
> pale eyes as if without fire.
>   (80/511:546)

[a] the South Wind is jealous.

The clue is in the Homeric tag, 'rosy-fingered dawn', for Venus is the morning star, and Pound sees it from his cell cradled in the moon. But despite the playfulness, the identification of Diana or Artemis with the proud and terrible aspect of Aphrodite is reinforced.

The elaboration of the person of Aphrodite in this manner prepares the reader for the varied theophanies contained in the *Pisan Cantos*, the first in canto 79, the second in canto 81, and the third in canto 82. The first and third are Eleusinian in form, and involve the double movement of birth and death. The second is more autonomous in character and secular in tone. It begins with a libretto containing the refrain, 'Lawes and Jenkyns guard thy rest/Dolmetsch ever be thy guest', which concludes:

> Hast 'ou fashioned so airy a mood
>   To draw up leaf from the root?
> Hast 'ou found a cloud so light
>   As seemed neither mist nor shade?
>   (81/520:555)

Pound follows this unexpectedly artful celebration of the power of song with an equally unexpected citation of the refrain of Chaucer's 'Merciless Beautee':

> Your eyen two wol sleye me sodenly
> I may the beauté of hem nat susteyne
>
> And for 180 years almost nothing.

The point would seem to be that Chaucer recognized the terrible power of female beauty—or, perhaps more properly, the close affiliation of love and death—and that this knowledge was not manifest again in England until the late sixteenth century. In any event the Libretto and 'Merciless Beautee' serve as the prologue for a remarkable lyrical passage, which in effect domesticates the earlier mythically-rendered theophanies of Aphrodite to Pound's situation at Pisa:

> Ed ascoltando al leggier mormorio[a]
>   there came new subtlety of eyes into my tent,
> whether of spirit or hypostasis,
>   but what the blindfold hides

[a] 'And listening to the light murmur'.

or at carneval
                    nor any pair showed anger
      Saw but the eyes and stance between the eyes,
colour, diastasis,
   careless or unaware it had not the
      whole tent's room
nor was place for the full *Ειδὼς*[a]
interpass, penetrate
      casting but shade beyond the other lights
         sky's clear
         night's sea
         green of the mountain pool
         shone from the unmasked eyes in half-mask's space.
(81/520:555–6)

Still 'in the land of Dione' Pound records here his own proper 'vision'. What he actually sees is perhaps no more than a peculiarly affecting quality of light in his tent, but in describing it as 'a new subtlety of eyes', he brings it into the context of earlier invocations of Aphrodite's eyes such as that in canto 74, 'The suave eyes, quiet, not scornful'. This is the revelation of 'the seen form', whence love emanates in 'Dona mi Prega', reduced to the evanescent and fugitive form in which it is commonly accessible to men. Earlier, in canto 76, Pound had recollected the Cavalcanti canzone, and the reminder is repeated in canto 77: 'nothing counts save the quality of the affection' (p. 466:496). Now, in canto 81, he picks up this sentiment for the 'Pull down thy vanity' lyric:

What thou lovest well remains,
                    the rest is dross
What thou lov'st well shall not be reft from thee
What thou lov'st well is thy true heritage
Whose world, or mine or theirs
                    or is it of none?
First came the seen, then thus the palpable
   Elysium, though it were in the halls of hell,
What thou lovest well is thy true heritage.
What thou lov'st well shall not be reft from thee

The ant's a centaur in his dragon world.
Pull down thy vanity, it is not man
Made courage, or made order, or made grace,
   Pull down thy vanity, I say pull down.

[a] seeing.

Learn of the green world what can be thy place
In scaled invention or true artistry,
Pull down thy vanity,
                    Paquin pull down!
The green casque has outdone your elegance.[45]
                                        (81/520–1:556)

This private and secular revelation is accessible to all readers, and is one of the most frequently quoted portions of the *Cantos*. It does not depend upon the religious apparatus of Eleusis for comprehension, but it and the Eleusinian machinery are both built upon the common base of 'Dona mi Prega' and the religion of love. It is an affirmation of faith in man's place in the universe as a fully sentient being who has access to 'paradise' through his commonalty with that universe. This faith in the possibility of communication between the self and the world is labelled by Allen Upward *Metastrophe*:

By this word I mean more than the archbishops have meant by their word metabolism. I mean, not growth and decay, but growth turning into decay, and decay turning into growth. I mean involution in the midst of evolution. I mean life turning inside out. And I mean more than life; I mean also the expression of life. Metastrophe is a mood, and in so far as we attain this mood, so will the Strength Within chime more and more sweetly with the Strength Without; not in dead unity, but in living unison, and the faint gladness of our earthly voices climb and thread the thunder music rolling out of Heaven.[46]

Pound set down his own beliefs with regard to divinity in 1921 in a little article called 'Axiomata'. They are not the same as Upward's, but neither are they in conflict with them, and it seems very likely that 'old Upward's' eccentric views had their impact on the young Pound. Be that as it may, 'Axiomata' provides a useful gloss on the vision and lyric of canto 81. The tone of the piece is highly sceptical —so much so that Pound's editor, A. R. Orage takes exception to his irreligion in the same number. However, an atheist would probably find Pound rather too ready to accept the notion of divinity. He begins with three basic propositions:

(1) The intimate essence of the universe is *not* of the same nature as our own consciousness.
(2) Our own consciousness is incapable of having produced the universe.

(3) God, therefore, exists. That is to say, there is no reason for not applying the term God, *Theos*, to the intimate essence.[47]

These basic propositions are close enough to Upward's notion of a Strength Within, and a Strength Without, although lacking the dynamism of his idea. In proposition (5) of the first section Pound denies the possibility of any knowledge of the Divine. In (7) he tells us that 'dogma is bluff based upon ignorance', and in (9) that 'belief is a cramp, a paralysis, an atrophy of the mind in certain positions'. Essentially all of this amounts to the very minimal belief that there exists both Self and Other, and that the Self cannot know the Other.

In section III, however, Pound allows the possibility that 'the consciousness may be affected by the theos'. And he describes, in an awkward parody of philosophical expression, in what manner the consciousness may be affected:

> The theos may affect and may have affected the consciousness of individuals, but the consciousness is incapable of knowing why this occurs, or even in what manner it occurs, or whether it be the *theos*; though the consciousness may experience pleasant and possibly unpleasant sensations, or sensations partaking neither of pleasure or its opposite. Hence mysticism. If the consciousness receives or has received such effects from the theos, or from something not the theos yet which the consciousness has been incapable of understanding or classifying either as theos or a-theos, it is incapable of reducing these sensations to coherent sequence of cause and effect. The effects remain, so far as the consciousness is concerned, in the domain of experience, not differing intellectually from the taste of a lemon or the fragrance of violets or the aroma of dunghills, or the feel of a stone or of tree-bark, or any other direct perception. As the consciousness observes the results of the senses, it observes also the mirage of the senses, or what may be a mirage of the senses, or an affect from the theos, the non-comprehensible.

It is some such consciousness of the divine that canto 81 attempts to convey, a mystic experience rooted in ordinary sensory experience. And it is, of course, just such a consciousness of the divine that represents Paradise for Pound: 'Le Paradis n'est pas artificial/but spezzato apparently/it exists only in fragments unexpected excellent sausage,/the smell of mint, for example'.

Canto 82 contains still another experience of the divine. This time Pound audaciously attempts to render his experience by means of the sense of touch instead of the traditional mystical sense of sight:

How drawn, O GEA TERRA,
what draws as thou drawest
till one sink into thee by an arm's width
embracing thee. Drawest,
truly thou drawest.
Wisdom lies next thee,
simply, past metaphor.
(82/526:561)

Gea Terra is, of course, the earth, half-personified as a goddess. This experience is at once that of death and of copulation. It is the experience of Odysseus lying with Circe, but removed from its mythical locale and conveyed as a personal experience. Here the poet himself becomes the victim, Adonis or Attis, the couch-mate of the goddess:

Where I lie let the thyme rise
and basilicum
let the herbs rise in April abundant
By Ferrara was buried naked, fu Nicolo
e di qua di la del Po,[a]
wind: 'εμὸν τὸν ἄνδρα[b]
lie into earth to the breast bone, to the left shoulder
Kipling suspected it
to the height of ten inches or over
man, earth: two halves of the tally
but I will come out of this knowing no one
neither they me
connubium terrae ἔφατα πόσις ἐμός[c]
ΧΘΟΝΙΟΣ, mysterium
fluid *ΧΘΟΝΟΣ* o'erflowed me
lay in the fluid *ΧΘΟΝΟΣ*;
that lie
under the air's solidity
drunk with '*ΙΧΩΡ* of *ΧΘΟΝΙΟΣ*
fluid *ΧΘΟΝΟΣ*, strong as the undertow
of the wave receding[48].
(82/526:561–2)

Pound weaves into this remarkable combination of copulation and

[a] late Nicolo and on this side and the other side of the Po.
[b] my man.
[c] she said, my husband.

death, recollections of Niccolo d'Este, his Renaissance Agamemnon, and Clytemnestra, wife and murderer of the classical Agamemnon. (He had reminded us of her at the beginning of the canto by having her announce—in a pastiche of Greek and Latin: 'My husband . . . dead by this hand.') It is, of course, the delirium of Niccolo d'Este in canto 20 that Pound had described to his father as 'a general paradiso'. Niccolo's delirium is brought on by his remorse over the execution of his bastard son, Ugo Aldovrandino, on Niccolo's own orders. He had discovered that his son and his wife, Parisina, had become lovers. His story, like that of Agamemnon, is one of love gone awry—although he is the executioner and not the victim. It is a story of the power of Aphrodite *deina*.

In the 'connubium terrae' Pound finds himself buried in the fluid of the earth ('fluid *CHTHONOS*'), and drunk with the ichor of the earth-born ('*ICHOR* of *CHTHONIOS*'). His vision is very different from Niccolo's, for he is himself the victim of Aphrodite, the mortal lover of Gea, Earth. Entry into paradise here is achieved through nothing other than death, seen as the sexual union of man and earth: 'the loneliness of death came upon me/(at 3 P.M. for an instant)'. Unlike Niccolo, Pound is not buried naked; he merely experiences at Pisa the despair of death: 'but I will come out of this knowing no one/neither they me'. However, like Odysseus, and like Dante, he experiences death without dying. Odysseus' visit to the dead under the protection of a goddess with whom he has lain is here short-circuited so that the two acts are one.

The 'connubium terrae' vision is Eleusinian in inspiration if not in detail. For Pound, the central rite of Eleusis 'is the coition and *not* the going to a fat-buttocked priest'. He incorporates this view of the matter in the *Pisan Cantos*, but so cryptically as to have puzzled even the astute editors of the *Annotated Index*. It is contained in two widely separated Greek lines: *ΚΟΡΗ*, *'ΑΓΛΑΟΣ 'ΑΛΑΟΥ* (74/442:470), and ἀγλαὸς ἀλάου πόρνη Περσεφόνεια (80/494:527). The *Index* translates *alaou* as 'blind man', and perceives a reference to Tiresias. However, *alaou* can also be translated as 'darkness', and I believe this to be the correct translation. The two passages would thus read, respectively, 'Kore [,] the shining of the dark', and 'the shining of the dark [,] whore [,] Persephone'. The word, *porne*, translates as 'whore', but does not, of course, necessarily imply the *selling* of sexual favours. Koré (daughter) is the Eleusinian name of Persephone. She is *porne* because she is the primal bed-mate, without benefit of clergy. She is 'of the dark' because she dwells in the Underworld. She is 'shining' because her annual return to earth from the Underworld is celebrated at Eleusis by the showing forth of a bright light amid the darkness of the Telesterion. (Her return is annual, but the festival was celebrated only every fourth year.) This light or brightness is identified with the act of coition in canto 36: 'Sacrum, sacrum, inluminatio coitu' ('A sacred thing, a sacred thing, the illumination of coition'). And this declaration is recollected in canto 74:

> *Χθόνια γέα, Μήτηρ,*
> by thy herbs menthe thyme and basilicum,
> from whom and to whom,
> will never be more now than at present
> being given a new green katydid of a Sunday
> emerald, paler than emerald,
> minus its right propeller
> this tent is to me and *ΤΙΘΩΝΩΙ*
> eater of grape pulp
> in coitu inluminatio.
>
> (74/435:462)

It is true that in canto 80 the Greek line is followed by Circe's reference to Tiresias, 'Still hath his mind entire', quoted earlier in canto 39 in Greek, and translated in canto 47. It is, no doubt, this collocation which prompted the *Index* to translate *ἀλάου* as 'blind man'. But the reference is not so much to Tiresias as it is to Odysseus' descent following his union with Circe. The preceding two lines refer both to Tiresias, and to death: 'Nothing but death, said Turgenev (Tiresias)/is irreparable'. In short, it is not Tiresias' blindness that Pound has in mind, but his dwelling in darkness among the dead with the gift of knowledge.

In the preceding canto (79) Pound created his own version of the Eleusinian nights signalled by a recollection of Circe's directions to Odysseus, 'Prepare to go on a journey'. He finds himself

> and on the hill of the Maelids
> in the close garden of Venus
> asleep amid serried lynxes
> set wreathes on Priapus *Ἴακχος, Io! Κύθηρα, Io!*
> having root in the equities
> Io!
>
> (79/489:521)

In the Eleusinian Mysteries the worshippers journeyed in procession from the Agrai in Athens to Eleusis shouting, 'Iacchos', the name of a youthful god sometimes identified with Dionysus. Priapus and Aphrodite are not known to have been invoked, but the phallic god and the goddess of love belong in Pound's Eleusis.

On the next page the Eleusinian character of the events described becomes unmistakable:

> *Ἴακχε, Ἴακχε, Χαῖρε, AOI*
> 'Eat of it not in the under world'
> See that the sun or the moon bless thy eating
> *Κόρη, Κόρη*, for the six seeds of an error
> or that the stars bless thy eating
>
> O Lynx, guard this orchard,
> Keep from Demeter's furrow.
>
> (79/490:522)

In the Homeric Hymn to Demeter, Persephone is doomed to remain one third of the year in the Underworld with Pluto, despite the best efforts of her mother and the gods of Olympus, because Pluto 'secretly gave her sweet pomegranate seed to eat'.[49] But Demeter tells her that 'when the earth shall bloom with the fragrant flowers of spring in every kind, then from the realm of darkness and gloom thou shalt come up once more to be a wonder for gods and mortal men'.[50] In Pound's version, however, Pluto seems not to have any role, and it is the Corn Goddess, Demeter, who appears to represent the threat of death: 'Keep from Demeter's furrow'.

Pound continues, invoking Pomona, a minor goddess of fruit trees, and places himself in an orchard 'That is named Melagrana/or the Pomegranate field'. He is among lynxes, animals identified as sacred to Dionysus in canto 2 where the god instructs Acoetes:

> 'From now, Acoetes, my altars,
> Fearing no bondage,
> fearing no cat of the wood,
> Safe with my lynxes,
> feeding grapes to my leopards,
> Olibanum is my incense,
> the vines grow in my homage.'
>
> (2/8–9:12)

Dionysus Zagreus is sometimes represented in the role of Pluto in vase paintings, but Pound does not name him in canto 79. He does suggest 'the fragrant flowers of spring' promised by Demeter:

> Cythera, here are lynxes
> Will the scrub-oak burst into flower?
> There is a rose vine in this underbrush
> Red? white? No, but a colour between them
> When the pomegranate is open and the light falls
> half thru it.
>
> (79/490:523)

But this is 'the close garden of Venus', and it is she who is addressed, not Koré. Dionysus' lynxes, which guard the orchard, are warned to 'beware of these vine-thorns', and are given the *glaukopis*, 'gleaming' or 'owl-like' eyes of Athena. Aphrodite is again addressed, and other foods than the pomegranate seed are mentioned —notably the acorns Circe fed to Odysseus' metamorphosed men:

> Kuthera, here are Lynxes and the clicking of crotales
> There is a stir of dust from old leaves
> Will you trade roses for acorns
> Will lynxes eat thorn leaves?
> What have you in that wine jar?
> ἰχώρ, for lynxes?
>
> (79/491:523)

Aphrodite appears to be offering drink, an act that does not occur in the Mysteries. However, the initiates do drink of the Kykeon as part of the rite. Pound seems to be recalling Circe's offer of 'dreadful drugs' to Odysseus, a drink which (were it not for Hermes' *moly*) would have changed him into a pig and put him in Circe's thrall, much as Persephone was put in Pluto's power by eating pomegranate seeds.[51]

Pound's ceremony does not correspond to what is known of the Eleusinian rites, but it would appear to be, none the less, his own synoptic version of the mystic nights wherein Aphrodite is the principal goddess. As at Eleusis, he waits three nights for the revelation:

> We are here waiting the sun-rise
> and the next sunrise
> for three nights amid lynxes. For three nights
> of the oak-wood

and the vines are thick in their branches
    no vine lacking flower

(79/491:523–4)

Finally, at sunrise, Aphrodite—or a statue of Aphrodite—is drawn into the pomegranate field:

Therein is the dance of the bassarids
    Therein are centaurs
And now Priapus with Faunus
    The Graces have brought *'Αφροδίτην*
    Her cell is drawn by ten leopards
        O lynx, guard my vineyard
        As the grape swells under vine leaf
        ῞Ηλιος is come to our mountain
        there is a red glow in the carpet of pine spikes.

(79/491–2:524)

The goddess drawn in procession is a recurrent motif in the *Cantos*, although it is somewhat different in each occurrence. In canto 17 Nerea is drawn in a boat 'without sound'; in 20 it is apparently Vanoka who is drawn by panthers; and in canto 4 it would seem that the Virgin Mary is drawn in procession.[52] This appearance of Aphrodite conforms more closely to these earlier processions in the *Cantos* than to anything known of Eleusis.

The whole concludes with an 'explanation' of Aphrodite's significance:

This Goddess was born of sea-foam
She is lighter than air under Hesperus
    δεινὰ εἶ, Κύθηρα[a]
terrible in resistance
    Κόρη καὶ Δήλια καὶ Μαῖα[b]
trine as praeludio
    Κύπρις 'Αφρόδιτη
a petal lighter than sea-foam
    Κύθηρα
        aram
        nemus
        vult[c]
O puma, sacred to Hermes, Cimbica servant of Helios.

(79/492:525)

[a] 'You are fearful, Cythera.'
[b] Koré and Delia and Maia.
[c] the grove needs an altar.

Although Aphrodite's cell is 'drawn by ten leopards', she herself is 'lighter than air', 'lighter than sea-foam'. She is, in short, an evanescent and fugitive apparition, in keeping with Pound's notion of paradise as 'spezzato'. Koré herself, Artemis, and Maia are apparently goddesses who somehow serve as prelude to Aphrodite. It is not possible to be certain in just what sense they do prepare one for Aphrodite. Koré is, of course, a daughter, a victim of rape, and is bound to Pluto and the Underworld by 'the six seeds of an error'. Artemis is the virgin huntress, of whom one might say that she has abjured entirely the rites of love in favour of the rites of death. Maia has no cult of her own, but is known as the couch-mate of Zeus and mother of Hermes. In cantos 4 and 5 Danaë was invoked as the mortal wife of Zeus—and she was also a victim of his love. But Maia is neither mortal nor a victim. She is merely the lover of Zeus and mother of Hermes, the messenger of the gods, transporter of souls, and patron of thieves. Perhaps it is in her extra-marital motherhood that we should seek her significance. We would then have three kinds of 'love' as a prelude to Aphrodite: enforced marriage, murderous virginity, and adultery.

It is probably as symbols or manifestations of three possible, but imperfect arrangements of human sexual relationships in an ascending scale, that these goddesses are to be understood. Aphrodite would then represent sexuality in a noumenal role, free of all social, physical, and reproductive functions. Such a reading would be in keeping with Pound's queries in 'Psychology and Troubadours':

> The problem, in so far as it concerns Provence, is simply this: Did this 'chivalric love' this exotic, take on mediumistic properties? Stimulated by the color or quality of emotion, did that 'color' take on forms interpretive of the divine order? Did it lead to an 'exteriorization of the sensibility,' and interpretation of the cosmos by feeling?[53]

The invented Eleusinian ceremony of canto 79 is an attempt to externalize, to express in impersonal terms, his faith in the primacy and sanctity of human perception. The mode would seem to be alien to the modern temperament, for which the gods and goddesses are dead. The very obscurity of the Eleusinian elements in the *Cantos* suggests a certain discomfort and uncertainty in the handling of such material on the part of Pound himself. The names of gods and goddesses are frequently talismans of an indecipherable significance—as the many divinities in the ceremony of canto 79. In general, the Eleusinian background has failed to communicate to readers and critics. Only Noel Stock has acknowledged the importance to Pound of Eleusis, and he finds it to be rather desperate and tendentious.[54]

I cannot agree with Stock's assessment of the religious or Eleusinian dimension of the *Cantos*, but his criticisms do have some point. The weakest aspect of the whole structure is Pound's insistence upon a bridge between his faith in the validity of the entire range of human experience (including the ineffable), and the existence in history of other groups sharing that faith. This insistence leads him to fictionalize history—not simply to make it fit a pattern such as that of the Trojan cycle, but to assert a continuity of belief where none can be shown to exist, as in the assertion of a continuity between the Albigenses and Eleusis. In itself such an unprovable assertion is harmless enough in a poem attempting to gather 'from the air a live tradition'. However, such a fictionalized history—which exceeds not only historical evidence, but also historical plausibility—may seriously interfere with the reader's willingness to accept the poem's secular history. That history, too, is fictionalized, but in a clearly poetic or structural way that renders it intelligible and meaningful within the poem. One can accept the fictionalization of secular history because it has an aesthetic and rhetorical function. The fictionalization of the religious history, on the other hand, is designed to enhance the credibility of the religious views expressed. In effect, the reader is asked to accept Pound's religious views because of their supposed antiquity.

Stock complains, drawing especially on the *Rock-Drill* section, of Pound's device of accepting similarities of a formal nature between different groups as evidence of identity:

> What does need saying about Pound's method, especially as he uses it in the later cantos, and as it is often used by other writers on the occult, is that there is no necessary connection between people who use the same ritual or symbols. The use, for instance, of a certain symbolism by Dante and its use again by some individual or group five hundred years later does not prove a connection between the two. It proves neither that there was a living tradition by which the symbolism was handed down, nor even basic similarities in belief. A tradition traced out by this method alone is based on nothing more solid than faulty reasoning.[55]

Stock's criticism of Pound's historiography is no doubt sound, but it is surely much too literal-minded to be applied to a work of the imagination. And it ignores Pound's claim to be writing morphological history on the model of anthropology, whose primary interest—at least in Pound's authors, Frazer and Frobenius—was in the discovery of analogy between the forms of ritual and myth in one culture and another, or one age and another. The validity of the Eleusinian tradition as the religion of the *Cantos* does not depend upon historical evidence, but rather upon the nature of the cult itself—or the nature it can plausibly be said to have had, since, after all, it remains a mystery. Thus Pound's claim of a historical continuity—and therefore Stock's criticism of that claim—is quite beside the point, except as criticism of Pound's rhetoric. The cryptic assertions of historical continuity in *Rock-Drill* and *Thrones*, however, are very often counter-productive.

In any event one cannot come to any understanding of a poem or a poet by complaining that he ought not to have done whatever it is that he has done. Pound's Eleusis is not a faith many could or would adopt. Like Yeats's mysticism, Pound's Eleusis is a key to his poetry, and one that is perhaps less remote from the mainstream of modern thought than Yeats's gyres and Faculties.

Eleusis is a cult of the chthonic, uniting in the doubled goddess and god the double process of death and birth. As we have seen, the rites lead to a revelation, something seen. Their *raison d'etre*, as it were, is to produce in the faithful a psychic experience, an encounter with the divine, which mystically transforms the lives of the initiates. Eleusis has no moral teaching, no theology, no cosmology, and no eschatology. It is thought to be, as practised at Athens, a survival of the most primitive religious sensibility.

The very rudimentary quality of the Eleusinian cult makes it appropriate to Pound's poetic and imaginative needs. The vast theological, metaphysical, and philosophical superstructure which Christianity erected around its own creed had been visibly crumbling since at least the sixteenth century, until for Pound and his contemporaries, belief in this enormous structure had become virtually impossible except at great, and often crippling intellectual effort.[56] But a primitive cult like Eleusis asks no more of its adherents than that they share in a psychic experience. And, moreover, that psychic experience—according to rumours at least—is closely associated with the universally known physical experience of sexual orgasm. In effect, by going back to Eleusis, Pound no doubt believed himself to be going back to the very rock bed of human religious sensibility. For most nominally Christian sensibilities, it is distasteful to associate religion with the erotic—even now, despite Freud, Jung, and D. H. Lawrence—unless the association is clearly metaphorical, as it can be seen to be in much devotional poetry and mystical writing. It is doubtful that anything can be said which would overcome a distaste based on two thousand years of culture. But it can be recognized, intellectually at least, that sexual orgasm must surely be the most significant psychic experience of men and women who live in their five senses and have neither time nor letters for abstract thought. It must be, then (as Frazer rather unwittingly demonstrated), that such a primal conception of ecstasy lies hidden below the collapsing superstructure of Christendom. Freud surely revealed the same possibility in his clinical discovery of the role of sexuality in human behaviour and thought, but without the historical method of Frazer.

Frazer saw the evidence of sexuality in the origins of religions as tending to discredit religion itself. Freud believed that civilization rested upon the successful sublimation of the primal sexual urge into other activities. Both of them regarded sexuality as a darkness within, which must be curbed lest men return to the ignorance and brutality of the past. However, the poet has never feared sexuality as do the philosopher and historian—perhaps because his mind is attuned to the discovery of correspondences whereas the philosopher seeks to draw distinctions. In poetry there is no 'either . . . or', but rather metaphor: 'this is also that'. The discovery that religion is founded on the erotic sensibility is not received by the poet as a discrediting of religion, but rather as a revelation that religion can be reconstructed from the rock bed of a universal experience.

D. H. Lawrence sought to elevate the ordinary sexual experience of men and women to the level of religious ecstasy in his novels. Pound's more historical imagination leads him to adopt the ancient mythical formulations of religious ecstasy, whose metaphorical base was human and animal sexuality. Lawrence is frequently misunderstood because his readers confuse his intention with that of the much more numerous novelists who deal in romantic erotica. Pound, too, is frequently misunderstood because his readers mistakenly assume that the mythical apparatus of the *Cantos* functions as a network of allusions to classical literature, when it is, in fact, an effort to reach back to the pre-classical religious sensibility:

I offer for Mr. Eliot's reflection the thesis that our time has overshadowed the mysteries by an overemphasis on the individual. . . . Eleusis did not distort truth by exaggerating the individual, neither could it have violated the individual spirit. Only in the high air and the great clarity can there be a just estimation of values. Romantic poetry, on the other hand, almost requires the concept of reincarnation as part of its mechanism. No apter metaphor having been found for certain emotional colours. I assert that the Gods exist.[57]

Even more clearly, he cites in 'Terra Italica' (where he argues that Eleusis persisted through the Albigenses to Cavalcanti) the following paragraph with approval:

Paganism, which at the base of its cosmogonic philosophy set the sexual phenomena whereby Life perpetuates itself mysteriously throughout the universe, not only did not disdeign [*sic*] the erotic factor in its religious institutions but celebrated it and exalted it, precisely because it encountered in it the marvelous vital principle infused by invisible Divinity into manifest nature.[58]

Fortunately it is not part of the task of the present study to convince its readers of the theological or historical verity of Pound's religious views. It is only necessary to understand that Pound sees himself to be returning to the psychic and historical well-head of religion in the adoption of Eleusis as his 'faith'. It is a faith which does not require the 'bluff based upon ignorance' of dogma, and asks only that one believe in the primacy of felt experience, *and* the testimony of extraordinary (or mystic, if you will) experience.

VIII · The Later Cantos

I. THE EARTHLY PARADISE

THE *Pisan Cantos* internalized the poem's search for an ideal polity, turning from the collective past of cultural achievement, from political and economic wisdom to a personal past of cultural awareness and political failure. For the first time in the poem everything is seen from the perspective of the speaker's immediate and actual situation. As discontinuous, allusive, and cryptic as ever, the *Pisan Cantos* reclaim the traditional rhetorical ground of coherence—a single speaking voice. And with that single speaking voice returns the emotional bond between reader and author so conspicuously absent from the poem until that point. The impersonal and multitudinous voices of the past are now heard through the filter of a single recollecting mind and voice. To come to the *Pisan Cantos* after the *Fifth Decad*, China, and Adams is to come home again to familiar human discourse after having been kept reeling in nightmarish vertigo by an unceasing babble of disembodied voices.

The *Pisan Cantos* demonstrate, with greater force than any critical argument, the rhetorical failure of Pound's technique of direct transcription of the historical record into his poem. That technique —begun with the Malatesta cantos, but not fully expunging the sense of a speaking voice until the *Fifth Decad*—deprives the reader of the only ground of rhetorical continuity possible in Pound's poem. In the large scale, the *Cantos*' rhetorical organization is like that of a drama—or, still better, a film—in which the scene and the speaking personae are constantly shifting and only occasionally aware of the existence of the other speakers on stage at the same time. Pound himself compared the poem to a radio drama in which you identify the speakers by 'the noise they make'. It is a *Waiting for Godot* with a cast of thousands, lasting for a dozen or more hours and with a specific lesson—or whole textbook of lessons—to teach. But there is no stage, no silver screen, no actors, and there is, of course, no story, no plot, no denouement. Without coherence of plot, setting, or character, without discursive development, the poem must rely for *rhetorical* coherence upon the speaking voice. With the exception of the mythical cantos, concerned with the Odysseus/Eleusis subject, that voice has been multitudinous until the *Pisan Cantos* and has not provided rhetorical coherence.

To argue that the *Cantos* failed to achieve rhetorical coherence before the *Pisan Cantos* is not, of course, to argue that the poem lacks rational coherence. Indeed, those parts of the poem which are least coherent rhetorically—the historical cantos—are the parts most obviously coherent on rational grounds. They depend upon Pound's economic reading of history, which is perfectly coherent and rational—however erroneous and partisan it may be. Conversely, rhetorical coherence does not guarantee rational coherence. One may babble any sort of nonsense in the strictest of couplets. The primary purpose of this study has been to elucidate the rational coherence of those portions of the poem that demonstrate the greatest rhetorical coherence.

Rhetoric is a term that has fallen into disuse except as one of condemnation implying a lack of sincerity in the use of language, or the organization of discourse on recognizable and disapproved models. But, of course, all speech is rhetorical, that is, organized to achieve some effect upon its auditor. A speaker or writer may utter the first thing that comes into his head, thereby avoiding that self-conscious and calculating organization of his utterance which he recognizes as rhetoric, but his auditor or reader will still be confronted with utterance that is organized somehow, and therefore possesses a rhetorical dimension. If the proverbial *n*th monkey fortuitously typed out *Hamlet*, it would have precisely the same rhetorical organization as the play written by Shakespeare. Only silence and gibberish are unrhetorical.

The poet may be distinguished from other men by the greater acuity of his senses, or the greater sensitivity of his soul, but his utterance can be distinguished from other men's only by its rhetoric. He may reveal to us the world of men, or of gods, or even our own hidden souls, but in so far as his revelation is conveyed in language, it is manifest in rhetoric. Hence, the primary critical issue for any poem is a rhetorical one. Pound's rhetoric, as we have seen, is based upon certain presumptions about the nature of the intelligible universe and the nature of human intellection. He assumes, following Plato, that the universe is of the same nature as the human mind, and further assumes that the patterns of the sensible universe reveal the patterns of the intelligible universe. On this epistemological theory, the patterns themselves are not directly knowable. They are revealed only through the congregation of particular sensible data. Hence one who is interested to learn must gather information and wait patiently for the patterns to reveal themselves. The progress of the *Cantos* mime this patient attendance upon revelation, and Pound repeatedly enjoins his readers to exercise patience.

As we have seen, the historical and economic revelation appears to Pound in canto 46 via Christopher Hollis, whose *Two Nations* provides the intellectual force field organizing Pound's congeries of particulars into a lucid pattern—or, at least, so Pound declares, substituting assertion for demonstration. But this intellectual revelation, retroactively 'explaining' much of the information contained in the poem, did nothing to resolve the problem of rhetorical coherence. Indeed, it is after the composition of canto 46 (dated 1935) that Pound begins to request patience of his readers who ask him to explain what it is all about. Committed by his epistemology and the artistic practice of his peers to the avoidance of plot or single story line, and of a single speaking voice, and further committed by the same factors to a discontinuous textual surface, Pound resorted to the desperate device of borrowing a species of rhetorical coherence from de Mailla's history of China and the *Works* of John Adams. This device achieved a limited rhetorical success in that the Chinese and Adams cantos are more accessible to the reader than earlier sections, but they are less worth reading. Such a degree of coherence as they possess is achieved at the cost of prolixity and simple blandness—not to mention the peculiarity that scarcely a line is of original composition.

It is not uncommon to praise the *Cantos* for the uncompromising variegation and discontinuity of their rhetorical surface.[1] And, indeed, it is both correct and necessary to praise the artistry of this rhetoric, and to describe the aesthetic pleasure it affords. A poem *is* rhetoric. If we reject the rhetoric, we reject the poem. Moreover, Pound's rhetorical theories and example have influenced profoundly three generations of poets. None the less, Pound's rhetoric was unable to generate the coherence required by a long poem without the introduction of the single speaking voice—a device he avoided until the *Pisan Cantos*. In other words, while it is correct to argue for the metrical and verbal brilliance of canto 4, or 20, or 45, it is wrong to ignore the failure of these cantos—taken singly or together—to achieve an acceptable level of rhetorical coherence. The standard of what *is* an acceptable level of rhetorical coherence for an unexampled poem like the *Cantos* can only be set by the poem itself, and that standard is set by the *Pisan Cantos*.

In the typescript of the *Pisan Cantos* at Yale the last line is the date, 'Oct. 1945'. On the 30th of that month Pound celebrated his sixtieth birthday. On the 18th of November he stepped off a plane in Washington, D.C., facing charges of treason. Of course, he never stood trial on those charges, being found mentally unfit. Asked at the court hearing from what delusions Pound suffered, Dr. Overholser replied: 'Well, I think they are both delusions of grandeur and delusions of persecution, both of which are characteristic of what we call the paranoid condition.'[2] A subsequent trial judged him of unsound mind, and he was committed to St. Elizabeth's in February of 1946. Pound remained in St. Elizabeth's until April of 1958 when the indictment for treason was withdrawn, and he was released in the care of his wife.

Pound's political and economic views did not undergo any significant change during his confinement. He attracted to himself not only a whole generation of younger writers, but also anti-Semites and right-wing extremists. He continued his reading in economics and history, and published translations, but no cantos beyond the Pisan section, until 1955 when canto 85 appeared in the *Hudson Review*. Asked about the *Cantos* while at St. Elizabeth's he replied:

> Well, you know, Grandpa can't do it all—he's gettin' old. Well, what I mean to say, Grandpa's burst his mainspring. Now it's up to your generation to raise the cultural status.
>
> All that quoting from different languages is just the easiest way to show that it's all been said before. If I don't translate as such, well, the same ideas in English are in the neighbourhood.
>
> It takes a while till you get your bearings—like a detective story—and see how it's going to go. I hit my stride in the *Fifth Decad of Cantos*.[3]

Nonetheless, he returned to the *Cantos*, writing *Rock-Drill* and most of *Thrones* before he left St. Elizabeth's. Given Pound's situation, one could hardly expect these later cantos to be predictable from what preceded them. The twenty-five cantos in these two sections were published between 1955 and 1959, and were probably written in a similar period—say six years—and when Pound was in his seventies. For all their shortcomings, they are among the most remarkable poetry ever written by a man of that age. In them the memorious reverie which had proved such an effective rhetorical device in the *Pisan Cantos*, becomes more obsessive, more garrulous, and more obscure. The historical documentation—which had descended to mere slavish redaction in the Chinese and Adams cantos—becomes in the later cantos nothing more than marginalia and underlinings of specific texts. But the subjects remain the same—now very nearly reduced to the simplicity of the formula: gold versus the gods. And beneath the nearly impenetrable surface of the old man's mumblings lies an astonishing—indeed obsessive—coherence. Even more remarkably, there is not a little poetry of great power.

Pound was, from his youth, an exceptionally bookish poet. He sought inspiration in what other men had experienced, and taught himself to imitate their voices when writing about their experiences. The *Cantos* are a record of Pound's mind—a palimpsest of a lifetime's reading. Even the intensely private *Pisan Cantos* effectively transform a personal disaster into a recollection of other poets and other poetry—both ancient and modern. The later cantos enter entirely into a world of books—perhaps escaping the intolerable environment of St. Elizabeth's, but also extending and intensifying a lifelong habit: 'Man reading shd. be man intensely alive. The book shd. be a ball of light in one's hand.'[4]

Any study of the *Cantos* must be a history of Pound's reading. The books he read are the ground upon which he traces the figures of his poetry. Sometimes the poetry is autonomous and independent of this ground—as in the *Pisan Cantos*. Very frequently it is not. There is nothing particularly unusual or vicious in the dependence of the *Cantos* on the European library. Indeed poetry has always been bookish—or at least was until the Age of Sensibility taught poets to be introspective. Shakespeare, Spenser, and Milton made poetry out of what they read as much as out of what they saw. The difference is that Pound made poetry only some of the time. All too often he is concerned only to teach, forgetting his obligation to delight and to move his readers.

But for all their bookishness, the later cantos maintain the single speaking voice of the *Pisan Cantos*, making them rhetorically much less dependent on their sources. At the same time, many cantos are literally marginalia on specific texts, and quite unintelligible without reference to those texts. Pound frequently identifies his sources, and even provides page references to them as he had not done before. This helpfulness amounts to an admission that the later cantos are intended to direct the reader to further study, and that they are not an autonomous work. In other words, the later cantos drop the pretence of including history, and merely make reference to other studies of history and economics, as well as to some documents of actual governmental regulation. They represent the nadir of the poem's didacticism—a mumbling over of unexplained verities, the *disjecta membra* of a political and religious philosophy known only to Ezra Pound.

Most of the sources not identified by Pound himself were identified by Noel Stock in *Reading the Cantos*, and have been copiously annotated in the pages of Eva Hesse's *New Approaches to Ezra Pound*, and in *Paideuma*. The bulk of this annotation now far exceeds that of the poetry itself, and it is some way from completion. The list of works on which Pound draws is formidable: cantos 85–6, *Chou King*, Texte chinoise avec une double traduction en français et en latin des annotations et un vocabulaire, par S. Couvreur, Sien Hsien: Imprimerie de la Mission Catholique, 1934 (4th ed.); cantos 88–9, T. H. Benton, *Thirty Years View*, New York: D. Appleton, 1854, 2 vols.; canto 91, Layamon, *Brut*, John Heydon, *The Holy Guide*, London, 1662, Philostratus, *The Life of Apollonius of Tyana*, trans. F. C. Conybeare, Loeb Classical Library; canto 93, L. A. Waddell, *Egyptian Civilization, Its Sumerian Origin*, London, 1930; canto 96, Paulus Diaconus, *De Gestis langobardorum* (in Migne's *Patrologia Latina*), *Eparchon Biblion: Le Livre du Préfet*, ed. Jules Nicole, Geneva: H. Georg, 1893 (text in Greek, Latin, and French); canto 97, Alexander Del Mar, *A History of Monetary Systems*, Chicago, 1896; cantos 98–9, *The Sacred Edict* of K'Ang-Hsi, ed. F. W. Baller, the China Inland Mission, Shanghai, 1924; canto 101, J. F. Rock, *The Ancient Na-Khi Kingdom of Southwest China*, Cambridge, 1948, 2 vols., *Memoirs of Mme de Rémusat*, trans. Mrs. Cashel Hoey and John Lillie, London, 1880, 2 vols.; canto 105, the life and works of Saint Anselm as in Migne's *Patrologia*; and cantos 107–9, Coke, *Institutes*, Catherine Drinker Bowen, *The Lion and the Throne*, Boston: Little, Brown, 1956. The list is not exhaustive, but indicates those works most heavily drawn upon.

It is not possible to read through *Thrones* and *Rock-Drill* with any comprehension unless one has some knowledge of their relationship to those works listed above. A careful study of any one of them will reveal that Pound excerpts phrases, sentences, and paragraphs which strike him as important or interesting, and interposes remarks of his own, or citations from other works such as the *Odyssey* or the *Commedia.* Christopher Hollis's history of the iniquity of banks remains a guiding light, and is supplemented by the monetary studies of the American, Alexander Del Mar. These two men, above all, guide Pound's hand and eye in his search of the historical record for the principles of good government. For that is the didactic purpose of *Rock-Drill* and *Thrones*: the elucidation of the principles of good government—as Pound himself suggests in the note at the end of canto 85, 'Kung said he had added nothing. Canto 85 is a somewhat detailed confirmation of Kung's view that the basic principles of government are found in the Shu, the History Classic.'

Astonishingly, Pound finds his models of good government in ancient China, in the Rome of Antoninus, in Byzantium, and in the England of Athelstan and Elizabeth. This odd collocation of governmental models is achieved by the application of economic touchstones: control of the issue of currency, low interest rates, the government acting as its own banker, government control of production and trade, and the promotion of the guild system of manufacture. The last two principles hark back to the guild socialism of A. R. Orage and the *New Age*, and through him to the medievalism in economics of Ruskin and William Morris. The first three come from Douglas, Hollis, and Del Mar. Villains—such as our old friends Biddle, Roosevelt, and Churchill—are identified by the application of the same touchstone.

The long, eclectic, and esoteric bibliography of sources of the later cantos reflects Pound's effort to validate his didactic message, as well as evincing a full retreat from the world in which he lived. But the message is much simpler and much less esoteric than the bewildering array of languages and references would suggest. It is put with considerable succinctness by the presiding master of these cantos, Alexander Del Mar:

That which has engaged the attention without harmonizing the convictions of such master minds as Aristotle, Plato, Tycho Brahe, Copernicus, Locke, Newton, Smith, Bastiat, and Mill, is surely a study which none can afford to approach with rashness, nor to leave with complacency. Money is perhaps the mightiest engine to which man can lend an intelligent guidance. Unheard, unfelt, unseen, it has the power to so distribute the burdens, gratifications, and opportunities of life that each individual shall enjoy that share of them to which his merits or good fortune may fairly entitle him, or, contrariwise, to dispense them with so partial a hand as to violate every principle of justice, and perpetuate a succession of social slaveries to the end of time.[5]

Pound learned from Del Mar that the coinage of gold was originally a sacred privilege, belonging to the Roman pontifex. Julius Caesar took the office of pontifex to himself, and thereby the right of coinage, which remained with the Roman emperor until the fall of Byzantium. The Muslim ruler, Habdimelich (Abd-el-Melik), of whom Paulus Diaconus speaks in canto 96, challenged this right by coining his own gold.

It is the right to coin gold (or print paper money) that bestows economic power, rather than the possession of gold:

Monometallism and bimetallism [that is, a gold standard of value, or a gold and silver standard] both imply that money consists of a metal or metals, and that this is what measures value. The implication is erroneous; the theory is physically impossible. Value is not a thing, nor an attribute of things; it is a relation, a numerical relation, which appears in exchange. Such a relation cannot be accurately measured without the use of numbers, limited by law, and embodied in a set of concrete symbols, suitable for transference from hand to hand. It is this set of symbols which, by metonym, is called money.[6]

The discovery that this right was originally a sacerdotal privilege, provides the aged Pound with a means of restructuring his history in terms of an opposition between the church and the state. When church and state were united in a single body—as in China, Byzantium, and England after the Reformation—justice and plenty would prevail. When they were divided—as in the Middle Ages after the fall of Byzantium—justice would depend upon the willingness of rulers to follow the advice of the Church. Anselm's difficulties with William Rufus (son of William the Conqueror) are a case in point:

Anselm versus damn Rufus
'Ugly? a bore,
          Pretty, a whore!'
                    brother Anselm is pessimistic,
digestion weak,
          but had a clear line on the Trinity, . . .
                                        (105/750:775)

When both church and state surrender the privilege of issuing money to private individuals, we have usurocracy, date: 1694.

Having selected ideal periods and heroes for his heavenly thrones, Pound seeks moral and religious nuggets of wisdom to elaborate his vision of an ideal polity. For example, in canto 85 (547:583) we find 'III. 6. xi, Right here is the Bill of rights', followed by seven Chinese characters. The numbers refer to Couvreur's edition of the *Chou King*, section xi of Chapter 6 of Part III:

> Un prince sans sujets n'aurait pas à qui commander; un peuple sans prince n'aurait pas à qui obéir. Ne cherchez pas à vous grandir en rabaissant les autres. Si un homme ou une femme du peuple n'a pas la liberté de s'appliquer de toutes ses forces (à faire le bien), le maitre du peuple aura un secours de moins, et le bien qu'il doit faire ne sera pas complet.

> A prince without subjects would not have anyone to rule; a people without a prince would not have anyone to obey. Do not try to improve your own lot by depriving others. If an ordinary man or woman is not free to apply himself with all his strength (to do good), the master of the people will have one less care, and the good which he ought to do will not be complete.

The Chinese characters translate literally: 'ordinary men and women seize full development for themselves'. The ideal reader who understands Chinese would get a much more liberal and egalitarian sense of the advice which I In (or Y Yin) gave to the emperor T'ai Kia than one who read the whole section in Couvreur. But even if we disregard Pound's distortion of I In's advice, the nature of the wisdom hardly justifies the labour of discovering it or the importance Pound attaches to it.

Clearly it is the *provenance* of fine sentiments and wise observations that is most important to Pound in the later cantos, and it is their provenance that he puts most clearly before his readers. It is important to him to construct a political and moral philosophy grounded in the past. In *Rock-Drill* and *Thrones* he pursues the same path with the philosophy of government that he had earlier pursued with religion. The Poundian view of a paternalistic government presiding over a nation of protected and contented farmers, craftsmen, and artists, free to pursue their skills without interference from the usurious 'hoggers of harvest' must, like Eleusis, be seen to be a *recovery* of lost wisdom, of an ancient light burning dimly on through the ages.

Pound does put his message in (for him) plain language from time to time, and this is a departure from earlier practice, reflecting the presence of a single speaking voice:

> But if you will follow this process
> 德[a]
> not a lot of signs, but the one sign
> etcetera
> plus always *Τέχνη*
> and from *Τέχνη* back to ςεαυτόν
> Neither by chinks, nor by sophists,
> nor by hindoo immaturities.
> (85/546:582)

Virtue from Confucius and technique (or science perhaps) from Aristotle will lead us back to self-possession. The dismissal of Sophists and Hindus reflects well-established Poundian judgements, but it is a surprise that the Chinese are also dismissed. Perhaps it is because they lacked *techné*. Four pages later he elaborates a little:

> ½ research and ½ *Τέχνη*
> ½ observation, ½ *Τέχνη*
> ½ training ½ *Τέχνη*.
> (85/550:586)

In canto 98 he adds more light, now borrowing from the *Sacred Edict*:

> The King's job, vast as the swan-flight:
> thought built on Sagetrieb:[a]
> civil, the soldier's
> suns rise, the sun goes into shadow
> Hsuan, in the first tone 示 proclaim[b]
> a filiality that binds things together.
> First the pen yeh 本[c]
> then *Τέχνη* 業
> and to philosophise in old age (Ari's χαθόλου)[d]

[a] Tê: 'Virtue'.
[a] oral tradition.
[b] hsuan: 'proclaim'.
[c] root or original occupation or possessions.
[d] in general.

'and that the Buddha abandoned such splendours,
    is it likely!' . . .[7]

(98/686–7:716–17)

Baller translates pen yeh as 'proper callings', but Pound gives it a different sense (one permitted by the Chinese):

What a government usefully COULD do.
False middles serve neither commerce
    nor the NOOS in activity
That fine old word (Stink Saunders' word) 'an Independence'
本
業 pen yeh
Homestead versus kolschoz,
    advice to farms, not control.

(104/744–5:770)[8]

Pound had recorded his admiration for 'an independence' fifteen years before:

Let us note that at the beginning of the Nineteenth Century the 'mercantile' concept still retained traces of decency. Adams judged it 'hardly mercantile' to do business on borrowed capital. At that time individualism had its own probity, a modest but secure income was called an '*independence*'.[9]

Thus, to simplify slightly, Pound leads us via China, Rome, Byzantium, and England to the Jeffersonian dream of a nation of independent farmer yeomen: '"an Independence"/ . . . /Homestead versus Kolschoz,/advice to farms, not control'. The paper money of China, the interest rates of Rome, the trade regulation of Byzantium, and the guilds of Athelstan, combined with the *techné* of Greece and the *Te* (Virtue) of a Confucian emperor will create the eighteenth-century dream of pastoral America.

It is not a little ironic that Pound, the lover of cities and sophistication, who found American presidents rather a dull lot in the early 1920s, and who was still celebrating a dream of empire in 1945, should finally turn to the pastoral dream of his forefathers—a dream he had scorned for so long. And it is characteristic that he should find his way to it by as devious and esoteric, and un-American a route as one could imagine. (Although, one must admit that American political thinkers have always had a fondness for the republican examples of Greece and Rome. And the Virgil who led him to China was the Harvard graduate, Ernest Fenollosa.)

It is easy to mock the massive labour of the later cantos bringing forth the mouse of a pastoral kingdom. It is not my intention to mock Pound, but it does him no service to pretend that the later cantos are the record of a mature and profound wisdom. They are rather—in so far as they are didactic—the obsessive ramblings of an aged mind poring over old volumes. The mind is old, obsessed, and without tact, but it is not mad. That is to say, the utterance in the later cantos is not incoherent babbling. It is rather a cryptic *pointing*. The old man in his library (actually in St. Elizabeth's) is saying: 'Look there. That proves I was right. Look *there*. I discovered that thirty years ago.' His eagerness to find corroboration encourages him to make truly fantastic historical links—as we have already seen in the Chinese cantos. And he is content to trust the truth of his sources even when they are demonstrably unreliable, such as L. A. Waddell.[10] But if the later cantos are not the babblings of a madman, no more are they the utterance of a perfectly balanced and clear mind. Much wisdom is, no doubt, to be found in Pound's sources—in the *Chou King* or Coke's *Institutes*, or perhaps even the *Eparch's Book*—but that wisdom is not Pound's. Pound's appeal to it is an appeal to the sanctity of age as a validation of *his* wisdom, resting precariously on the jerry-rigged foundation of I In, Leo the Wise, and Coke, to mention only a few of his sages.

2. PARADISO

After completing the Adams section, Pound said that he wished to turn to questions of belief, and in 1944 he described the *Cantos* as a poem 'which begins "In the Dark Forest", crosses the Purgatory of human error, and ends in the light, *fra i maestri di color che sanno* [among the masters of those who know].'[11] Clearly he was preparing his readers for a concluding paradisal section of the *Cantos* on the model of Dante's *Commedia*. But, as we have seen, the *Cantos* do not in fact imitate Dante's processional movement through the tripartite world of the dead. Pound has no machinery whereby he can create a paradiso. Indeed, his whole conception of divinity militates against the notion of paradise as a *place* of bliss in the eternal presence of god. Just after the publication of *Thrones*, he described the relation he saw between the *Cantos* and the *Commedia*:

I was not following the three divisions of the *Divine Comedy* exactly. One can't follow the Dantesquan cosmos in an age of experiment. But I have made the division between people dominated by emotion, people struggling upwards, and those who have some part of the divine vision. The thrones in Dante's *Paradiso* are for the spirits of the people who have been responsible for good government. The thrones in the *Cantos* are an attempt to move out from egoism and to establish some definition of an order possible or at any rate conceivable on earth. One is held up by the low percentage of reason which seems to operate in human affairs. *Thrones* concerns the states of mind of people responsible for something more than their personal conduct.[12]

If we take this description at face value, Pound's paradiso would be some sort of account of people 'who have been responsible for good government', and of people 'who have some part of the divine vision'. The first group we have already found in Pound's marginalia on a number of books. Even if we grant that Pound's collection of *i maestri di color che sanno* belong in paradise, a network of cryptic allusions to them constitutes a highly tangential imitation of Dante. It is not clear that Pound would distinguish between the governors and the visionaries, but it is possible to distinguish between the didactic and visionary aspects of the later cantos. And it is in the visionary portions of the poem that we find poetry achieving rhetorical success comparable to the *Pisan Cantos*. Here the subjective lyric voice once again comes into its own because its subject is appropriate to its rhetoric, as the subject of the principles of good government is not.[13]

We do not encounter the lyric voice in *Rock-Drill* until canto 90:

> from under the rubble heap
>   m'elevasti
> from the dulled edge beyond pain,
>   m'elevasti
> out of Erebus, the deep-lying
>   from the wind under the earth
>   m'elevasti.
>   (90/606:640)

This lambent voice speaking of an emergence from rubble and oblivion must surely announce the beginning of the ascent into a paradiso.[14] An expectation which is reinforced by the following light and water imagery, and the metamorphosis of tree into stone—

ideograms of some kind of paradisal world, established in cantos 2, 4, and 20. Certainly we have emerged from the repetitive round of history into a bright, subjective, and pastoral world. But the penultimate passage of canto 90 repeats the motif of ascension with allusions that give rise to some uncertainty about the purely paradisal nature of the world into which one is emerging:

> out of Erebus, the delivered,
>   Tyro, Alcmene, free now, ascending
> e i cavalieri,
>   ascending,
> no shades more,
>   lights among them, enkindled,
> and the dark shade of courage,
>   *'Ηλέκτρα*
>   bowed still with the wrongs of Aegisthus.
> Trees die & the dream remains.
>
> (90/608–9:642)

Both these passages describing ascension allude to canto 1 through the phrase 'out of Erebus'. Canto 1 is, of course, a translation of the Homeric *nekuia* or calling forth of the dead (*Odyssey*, XI). When Odysseus pours blood into the ditch he has dug, there arise

> Souls out of Erebus, cadaverous dead, of brides
> Of youths and of the old who had borne much;
> Souls stained with recent tears, girls tender,
> Men many, mauled with bronze lance heads,
> Battle spoil, bearing yet dreory arms,
> These many crowded about me; . . .
>
> (1/3–4:7–8)

In canto 1 the souls are in no sense ascending into a paradise. They are merely shades, 'the impetuous, impudent dead' in Pound's phrase. In canto 90 they are 'no shades more'; they are delivered, 'free now, ascending'. Clearly it is an escape from death that is being described, but it would appear to be an escape into a world which contains 'the dark shade of courage' and '*Electra*,/bowed still with the wrongs of Aegisthus', that is to say, into a world far short of unadulterated heavenly bliss.

The two women, 'free now', and 'ascending', Tyro and Alcmene, are two of the shades to whom Odysseus spoke in the Underworld.

Tyro is given a place of honour in canto 2 where Poseidon's watery rape of her is described, but Alcmene, mother of Heracles, is not mentioned before the *Pisan Cantos*:

> between NEKUIA where are Alcmene and Tyro
> and the Charybdis of action
> to the solitude of Mt. Taishan
> femina, femina, that wd/ not be dragged into paradise by the hair,
> under the gray cliff in periplum
> the sun dragging her stars
> a man on whom the sun has gone down.
> (74/431:457–8)

Both women are 'brides' of gods although themselves mortals. They have both, as it were, tasted of paradise although they are in the Underworld. Although raped by gods, they have remained in the world of mortals because they were unable or unwilling to join the gods in paradise: 'femina, femina, that wd/not be dragged into paradise by the hair'. The grey cliff under which the poet finds himself is undoubtedly the cliff at Terracina on whose heights Pound claims the statue of Venus was once to be found. In the water at the foot of these sea-cliffs the poet is in an unpleasant state of suspension, a *periplus* which must be, in this context, an aimless wandering *between* the positive acts of raising the dead and actively confronting hostile forces: 'between NEKUIA . . . and the Charybdis of action'. Mount Taishan, the sacred mountain in China, is symbolically equivalent to the heights at Terracina; it is the dwelling place of the divinities, that is to say, paradise.

The ascent 'out of Erebus' in canto 90 is thus not clearly an ascent into paradise. In so far as the allusions to cantos 1 and 74 determine the sense of the descriptions of ascent in canto 90, the ascent is *from* death and it is into a world which contains both Electra still vengeful toward the murderers of her father, and 'i cavalieri', the knights of old whom Dante saw in the second circle of Hell.[15] It is true that Tyro, Alcmene, and Dante's knights are 'free now', 'no shades more', and are ascending, but an ascent is not a paradiso. And there is the inescapable and inharmonious 'Electra/bowed still with the wrongs of Aegisthus'.

The ascension is more like the return to the daylight world of the Eleusinian initiate, who, according to Plutarch, 'lives with pure and holy men', and 'sees on earth the crowd' of the uninitiated 'crush and jostle themselves in the mud and darkness'. The motif is continued in canto 91 together with the unmistakable allusions to Aphrodite, the touchstone for the paradisal motif in the *Cantos*:

> that the body of light come forth
>   from the body of fire
> And that your eyes come to the surface
>   from the deep wherein they were sunken,
> Reina—for 300 years
>   and now sunken
> That your eyes come forth from their caves
>   & light then
>   as the holly-leaf
>   qui laborate, orat
> Thus Undine came to the rock,
>   by Circeo
> and the stone eyes again looking seaward.
>   (91/610:644)

Reina, or 'the Queen' rises from the sea like Aphrodite herself—although her rising would appear to be a rebirth like that of Tyro and Alcmene, on the model of Persephone, but from the sea rather than from underground. It would not, I think, be profitable to attempt to attach a specific identity to Reina. She is, after all, not given a proper name, and can attract to herself the characteristics of Aphrodite, Persephone, Diana, Tyro and Alcmene, Miss Tudor, or the Princess Ra-Set. The importance of the passage for this discussion is the continuation of the motif of resurrection from canto 90, and the implication that the poem is moving into its paradiso.

Undine is said to have come 'to the rock' as did Reina ('Thus Undine came to the rock'). She is a water sprite or *ondine* whom Pound presumably remembers from Fréderic de la Motte Fouqué's tale, *Undine*.[16] In the tale she marries a mortal who is unfaithful to her, thus bringing down a fatal curse upon himself. Perhaps he too, like Tyro and Alcmene, has failed to enter paradise. However, Pound does not make use of Undine's story (there is only one further reference (93/623:656). He does make extensive use of Apollonius of Tyana who is the next figure introduced in the passage: 'Thus Appollonius /(if it was Apollonius)'.

Apollonius of Tyana was a first-century sage and miracle worker whom some put forward as a rival to Christ. As a Pythagorean and sun worshipper he ate no meat, disapproved of blood sacrifice, and wore clothes of pure linen only, not permitting animal skins or fabrics to touch his own skin. Pound's principal source for his treatment of Apollonius is F. C. Conybeare's Loeb translation of Philostratus' *Life of Apollonius of Tyana.*[17] Apollonius is particularly interesting because he has been everywhere that the *Cantos* have been. As reported in Philostratus' *Life*, he travels extensively throughout the ancient world (like Odysseus); he advises kings and emperors (as Pound imagined himself to be advising dictators and presidents); and (again like Pound) he is arrested and charged with treason—on two occasions, once by Nero and again by Domitian.

Apollonius is introduced into the poem as a lone male mortal in the company of ascending goddesses and mortal women, among them Helen of Tyre, remembered from Mead's lecture. Clearly he must somehow partake of this ascension, although a mortal and a man; in other words, Apollonius is part of the uncertain movement into 'paradise', is perhaps one who has attained whatever degree of paradisal repose is available in the *Cantos*. Certainly his recurrence on the next page is in the midst of imagery associated with the theophany of Aphrodite:

> Light & the flowing crystal
> never gin in cut glass had such clarity
> That Drake saw the splendour and wreckage
> in that clarity
> Gods moving in crystal
> ichor, amor
> Secretary of Nature, J. Heydon.
> Here Apollonius, Heydon
> hither Ocellus.
> (91/611:645)

Despite the fact that they are gods, not goddesses, 'moving in crystal', this passage inescapably echoes that in canto 23 (based on the *Hymn to Aphrodite*) where Aphrodite appears to Anchises, the father of Aeneas, disguised as the daughter of Otreus. As the groom of a goddess, Anchises is the male analogue of Tyro and Alcmene, 'brides' of gods. Those women are 'free now, ascending'. Apollonius, like Drake, may be supposed to have seen 'the splendour and wreckage/in that clarity'.

Pound has said that he 'made the division between people dominated by emotion, people struggling upwards, and those who have some part of the divine vision'. Apollonius is perhaps, one of *i maestri di color che sanno*, one of the masters of those who know.

But Apollonius is not the groom of a goddess like Anchises or Odysseus. His vision of paradise, his 'bust thru from quotidien into "divine or permanent world"' is of a different nature and is achieved in a different manner. Through Apollonius the *mythos* or 'story' of the *Cantos* is revisited and restructured; we move away from the Odyssean 'Charybdis of action' (which is history) toward a subjective world which is sometimes lyrical, sometimes visionary, and sometimes (as with Apollonius) magical. With Apollonius we encounter a third *nekuia* different from that of canto 1, and different also from the personal, memorious *nekuia* of the *Pisan Cantos*:

> That he passed the night on the mound of Achilles
> 'master of tempest and fire'
>   & he set up Palamedes
> an image that I, Philostratus, saw
>   and a shrine that will hold ten people drinking.
> 'It was not by ditch-digging and sheep's guts . . .
>   'in Aeolis close to Methymna'
> in the summer lightning, close upon cock-crow.[18]
>   (94/638:671)

Apollonius' *nekuia* is effortless and without either violence or fear, 'it was not by ditch-digging and sheep's guts'. Odysseus visits the dead in order to learn of his fate and how he may return home and restore Ithaca. He learns what he needs to know and does return home, but only after a perilous and uncertain journey. Apollonius, on the other hand, visits Achilles more out of respect than curiosity, and only incidentally learns of the neglect of Palamedes' tomb. Moreover, his restoration of Palamedes' statue—an act formally equivalent to Odysseus' restoration of Ithaca—is accomplished effortlessly and, in Philostratus' account, almost magically. Even though the episode of Palamedes' statue is given only cryptic treatment, it must be placed in juxtaposition with earlier historical action if it is to be properly understood. One need only bring to mind the great difficulties Malatesta encountered, and the dubious behaviour into which he fell in his effort to construct the Tempio, in order to understand that Apollonius enjoys a more perfect state of being. He is not—as Odysseus, Malatesta, and all the other earlier heroes of the poem are—engaged in the 'Charybdis of action'.

The historical action of the *Cantos* is concerned with what Gaudier Brzeska once called 'the incessant struggle in the complex city'. Apollonius seems to enjoy some kind of remission from that struggle, a remission which was not granted to Odysseus. But at the same time, Apollonius still inhabits a world where statues fall and need to be erected once again, where sages can be arrested by emperors and charged with treason; a world, in short, which is not in any of the usual senses paradisal; a world where Electra is 'bowed still by the wrongs of Aegisthus'.

As a sage and miracle-worker—or wizard, as his accusers called him—Apollonius is in the world, but not of it. This amphibious nature of the sage is never more clearly illustrated than in the incident of his arrest and trial for treason by the emperor Domitian. He submits himself to arrest, and comes to Rome to plead his case. Philostratus copiously reports the eloquent defence which reduces his accusers to silence. But at the end of it all Apollonius says to the court, 'For thou shalt not slay me, since I tell thee I am not mortal', and magically vanishes.[19] Philostratus does not fail to draw the implication that however just his cause, Apollonius could not hope to receive justice. Clearly the Roman Empire under Domitian is not paradise.[20]

Pound makes only one direct reference to the whole business of Apollonius' arrest and trial. As Apollonius is waiting to enter the court-house, a secretary comes up to him and says, '"Man of Tyana, you must enter the court with nothing on you." "Are we then to take a bath," said Apollonius, "or to plead?"'[21] This witticism appears without explanation in canto 91:

> 'Is this a bath-house?'
> *ἄλλοτε δ'αὖτ' Εὖρος Ζεφύρῳ εἴζασκε διώκειν*
> 'Or a Court House?'
> Asked Apollonius.
>
> (91/616:649)

Despite the paucity of reference, this incident from Philostratus is an important one for both *Rock-Drill* and *Thrones*, for it is in the context of Apollonius' difficulties that Pound is directed by Philostratus to the episode of Leucothea in the *Odyssey*.

Leucothea is the sea nymph who rescues Odysseus in Book V after his boat has been wrecked in the storm. She is identified also as Ino, the daughter of Cadmus. She appears to Odysseus in the midst of the storm, and tells him to discard the gorgeous clothes given to him by Calypso, and don instead her scarf (*kredemnon*) which will save him from drowning. He is instructed to return the scarf when he is safely ashore, and does so when, after much difficulty, he is thrown up exhausted on the Phaecian coast.

Damis, a disciple of Apollonius, alludes to the Leucothea episode when he learns that Apollonius is to be charged with treason and wizardry. It is only by some such divine intervention, Damis believes, that Apollonius can possibly escape an unhappy fate:

> Now I am ready to believe that Leucothea did really give her veil to Odysseus, after he had fallen out of his ship and was paddling himself over the sea with his hands. For we are reduced to just as awful and impossible a plight, when some god, as it seems to me, stretches out his hand over us, that we fall not away from all hope of salvation.[22]

Beside this passage the Loeb edition gives a reference to *Odyssey*, V. 333 where Leucothea is introduced as daughter of Cadmus (*Kadmou Thugater*). The Greek line in the passage cited above from canto 91 is *Odyssey*, V. 332, describing the buffeting of Odysseus' boat by the East and West Winds. Taking the hint from Philostratus, Pound develops the Leucothea episode as a paradigm for his uncertain paradiso.[23]

Leucothea first appears just before Apollonius' bath-house joke. She is placed in the context of light which surrounds the ubiquitous and deliquescent goddess of these cantos:

(to the tough guy Musonius: honour)
Rose, azure,
the lights slow moving round her,
Zephyrus, turning,
the petals light on the air
Bright hawk whom no hood shall chain,
They who are skilled in fire
shall read 旦 tan the dawn.
Waiving no jot of the arcanum
(having his own mind to stand by him)
As the sea-gull Κάδμου θυγάτηρ said to Odysseus
KADMOU THUGATER
'get rid of parapernalia'
TLEMOUSUNE.
(91/615:649)

Leucothea, like Undine at the beginning of this canto, is a lesser analogue of Aphrodite herself. Her appearance to Odysseus amounts to a form of salvation, but it is clearly not equivalent to entry into paradise. The last word of the passage cited, *tlemousune* ('misery', 'endurance')—which does not occur in the local context of either Homer or Philostratus—is a reminder that Odysseus had still to endure many hours of pain and uncertainty in the storm-tossed sea before he would be thrown up, half-dead, on the Phaecian coast. A divinity stretches out her hand to Odysseus, but he does not thereby transcend the pain and suffering of the 'Charybdis of action'.

Apollonius scolded Damis for being so faint-hearted as to expect divine intervention such as Odysseus' rescue by Leucothea:

> How long will you continue to cherish these fears, as if you could never understand that wisdom amazes all that is sensible of her, but is herself not amazed by anything?[24]

And he is not moved by Damis' sensible reply that Domitian 'is quite insensible, and . . . not only cannot be amazed by us, but would not allow anything in the world to amaze him'. Yet, in the event, Apollonius follows the route of Odysseus, when confronted with overwhelming and insensible worldly forces, by causing himself to disappear from the courtroom. Pound could not fail to be reminded of his own difficulties with the American authorities when reading of Apollonius' adventures. That the parallel is inexact is an imperfection which need not detain us here. From all reports it would seem that Pound initially possessed something of the confidence expressed in Apollonius' reproach to Damis—a confidence which played no small part in the medical judgement that he was of unsound mind. He soon learned that neither military nor civil authorities are easily amazed by wisdom.

But even if Pound's self-confidence did reach the limits of madness, within the *Cantos* he is much closer to the more sensible, if less noble, fear of Damis than he is to the contemptuous courage of Apollonius. Indeed, in the *Pisan Cantos* he turns, like Damis, to the Odyssey for comfort and guidance. He speaks first of Odysseus' attack on the Cicones, and its unhappy consequence for him:

> care and craft in forming leagues and alliances
> that avail nothing against the decree
> the folly of attacking that island
> and of the force ὑπὲρ μόρον[25].

and continues with an allusion to Odysseus' shipwreck:

> Je suis au bout de mes forces/
> That from the gates of death,
>
> . . . . .
>
> hast 'ou swum in a sea of air strip
>   through an aeon of nothingness,
> when the raft broke and the waters went over me.
>
> (80/512–13:547)

Although Pound remembers Odysseus' shipwreck at Pisa, he does not recall Leucothea. However, a goddess does appear to him in canto 81. The goddess is not identified, but she has Aphrodite's eyes: 'there came new subtlety into my tent, . . . Elysium though it were in the halls of hell.' Some divinity (for Pound as for Odysseus) stretches out her hand so that the sufferer fall not away from all hope of salvation. But the divinity stretches out her hand in the midst of adversity.

The remission from the struggle granted to Pound in his tent at Pisa is not so much paradisal as ecstatic. It is the '"magic moment" or moment of metamorphosis, bust thru from quotidien into "divine or permanent world"'. The *Pisan Cantos*, of course, are not intended as a delineation of the paradisal state. But the paradisal motif in the later cantos never escapes this paradigm of the ecstatic moment, the moment of theophany, or of metamorphosis, or whatever one wishes to call it. It has been identified with the theophany of Aphrodite, and it is parallel to the Eleusinian *epopteia*. The ecstatic moment is just that, a moment, fugitive, ungraspable, and unrelated to mundane matters such as pain or well-being, death or life. The sage Apollonius represents, perhaps, one who has absorbed the *eidous* of the ecstatic moment, and has thus become immune to the dangers and vagaries of this world. He is, as it were, an initiate into the Mysteries.

However, Pound does not show us Apollonius' miraculous escape, and thereby barely avoids the desperate expedient of incorporating into his poem a miraculous and unbelievable ascension into paradise. Instead he invokes 'the tough guy, Musonius', another sage who ran foul of the state. Musonius is first mentioned in canto 91 in the passage cited above alluding to Leucothea. Philostratus tells us that:

> Musonius of Babylon, a man only second to Apollonius, was thrown into prison for the crime of being a sage, and there lay in danger of death; and

he would have died for all his gaoler cared, if it had not been for the strength of his constitution.[26]

Unlike Apollonius, Musonius does not escape his imprisonment by magic. He suffers the hardships of prison, and (like Pound at Pisa and St. Elizabeth's), survives them only because of the strength of his constitution and confidence in the rectitude of his own actions and beliefs. It is Musonius whom we find, in apposition with Leucothea's advice to Odysseus, '(having his own mind to stand by him)'. Pound's phrase echoes a letter Musonius wrote from prison to Apollonius:

> For your solicitude on my behalf, I shall never do anything but commend you: but he who has strength of mind to defend himself, and has proved that he has done no wrong, is a true man.[27]

Musonius would appear to have little to do with ecstasy or paradise, condemned as he is to labour cutting a canal through the Isthmus to join the Aegean and Adriatic seas. There is no miraculous escape for him, no god stretching out his hand, not even 'a subtlety of eyes'. But, like Odysseus, he endures; it is to him, as much as to Odysseus, that the epithet *tlemousune* applies; and it is he who answers the question Pound poses at the end of canto 93: 'Without guides, having nothing but courage/Shall audacity last into fortitude?' He also provides an ironic commentary on Apollonius' pious reminder that 'the whole earth affords secure ground for the doers of holiness, and that the sea is safely traversed not only by people in ships but even by people attempting to swim'.[28] Pound picks this up in canto 94 where he quotes Philostratus' Greek and provides his own translation (characteristically the Greek is incomplete and unintelligible by itself):

> δὲ τοῖς ὅσια πράττουσι
> for the doers of holiness
> γῆν μὲν πᾶσαν ἀσφαλῆ
> they may ship or swim, being secure.
> We have already raised our stele to Musonius,
> the man with the spade.
> (94/638–9:671–2)

Apollonius would appear to be one who travels dry and comfortable in a ship, Odysseus one who is forced to swim, and Musonius one whose security resides only in Stoic indifference to misfortune.

Musonius serves to remind us that the reader is not being led out of Purgatory into Paradise, but is being led out of the world of effective action into a world of sensitive awareness, out of history into contemplation, out of *periplus* into vision, out of epic into lyric. The lyric world of vision and contemplation does not, in the *Cantos*, transcend the world of action; it merely interpenetrates, providing a momentary remission from pain:

> Le Paradis n'est pas artificiel
>   but is jagged
> For a flash,
>   for an hour.
> Then agony,
>   then an hour,
>   then agony,
> Hilary stumbles, but the Divine Mind is abundant
>   unceasing,
>   *improvisatore*
> Omniformis
>   unstill.
>
> (92/620:653)

In the middle of his borrowings from Philostratus in canto 94 Pound quotes himself in an intriguing little passage that is intended, I think, to direct us to the Leucothea episode as the touchstone for his paradisal theme:

> So that walking here under the larches of Paradise
> the stream was exceedingly clear
>   & almost level its margin
> 'was thrown in my way a touch-stone
> *γὰρ βάσανος χαθαρὸν χαὶ ἀπ' οὐδενὸς θνητοῦ.*
>
> (94/638:671)

The speaker of the first three lines must be Pound himself. (Is he perhaps picking up the enigmatic 'So that:' with which he concluded canto 1 so many pages and years ago?) The phrase, 'under the larches of Paradise' is from 'The Alchemist: Chant for the Transmutation of Metals' written for *Ripostes*, but not published until 1920. In that poem many dead women are invoked by name to arise and aid in the transmutation of metals:

> Out of Erebus, the flat-lying breadth,
> Breath that is stretched out beneath the world:

Out of Erebus, out of the flat waste of air, lying
    beneath the world;
Out of the brown leaf-brown colourless
        Bring the imperceptible cool.[29]

These women, dwelling in Erebus, are said to move 'under the larches of Paradise', as if in 'The Alchemist' Erebus, the upper reaches of the Underworld, were identified with the Elysian Fields. The clear, level stream, however, is not found in 'The Alchemist'; rather it reminds one of the clear stream in Dante's Earthly Paradise (*Purgatorio*. xxviii).[30]

Whether the paradise named in these lines be thought to be Erebus, the Elysian Fields, the Earthly Paradise, or Heaven, the reader is being informed unequivocally that the locus of the speaker is Paradise, and that while walking there a touchstone was thrown in his way. The fourth line of the passage is in quotation marks because it is Apollonius, not Pound, speaking. Learning that he must go to Rome to face charges of treason—brought against him by Nero this time—Apollonius receives the news as a blessing:

Well, of all the blessings which have been vouchsafed to me by the gods . . . this present one, I may say, is the greatest that I have ever enjoyed; for chance has thrown in my way a touchstone to test these young men. . .[31]

It turns out that twenty-six of Apollonius' followers are of false metal: they decline to accompany him to Rome.

The final Greek line would translate: 'for a pure touchstone [made] from no dead matter'. It, too, is Apollonius speaking, but the line is a pastiche, the first two words taken from the passage on page 435 cited above, and the rest from page 444 where Apollonius is speaking of his clothing, which he says is pure because it is not made from dead matter, that is, animal skins or fibres, but is of linen.

Since the touchstone turns out to be Apollonius' linen garments, it is tempting to identify Pound's touchstone with Leucothea's injunction to Odysseus, 'get rid of parapernalia', that is, 'discard the gorgeous garments of Calypso and take my veil'. She is heard repeating the advice after Apollonius' witticism about entering the court-house naked:

. . . Apollonius unpolluted
and the whole creation concerned with 'FOUR'
        'my bikini is worth your raft'.
                (91/616:650)

What Leucothea reveals to Pound is that 'a stage set *á* la Dante' is not needed for his paradiso, that he can go naked like Odysseus though tossed by the storms of life, and still be thrown up on the further shore: 'for the doers of holiness/they may ship or swim, being secure'.

Leucothea also permits Pound to unite the Odyssean plot with his subjective lyric by transforming Odysseus from the resourceful conqueror of Circe to the pious supplicant of Leucothea. The courage and mental alertness he brought to the Underworld are seen to be unnecessary and messy: 'it was not by ditch-digging and sheep's guts'. Odysseus' rescue by Leucothea is a paradigm of the paradisal possibilities in the *Cantos*; the goddess appears but briefly in the midst of Hell, and then disappears:

> 'Unhappy man, how is it that Poseidon, the earth-shaker, has conceived such furious wrath against thee, that he is sowing for thee the seeds of many evils? Yet verily he shall not utterly destroy thee for all his rage. Nay, do thou thus; and methinks thou dost not lack understanding. Strip off these garments, and leave thy raft to be driven by the winds, but do thou swim with thy hands and so strive to reach the land of the Phaecians, where it is thy fate to escape. Come, take this veil, and stretch it beneath thy breast. It is immortal; there is no fear that thou shalt suffer aught or perish. But when with thy hands thou has laid hold of the land, loose it from thee, and cast it into the wine-dark sea far from the land, and thyself turn away.'
>
> So saying, the goddess gave him the veil, and herself plunged again into the surging deep, like a sea-mew; and the dark wave hid her.[32]

Pound closes *Rock-Drill* with this incident:

> That the wave crashed, whirling the raft, then
> Tearing the oar from his hand,
> broke mast and yard-arm
> And he was drawn down under wave,
> The wind tossing,
> Notus, Boreas,
> as it were thistle-down.
> Then Leucothea had pity,
> 'mortal once
> Who now is a sea-god:
> νόστου
> γαίης Φαιήχων, . . .'[a]
>
> (95/647:680)

[a] try to reach Phaecia.

These lines 'rhyme' with the theophany of Aphrodite in canto 74 (74/443:471).

The *Cantos* might well have ended with Leucothea's rescue of Odysseus, since it brings him as close to Ithaca as he can possibly get in our age; nor can there be any orderly Dantescan rising into the resplendent paraphernalia of a Paradiso. But Pound was in no mood to end his poem. *Rock-Drill* was just the first instalment in this late outburst of poetic activity. (Canto 96 appeared in the Spring 1956 number of *Hudson Review*, while *Rock-Drill* was still being reviewed.)

Thrones is less successful than *Rock-Drill*, suffering more severely from the endemic infection of what one reviewer called 'flash card poetry'. Even when he is not writing marginalia on the books he is reading, Pound offers his readers little more than invitations to trace allusions to earlier cantos. Much of the volume is hopelessly obscure even when one has traced the allusions, translated the foreign phrases, and studied the rest of the poem carefully. It contains a discontinuous poetry of inference which has become so abbreviated and so intensely private as to be indecipherable. But, granting the volume's egregious obscurity, one can still find within it the continued ingenious reworking of old themes. Odysseus and Dante still occupy his mind.

The volume opens with an allusion to the Leucothea episode:

> Κρῄδεμνον . . .
> χρῄδεμνον . . .
> and the wave concealed her,
> dark mass of great water.
> (96/651:683)

And moves from there into Paulus Diaconus' history of the Lombards via a little creative lexical metaphor:

> Aestheticisme comme politique d'église, hardly religion.
> & on the hearth burned cedar and juniper . . .
> that should bear him thru these diafana
> Aether pluit numismata
> Tellus vomit cadavera,
> Thusca quae a thure,
> from the name of the incense, in this province is
> ROMA *quae olim* . . .
> In the province of Tuscany is Rome, a city which formerly. . . .

In the Latin ('The air rains coins/the earth throws up corpses,/ Tuscany which is from frankincence (*thure*)'), the similarity between 'Thuscae' and 'thure' permits Pound to postulate an association between Tuscany and another semi-divine female with a name very similar to Leucothea. This is Leucothoë, beloved of Apollo, and buried alive by her father for succumbing to the god. Apollo rescued her by metamorphosing her into an incense bush. As Leucothea is a lesser analogue of Aphrodite, Leucothoë is a lesser analogue of Persephone. One issues from water into the bright air, the other from earth into the bright air.

Pound introduced Leucothoë in canto 95 in another bit of lexical metaphor:

> Queen of Heaven bring her repose
> *Κάδμου θυγάτηρ*[a]
> bringing light *per diafana*
> λευχὸς Λευχόθοε[b]
> white foam, a sea-gull
>
> . . . . .
>
> That the crystal wave mount to flood surge
> c 近 chin[4]
> d 乎 hu[1]
> e 仁 jên[2]
> The light there almost solid.[33]
>
> (95/644:677)

The name, Leucothea, means 'white or bright goddess'. Leucothoë's name has the same Greek root, meaning 'white, bright, or light', but it is not of Greek provenance. She would appear to be an invention of Ovid's. At least the only references to her are in the *Metamorphoses* (IV. 220 ff.). In any case, Pound adopts her as a bright, chthonic semi-divinity to associate with the bright, aquatic semi-divinity, Leucothea. Indeed, he gives to her Leucothea's advice to Odysseus: '"My bikini is worth yr/raft". Said Leucothoe'. (95/645: 678).

However, the associations of Leucothea/Leucothoë are even more

[a] daughter of Cadmus, i.e. Leucothea.
[b] light Leucothöe.
[c] to approach.
[d] an intensive:!
[e] love, humanitas.

tangled in the obsessively echoic world of the late cantos. For Pound follows the words just quoted with: 'And if I see her not/No sight is worth the beauty of my thought'. These lines refer the reader back to canto 92 where Pound essays a beatific vision in the mode of *Paradiso*, xxxiii. There he cites *Paradiso*, xxvii ('e piove d'amor': 'and rained down love'), and *Paradiso*, ix, where Folquet of Marseilles in the third heaven (that of Venus) addresses Dante: 'in questa lumera appresso' ('in this radiance that sparkles'). He also invokes Danaë from canto 4 (whom Zeus visited as a shower of gold: 'To another the rain fell as of silver./La Luna Regina./Not gold as in Ecbatan'), Montségur, and Aphrodite (whose marine birth is mentioned in Latin and Greek: 'ex aquis nata/*τά ἐχ τῶν ὑδάτων γενόμενα*'). He also throws in his invented Egyptian goddess, Ra-Set, and Anubis to lead up to:

> 'And if I see her not,
>   no sight is worth the beauty of my thought.'
> Then knelt with the sphere of crystal
> That she should touch with her hands,
>   Coeli Regina,
> The four altars at the four coigns of that place,
> But in the great love bewildered.
>   (92/619:652)

This vision is concluded with a passage admitting the momentary and ecstatic nature of paradise as well as of vision as cited above: 'Le paradis n'est pas artificiel/but is jagged'. Much more could be said about the beatific vision of canto 92. It is an astonishing *tour de force*, bringing together as it does all of Pound's goddesses within a framework imitative of Dante's beatific vision, and at the same time maintaining—even through a quotation from Dante—his own metaphor of a rain of light from heaven to earth.[34] Indeed, it goes further than that, for the passage Pound cites from *Paradiso*, xxvii describe the universe as an emanation of the divine mind:

> 'La natura del mondo, che quieta
> il mezzo e tutto l'altro intorno move.
> quinci comincia come da sua meta;
> e questo cielo no ha altro dove
> che la mente divina, in che s'accende
> l'amor che il volge e la virtù ch'ei piove[.]

The nature of the universe, which holds the centre still and moves all else round it, begins here as from its starting-point, and this heaven has no other *where* but the Divine Mind, in which is kindled the love that turns it and the virtue which it rains down.

(*Paradiso*, xxvii. 106–11)

Pound adapts this to

Hilary stumbles, but the Divine Mind is abundant
unceasing
improvisatore
Omniformis
unstill.

And the 'omniformis' is a recollection of the heading for chapter 13 of Porphyry's *De Occasionibus*, 'Omnis intellectus est omniformis', which Pound had cited nearly forty years earlier in the 1917 *Poetry* version of 'Canto Three':

And then comes John Heydon!
'I have seen John Heydon.'
Let us hear John Heydon!
'*Omniformis*
Omnis intellectus est'—thus he begins, by spouting
half of Psellus.
(Then comes a note, my assiduous commentator:
Not Psellus *De Daemonibus*, but Porphyry's *Chances*,
In the thirteenth chapter, that 'every intellect is
omniform.')

The first pages of canto 98 are among those pages of pastiche, so frequent in *Thrones*, which have the echoic quality of the lyric sections, without any rhetorical coherence. They precede a long redaction from Baller's edition of the *Sacred Edict*, which occupies the rest of canto 98 and all of canto 99. In it we find Ra-Set (the goddess Pound created out of two male divinities, Ra and Set[35]), Ocellus on light, three of the names of Wagadu, and Tching Tang's injunction to 'make it new' from canto 53. All of these also occur elsewhere in the later cantos. Here they lead up to Leucothea and another Odyssean allusion:

Τὰ ἐζ Αἰγύπτου φαρμαχα[a]
Leucothea gave her veil to Odysseus
Χρόνος[b]
πνεῦμα θεῶν[c]
χαι ἔρως σοφίας[d]
The Temple (hieron) is not for sale.
Getting the feel of it, of his soul,
while they were making a fuss about Helen.
(98/684:714)

The Greek about Egyptian drugs is from Philostratus (II, p. 208) just before Damis' reference to Leucothea. Apollonius has just left the law court and proposes that he and Damis speak to their fellow prisoners. Damis asks, 'Will they not think us babblers ... and bores, if we interrupt them in the preparation of their defence, and moreover, it is a mistake to talk philosophy with men so broken in spirit as they are.' Apollonius replies, 'Nay, ... they are just the people who most want someone to talk to them and comfort them. For you may remember the verses of Homer in which he relates how Helen mingled in the bowl of wine certain drugs from Egypt in order to drown the heart-ache of the heroes.'[36] Apollonius goes on to say that he thinks she must have sung spells to ease their hearts, as his words would ease those of his fellow prisoners.

By 'rhyming' Leucothea with Helen's Egyptian drugs, Pound suggests that supernatural aid is psychological like that of drugs. We are also reminded of Circe's 'dreadful drugs' mentioned in canto 39, of the wine jar 'ichor for lynxes' in canto 79, and of the lotus-eaters of canto 20. Circe's drugs and the lotus leaf are dangers for Odysseus and his men, seducing them into a world of easeful languor and away from their proper task. Helen's drugs are similar in their effect, but they are administered when men require solace from the world's horrors. Homer tells us that 'whoso should drink this down, when it is mingled in the bowl, would not in the course of that day let a tear fall down over his cheeks, no, not though his mother and father should lie there dead, or though before his face men should slay with the sword his brother or dear son, and his own eyes beheld it' (*Odyssey*, IV. 222–6).

[a] It out of Egyptian drugs.
[b] Time or the god, Chronos.
[c] godly soul.
[d] and the wisdom of love.

This rather surprising collocation of drugs, Leucothea, and unidentified Greek phrases referring to Chronos, godly souls, and the wisdom of love parallels the puzzling paradiso of canto 20. Pound described that canto to his father (without the first two pages) as follows:

The whole reminiscence jumbled or 'candied' in Nicolo's delirium. Take that as a sort of bounding surface from which one gives the main subject of the Canto, the lotophagoi: lotus eaters, or respectable dope smokers; and general paradiso.[37]

Niccolo's delirium is brought on by remorse after he has had his son, Ugo, and his wife, Parisina, executed for having become lovers. Pound mixes in allusions to other sexual disasters, especially the Trojan story and Lope da Vega's *Las Almenas da Toro*. It has always seemed strange to me that he should lead up to 'a general paradiso' by a delirium induced by remorse for an act of vengeance, and by a delirium induced by drugs. The lotophagoi are floating

> Each man in his cloth, as on raft, on
>   The high invisible current;
> On toward the fall of water;
> And then over that cataract.
>
> (20/92:96–7)

They are floating, unaware, toward death and disaster:

> Lotophagoi of the suave nails, quiet, scornful,
> Voce-profondo:
>   'Feared neither death nor pain for this beauty;
> If harm, harm to ourselves.'
> And beneath: the clear bones, far down,
> Thousand on thousand.

And Pound has them speak scornfully of the rewards to be derived from Odysseus' struggle: 'What gain with Odysseus,/ . . . /Give! What were they given?/Ear-wax./Poison and ear-wax,/and a salt grave by the bull-field'.

Canto 20 would suggest that paradise is a refuge from the pain, from the *tlemousune* of life. In 1926, when he wrote canto 20, Pound was not prepared to approve the false, drug-induced paradise of the lotophagoi. But, none the less, he saw an affinity between a pharmacological escape from pain and ugliness into beauty, and less contrived heightening of perception. In the *Pisan Cantos* he laments:

I don't know how humanity stands it
    with a painted paradise at the end of it
    without a painted paradise at the end of it
the dwarf morning-glory twines round the grass blade
magna NUX animae   with Barabbas and 2 thieves beside me.
(74/436:463)

In canto 45 Pound wrote, 'With usura/hath no man a painted paradise on his church wall.' In canto 74, he is saying that even a world reformed to permit the creation of artistic beauty would remain a painful place. He later transforms 'painted paradise' into 'paradis peint', and insists that it is not 'artificiel'. This same passage in canto 74 links to both canto 20 and canto 98 through the mention of the mystic's 'dark night of the soul'. The beatific vision of the mystic is preceded by darkness and bewilderment equivalent to the darkness and confusion experienced by the initiate at Eleusis. In other words, paradise can be seen only from out of pain. It is this awareness—an entirely traditional one, imaged by Dante as the *selva oscura*—which accounts for Pound introducing his paradiso in canto 20 through Niccolo's remorse-induced delirium.

Thus, the elements of the ecstatic sense of paradise developed in the *Pisan Cantos*, and a paradise even further restricted to ecstasy in *Rock-Drill*, were already there very early in the poem. But the earlier presence of ecstatic vision was ambivalent. Odysseus remained masterful; he did not eat of the lotus, and drank of Circe's drugs only after he had protected himself with Hermes' *moly*. Odysseus sets the standard of heroic action in the Cantos, and there was no *paradis peint* for him—not even in the *Pisan Cantos*. In *Rock-Drill* he must be content with enough paradise to save his skin. In canto 98, it seems that he would be content to take Helen's drug and its boon of freedom from human cares in order to contemplate his soul: 'Getting the feel of it, of his soul,/while they were making a fuss about Helen.'

Lower down the page in canto 98 Pound invokes Sabine and Italic customs, and Demeter:

ius Italicum, *more Sabello*,
    no more black shawls in the Piazza
more Sabello, for Demeter.
    'Ut facias pulchram'[a]

[a] Thus thou makest beauty.

there is no sight without fire.
Thinning their oar-blades
θῖνα θαλάσσης[a]
nothing there but an awareness.
(98/684:714)

The black shawls are those he says (in canto 102) were 'still worn for Demeter/in Venice,/in my time,/my young time', but are no longer. They represent a persistence of Eleusis into modern times, that is, of the cult of beauty: 'Ut facias pulchram'. 'θῖνα θαλάσσης'' echoes canto 96: 'After 500 years, still sacrificed to that sea gull,/a colony of Phaeacians θῖνα θαλάσσης'. 'That sea gull' is, of course, Leucothea, but I do not know where Pound learned that she was still worshipped in Phaecia 500 years after Odysseus' miraculous rescue. In any case, with Demeter and Leucothea there is 'nothing there but an awareness'—no dogma, no monuments, no paradise, painted or otherwise.

Pound proceeds via a little economic and governmental awareness to a supposed persistence of the Eleusinian awareness within the Christian tradition:

In Byzantium 12 % for a millennium
The Manchu at 36 legal, their Edict
the next pass.
Anselm: that some is incarnate awareness,
thus trinitas; some remains spiritus.
'The body is inside.' Thus Plotinus,
But Gemisto: 'Are Gods by hilaritas';
and their speed in communication.
et in nebulas simiglianza[b]
χαθ' ὁμοίωσιν Deorum[c]
a fanned flame in their moving[.]

It is not clear who 'they' in this passage are, but one might suppose them to be the divinities and masters whose manifestation and awareness, respectively, make in the darkness of human misery and ignorance 'a fanned flame in their moving'. Presumably we are also meant to understand that the kind of awareness exemplified by Anselm, Plotinus, and Gemisto Plethon is also manifest in the

[a] sea shore.
[b] and in the likeness of darkness.
[c] made like God.

Byzantine maintenance of interest rates at 12 per cent for a millennium, and in the *Sacred Edict* (whose wisdom will form the bulk of this canto and the next) which will correct the Manchu interest rate of 36 per cent.

Leucothea and Leucothoe are meant to be a 'mythological exposition' and concentration of this whole complex of religious, economic, and political awareness:

> And that Leucothoe rose as an incense bush
> —Orchamus, Babylon—
>   resisting Apollo.
> Patience, I will come to the Commissioner of the Salt Works
>   in due course.
> Est deus in nobis.[a]   and
>   They still offer sacrifice to that sea-gull
> est deus in nobis
>   *Χρήδεμνον*
> She being of Cadmus line,
>   the snow's lace is spread there like sea foam.
>
> (98/685:715)

The Commissioner of the Salt Works is K'ang-hsi whom we meet later on in the canto (p. 688:718). Leucothea and Leucothoe are, perhaps, manifestations of the god that is in us, and therefore, less resplendent and less potent than Aphrodite and Persephone who are manifestations of the *nous*. But there is probably no precise theological or philosophical interpretation of Pound's meaning here. He is working out his own relationship with the world and with the divine in mythological terms, because that is the only language possible for him. The point to be taken is that Leucothea and Leucothoe, as manifestations of divinity, represent a much lower level of expectation than Aphrodite and Persephone.

Odysseus, too, is diminished. In canto 102, via maddeningly cryptic (and inaccurate) Greek, he is given the characteristics of the saint rather than the hero:

>   and as to why Penelope waited
> keinas . . . e Orgei. line 639. Leucothoe
> rose as an incense bush,
>   resisting Apollo,
>
> . . . . .
>
>   OIOS TELESAI ERGON . . . EROS TE.
>
> (102/728:754)

[a] God is in us.

The first bit of Greek is from *Odyssey*, IV. 693 (not 639) where Penelope berates the suitors and tells them that Odysseus 'never wrought iniquity to any man', Pound cites only 'wrought' (*keinas*) and 'any' (*eorgei*). And the last is from *Odyssey*, II. 272, where Athena (disguised as Mentor) tells Telemachus that Odysseus was a man 'to fulfil [*telesai*] both word [*epos* (*eros* is an error)] and deed [*ergon*]'. Thus it would seem that Penelope waited for Odysseus because he was kind and honest. The diminished Odysseus belongs with Leucothoe, the diminished Persephone, but I cannot read any more specific meaning into the juxtaposition.

Odysseus' last act in the *Cantos* is to throw Leucothea's veil back out to sea:

> So that the mist was quite white on that part of the sea-coast
> Le Portel, Phaecia
> and he dropped the scarf in the tide-rips
> KREDEMNON[a]
> that it should float back to the sea,
> and that quickly
> DEXATO XERSI
> with a fond hand
> AGERTHE.
> (100/716–17:744)

This is based on *Odyssey*, V. 458–63:

> But when he [Odysseus] revived, and his spirit returned [*agerthe*] again into his breast, then he loosed from him the veil of the goddess and let it fall into the river that murmured seaward; and the great wave bore it back down the stream, and straightway Ino received it in her hands [*dexato chersi*].

This is not the last appearance of either Odysseus or Leucothea in the *Cantos*—indeed, Leucothea is twice invoked (as Ino Kadmeia) on the last page of *Thrones*—but it is Odysseus' last *act*. He surrenders the talisman of divine aid to the sea whence it came, and thereby re-enters the world of men, naked and exhausted.

[a] veil.

IX · Conclusions

POUND was in his seventy-third year when the *Thrones* volume was published. He had by then been engaged in the composition of the *Cantos* for at least 44 years, and had 107 cantos in print (109 minus the missing cantos 72 and 73). But the poem remained incomplete and unconcluded. It seems clear now that it never could have been completed. But Pound continued to compose new cantos, publishing 113, part of 115, and 116 in 1962. After that his health broke, and the old man fell into silence. Despite his silence and poor health, a new section was long promised, but all that was forthcoming was *Drafts & Fragments* published in 1969, containing the 1962 cantos, some previously unpublished cantos and fragments of cantos, and two fragments from 1941, now labelled 'Addendum for Canto C'. This volume announced the terminus of the poem in an appropriately indirect, but rather pathetic manner.

Of these last cantos, only 113 and 116 are of very great interest. Canto 116 stops just short of being a palinode, admitting the failure of the poem, but asserting the truth of the vision:

> Came Neptunus
>   his mind leaping
>   like dolphins,
> These concepts the human mind has attained.
> To make Cosmos—
> To achieve the possible—
> Muss., wrecked for an error,
> But the record
>   the palimpsest—
> a little light
>   in great darkness—
> cuniculi—[1]
>
> (116/795)

Pound's mind indeed leaps like dolphins, and it is the restless galvanic energy of his mind that both fascinates and irritates

Although retaining a remarkable consistency of purpose and an obsessive singularity of view in the poem, Pound seemed incapable of dealing with one subject at a time. He sought to make a virtue of his proclivity for wide-ranging metaphor and analogy through the rhetorical technique of juxtaposition without links and by broader techniques of implication.[2] But the technique did not work:

> I have brought the great ball of crystal;
> who can lift it?
> Can you enter the great acorn of light?
> But the beauty is not the madness
> Tho' my errors and wrecks lie about me.
> And I am not a demigod,
> I cannot make it cohere.
> (116/795–6)

The restlessness of his mind finally became a kind of torture for him, a ceaselessly turning wheel to which he is bound:

> Out of dark, thou, Father Helios, leadest,
> but the mind as Ixion, unstill, ever turning.
> (113/790)

No longer the suffering, wandering, conquering Odysseus, 'sailing after knowledge', Pound finally sees himself as Ixion, punished by the gods for his insolence with eternal restlessness. But even though canto 113 closes with a rather uncomfortable image, it opens on a note of serenity and pathos:

> Thru the 12 Houses of Heaven
> seeing the just and the unjust,
> tasting the sweet and the sorry,
> Pater Helios turning.
> 'Mortal praise has no sound in her ears'
> (Fortuna's)
> *Θρῆνος*[a]
> And who no longer make gods out of beauty
> *Θρῆος* this is a dying'.
> (113/786)

Fortuna is a goddess frequently invoked in the later cantos—an

[a] lamenting.

admission of irrationality in the affairs of men that Pound had long denied, seeing both good and evil as volitional. He frequently repeats the formula, 'all 'neath the moon, under Fortuna', thus accounting for his own misfortunes, and perhaps abjuring his belief that the western world is controlled by malevolent bankers. But the importation of Fortuna into the poem's pantheon is, at best, a pale reversion of earlier confidence and condemnation. Still, Pound here renounces the role of divine scourge, and acquiesces in Pater Helios' serene contemplation of 'the just and the unjust', 'the sweet and the sorry', contenting himself with the insistence that one should worship beauty.

Canto 113 is a dream of heaven, of a garden where one may walk with the esteemed dead:

Yet to walk with Mozart, Agassiz and Linnaeus
'neath overhanging air under sun-beat
Here take thy mind's space
And to this garden, Marcella, ever seeking by petal,
by leaf-vein
out of dark, and toward half-light.
(113/786)

But it is a dream he cannot sustain, returning always to the circumambient and faulted world:

Canals, bridges, and house walls
orange in sunlight
But to hitch sensibility to efficiency?
grass versus granite,
For the little light and more harmony
Oh God of all men, none excluded
and howls for Schwundgeld in the Convention
(our Constitutional
17 . . . whichwhat)
Nothing new but their ignorance,
ever perennial.
(113/788)

But in canto 116, which I take to be Pound's final statement, there is no question of walking in paradise. There paradise is only the ecstatic vision that it had always truly been for Pound—although he had tried, as he says in the 'M'amour' fragment, 'to make a paradiso/ terrestre':

again is all 'paradiso'
    a nice quiet paradise
        over the shambles,
and some climbing
    before the take-off,
to 'see again',
the verb is 'see', not 'walk on'
i.e. it coheres all right
    even if my notes do not cohere.
(116/796–7)

Pound admits in this canto that his poem is no more than notes, the material for a poem, but not an achieved work of art. He also calls the *Cantos* a palimpsest—a piece of parchment with a number of texts erased and written over. Palimpsest is a very apt analogy for the *Cantos*, for Pound has indeed traversed the same ground many times in the poem—each passage intended to alter and correct the previous one. China, America, and Europe are examined and explained once in *A Draft of XXX Cantos*, again in cantos 31–71, and still again in the later cantos. His economic views are at first Douglas's, then Douglas plus Hollis and Gesell, and finally Del Mar is added to the mixture. The three variant perspectives are represented in the same three divisions of the poem as the historical perspectives. His developing understanding of history and economics is not erratic or self-contradictory, but the beginning does not foresee the end. He was therefore obliged to repeat and correct himself.

But while he was, as it were, erasing and recopying the matter of his poem, he was able to develop and transform its poetic or mythical vehicle. The figure of Odysseus and the sense of divinity as something manifest in the beauty and fertility of nature (which sense of divinity Pound called Eleusis) proved capable of dynamic transformation, as his understanding of economics and history was not. The coherence he claims is the coherence of that poetic and mythical vehicle. To put it another way, there is no great imaginative gap between the vision of John Heydon, rendered in 'Canto Three', and the appearance of Leucothea to Odysseus or the vision of canto 106:

                Circe, Persephone
so different is sea from glen that
                    the juniper is her holy bush

between the two pine trees, not Circe
but Circe was like that
coming from the house of smoothe stone
'not know which god'
nor could enter her eyes by probing
the light blazed behind her
nor was this from sunset.
(106/753–4:778–9)

Heydon's vision in the *Lustra* version of 'Canto Three' is rendered as follows:

Another one, half-cracked: John Heydon,
Worker of miracles, dealer in levitation,
'Servant of God and secretary of nature,'
The half transparent forms, in trance at Bulverton:
'Decked all in green', with sleeves of yellow silk
Slit to the elbow, slashed with various purples,
(Thus is his vision). Her eyes were green as glass,
Her foot was leaf-like, and she promised him
Dangling a chain of emeralds, promised him
The way of holiest wisdom.

Heydon was almost certainly a charlatan. The preface to *The Holy Guide* (whence Pound derives the vision) lifts matter verbatim from Sir Thomas Browne's *Religio Medici*, and borrows a good deal from Philostratus' life of Apollonius as well. He repeats the vision in *The Harmony of the World* and in *The Temple of Wisdom* (whose preface is almost entirely lifted verbatim from Plutarch's *Isis and Osiris* except that Heydon changes the names of the divinities). Pound dropped this vision from the poem, but revived John Heydon in *Rock-Drill* as one of his guides. This revival is rather odd because Heydon's vision of the goddess (variously called Beata, Euterpe, or Hester Heaton) is not revived, and because I cannot agree with Walter Baumann's assessment of Heydon as one who can be taken seriously.[3]

But Heydon is interleaved in canto 91 with Apollonius and the Leucothea episode—everything between 'to ascend those high places' and '"before my eyes into the aether of Nature"' being taken from *The Holy Guide*, with the exception of the lines: 'Formality. Heydon polluted. Apollonius unpolluted' and '"my bikini is worth your raft"'. Clearly Pound is attracted by Heydon's gleanings from rummaging about in Hermetic sources—gleanings he had characterized in the *Lustra* 'Canto Three' as 'munching Ficino's mumbling Platonists'. In his old age he returns to the rich metaphorical world of the occult and the mystical into which Yeats and Mead had introduced him. He had been fascinated by that world, but had maintained a sceptical attitude toward it. Both the scepticism and the fascination are there in 'Canto Three' where he follows Heydon's 'mumbling Platonists' with 'Valla, more earth and sounder rhetoric'. Now that scepticism is replaced—if not by belief, at least by a desire for belief.

For example, Heydon writes, 'let us know first, that the minde of man being come from that high City of Heaven, desireth of her self to live still that heavenly life'.[4] This is a very common Christian Neoplatonic sentiment, familiar from Wordsworth's 'Ode: Intimations of Immortality'. Pound entirely transforms it in canto 91 to: 'and if honour and pleasure will not be ruled/yet the mind come to that High City . . .'. He takes Heydon's statement that men desire heaven, and turns it into an assertion that the mind can attain heaven. That he is unfaithful to Heydon's text here is of no importance in itself, but it indicates a desire to extract from Heydon a statement of the possibility of transcendence or at least of communication with the transcendent.

Indeed, Heydon invariably promises to show his readers the way to long life, health, and power through the alchemical recipes which make up the text of each of his books. The following passage, from which Pound paraphrases the italicized clause, is typical:

> . . . that *Pulchritude* is conveyed indeed by the outward senses unto the soul, but a more intellectual faculty is that which relishes it . . . it is more rational to affirm, that some intellectual principle was the Author of this *Pulchritude* of things than that they should be thus fashioned without the help of that principle: And to say there is no such thing as *Pulchritude*, *and some say*, *there is no way to felicity*: . . . But that there is such a thing as *The Holy Guide*, *Long Life*, I will demonstrate, I will shew you anon in this Book. . . .[5]

The way to felicity turns out to be numerology and alchemy—recipes that did not interest Pound, although he does paraphrase II, p. 39 ('and the whole creation concerned with "FOUR"'):

> . . . and both Philo and Plotinus out of the Pythagoreans, affirm that the Number four is a Symbole of justice, all which makes towards what I drive at, that the whole Creation is concerned in this Number four, which

is called the fourth day . . . all the numbers are contained in four vertually . . . ten . . . is made by the scattering of the parts of four thus, one, two, three, four; put these together now and they are ten.

Baumann tells us that Pound borrowed *The Holy Guide* from Mrs. Yeats while writing *Rock-Drill* at St. Elizabeth's. No doubt he hoped to find in it means of regaining that faith in the transforming power of beauty—particularly the beauty of women—which had sustained the poem for so long. He must have been disappointed in what he found in Heydon. He could not have failed to perceive that Heydon's vision of Euterpe, and his Neoplatonic and Rosicrucian doctrine were used simply as means of selling his books. As a result, he entirely alters Heydon in the pastiche at the end of canto 91, and even unfavourably contrasts Heydon with Apollonius: 'Heydon polluted. Apollonius unpolluted.'

Heydon's dream vision no longer interests him. He does not revive it, but cites only the disappearance of Heydon's 'best beloved', Euterpe: 'before my eyes into the aether of Nature'. None the less, it is worth quoting Heydon's vision, for it is that, rather than his alchemy or numerology or astrology, that caught Pound's interest:[6]

Walking upon the plain of *Bulverton Hill* . . . I could see between me and the light, a most exquisite Divine beauty; her frame neither long nor short, but a mean decent stature; attir'd she was in thin loose Silks, but so green that I never saw the like, for the color was not earthly, in some places it was fancied, with gold & silver Ribbands, which look'd like the Sun and Lyllies in the field of grass; . . . her eyes were quick, fresh, and Celestial, but had something of a Start, as if she had been puzzled with a suddain occurrence.

[She approaches him and gives him her key and signet with which he can open the secrets of the Rosie-Cross, especially the virtue of numbers.]

. . . but her hour of Translation was come, and taking as I thought our last leave, she passed before my eyes into the aether of Nature.[7]

In harking back to Heydon, and to Apollonius, Pound was trying to get back to the beginnings of the poem, to the confidence in the power of beauty and imagination of his London years under the tutelage of Yeats. Heydon failed him, but for all that, is thrust into the poem as if Pound were incapable of keeping anything out at this stage. Apollonius proved more fruitful, providing an analogy for Odysseus and for Pound himself in his solitary conflict with a hostile and uncomprehending world. But if Pound found that he could not revive Heydon's Beata, he echoes her eyes (those eyes of goddesses which are ubiquitous in the *Cantos*), and her location 'between me and the light' in the theophany of canto 106: 'nor could enter her eyes by probing/the light blazed behind her/nor was this from sunset'.

Pound had originally discarded Heydon because he had found his hero in Odysseus, perceived as an Eleusinian initiate who could brave both the terrors of the Underworld, and the bed of the Goddess—a figure uniting the three subjects of the poem: the descent, the repeat in history, and 'the bust thru from quotidien into the divine'. As we have seen, Odysseus is progressively diminished until in *Rock-Drill* he no longer has access to the divine world, and the repeat in history has become a recurrence of usurious exploitation in which Odysseus has no role. Odysseus and his warrior/lover analogues (Malatesta, Niccolo d'Este, and Austors de Maensac) are replaced by men of wisdom and little passion: Jefferson, Adams, Ngan, *et al.* Such men have no contact with the bust through into the divine, nor even with the creation of beauty. They converse with the dead only through books. For them Odysseus cannot draw his great bow in Ithaca and slaughter the impudent suitors. For them he cannot lie with the goddess and take on her power. For such men who battle with the pen, not against fear, but against ignorance, Odysseus can only be ignominiously rescued by a marine nymph from the storm-tossed sea.

With the three subjects of the poem no longer united in the figure of Odysseus, Pound seeks to draw the poem back together with the third subject alone, the bust through into the divine—a theophany detached from Odysseus, from Eleusis, and not even of any particular divinity, but remembering Circe and Aphrodite's eyes: 'not Circe/but Circe was like that'. He says it all in the weary measure of canto 113:

> The long flank, the firm breast
> and to know beauty and death and despair
> and to think that what has been shall be,
> flowing, ever unstill.
>
> Then a partridge-shaped cloud over dust storm.
> The hells move in cycles,
> No man can see his own end.
> The Gods have not returned. 'They have never left us.'
> They have not returned.
> Cloud's processional and the air moves with their living.

Notes

CHAPTER I

1. The British Library catalogue does not record any works by Bertold Lomax. Pound probably invented him.
2. First published in *A Lume Spento*, Venice, 1908. It is not collected in *Personae*, but is in *A Lume Spento and Other Early Poems*, London: Faber & Faber, 1965.
3. *A Lume Spento and Other Early Poems*, p. 38.
4. Donald Hall, 'Ezra Pound: An Interview', *Paris Review*, 28 (Summer–Fall 1962), p. 23. The interview was actually given in January or February 1960.
5. This hypothesis is at least as likely as Hugh Kenner's that Pound was referring to an undated conversation with Professor Ibbotson reported by Charles Norman in *Ezra Pound: A Biography*, London: MacDonald, 1969 (p. 356). Hugh Kenner, *The Pound Era*, Berkeley and Los Angeles: The University of California Press, 1971, pp. 354–5.
6. See Faubion Bowers, 'Memoir Within Memoirs', *Paideuma*, 2 (Spring 1973), pp. 53–66, and Norman, pp. 27–9.
7. *The Letters of Ezra Pound*, ed. D. D. Paige, London: Faber & Faber, 1951, p. 385.
8. See Myles Slatin, 'A History of Pound's *Cantos* I-XVI, 1915–1925' *American Literature*, 35 (1963/4), pp. 183–95.
9. *Selected Cantos of Ezra Pound*, London: Faber & Faber, 1967, p. 9.
10. Robert Browning, Foreword to the republication of *Sordello* in *Browning Poetical Works*, ed. Ian Jack, London: Oxford University Press, 1970, p. 156.
11. Ezra Pound, *The Spirit of Romance*, Norfolk, Conn.: New Directions, n.d., p. 16. It should be noted that this work was first published in 1910, and thus antedates 'Canto One' by seven years.
12. *Sordello*, III. 976–85, Browning, *Poetical Works*, p. 234.
13. The text used is *The Cantos of Ezra Pound*, New York: New Directions, [1970]. This edition is complete, containing all the printed cantos including *Drafts and Fragments*. References will be made by canto and page number thus, (5/17:21). The second number after the slash is the corresponding page number in the English edition of the *Cantos*, *Cantos 1–109*, London: Faber & Faber, 1964. For cantos beyond 109 only the New Directions page numbers are given. Although the English and American editions are not identical, there are no textual issues of significance.
14. *Sordello*, VI. 184–94, Browning, *Poetical Works*, p. 292.
15. Hall, 'Ezra Pound: An Interview', *Paris Review*, 28 (Summer–Fall 1962), p. 48.

16. 'Three Cantos: II' *Poetry*, X, no. 4 (July 1917), p. 188.
17. 'Three Cantos: III', *Poetry*, X, no. 5 (Aug. 1917), p. 248.
18. Yale Collection, no. 538, 13 Dec. 1919. All references to 'Yale Collection' are to the carbons of the Paige Smith transcriptions of Pound's letters, courtesy of the Beinecke Library and the Pound Estate.
19. Forrest Read, *Pound/Joyce: The Letters of Ezra Pound to James Joyce with Pound's essays on Joyce*, New York: New Directions, 1967, p. 193. Read develops this argument more fully in 'Pound, Joyce, and Flaubert' in Eva Hesse, *New Approaches to Ezra Pound*, London: Faber & Faber, 1969, pp. 125–44.
20. *Guide to Kulchur*, Norfolk, Conn.: New Directions, n.d., p. 96. The phrase 'age of usury' reminds us that Pound had met Major Douglas in 1918.
21. *Letters*, p. 234.
22. T. S. Eliot, 'Ulysses, Order, and Myth', *The Dial*, 75 (Nov. 1923), p. 483.
23. Pound wrote to his father in August 1922, 'Have now a rough draft of 9, 10, 11, 12, 13. IX may swell out into two.' Yale Collection, no. 616, p. 1. Canto IX did swell, but into four cantos, not two.
24. Myles Slatin, op. cit., p. 193.
25. Daniel D. Pearlman, (*The Barb of Time*, New York: Oxford University Press, 1969) cites the following note (Appendix A: p. 301): 'I send four cantos. Canto IV is O.K. by itself, Cantos V, VI, VIII shd. appear together as the Lorenzacchio Medici begins in V and ends the VII.'
26. Yale Collection, no. 643.
27. *Letters*, pp. 284–5.
28. W. B. Yeats, 'A Packet for Ezra Pound', in *A Vision*, New York: Macmillan, 1961, p. 4.
29. Yeats, *A Vision*, p. 4.
30. *Letters*, p. 247; *Letters*, p. 385; *Letters*, p. 418; Hall, 'Ezra Pound: An Interview', p. 49.
31. Hall, 'Ezra Pound: An Interview', p. 48.

CHAPTER II

1. Ezra Pound, *Personae*, New York: New Directions, n.d., p. 132.
2. The notes Eliot added to *The Waste Land*, and his ambivalent attitude toward them, suggest some unease about the status of the inferential technique used in his poem. As is well known, several of the notes are ironic, but, at the same time, many of them are of real assistance in making apparent unstated assumptions in the poem. In themselves the notes constitute an external mechanism—but one that Eliot seems to be unhappy about. Of course, he claims they were added to achieve sufficient bulk for a one poem book, but he would not have permitted such a device if it had been merely expedient.
3. Yale Collection, no. 702, To Homer Pound, 29 Nov. 1924.
4. Ezra Pound, 'Early Translators of Homer', in *Literary Essays*, p. 267.
5. Pound assumes that his readers know 'Peire Vidal, Old', in *Personae*, pp. 30–32.
6. Walter Baumann, *The Rose in the Steel Dust*, Berne: Francke Verlag, 1967.

7. Translated by the author from the modern French as found in *Les Troubadours* II *Le Trésor de l'Occitanie*, Texte et traduction par René Nelli et René Lavaud, Desclée de Brower, 1966, p. 317.
8. 'Three Cantos: The Sixth Canto', *Dial*, 71 (Aug. 1921), p. 202.
9. See 'Mœurs Contemporaines, VII', in *Personae*, p. 181, and *Literary Essays*, p. 295.
10. Letter to John Quinn as quoted in Daniel D. Pearlman, *The Barb of Time*, New York: Oxford University Press, 1969, p. 302.
11. This section of Chapter II and the first section of Chapter III appeared in *Paideuma*, 3 (Fall 1974), pp. 191–216 as 'A Light from Eleusis'.
12. I cannot pretend to have read the some sixty titles in Péladan's bibliography nor is there any reason to suppose that Pound had done so. Very helpful in assessing Péladan's work is Édouard Bertholet, *La Pensée et les secrets du Sar Joséphin Péladan*, Lausanne: Éditions Rosicruciennes, 4 vols., 1952, 1955, 1958. Bertholet's work is intended to restore—or rather create—Péladan's reputation, but by providing a summary of virtually all of his publications, it permits one to arrive at a fairly confident estimate of the quality of his mind and work. René Louis Doyon's biography (*La Douloureuse Aventure de Péladan*, Paris: La Connaisance, 1946) is much more objective in its assessment of the man, and points out that Péladan leaned very heavily without acknowledgement on two books by one E. Aroux, *Dante Hérétique* (1854), and *Les Mystères de la chevalerie et de l'amour platonique au moyen-âge* (1858). Aroux was interested in exposing Dante as a heretic. He was himself a Catholic who wished to root out all traces of heresy from the Church, and endeavoured to demonstrate that Dante was in fact 'Pasteur de l'église Albigeoise dans la ville de Florence, affilié à l'Ordre du Temple'. He provides the essentials of Péladan's hypothesis of a religion of *amor* (indeed, in much more detail than Péladan), but there is nothing in his work to suggest that Pound ever read him. Remy de Gourmont does, however, mention Aroux—rather disparagingly—in a note (p. 5) in his little book, *Dante, Béatrice et la poésie amoureuse* (Paris: Mercure de France, 1921), which Pound most likely had read.
13. 'Interesting French Publications', *The Book News Monthly*, 25 (Sept. 1906), p. 54.
14. *The Spirit of Romance*, p. 90. This chapter, 'Psychology and Troubadours', was first published in *The Quest*, 4 (Oct. 1912), pp. 37–53, a periodical edited by G. R. S. Mead.
15. 'Terra Italica', *New Review*, 1 (Winter 1931/2), p. 388.
16. 'Credo', *Front*, 1 (Dec. 1930), p. 11.
17. For a discussion of the Edwardian fascination with the occult see Samuel B. Hynes, *The Edwardian Turn of Mind*, Princeton: Princeton University Press, 1968.
18. Joséphin Péladan, *Le Secret des troubadours: de Parsifal à Don Quichotte*, Paris: E. Sansot, 1906, pp. 44–6. Translated from French by the author.
19. René Nelli and René Lavaud, op. cit., pp. 258–9. Translated by the author

CHAPTER III

1. Noel Stock (*Poet in Exile*, Manchester University Press, 1964) devotes a chapter to 'The Pagan Mystery Religions'. He acknowledges the importance of Eleusis to the *Cantos*, but unaccountably regards Pound's paganism as a weakness and 'a detour, an attempt to avoid the main claims of orthodox Christianity' (p. 15). Boris de Rachewiltz ('Pagan and Magic Elements in Ezra Pound's Work', in Hesse, *New Approaches*, 174–97) throws much light on the mystery religion elements of the later cantos.
2. 'Three Cantos: I', *Poetry*, X (June 1917), p. 119. 'O Virgilio mio' is obviously a reference to the *Commedia*—although this precise expression occurs nowhere in Dante's poem.
3. The first nineteen lines of canto 3 are lifted from 'Canto One' where they are found scattered over several pages. Of course the lines have been considerably revised, and Pound has made some additions—most notably the line, 'And peacocks in Koré's house, or there may have been'.
4. The descent under the earth down a staircase, and the 'tree of the bough' surely allude to Book VI of the *Aeneid*. The quiet air, on the other hand, derives from the fourth canto of the *Inferno* and the description of Limbo. Of course, Dante himself borrows some details of his Limbo from Virgil. Pound would not appear to have drawn on Dante's descent through the gate of Purgatory (*Purgatorio*, ix. 95–108). The whole passage, and others like it, suggests a pictorial inspiration—perhaps a specific painting or a *mélange* of several Pound had seen.
5. *Letters*, p. 285.
6. Yale Collection, no. 745.
7. Ezra Pound, *The ABC of Reading*, A New Directions Paperbook, n.d., p. 44.
8. *Poetry*, X, pp. 120–1. Simonetta is the woman who some say modelled for the painting.
9. It should be understood that the Mysteries remain a mystery to this day. A great deal is known about them, but the precise nature of the *epopteia* is not known. My principal authority is C. Kerenyi, *Eleusis: Archetypal Image of Mother and Daughter*, trans. Ralph Mannheim, Bollingen Series, LXV. 4, Pantheon Books, 1967.
10. I had the geography of Circeo and Terracina wrong in 'A Light from Eleusis' (*Paideuma*, 3, p. 204). I am indebted to Hugh Kenner for pointing out my error and correctly identifying the localities. However, Kenner did not mention the probable source in Bérard (Victor Bérard, *Les Phéniciens et l'Odyssée*, 2 vols., Paris: Libraire Armand Colin, 1902, 1903. For Feronia see especially II, pp. 285–7.)

    Bérard's identification of Circe with Feronia, and that goddess's role in the manumission of slaves may account for Pound's continuing interest in Sordello's mistress, Cunizza da Romano even after Sordello himself had been virtually expunged from the poem. She is first mentioned, rather incidentally, in canto 6, closing a brief account of Sordello's life. Sordello

    > . . . went to the court of Richard Saint Boniface
    > And was there taken with love for his wife
    > Cunizza, da Romano,

That freed her slaves on a Wednesday
Masnatas et servos. . . .

(6/22:26)

She reappears in canto 29, and then is recalled four times in the *Pisan Cantos* (74:438:465, 443:471, 76/452:480, and 78/483:514), always in association with theophanies. However, it may be that Pound simply admired her kindness. He writes in *Guide to Kulchur* (p. 108): 'There was nothing in Créstien de Troyes' narratives, nothing in Rimini or in the tales of the ancients to surpass the facts of Cunizza, with, in her old age, great kindness, thought for her slaves.'

11. The Anchises reference is to canto 23 where Pound alludes to the Homeric hymn to Aphrodite and its account of Aphrodite's 'marriage' to Anchises in the guise of the daughter of the Phrygian king, Otreus:

'King Otreus, of Phrygia,
'That king is my father.'
and saw then, as of waves taking form.
As the sea, hard, a glitter of crystal,
And the waves rising but formed, holding their form.
No light reaching through them.

(23/109:114)

The Faber edition has:

And she said: 'Otreus of Phrygia,
'That king is my father . . .'
and I saw then, as of waves taking form.

12. Kerenyi, op. cit., pp. 117–18. Lewis Farnell (*The Cults of the Greek States*, vol. III, Oxford at the Clarendon Press, 1907) mentions Aphrodite not at all, and Paul Foucart (*Les Mystères d'Eleusis*, Paris: Auguste Picard, 1914) expressly states that Aphrodite had no role at all in the nocturnal rites of initiation (p. 392).

13. Foucart, op. cit., p. 391. He quotes Lenormant: 'On peut, je crois, conclure sans hésiter . . . qu'une apparition de Vénus faisait partie des spectacles d'Eleusis, et, de même que la vue de la statue de Démeter inaugurait la représentation, qu'elle se terminait par l'intervention de Vénus, au moment ou l'on voulait que l'extase de l'initié arrivat à son comble.'

14. Cited by Paul Foucart, op. cit., p. 393. Translated from French by the author. Farnell cites the same passage (*Cults*, III, p. 179), but attributes it to one Themistius, and then calls Themistius' reliability into question. I 'can nat bult it to the bren', and merely note this as a curiosity.

15. The interpretation of canto 39 and the Odyssean role in the *Cantos* given here differs materially from that so convincingly argued by Forrest Read in 'A Man of no Fortune' (in *Motive and Method in the Cantos of Ezra Pound*, ed. Lewis Leary, New York: Columbia University Press, 1954, pp. 101–23). Read quite correctly argues for the importance of the Odyssean parallel. Where we differ is in his assumption that it is the *nostos* or return journey which is most significant for the *Cantos*, and my contention that it is the descent which is most important, and further, that the return to Penelope and Ithaca does not apply to the *Cantos*. I would also take issue with Read's tendency in his article to allegorize canto 39. I find nothing in canto 39 or

elsewhere in the poem to justify his assertion, for example, that 'Eurilochus is the destructive side of Odysseus' nature' or that 'Elpenor is the perversion of passion'.

16. Homer, *The Odyssey*, with an English translation by A. T. Murray, London: William Heinemann, 1966, x. 333–5.
17. The incomplete Latin is from the Clark and Ernestus translation of the *Odyssey*. Pound more or less translates it in the following line. It is actually Odysseus speaking, asking if anyone has ever been to Hell in a black ship and returned.
18. The *Annotated Index* gives a reference for *sub nocte* to *Aeneid*, VI. 268. There Aeneas and the Sibyl are just entering the Underworld: 'Dimly through the shadows and dark solitudes they wended,/Through the void domiciles of Dis, the bodiless region'. (*Aeneid*, VI. 268–9.)
19. Lilian Feder ('The Voice from Hades in the Poetry of Ezra Pound', *Michigan Quarterly Review*, 10 (1971), pp. 167–86) has anticipated some of the observations recorded here—particularly the association of love and death. However Feder does not connect what she calls the image of death with Eleusis. Instead she tends to psychoanalyze Pound's 'preoccupation' with death: 'Yet, perhaps in spite of himself, the mythical voices Pound adopts, especially the voice from Hades, expose a chaos within the speaker deeper and more threatening than even the rage he projects on the people and the societies he judges and condemns.' (p. 167.)
20. Forrest Read, 'A Man of no Fortune' and *Pound/Joyce*, p. 193. Read's hypothesis of the *nostos* is both well argued and influential. I do not pretend to refute it with these few words, but rather with the substance of my own argument.
21. Ezra Pound, *A Lume Spento and Other Early Poems*, London: Faber & Faber, 1965, pp. 65–6. The poem is dedicated to Swinburne.

    Walter Baumann (*The Rose in the Steel Dust*) has taken note of this poem (p. 105) and the dedication and has concluded that it 'may lead one to assume that Pound's mythological and paganistic preoccupations were inspired, to a high degree, by his enthusiastic admiration for Swinburne's poetry'. Thus may a man's juvenilia come back to haunt him.

    It is true that Swinburne has three Eleusinian poems in *Poems and Ballads* ('Hymn to Proserpine', 'The Garden of Proserpine', and 'At Eleusis'), but none of them could have suggested 'Salve O Pontifex', much less the mythology of the *Cantos*.

    Pound probably did read at least 'Hymn to Proserpine' because he borrows the phrase 'pale galilean' from it, and may have borrowed the Greek phrase from Epictetus on page 44 of canto 77 from this poem as well.

    Swinburne's other 'Hellenics' are not of a character to have inspired Pound's 'mythological and paganistic preoccupations', and Baumann does not produce any further evidence to support his discovery.
22. *The Spirit of Romance*, p. 127.
23. In fact, they may have been Manichaeans. At least both Pierre Belperron, *La Croisade contre les Albigeois* (Paris, 1942) and Zoé Oldenbourg, *Massacre at Montségur* (New York, 1961) argue that the Albigenses held the Mani-

chaean belief that the world was created by the devil and was therefore inherently evil. However, a Gnostic influence seems more likely.

24. *Letters*, p. 432. Jan. 1940. For a comprehensive discussion of Erigena in the *Cantos* see Walter B. Michaels, 'Pound and Erigena', *Paideuma*, 1 (Spring–Summer 1972), pp. 37–54.
25. The image of the stone knowing the form first occurs in the Cavalcanti essay: 'The god is inside the stone, *vacuos exercet aera morsus*. The force is arrested, but there is never any question about its latency, about the force being the essential and the rest "accidental" in the philosophical technical sense.' *Literary Essays*, p. 152. Erigena was not dug up. See W. B. Michaels for an account of Pound's error (p. 43).
26. *The Spirit of Romance*, n. 3, p. 91.
27. G. R. S. Mead, *Simon Magus: An Essay*, London: Theosophical Publishing Society, 1892, pp. 19–20.
28. Mead, op. cit., pp. 20–1.
29. G. R. S. Mead, *Fragments of a Faith Forgotten*, London and Benares Theosophical Publishing Society, 1906, 2nd edition, pp. 167–8.
30. Mead, *Simon Magus*, p. 75.
31. *Letters*, p. 397. Pound was so explicit that Mr. Paige found it necessary to replace the key word with four dashes. But even with the elision, the statement is sufficiently clear, I think.
32. She appears in 'Canto Two' (*Poetry*, X, p. 186):

    The kernelled walls of Toro, *las almenas*;
    Afield, a king come in an unjust cause.
    Atween the chinks aloft flashes the armored figure,
    Muy linda, a woman, Helen, a star,
    Lights the king's features . . .,
    'No use, my liege—
    She is your highness' sister,' breaks in Ancures;
    'Mal fuego s'enciende!'
    Such are the gestes of war 'told over and over.'

    The same incident has been retained in the poem, but pushed back to canto 20, and now described by Pound as 'subject rhyme with Helen on Wall', as in canto 7:

    Under the battlement
    (Epi purgo) peur de la hasle,
    And the King said:
    'God what a woman!
    My God what a woman' said the King telo rigido.
    'Sister!' says Ancures, ''s your sister!'
    Alf left that town to Elvira, and Sancho wanted
    It from her, Toro and Zamora.
    (20/91:95)

    The second version is both more cryptic and more firmly attached to the theme of a city destroyed by a woman.
33. *Letters*, p. 130.
34. However, Herbert N. Schneidau suggests on the evidence of an unpublished and unquoted letter that Pound heard this lecture in December 1911 (*Ezra*

Pound: The Image and the Real, Baton Rouge: Louisiana State U.P., 1969, p. 119).

35. Canto 5/18:22. The story is scarcely intelligible in this version. Pound gives a more complete prose version of the *vida* in 'Troubadours—Their Sorts and Conditions' (*Literary Essays*, pp. 95–6):

> The monk, Guabertz de Poicebot, 'was a man of birth; he was of the bishopric of Limozin, son of the castellan of Poicebot. And he was made monk when he was a child in a monastery, which is called Sain Leonart. And he knew well letters, and well to sing and well *trobar*. And for desire of woman he went forth from the monastery. And he came thence to the man to whom came all who for courtesy wished honour and good deeds—to Sir Savaric de Mauleon—and this man gave him the harness of a joglar and a horse and clothing; and then he went through the courts and composed and made good canzos. And he set his heart upon a donzella gentle and fair and made his songs of her, and she did not wish to love him unless he should get himself made a knight and take her to wife. And he told En Savaric how the girl had refused him, wherefore En Savaric made him a knight and gave him land and the income from it. And he married the girl and held her in great honour. And it happened that he went into Spain, leaving her behind him. And a knight out of England set his mind upon her and did so much and said so much that he led her with him, and he kept her long time his mistress and then let her go to the dogs (malamen anar). And En Gaubertz returned from Spain, and lodged himself one night in the city where she was. And he went out for desire of woman, and he entered the *alberc* of a poor woman; for they told him there was a fine woman within. And he found his wife. And when he saw her, and she him, great was the grief between them and great shame. And he stopped the night with her, and on the morrow he went forth with her to a nunnery where he had her enter. And for this grief he ceased to sing and to compose.'

36. It may be that Pound drew upon Sir James Frazer for the particular conception he has of a divine marriage in cantos 39 and 47. Frazer has little to say about Eleusis, but what he does say could well have led Pound in the direction he takes in these two cantos:

> In the great mysteries solemnized at Eleusis in the month of September the union of the sky-god Zeus with the corn-Goddess, Demeter appears to have been represented by the union of the hierophant with the priestess of Demeter, who acted the parts of god and goddess. But their intercourse was only dramatic or symbolical.
>
> After a time the hierophant reappeared, and in a blaze of light silently exhibited to the assembly a reaped ear of corn, the fruit of the divine marriage. (Sir James Frazer, *The Golden Bough*, vol. II, London: Macmillan, 1890, p. 138.)

In vol. VII Frazer modifies this statement admitting that the god should perhaps be Zeus Chthonius and the goddess, Persephone, but is still confident that some sort of sacred marriage took place (pp. 67–9).

37. Kerenyi tells us that the Eleusinian nights of Alexandria, where a sacred marriage was performed, were remote from the nights of Eleusis where no such performance took place. Frazer, however, accepted the Alexandrian rites as true for Eleusis as well. (Kerenyi, op. cit., pp. 117–18).

38. Canto 116/795–6. Compare with this the remark in *Guide to Kulchur*: 'Properly we shd. read for power. Man reading shd. be man intensely alive. *The book shd. be a ball of light in one's hand.*' (p. 55; my italics.)

CHAPTER IV

1. Daniel Cory, 'Ezra Pound: A Memoir', *Encounter*, 30 (May 1968), p. 38.
2. The typography is as in the *Paris Review*, 28 (Summer–Fall 1962), 'Two Cantos by Ezra Pound' (canto 116), pp. 14–15. The text is the same in *Drafts and Fragments*, but the lines are set up a little differently. There is an obvious typographical error in the *Paris Review* ('there verb' for 'the verb') which I have corrected.
3. Richard Ellmann, 'Two Faces of Edward', in *Edwardians and Late Victorians*, New York: Columbia University Press, 1960, pp. 197–8.
4. 'Postscript to *The Natural Philosophy of Love* by Remy de Gourmont', in *Pavannes and Divagations*, Norfolk, Conn.: New Directions, 1958, p. 214.
5. 'An Introduction to the Economic Nature of the United States', in *Impact*, Chicago: Henry Regnery, 1960, p. 15.
6. It is of some interest to note in this connection that there is only one *maestro di color che sanno* in the *Commedia*, and that is Aristotle, whom Dante sees in Limbo (*Inferno*, iv. 131). The wise are indeed found in the first circle of Heaven, but Dante does not call them 'the masters of those who know'.
7. He had previously published *The Sonnets and Ballate of Guido Cavalcanit with Translation and Introduction*, Boston: Small, Maynard and Company, 1912.
8. George Dekker, *Sailing After Knowledge*, London: Routledge & Kegan Paul, 1963, pp. 111–41.
9. Noel Stock, *Reading the Cantos*, New York: Pantheon Books, 1966, pp. 26–7. In both this book and the earlier *Poet in Exile*, Stock argues that the *Cantos* are radically flawed, and are, indeed, 'nothing like advertised'. There is a good deal of sane common sense in his position, but he over-reacts to the poem's undeniable imperfections with the zeal of the fallen disciple.
10. W. B. Yeats, *Letters*, ed. Allan Wade, London: Rupert Hart-Davis, 1954, p. 739.
11. J. E. Shaw, *Guido Cavalcanti's Theory of Love: The Canzone d'Amore and Other Related Problems*, Toronto: The University of Toronto Press, 1949, p. 213.
12. *The Spirit of Romance*, pp. 91–2.
13. The review appeared originally in *Criterion* (Oct. 1932, 12, pp. 106–12), but is reprinted in *Ezra Pound: The Critical Heritage*, ed. Eric Homberger, London: Routledge & Kegan Paul, 1972, pp. 273–9.
14. James J. Wilhelm argues ('Guido Cavalcanti as a Mask for Ezra Pound', *PMLA*, 89 (Mar. 1974), pp. 323–40) that Pound's translation is defensible. Wilhelm uses the Italian critic Bruno Nardi to defend Pound's Averroistic reading of Cavalcanti, and as an answer to J. E. Shaw's criticisms.

    However, Wilhelm notes that Pound's translation 'utterly ignores the key phrase *poco soggiorna* (l. 48), "last but a little", where Cavalcanti insists upon the brevity of love. Similarly, Pound overlooks verse 56, which stipulates that in love as actuality there is 'no great wisdom' (*né . . . gran saver*)' (p. 339). These omissions reinforce my contention that Pound deliberately altered the sense of the poem to suit the needs of his own poetic enterprise.

See also George M. Gugelberger, 'The Secularization of "Love" to a Poetic Metaphor: Cavalcanti, Center of Pound's Medievalism', *Paideuma*, 2 (Fall 1973), pp. 159–73. Gugelberger discusses the sonnets as well as 'Dona mi Prega'.

15. *The Spirit of Romance*, pp. 96–7. In this comment one can see the rationale of the *Pisan Cantos*.
16. 'Cavalcanti', in *Literary Essays*, p. 151. This essay consists of the apparatus from *Guido Cavalcanti Rime* together with the Italian text and Pound's translation.
17. See Stuart Y. McDougal's analysis of the influence of Provençal poetry on Pound in *Ezra Pound and the Troubadour Tradition*, Princeton: Princeton University Press, 1972. Of particular interest in this connection is his analysis of 'The Flame' (pp. 94–7). He finds that 'the sexual experience symbolized by the "flame" is apparently a prelude to visionary knowledge. This knowledge permits one to converse with the gods, and to visit "places splendid"' (p. 97). See also Hugh Witemeyer, *The Poetry of Ezra Pound: Forms and Renewal, 1908–20*, (Berkeley and Los Angeles: The University of California Press, 1969), and Herbert N. Schneidau, *Ezra Pound: The Image and the Real* (Baton Rouge: Louisiana State U.P., 1969). All three books give a similar analysis of Pound's association of vision and sexuality, and demonstrate severally the complexity and persistence of this notion in Pound's aesthetic. My own analysis parallels aspects of those by Schneidau, Witemayer, and McDougal, but is independent of them.
18. In 'Religio or The Child's Guide to Knowledge', from *Pavannes and Divisions* (1918), Pound's conception of the nature of divinity is quite clearly stated: '"What is a god?" "A god is an eternal state of mind." "When is a god manifest?" "When the states of mind take form." "By what characteristics may we know the divine form?" "By beauty." "In what manner do gods appear?" "Formed and formlessly." "To what do they appear when formed?" "To the sense of vision."' (pp. 96–7). Mead's Gnostic texts sort well with such views.
19. *Literary Essays*, p. 160. Translated from French by the author. Pound also cites some fragments from Robert Grosseteste's *De Luce* suggesting that Cavalcanti may have read this neo-Platonic essay on light. For a full discussion of Grosseteste's presence in the *Cantos* and the text of *De Luce* (in Latin and English) see Carroll F. Terrell, 'A Commentary on Grosseteste with an English version of *De Luce*', *Paideuma*, 2 (Winter 1973), pp. 447–70
20. G. R. S. Mead, *Simon Magus*, p. 71.
21. 'In the Wounds: Memoriam A. R. Orage', *Impact*, pp. 157–8.
22. Quoted by C. B. Macpherson, *Democracy in Alberta*, Toronto: University of Toronto Press, 1953, p. 120. Until recently the best discussion of Douglas and Social Credit, Macpherson's book has now been superseded by John L. Finlay, *Social Credit: The English Origins*, Montreal and London: McGill–Queen's University Press, 1972. Finlay traces the background to Social Credit in English radical economic thought as Macpherson does not. He traces the theory of underconsumption back to John Ruskin and up to J. M. Keynes.

    Douglas first developed his ideas fully in the series of essays, 'Economic Democracy', appearing in the *New Age* from June to August of 1919. This was quickly followed by 'Credit-Power and Democracy' also in the *New Age* (February 1919 to August 1920), running concurrently with Pound's shorter 'Revolt of Intelligence' endorsing Douglas's views. Both of Douglas's series of articles appeared as books under the same titles in 1920. His major statement was *Social Credit*, published in 1924 (London: Cecil Palmer). He also went about the country giving lectures—some of which appear in *The Control and Distribution of Production* (London: Cecil Palmer, 1922).

23. The Labour Party, *Report of Committee on the Douglas–'New Age' Credit Scheme*, 1922, p. 15. This committee included among its members G. D. H. Cole, J. A. Hobson, and R. H. Tawney.
24. John Kenneth Galbraith, *Money: Whence It Came, Where It Went*, London: André Deutsch, 1975, p. 168.
25. Much of Douglas's writing in the thirties and forties appears in Social Credit journals, but *The Brief for the Prosecution* (Liverpool: K. R. P. Publications, 1945) provides sufficient evidence of his paranoia. There is no difference in quality or content from Pound's fulminations of the 1940s.
26. Earle Davis, *Vision Fugitive: Ezra Pound and Economics*, Lawrence: University of Kansas Press, 1968. Davis discusses much of the literature on Pound's politics and economics. The best study of Pound's political views is William M. Chace, *The Political Identities of Ezra Pound and T. S. Eliot*, Stanford, California: Stanford University Press, 1973. Chace's discussion is thorough and fair minded, but his arguments are biographical and psychological.
27. John Maynard Keynes, *The General Theory of Employment, Interest, and Money*, London: Macmillan, 1936, p. 18.
28. Galbraith, pp. 218–19.
29. Galbraith, p. 220.
30. Keynes, pp. 32–3.
31. 'The Mechanism of Consumer Control', *New Age*, 28 (23 Dec. 1920), p. 88.
32. Keynes, p. v.
33. Keynes, pp. 370–1.
34. Keynes, pp. 353–8.
35. Canto 74/441:468–9. It is not clear from this account that Wörgl's money was stamp scrip, but Pound calls it Gesellist money in 'A Visiting Card' (*Impact*, p. 51):

> In the early 1930's the small Tyrolean town of Wörgl sent shivers down the backs of all the lice of Europe, by issuing its own Gesellist money (or rather the Gesellist variety of Mazzinian money). Each month every note of this money had to have a revenue stamp affixed to it of a value equal to one per cent of the face-value of the note. Thus the municipality derived an income of twelve per cent per annum on the new money put into circulation.
>
> The town had been bankrupt: the citizens had not been able to pay their rates, the municipality had not been able to pay the schoolteachers, etc. But in less than two years everything had been put right, and the townspeople had built a new stone bridge for themselves, etc. All went well until an ill-starred Wörgl note was presented at the counter of an Innsbruck bank. It was noticed, all right—no doubt about that. The plutocratic monopoly had been infringed. Threats, fulminations, anathema! The burgomaster was deprived of his office, but the ideological war had been won.

36. Galbraith, pp. 206–9.
37. 'The Mechanism of Consumer Control', p. 78.
38. 'A Visiting Card', *Impact*, p. 48.
39. C. H. Douglas, *The Brief for the Prosecution*, Liverpool: K. R. P. Publications, 1945, p. 66. Douglas does not name Keynes, but it is obviously Keynesian policies he has in mind. This book is definitely crazy, blaming even the 1929 crash on the deliberate action of the banks, who, he says, called in their loans and overdrafts in a fit of pique because industry was becoming so prosperous that it was slipping out of their control. Of course, the banks did call in their loans in 1929, contributing to the crash, but their action was part of the general panic, and certainly not a deliberate attempt to destroy the American economy.
40. 'The Enemy is Ignorance', *Impact*, p. 112.
41. Karl Marx, *Capital*, Moscow: Progress Publishers, vol. I, p. 130.
42. Pound could have read intelligent criticisms (from a Social Credit perspective) of the economic policies of Hitler and Mussolini in the pages of the *New English Weekly* had he wished to. He preferred to praise the Fascists—including Father Coughlin and Huey Long—and damn Roosevelt in his own weekly item, 'American Notes' (beginning in the first number of the *N.E.W.* for 1935). Pound's contributions to the *N.E.W.* are markedly more virulent and excited than those of any other writer. Orage tried to steer him to literary subjects, but Pound clung to his platform for vituperation in the one column allowed him for 'American Notes'.
43. C. H. Douglas, *The Control and Distribution of Production*, London: Cecil Palmer, 1922, p. 79.
44. 'The Revolt of Intelligence: VII', *New Age*, 26 (4 March 1920), p. 287.
45. Christopher Hollis, *The Two Nations: A Financial Study of English History*, London: Routledge, 1935.
46. Hollis, p. 30. Hollis does not give any source for the remark.
47. Hollis, p. 19.
48. Hollis, pp. 9–10. The quantitative theory Hollis refers to is the theory of money elaborated by the American economist, Irving Fisher. It is substantially the same theory as that subscribed to by Douglas. As Galbraith describes it:

    Fisher made prices dependent on the volume of cash or circulating money and the rate at which it turned over, together with the volume of bank deposits and the rate at which they turned over, all adjusted for the volume of trade. (Galbraith, p. 208).

    In effect, the quantity theory of money acknowledges that if prices are to remain stable, and economic activity fostered, an increasing capacity to deliver goods and services must be matched by an increasing volume of circulating money.
49. Hollis, pp. 130–1.
50. Hollis, *The Seven Ages: Their Exits and Their Entrances*, London: Heinemann, 1974, p. 133.
51. In *Pavannes and Divagations*, pp. 213–14.
52. For a discussion of Agassiz's thought and Pound's debt to him see the introduction to *The Intelligence of Louis Agassiz* by Guy Davenport (Boston: Beacon Press, 1963).

53. 'Postscript', loc. cit., p. 212.
54. *Guide to Kulchur*, p. 299.
55. The Italian translates: 'In your belly, or in my mind'.
56. Or when compared to the contemporary theories of Henri Bergson, Chardin's acknowledged master. Oddly, Pound appears to have been quite ignorant of Bergson despite his great vogue before the First World War. He may, however, have absorbed some Bergsonian ideas from T. E. Hulme, and T. S. Eliot. He mentions Hulme's lectures on Bergson in a letter to his parents (Yale Collection, no. 232).
57. The creativity of the act of perception is a familiar Romantic notion, most uncompromisingly held by William Blake, but most influentially expressed in Coleridge's theory of the imagination. It is, of course, the meaning of the lines quoted above from canto 51:

    That hath the light of the doer, as it were
    a form cleaving to it
    Deo similis quodam modo
    hic intellectus adeptus
    [God-like, in a way, this intellect that has grasped.]

    And it is also part of the sense of the lines: 'Cometh of a seen form which being understood/Taketh locus and remaining in the intellect possible'.
58. Ernest Fenollosa, *The Chinese Written Character as a Medium for Poetry*, ed. Ezra Pound, San Francisco: City Lights Books, n.d., pp. 22–3.
59. Pound reported to W. C. Williams that he had the notes in his hands on 19 December 1913 (*Letters*, p. 65). Noel Stock (*The Life of Ezra Pound*, p. 148) reports the first meeting of Pound and Mrs. Fenollosa.

    It is interesting to note in passing the association Norman Holmes Pearson observes between Fenollosa and Agassiz:

    > It was he [Louis Agassiz] in his laboratory at Harvard who trained Edward S. Morse, the Salem natural scientist who taught at the Imperial University of Tokyo and became the influential collector and curator of Oriental art in this country, not forgetting to carry over the lessons of Agassiz into the new field. And it was Morse who in turn persuaded Ernest Fenollosa, also from Salem and fresh from Harvard, to go out as instructor in rhetoric to the Imperial University, where Fenollosa's interest like that of Morse expanded to include the stimulation of Oriental culture. (Review of Square $ Series, *Shenandoah*, 7 (Autumn 1955), pp. 81–2.)
60. *ABC of Reading*, p. 22.
61. *Spirit of Romance*, pp. 92–3. Pound may well have been influenced toward such a view by A. R. Orage, editor of the *New Age* in which Pound published regularly from 1911 to 1921, both under his own name and a variety of pseudonyms (William Atheling for music criticism and B. H. Dias for art criticism). In *Consciousness: Animal, Human, and Superman* (London and Benares: The Theosophical Publishing Society, 1907) Orage begins his argument from the assumption that 'my present human consciousness is only a superior degree of animal, plant, or mineral consciousness' (p. 12).
62. The last line brings in Amor by way of the persons of Aphrodite, Malatesta's mistress, Isotta degli Atti, and a representation of the Virgin Mary. They, like the stone, know the form imparted to them by their lovers/worshippers.
63. Fenollosa, op. cit., p. 23.

64. 'The Teacher's Mission' (1934), in *Literary Essays*, p. 61.
65. Donald Hall, 'Ezra Pound: An Interview', p. 48.
66. Letter to the Editor, *New English Weekly*, 3 (11 May 1933), p. 96.

    The categories (permanent, recurrent, and casual) he suggests are those mentioned in 'Patria Mia' (1912), but there he was speaking of reasons for studying the past, not of the *Cantos*, which were not yet even in embryo. (It is true that Pound assigns the date, 1912 to the first lines of 'Canto One' in his foreword to *Selected Cantos*, but there is no evidence dating from 1912 to support so early a date.)
67. *Letters*, p. 330 (14 Sept. 1933).
68. *Letters*, p. 259.
69. John Drummond ('The Italian Background to The Cantos', in *An Examination of Ezra Pound*, ed. Peter Russell, New York: New Directions, n.d., pp. 100–18) provides considerable assistance in unravelling the history of the period, but even with his help, it remains sorely complex. Pound's principal source is Charles Yriarte, *Un Condottiere au xv*[e] *siècle*, Paris: J. Rothschild, 1882. Yriarte includes Malatesta's letters and his poetry.
70. Letter to John Quinn, 10 Aug. 1922. Quoted by Daniel Pearlman, *The Barb of Time*, p. 302.

    Later in the same letter, Pound advises Quinn, 'don't you never try to write a epict, it is too bloody complicated'. This remark, casual as it is, must be placed against the disclaimer of epic status from 1924 cited above.
71. *Guide to Kulchur*, p. 159.
72. *Guide to Kulchur*, p. 159.
73. *Gaudier-Brzeska: A Memoir*, The Marvell Press, 1960, p. 91. This chapter (11) is reprinted from the *Fortnightly Review*, 96 (1 Sept. 1914).

CHAPTER V

1. L. D. Peterson, 'Ezra Pound: The Use and Abuse of History', *American Review*, 17 (1965), pp. 33–47; Noel Stock, *Reading the Cantos*; and Ronald Baar, 'Ezra Pound: Poet as Historian', *American Literature*, 42 (Jan. 1970) pp. 531–43. Each of these studies finds Pound either wilfully or unwittingly guilty of misrepresenting the facts of history. Peterson's argument is that Pound's view of history is not disinterested, and is therefore unsound. His premise is certainly true, but his argument is based on the further assumption that only disinterested history is sound—an ideal assumption which would vitiate the vast bulk of historical writing. Stock's argument is essentially the same as Peterson's.

    Ronald Baar compares Pound's treatment of the Bank War in the United States in cantos 37, 88, and 89 with academic histories, and finds Pound's representation to be distorted. He does not, however, examine Pound's sources, the *Autobiography* of Martin Van Buren and Thomas Hart Benton's *Thirty Years' View*. These sources are biased accounts by participants in the Bank War, but they are legitimate first-hand accounts. Pound, of course, believes the academic historians to be biased. In any event, Pound is not falsifying history in following biased contemporary accounts.

    In sum, all three of these critics apply to Pound's historical material the single standard of disinterestedness—an attribute he has never claimed for his 'history'—and they dismiss it when it (predictably) fails to meet that standard. Anyone familiar with historical writing will realize that such a standard is rarely, if ever, achieved even in professional historical writing (viz. the Whig and Tory histories of Britain, or, more recently, liberal and socialist histories), and is never achieved, nor desired, in poetic histories.

2. William M. Chace, 'Ezra Pound and the Marxist Temptation', *American Quarterly*, 22 (1970), pp. 714–25. Chace argues that Pound was driven mad by the conflict between his reactionary bourgeois elitism and his revolutionary social and artistic aims.
3. Harvey Gross, 'Pound's *Cantos* and the Idea of History', *Bucknell Review*, 9 (1960) pp. 14–31. Gross tells us that 'history as Pound presents it and interprets it, is no longer an ordering form; it is no longer an instrument for viewing reality' (p. 27). His argument is essentially the same as that of Wyndham Lewis in *Time and Western Man*, although it is more pointed. Both men are unhappy with an artistic representation that lacks the fixity and coherence of a sculptural object. It would be beyond the scope of this note to argue with their intellectual and aesthetic assumptions, but it is worth observing that the history in the *Cantos* can hardly be both fantastical and incoherent, and at the same time, narrow and tendentious.
4. Roy Harvey Pearce, 'Pound, Whitman, and the American Epic', in *Ezra Pound: A Collection of Critical Essays*, ed. Walter Sutton, Englewood Cliffs, N.J.: Prentice-Hall, 1963, pp. 163–77.
5. Pearce, op. cit., p. 174.
6. *Guide to Kulchur*, p. 195.
7. Ibid., p. 60.
8. Ibid., pp. 51–2.
9. Ibid., p. 129.
10. Ibid., p. 53.
11. Ibid., p. 53.
12. Karl Popper is perhaps the most cogent critic of the use of explanatory principles in history, which he calls 'historicism'. See *The Poverty of Historicism*, London: Routledge & Kegan Paul, 1957, and *The Open Society and its Enemies*, 2 vols., London: Routledge, 1945.
13. T. S. Eliot, 'Ezra Pound', in *Ezra Pound*, ed. Walter Sutton, p. 23. The essay was first published in 1946.
14. Ezra Pound, *Patria Mia*, London: Peter Owen, 1962, pp. 48–9. This book, not published until 1950, is based on two series of articles published in the *New Age*: 'Patria Mia', 5 Sept. 1912 – 14 Nov. 1912; and 'America: Chances and Remedies', 1 May 1913–5 June 1913. This quotation is from 'Patria Mia VI'.
15. *Letters*, p. 321.
16. *Confucius: The Great Digest & Unwobbling Pivot*, translation and commentary by Ezra Pound, London: Peter Owen, 1968, p. 36.
17. Guy Davenport, 'Pound and Frobenius', in *Motive and Method in the Cantos of Ezra Pound*, ed. Lewis Leary, p. 52.
18. A. Alvarez ('Craft and Morals', in *Ezra Pound: Perspectives*, ed. Noel Stock, Chicago: Henry Regnery, 1965) complains that 'the poet himself seems

hardly to exist' (p. 51). John Berryman ('The Poetry of Ezra Pound', *Partisan Review*, 16 (1949), pp. 377–94), on the other hand, observes that the *Cantos* 'seem to be only apparently an historical or philosophical epic, actually a personal epic', and suggests *The Prelude* as a parallel (p. 394).

19. *Patria Mia*, p. 49.
20. *Patria Mia*, pp. 13–14.
21. *Letters*, pp. 256, 257.
22. [April] 1924. Yale Collection, no. 669, p. 1. The following discussion is revised from 'The City of Dioce, U.S.A.: Pound and America', *Bucknell Review*, 20 (Fall 1972), pp. 13–34.
23. 20 May 1924. Yale Collection, no. 681, p. 1.
24. 25 October 1924. Yale Collection, no. 698.
25. 1 November 1924. Yale Collection, no. 700.
26. Oddly, Pound reports (Yale Collection, no. 885) that he is 'blocking in Cantos 28–30 but they won't affect the present volume'. These are the three cantos he added to the first two sections to form *A Draft of XXX Cantos*, published in 1930. I have never been able to understand the rationale behind the collection of the first two sections into a single long section of thirty cantos. Obviously Pound did not think of cantos 28 to 30 as an integral part of *Cantos 17–27*. See also Hugh Kenner, 'A Scheme for XXX Cantos', *Paideuma*, 2 (Fall 1973), p. 201.
27. Yale Collection, no. 702.
28. Yale Collection, no. 745.
29. Pound reported to Guy Davenport that it was about this time he began reading Frobenius. 'Pound and Frobenius', in *Motive and Method in the Cantos of Ezra Pound*, p. 35. Davenport's article remains the best discussion of the influence of Frobenius on Pound. Robert J. Welke has added a brief commentary on Frobenius's system in 'Frobenius: Pound—Some Quick Notes', *Paideuma*, 2 (Winter 1973), pp. 415–17.
30. *Guide to Kulchur*, pp. 57–8.
31. Robert J. Welke, 'Frobenius: Pound—Some Quick Notes', *Paideuma*, 2 (Winter 1973), p. 415.
32. Letter to Homer Pound, 11 Jan. 1927, Yale Collection, no. 846.
33. Leo Frobenius, *Erlebte Erdteile*, 7 vols. Frankfurt-on-Main, 1925–9.
34. Leo Frobenius, *The Voice of Africa*, trans. Rudolph Blind, London: Hutchinson, 1913, p. 337. The 'Templum' is Frobenius's term for the Yoruban world view in which the city of Ilife and its central temple represent a microcosm of creation.
35. 'The Jefferson–Adams Letters as a Shrine and a Monument', *Impact*, p. 171.
36. 'Date Line', *Literary Essays*, p. 85.
37. 'Terra Italica', *New Review*, 1 (Winter 1931/2), p. 388.
38. 'A Visiting Card' (1942), *Impact*, p. 55.
39. *Guide to Kulchur*, p. 264.
40. *Letters*, p. 434.
41. 'For a New Paideuma', *Criterion*, 17 (Jan. 1938), p. 205.
42. *Guide to Kulchur*, p. 44.

CHAPTER VI

1. W. E. Woodward, *George Washington: The Image and the Real*, New York: Boni and Liveright, 1926.
2. *Jefferson and/or Mussolini*, New York: Liveright, 1970, p. 12. Originally published in 1935.
3. This quotation is taken verbatim from a letter of 13 July 1813 from Adams to Jefferson (*The Life and Works of John Adams*, ed. Charles Francis Adams, Boston: Little, Brown & Co., 1856, vol. X, p. 53). Like many of the letters in these three cantos it is from the correspondence between Adams and Jefferson taken up in their old age after the rancours of their political opposition had subsided.

   The conversation must have taken place in 1780 when Adams returned to France with his sons, and when the Marquis de Lafayette was also in Paris. At this time the noble hero of the American revolutionary war would have been only twenty-three, and hardly a scholar.

   Pound's elision removes a reference to Napoleonic reforms, Napoleon not yet in Pound's favour: 'Cul de Sac, at Paris, and developed the plans now in operation to reform France, though I was silent as you was, I then thought I could say something new to him.'
4. 'The Jefferson–Adams Letters as a Shrine and a Monument', *Impact*, p. 168.
5. 'National Culture: A Manifesto', *Impact*, p. 3. Pound modestly refrains from mentioning himself as one of those heroic emigrants in the tradition of Whistler, and Henry James.
6. 'The Jefferson–Adams Letters as a Shrine and a Monument', *Impact*, pp. 166–7.
7. William Vasse, 'Aspects of the Cantos: II: American History and the Cantos', *Pound Newsletter*, 5 (Jan. 1955), p. 15. Vasse's brief article provides the best guide to annotation of American history in the *Cantos*. Canto 33 has been exhaustively annotated by William M. Chace, 'The Canto as Cento: A Reading of Canto XXXIII', *Paideuma*, 1 (Spring–Summer 1972), pp. 89–100. And Ronald Baar has studied canto 37 carefully, with a view to discover if Pound is a reliable historian, in 'Ezra Pound: Poet as Historian', *American Literature*, 42 (Jan. 1970), pp. 531–43. He finds that Pound is not a responsible historian, and throws some light on the Bank War of Jackson's administration, but does not annotate the canto thoroughly. Apart from these three articles and my own 'The City of Dioce, U.S.A.', the American aspect of the *Cantos* has received little scholarly attention, although brief critical pronouncements defining their importance or lack of it are not rare. Roy Harvey Pearce's article, 'Toward an American Epic' (*Hudson Review*, 12, Autumn 1959, pp. 362–77) is not specifically concerned with the American *content* of the *Cantos*, but should perhaps be mentioned here. Pearce argues in this excellent article that the American-ness of the *Cantos* is that Pound 'would create, not confirm, the hero if his epic' (p. 371).
8. *The Autobiography of Martin Van Buren*, Annual Report of the American Historical Association, 1918, vol. II. Pub. by Gov't. Printing Office, Washington, D.C., 1920. Van Buren dates it 1854, and Pound alludes frequently to the 'delay in publishing' it.

9. The first part of this quotation is from pp. 639–40 of Van Buren's autobiography:

> ... the plan which was carried out with such unrelenting vigor,—that of *employing the vast means at the disposal of the bank in deranging the credits of the Country* and of embarrassing business concerns to an extent sufficient to create wide spread distress and to infuse intense alarm for the safety of its every interest into all the ramifications of a great community—to excite public indignation against the Executive branch of the Government by imputing these disastrous occurrences to the interposition of the President's *Veto* and to the necessity he had wantonly imposed on the bank of preparing to wind up its affairs, the evils of which they (the bank leaders) had foretold, and to obtain, *by means of the extensive panic thus produced, a control over the action of the public mind* which would enable the protectors of these criminal schemes not only to mark out for the newly elected House of Representatives the course it should pursue but to gain in the sequel, possession of the General Government. [My italics, except for '*Veto*'.]

The second quotation is from p. 641:

> [Steps] were taken to supersede the action of *the regular and only board of directors* authorized by the charter in regard to all the important movements of the bank which it desired to conceal from the knowledge of the Government; of these the most important were the substitution of what was called the 'Exchange Committee', composed of only five directors, of whom the President of the bank was one and the other four were selected by him, and the bestowment of all but unlimited power on this Committee, whose doings were confidential and *from whose councils the Government directors were invariably excluded.* [My italics.]

In these pages Van Buren is discussing the behaviour of the Bank during 1832 and 1833 under Nicholas Biddle with respect to both management and control of its affairs. His argument is that the Bank's actions were undertaken with the deliberate intention of acquiring funds with which to suborn both the press and elected representatives. But the editor's notes observe that the Bank was, indeed, short of funds with which to meet its own obligations.

Obviously Pound ignores the editor's caution, but more disturbingly, he has adopted the device of quotation with such extreme elision as to approach, if not achieve, blank unintelligibility. The entire canto is constructed in the manner of these five lines, forcing the conscientious reader to become an industrious exegete, unless he is that mythical reader of quick wit, brilliant imagination, and unflagging attention that Pound apparently wrote for. Perhaps John Wain's suggestion that one read the *Cantos* in a semisomnolent state would get one through the American cantos happily.

10. *Jefferson and/or Mussolini*, p. 34.
11. *The Life and Works of John Adams*, vol. X, p. 197.
12. 'American History and the Cantos', *Pound Newsletter*, 5 (Jan. 1955), p. 14.
13. *Patria Mia*, p. 49.
14. C. F. Terrell has printed the Greek text and translation of Hanno's *Periplus* in 'The Periplus of Hanno', *Paideuma*, 1 (Fall–Winter 1972), pp. 223–30.
15. *Letters*, p. 386.
16. Giuseppe Galigani, 'Montis Pascuorum', *Yale Literary Magazine*, 126 (1958), pp. 18–23, provides an excellent annotation of these two cantos.
17. Giuseppe Galigani, op. cit., p. 19.

18. 'An Impact, 1935', *Impact*, p. 147.
19. Most of this is drawn from Christopher Hollis, *The Two Nations: A Financial Study of English History*, London: George Routledge & Sons, 1935. Hollis cites Paterson's remark on p. 30, but gives no source. The perfidious role of Regius professorships is also from Hollis (pp. 37–40).

    The Macmillan commission is doubtless the 1930 commission on Finance and Industry which heard C. H. Douglas as an expert witness, but did not take his advice.
20. Pound's source is Antonio Zobi, *Storia civile della Toscana*, Florence, 1850.
21. 'Semiramis' is the ship on which Marie Anne Elisa departed from Italy. Merinos are a breed of sheep, also mentioned in an Adams letter cited in canto 33 (p. 10:160).
22. 'Goodth' is 'goods', that is, Napoleon's economic sense was one of barter rather than credit and finance, hence a formidable opponent to the wicked bankers who speak with a lisp.

    Pound later accepts Brooks Adams's evaluation of Napoleon as the last challenge of the military and artistic type to the economic and usurious type. In this quotation from the *Pisan Cantos*, Mussolini is elevated to another such challenger. But Pound would not appear to have read *The Law of Civilization and Decay* before 1940, and therefore could not have had Brooks Adams in mind in canto 44.

    Pound does refer to 'B. Adams' in a 1930 letter to *Hound and Horn*, but does not otherwise refer to him until the 1940s when Brooks Adams becomes one of his 'discoveries'.

    Christopher Hollis also refers to Waterloo as a victory for the usurers (p. 88).
23. Noel Stock has described the background to these lines in *Reading The Cantos*, pp. 49–50. I have drawn on his account.
24. These dates are based on Yale Collection, nos. 1520, 1696, 1757.
25. Yale Collection, no. 1757.
26. The source of canto 49 remained a puzzle for many years until Daniel Pearlman discovered that it was based on a book of Homer Pound's containing seven Chinese and seven Japanese poems with illustrations. (*The Barb of Time*. Pearlman prints a translation of these poems in an appendix.)

    Hugh Kenner identified the English translation from which Pound worked in 'More on the Seven Lakes Canto', *Paideuma*, 2 (Spring 1973) pp. 43–6. And Angela Palandri identified the translator in 'The Seven Lakes Canto Revisited', *Paideuma*, 3 (Spring 1974), pp. 51–4. It was a Miss Tseng who visited the Pounds in 1928.
27. Hugh Kenner, *The Pound Era*, p. 434.
28. *Guide to Kulchur*, pp. 294–5.
29. Moyriac de Mailla, *Histoire générale de la Chine ou Annales de cet empire*, traduits du *Tong-Kien-King-Mou* par le feu père Joseph Anne-Marie de . . ., 12 vols., Paris 1777–83. The *Annotated Index* has a thirteenth volume by l'Abbé Grossier, and a final date of 1785, but the edition possessed by the Bodleian Library has no thirteenth volume.
30. I do not know the source of Pound's *Li Ki* fragment, but it is not de Mailla, nor is it from Pauthier or Couvreur, the other translations of Confucian

texts in his possession. William Tay does not identify the text Pound uses, but tells us that Pound's adaptation is primarily from chapter five of the *Li Ki*. William Tay, 'Between Kung and Eleusis', *Paideuma*, 4 (Spring 1975), pp. 37–54.

31. *Confucii Chi King, sive Liber Carminum* ex Latina P[ére] Lacharme interpretatione, edidit Julius Mohl, Stuttgartiae et Tubingae, 1830, p. 308.

32. Lacharme, p. 188. It is interesting to compare this rendering from the Latin with Pound's later translation directly from the Chinese (albeit with the aid of cribs):

    Many and thick moved the king's troops
    as the wings of birds flying
    (as the red plumes of the pheasant);
    as flood of the Kiang and Han,
    as the gnarled roots of the mountains,
    as rivers o'er flowing.

    Ezra Pound, *The Confucian Odes*, New York: New Direction Paperbook, 1959, Ode 263, p. 193.

33. In *The Confucian Odes* this is rendered:

    Splendid, dire, terrible in magnificence
    the Imperial operation royally
    stretched out, supported, aroused
    with no gaps and no straggling,
    ever deploying and prodding.

    The fulsome praise has been transferred from the emperor to his conduct of the campaign.

34. Lacharme, II. 3; Ode 10, p. 94.
35. De Mailla, V, pp. 57–8.
36. Pound's account is based on pp. 256–311 of vol. VIII.
37. *Confucius: The Great Digest and Unwobbling Pivot*, translation and commentary by Ezra Pound, London: Peter Owen, 1968, p. 19.
38. De Mailla, VIII, p. 278. The second line following the passage cited above from the *Cantos*, ('Died now the master of Nenuphar') refers to the death of Tcheou Tun-y, known as the 'master of nenuphar', because of a house he built in a place 'fort agréable, rempli de nénuphar'.
39. C. F. Terrell cites this passage and prints *De Luce* in Latin and English in 'A Commentary on Grosseteste with an English Version of *De Luce*', *Paideuma*, 2 (Winter 1973) pp. 449–70.
40. Lacharme, pp. xi–xii.
41. From a letter quoted by Charles Norman, *Ezra Pound*, p. 375.
42. Pound's selection is very remote from any I should make since it omits virtually all the Odysseus/Eleusis dimension of the poem and stresses the history and economics.
43. The University of Maine Press is advertising *John Adams Speaking: Pound's Sources for the Adams Cantos* by Frederick Sanders. I have not seen this work. It cannot help but reveal the slavish adherence to the organization of *The Life and Works* outlined in note 48 below.
44. The first line seems to reflect amusement at Charles Francis Adams's turn of phrase in his account:

At about nine o'clock of the night on which Lord North declared himself impassible to menace. . . . It was moonlight, and a light coating of fresh snow. . . . [Pound picks up King St. and Boston from the previous sentence.] There had been noise and commotion. . . . and at Murray's barracks, in what is now Brattle Street, where the twenty-ninth regiment was stationed. . . . In this case it was a barber's boy whose thoughtless impertinence opened the floodgates of passion in this town . . . (*Works*, I, pp. 97–8.)

45. Pound alludes to this in canto 65 (367:386):

    'Mr. Jefferson, you can write ten times better than I can'
    Cut about 1/4th and some of the best of it
    I have often wondered that J's first draft has
                                                                        not been published
    suppose the reason is the vehement phillippic
                                                                        against negro slavery'

    This is from a note which prints a letter by John Adams giving an account of the origin of the Declaration of Independence. *Works*, III, p. 514.

46. Pound gives this role, and indeed, the entire revolutionary war, scant attention: 'June 12th. J. Adams head of the Board of War/till Nov. eleventh '77' (65/368:386).

47. The first line of this quotation is from the entry for 14 May 1799 (*Works*, III, p. 202), and the second line is from the entry for 14 December 1799 (*Works*, III, p. 233).

48. His source is *The Life and Works of John Adams*, ed. Charles Francis Adams, 10 vols. Boston: Little, Brown & Co., 1852–65. In an appendix to 'American History and the Cantos' (*Pound Newsletter*, 5, Jan. 1955) William Vasse prints a table showing the volume and page corresponding to selected items in the poem (p. 19). It is clear from this list that Pound simply followed the order of material in the *Works*. The result is a peculiar dislocation of chronology. Cantos 62 and 63 trace Adams's career via Charles Francis Adams's biography up to the election of John Quincy Adams in 1825. Then, at the top of page 352 (369) we read 'Vol Two (as the protagonist saw it:)'. Volume II of *The Life and Works* begins John Adams's Diary, and Pound picks it up at its beginning in 1758. He continues to follow the Diary until it ends with an entry for 8 Sept. 1796 on page 424 of vol. III. The last line from the Diary is 'they wanted Hamilton for vice president/I said nothing' (66/381:402). But Charles Francis Adams had printed excerpts from the debates of the Continental Congress of 1775 at the end of vol. II. Instead of skipping them to follow the Diary, Pound includes them as well, beginning with 'Committee to purchase woollen goods for the Army' (65/365:383), down to 'Hooper of North Carolina said: I wish to see a day/when slaves are not necessary' (65/367:385). The debates run from page 445 to page 498 of vol. II.

    Having worked his way through the Diary by the second page of canto 66, Pound moves immediately into a redaction from Adams's published works in the order Charles Francis prints them, beginning with the 'Dissertation on the Canon and Feudal Law' first published in August of 1765 in the *Boston Gazette*. The balance of canto 66, canto 67, and canto 68 up to 'Commission to France '77' (68/396:417) is made up of redactions from Adams's works as printed in vols. III, IV, V, and VI of *The Life and Works*.

The rest of the section is based on the letters as printed in vols. VII, VIII, IX, and X, the letters beginning in 1777 and ending in 1818.

49. *Letters*, p. 418.
50. 'America and the Second World War', *Impact*, p. 185. Woodward discusses the currency issue in *A New American History*, New York: Garden City, 1938, pp. 107–25. Commenting on the prohibition of colonial paper money, he writes:

    The result was an excessive deflation; a pronounced drop in prices and wages. When the paper money was suppressed there was simply not enough coin in the colonies to carry on ordinary commerce. Britain's failure to settle the colonial currency problem satisfactorily was one of the material causes of the American Revolution. (p. 125)

51. *Impact*, p. 17: 'Adams faced the terrors of inflation by saying that a diminishing buying power of the paper money functioned as an unevenly distributed tax, a tax that hit those with a fixed salary, or living on an income; that the businessmen would have the best of it; and that, in any event, an inflation of this kind would not have created a public debt *with interest*.'
52. *Impact*, p. 95.
53. Woodward, *A New American History*, p. 167.
54. *Works*, VII, pp. 357–8.
55. By removing the punctuation, Pound has made it appear that the merchants, farmers, etc. are the moneyed men, whereas Adams is distinguishing them from those who have money at interest.
56. *Works*, IX, pp. 638–9. Letter to Benjamin Rush, 28 August 1811.
57. *Impact*, p. 94. Earle Davis (*Vision Fugitive*) notes this discrepancy of view, but excuses Pound: 'Pound felt that mentioning Adams' objections to paper money would distract attention from what he considered to be the main point, and he is probably right.' (p. 144)
58. *Works*, X, pp. 375–6.
59. 'A Visiting Card', *Impact*, p. 45.

CHAPTER VII

1. Quoted by Forrest Read, *Pound/Joyce*, p. 228.
2. *Letters*, p. 424.
3. *Drafts & Fragments of Cantos CX–CXVII*, New York: New Directions, 1968, pp. 28, 29.
4. Noel Stock (*The Life of Ezra Pound*, p. 404) says that Pound wrote two cantos in Italian (72 and 73) while at Sant' Ambrogio, but says they have not been published, and does not appear to have seen them himself.
5. The typescript at Yale indicates that the section has been considerably shortened, for after continuous pagination from '2' to '8', the following page is numbered in type '9 MS 77', and '10' in the final, pencilled pagination. The MS. pagination uses only alternate numbers. On the basis of the numbering of the typescript, about 40 pages seem to have been cut.
6. Noel Stock, *Reading the Cantos*, p. 80. Stock maintains the same view of the *Pisan Cantos* in *The Life of Ezra Pound*. See especially pp. 411–12.
7. *The Spirit of Romance*, p. 153, and p. 216.

8. T. S. Eliot, *Collected Poems, 1909–1962*, London: Faber & Faber, 1963, p. 92.
9. Leo Frobenius and Douglas C. Fox, *African Genesis*, New York: Stockpole Sons, 1937, pp. 97–110. Guy Davenport first drew attention to the legend in his 1953 English Institute essay, 'Pound and Frobenius', reprinted in *Motive and Method in the Cantos of Ezra Pound*. Davenport's argument in the latter part of that essay anticipates the general thrust of my argument in these pages, but is somewhat different in detail.

   In a more recent article, 'Persephone's Ezra' (in Hesse, *New Approaches*, pp. 145–73), Davenport returns to a consideration of the city theme, particularly as it is further developed in the later cantos.
10. Frobenius and Fox, pp. 97–8.
11. Frobenius and Fox, p. 98. The discrimination of the sexes in the last line of this passage is reminiscent of canto 29, '"Nel ventre tuo, o nella mente mia,/ "Yes, Milady, precisely, if you wd./have anything properly made."'
12. Gassire of the legend is son of Nganamba, king of Dierra. Nganamba is particularly long-lived, and Gassire becomes impatient to claim his patrimony. However, he is told by a wise man that 'Nganamba will die; but he will not leave you his sword and shield: You will carry a lute. Shield and sword shall others inherit. But your lute shall cause the loss of Wagadu' (Frobenius and Fox, p. 100). And so it comes to pass. Gassire is thus the original bard who brings about the first disappearance of Wagadu, and he accomplishes it by involuntarily bathing his lute in the blood of his sons.

   Pound might have used this legend as an analogue of his own situation, substituting the dead friends and fellow artists he elegizes in the *Pisan Cantos* for Gassire's sons. But it is the fourth and final appearance of Wagadu that he chooses to incorporate into his poem—stressing the internalization of the city rather than the fearful price exacted of the artist by the world.
13. There are, in all, eight allusions to *Gassire's Lute* in the *Cantos* from 74 on. They are: 74/427:454, 429:455, 430:457, 442:470; 77/465:494; 94/635:668; 98/636:714; 105/749:774. The references cited above constitute all the substantial ones.
14. The allusion is in canto 48, where Pound crosses the Albigensian motif with his own memories of a walking tour in the region of Montségur. See above, pp. 29–30, 38–9, 145–6.
15. *Gaudier-Brzeska*, p. 89.
16. *Formato locho* is translated as 'that forméd trace' in canto 36 (p. 178:184). 'To forge Achaia' is a quotation from 'Hugh Selwyn Mauberly':

   > Colourless
   > Pier Francesca,
   > Pisanello lacking the skill
   > To forge Achaia.
   >
   > (Second Series, I, *Personae*, p. 198)

   Pisanello created forgeries of Greek medals. The point of the allusion would seem to be that the images, the ikons, remain in the mind, but require skill to be successfully re-created or 'forged'.
17. *Literary Essays*, p. 9.
18. Erigena's work, *De Divisione Naturae*, was condemned in 1225, during the Albigensian Crusade, but his remains were not disinterred. Of course, my

commentary is intended as an interpretation of the lines quoted from canto 83, and not as an accurate representation of the views of either Yeats, Erigena, or the Church.

19. Étienne Gilson, *History of Christian Philosophy in the Middle Ages*, New York: Random House, 1955, p. 119. Pound used the French edition (1922), but the English translation is close enough to the original French for the purposes at hand.
20. Gilson, p. 120.
21. 'Medical Report on Pound', in *A Casebook on Ezra Pound*, eds. William Van O'Connor and Edward Stone, New York: Thomas Y. Crowell Co., 1959, p. 25.
22. The reference to Upward continues:

        his seal Sitalkas, sd/the old combattant: 'victim,
    withstood them by Thames and by Niger with pistol by Niger
        with a printing press by the Thomas bank'
        until I end my song
            and shot himself.

(74/437:464)

A. D. Moody suggests that the Sitalkas seal is that stamped on the boards of *Some Personalities*—a figure Upward himself identifies as John Barleycorn ('Pound's Allen Upward', *Paideuma*, 4 (Spring 1975) pp. 55–70).

Bryant Knox first drew attention to Upward ('Allen Upward and Ezra Pound', *Paideuma*, 3 (Spring 1974) pp. 71–84). Knox gives what biographical information is available, drawing on *Some Personalities* (London: John Murray, 1921), an extraordinarily egocentric memoir published by Upward in his fifty-eighth year, five years before his death.

The middle two lines of Pound's tribute are a paraphrase of lines from Upward's 'The Discarded Imagist', (*The Egoist*, June 1915, p. 98):

I withstood the savages of the Niger with a revolver
I withstood the savages of the Thames with a printing press.'

The printing press was the Primrose (later, the Orient) Press founded by Upward and Byng in 1904. Their first publication was Upward's *Sayings of Confucius* (1904), beginning a series called *Wisdom of the East*, continued for many years by John Murray.

23. Allen Upward, *The Divine Mystery: A Reading of the History of Christianity down to the Time of Christ*, Boston and New York: Houghton Mifflin Co., 1915. It is interesting to note that Upward argues that Christianity predates Christ, but attached itself to the person of Christ as the expected saviour through the work of the evangelists. This hypothesis has been strengthened by the discovery of the Dead Sea Scrolls. It was a matter of conviction in Mead's theosophical circle whence Upward derived many of his ideas.
24. Quoted by Ezra Pound in 'The Divine Mystery', *The New Freewoman*, 1 (15 Nov. 1913), p. 207. On p. 436 (463) of canto 74 Pound repeats a motif from canto 38 (189:196):

        Frobenius der Geheimrat
    der im Baluba das Gewitter gemacht hat
    [Frobenius of Geheimrat/who made the tempest
    in Baluba].

Frobenius, one of Pound's culture heroes, succeeded in accomplishing the same stunt that Upward had seen performed in Nigeria. Pound cites this incident (also 53/264:274 and 77/465:494) as evidence of the acuity of Frobenius's sensibility.

25. Ezra Pound, *The ABC of Reading*, pp. 81, 83.
26. *The Spirit of Romance*, p. 92.
27. Mary de Rachewiltz, *Discretions*, London: Faber & Faber, 1971, p. 245.
28. Allen Upward, 'Karos the God', *The New Freewoman*, 1 (15 Dec. 1913), pp. 242–3.
29. Dante Alighieri, *The Divine Comedy*, *Purgatorio*, xxxi. 90–104. Prose translation by John D. Sinclair.
30. The feminine form, 'vieille', indicates that a woman is being addressed. One can only guess at her identity. It may be Dorothy, his wife, or Olga Rudge, his 'other wife', or, indeed, Katherine Ruth Heyman. Whoever it might be, one is reminded of 'Scriptor Ignotus' where Pound—or rather his persona—imagines his beloved grown old as he brings his 'forty-year epic' to completion.
31. It would lead the discussion far astray to enter into the question of sense of time in the *Cantos* at this point, but it would be dereliction of duty not to mention Daniel Pearlman's book, *The Barb of Time*. Pearlman's argument is that the major form of the *Cantos* is to be found in its preoccupation with the problem of time. Pound is, of course, playing fast and loose with ordinary notions of progressive chronology—as Pearlman argues—and Mircea Eliade's notion of 'sacred time'—which Pearlman cites—seems to me an excellent model for the temporal sense of the poem. However, I would argue that the character and content of Pound's sacred moments—which are said to be 'out of time' or 'in illo tempore'—are more crucial to the poem's form than Pearlman's argument would allow.
32. See J. P. Sullivan, *Ezra Pound and Sextus Propertius*, Austin: The University of Texas Press, 1964, p. 150.
33. 'Homage to Sextus Propertius', IX. 2, in Sullivan, op. cit.
34. 'Ac ferae familiares' is the key phrase which links this passage with canto 20. It occurs nowhere else in the poem until canto 90.
35. G. R. S. Mead, *Orpheus*, London: John M. Watkins, 1965 (first edition, 1896), p. 149.
36. Mead, *Orpheus*, p. 188.
37. Mead, *Orpheus*, p. 149.
38. Unfortunately Mead cannot help us to understand the significance of the three goddesses, Thetis, Maia, and Aphrodite. Thetis and Aphrodite are mothers of heroes begotten by mortal fathers, and hence can be seen as emblems of the union of body and spirit. Aphrodite's 'marriage' with Anchises is, of course, alluded to on a number of occasions already discussed. Maia, however, is the mother of the god, Hermes, by Zeus, and therefore does not fit such a pattern. It is true that she is a nymph like Thetis rather than a true goddess, but still she is an immortal, and her son a god rather than a hero. Perhaps Maia is included because of Hermes' role as psychopomp or bearer of souls into the Underworld. See also the discussion of canto 79 below.

39. 'Benecomata dea', 'the fair-tressed goddess' is an epithet of Circe introduced in canto 74, 'nec benecomata Kirke' (p. 437:464).
40. Noel Stock (*Reading the Cantos*, p. 88) says that this girl, to whom Pound speaks in Italian, is Pound's daughter, Mary. However, Mary de Rachewiltz makes no mention of the conversation in her memoir, *Discretions*.
41. *Guide to Kulchur*, p. 127.
42. Cunizza is she 'that freed her slaves on a Wednesday' (6/22:26). We encounter her also at 29/141:146, 74/438:465, 443:471, 76/452:480, and 78/483:514. Her signature in the *Pisan Cantos* is 'al triedro', 'in the corner', and she is associated with Artemis.

    Isotta is introduced in canto 9/38:42; mentioned on 20/94:98, and appears in the *Pisan Cantos* as 'Ixotta', 74/448:478, 76/452:480, 76/459:487, and 76 462:491.
43. Pallas Athena could be added to the list as another virgin goddess—of whom Pound complains 'Athene cd/have done with more sex appeal' (79/486:518).
44. This destructive aspect of Aphrodite is underlined later in canto 84: 'and at Ho Ci'u destroyed the whole town/for hiding a woman, *Κύθηρα δεινά*' (84/538:573–4). The reference to Ho Ci'u is obscure, but the parallel with Troy is clear enough.
45. Paquin is a Parisian dress designer, presumably representing in his craft the embodiment of vain artificiality.
46. Allen Upward, *The New Word*, New York: Mitchell Kennerley, 1910, pp. 204–5. Donald Davie makes very large claims for the influence of this notion on Pound in *Pound*, Fontana Modern Masters, 1975, pp. 62–74—far too large, I think.
47. Ezra Pound, 'Axiomata', *New Age*, 38 (13 Jan.)1921), p. 125. The article is only two pages long, therefore no further page references will be given.
48. There is much that requires glossing in this passage beyond the requirements of the argument. 'Niccolo' is Niccolo d'Este, an analogue of Agamemnon, mentioned in canto 8 as of a family called Atreides (the family name of Agamemnon and Menelaus). In canto 24 (p. 113:118) we are told that he was buried naked. *Emon ton andra* is from Theocritus, *Idyll*, II, cited earlier at 81/518:554. I do not understand the reference to Kipling. The second Greek phrase is doubtless meant to be Clytemnestra speaking after she has murdered Agamemnon although this specific phrase is not to be found in the *Agamemnon*. See 82/523:558 where Clytemnestra unmistakably speaks: '*EMOS POSIS . . . CHEROS*'.
49. 'Hymn to Demeter', 11. 370–1. Loeb translation.
50. 'Hymn to Demeter', 11. 401–3.
51. The sharing of food was part of the Greek marriage rite, and was thought to bind the two parties indissolubly. See Le Comte Goblet d'Alviella, *Eleusinia*, Paris: Ernest Leroux, 1903, p. 48. See also Pound's reference to Helen's Egyptian drugs in canto 98, discussed below.
52. On this last procession Pound has written a rather puzzling comment in a letter to his father (Yale Collection, no. 511, p. 2, 1919):

    The worms of the procession had three large antennae, and I hope to develop the motive later, [*sic*] text clearly states that this vermiform object circulated in the crowd at the Church of St. Nicholas in Toulouse. Not merely mediaeval but black central African superstition and voodoo energy squalling infant, general murk and epileptic religious hog wash with chief totem being magnificently swung over whole.

This description of canto 4 does not quite fit either published version, in neither of which is the location 'clearly stated'. He is apparently describing some procession on a Catholic feast day which he actually observed. What is surprising is the indication that his intent was to satirize this and other religious processions. It is impossible to believe that such processions have a satirical force throughout the *Cantos*. The crowd is praying to the Virgin Mary, and it is perhaps the unnatural notion of the virgin birth that Pound means by 'general murk and epileptic religious hogwash'. The bulk of the canto is concerned with various acts of sexual violence, and includes Danaë, 'the god's bride', who 'lay ever, waiting the golden rain'.

53. *The Spirit of Romance*, p. 94.
54. *Reading the Cantos*, esp. Chapter 2, pp. 15–28.
55. Noel Stock, *Poet in Exile*, pp. 26–7.
56. T. S. Eliot is a case in point. Few—certainly not this writer—would argue that Eliot's conversion to Anglicanism was intellectually crippling, but there is little question about the great intellectual effort Eliot was compelled to devote to religious matters in order to accomplish and maintain his conversion. No one of Pound and Eliot's generation could simply accept Christianity as a birthright.
57. *Guide to Kulchur*, p. 299.
58. 'Terra Italica', *New Review*, 1 (Winter 1931/2), p. 386. Pound does not identify the source of the citation.

CHAPTER VIII

1. Hugh Kenner is the paterfamilias if not only-begetter of this view. It is ably argued by Donald Davie in his recent study, *Pound*, Fontana Modern Masters, 1975, pp. 82 ff. As with Kenner, his argument depends rather heavily upon the imputation of impercipience and sloth to those who complain of the *Cantos*' rhetoric.
2. Cited by Charles Norman, *Ezra Pound*, p. 421.
3. Quoted by Norman, p. 444.
4. *Guide to Kulchur*, p. 55.
5. Alexander Del Mar, *A History of Monetary Systems*, Chicago: Charles Kerr, 1895, p. 5. Pound cites this passage in canto 97: '"That most powerful engine" says Del Mar'. For a detailed annotation of canto 97's borrowings from Del Mar see Daniel Pearlman, 'Alexander Del Mar in *The Cantos*', *Paideuma* 1 (Fall–Winter 1972), pp. 161–80.
6. Del Mar, *Systems*, pp. 7–8.
7. For the relationship to the *Sacred Edict* see David Gordon, 'Pound's Use of the Sacred Edict in Canto 98', *Paideuma*, 4 (Spring 1975), p. 126.
8. Stink Saunder's word is first cited in canto 87 (575:611). He taught Pound chemistry in high school.
9. 'An Introduction to the Economic Nature of the United States', *Impact*, p. 18.

10. For Pound's use of Waddell see Boris de Rachewiltz, 'Pagan and Magic Elements in Ezra Pound's Works', Hesse, *New Approaches*, pp. 174–97. For some of the rather imaginative history in canto 91 see Christine Brooke-Rose, 'Lay me by Aurelie: An Examination of Pound's Use of Historical and Semi-Historical Sources', also in Hesse, *New Approaches*, pp. 242–79. Virtually all the studies of Pound's sources in the later cantos show him inventing political, philosophical, and religious traditions to validate his own beliefs and preoccupations. But, for the most part, the commentators remain more impressed with Pound's ingenuity than disturbed by his inventiveness. He remains ever the poet—discovering correspondence and ignoring the fatal knife of analytical distinction.
11. *Impact*, p. 15.
12. 'Ezra Pound: an Interview', pp. 48–9.
13. Much of the following discussion has appeared in *Hudson Review*, 27 (Winter 1974–5), pp. 491–510. James Neault subsequently published an independent study of Pound's use of Apollonius, 'Apollonius of Tyana', *Paideuma*, 4 (Spring 1975), pp. 3–36.
14. Hugh Kenner, for one, states that the 'lyric Paradiso' begins here in canto 90. 'Under the larches of Paradise', in *Gnomon*, New York: McDowell Oblensky, 1958, p. 293.
15. It should be noted, however, that the phrase, 'e i cavalieri' also occurs in canto 20, which canto Pound has himself described as 'a general paradiso' (*Letters*, p. 285). 'La donna antiche e i cavalieri' (the knights and ladies of old) are placed in Hell by Dante because of their well-publicized sins of passion. Pound very clearly does not share the Catholic disapproval of amorous adventure in which Dante was obliged to acquiesce. This allusion to the *Inferno* (v. 71), therefore, by no means gives warrant for regarding canto 90 as infernal.

    I doubt that Pound had Dante in mind when he introduced Electra into the passage, but she too is given her appropriate place in the *Divine Comedy*: in limbo.
16. There is also a play by Jean Giradoux, *Ondine*, based on the tale, and first performed in Paris in May 1939.
17. Philostratus, *The Life of Apollonius of Tyana*, with an English translation by F. C. Conybeare, 2 vols., London: William Heinemann, 1912. Hugh Kenner is the first scholar to have given this work any attention, as he does with characteristic brilliance in 'Under the Larches of Paradise', in *Gnomon*, pp. 280–96. Kenner points out that Pound also used G. R. S. Mead's *Apollonius of Tyana* (London, 1901).
18. In this passage Pound draws on Philostratus, vol. I, bk. IV, chapters xi–xvi. In the following account I italicize those parts echoed or repeated in the passage cited from the *Cantos*.

    Apollonius and his company stop off at Troy on their way from Ephesus to Athens. Apollonius announces his intention to pass a night alone on the mound of Achilles in order to have converse with him (p. 367). In chapter xiii we are told that many people rushed to board Apollonius' ship 'for it was already autumn and the sea was not much to be trusted. They all regarded Apollonius as one who was *master of the tempest and of fire* and of perils of all sorts, and so wished to go on board with him . . .' (p. 371).

In the same chapter Apollonius tells them to sail 'towards *the country of Aeolians*, which lies over against Lesbos, *and then to turn as close as he could to Methymna*, and there to cast anchor' (p. 373). It is there that Achilles has told Apollonius that Palamedes is buried.

Philostratus continues, 'they then had hardly leapt out of the ship, when he hit upon the tomb and found the statue buried beside it. And there were inscribed on the base of the statue the words: 'To the divine Palamedes'. *He accordingly set it up again in its place, as I myself saw*; and he raised a shrine around it of the size which the worshippers of the goddess of the crossways, called Enodia, use: for *it was large enough for ten persons at once to sit and drink* and keep good cheer in' (p. 373).

Finally, in chapter xvi, Apollonius describes his conversation with Achilles. He begins by remarking, 'Well, *it was not by digging a ditch* like Odysseus, *nor by tempting souls with the blood of a sheep*, that I obtained a conversation with Achilles' (p. 377). As a Pythagorean, Apollonius says, he does not believe that Achilles is dead, and so merely calls upon him to make an appearance.

Apollonius closes his account of the conversation by telling his audience that 'Achilles vanished with a flash of summer lightning, for indeed the cocks were *already beginning their chant*' (p. 385).

19. The whole episode occupies pp. 195–283 of vol. II. The quotation is from p. 283.
20. Pound, in a manner characteristic of his late cryptic style, gives only two lines to indicate the character of Domitian's rule: 'And that even in the time of Domitian/one young man declined to be bugger'd'. This is a reference to an unnamed Arcadian youth who was thrown into prison for refusing to become Domitian's lover (II, pp. 263–5).
21. Philostratus, II, p. 277.
22. Philostratus, II, p. 211.
23. Since Leucothea is a new figure in the *Cantos* and is referred to on a number of occasions in both *Rock-Drill* and *Thrones*, she has drawn a good deal of critical attention. Hugh Kenner's review article, 'Under the Larches of Paradise', was the first to draw attention to her. Kenner returns to Leucothea in an article focusing on Pound's lexical technique, 'Leucothea's Bikini: Mimetic Homage', in *Perspectives*, ed. Noel Stock, Chicago: Henry Regnery, 1965, pp. 25–40. K. L. Goodwin has written a comprehensive discussion of her occurrence in *Rock-Drill* and *Thrones*, 'The Structure of Ezra Pound's Later Cantos', *Southern Review*, 4 (1971) pp. 300–7. For some reason Goodwin makes no reference to Kenner's two earlier articles. The best and most complete discussion of Leucothea is to be found in Christine Brooke-Rose, *A ZBC of Ezra Pound* (London: Faber & Faber, 1971; especially pp. 138–56). Brooke-Rose builds upon Kenner's two articles.

    None of these discussions note the reference to the Leucothea episode in Philostratus, nor do any of them read the episode in the context of Pound's reformulation of his paradisal motif in the later cantos.
24. Philostratus, II, p. 211.
25. *Pisan Cantos*, 80/518:547. The Greek phrase means 'beyond what is des-

tined', as in *Odyssey* I. 32–4: 'Look you now, how ready mortals are to blame the gods. It is from us, they say, that evils come, but they even of themselves, through their own blind folly, have sorrows *beyond that which is ordained*' (Loeb translation).

Pound thought that 'the perfectly useless, trifling, unprovoked sack of the Cicones' gave the *Odyssey* 'a crime and punishment motif' (*Literary Essays*, p. 212).

26. Philostratus, I, p. 431.
27. Philostratus, I, p. 461.
28. Philostratus, I, pp. 501–3.
29. *Personae*, p. 76.
30. There are a number of allusions in *Rock-Drill* to *Purgatorio*, xxviii, just as there are a number of allusions to the *Paradiso* and the *Inferno*. In themselves they do nothing to fix the nature of Pound's 'paradiso'. The opening lines of canto 92 echo *Purgatorio*, xxviii. 109–20. And the last half-line of canto 93 is from the same canto (l. 29) where Dante says that Matilda reminds him of Proserpine.
31. Philostratus, I, p. 435.
32. *Odyssey*, V. 339–53. Loeb translation.
33. The Chinese, and the last line first appear in canto 93/628–9:661–2, concluding a lyric on compassion. The Chinese sentence there has four characters, and Pound translates it: 'energy is near to benevolence'. The character for 'Energy' (hsing^2) is omitted in canto 95.
34. One hidden infelicity is the prominent role of Folquet of Marseille as a sanguinary persecutor of the Albigenses—not noted by Dante, and perhaps unknown to Pound. Folquet became Bishop of Toulouse (1205–31), discarding his youthful life as a singer of 'gai savoir'.
35. It would be quite impractical to explain all the allusions and references in the later cantos even if I possessed all the necessary information. The *Annotated Index* does not cover *Thrones* and *Rock-Drill*, but one can garner a good deal of annotation from the pages of *Paideuma: A Journal Devoted to Ezra Pound Scholarship*, and in *New Approaches to Ezra Pound*, ed. Eva Hesse. For commentary on Ra-Set and other Egyptian elements, see Boris de Rachewiltz, 'Pagan and Magic Elements in Ezra Pound's Works', in Hesse, pp. 174–97. Boris de Rachewiltz is Pound's son-in-law and, no doubt, the source of much of the Egyptian lore in the *Cantos* since he is an Egyptologist.
36. Philostratus, II, pp. 209, 211.
37. *Letters*, p. 285.

CHAPTER IX

1. 'Cuniculi' are underground passages. They are first mentioned in canto 101/724:750–1, '(Del Pelo Pardi/came on cuniculi)'. According to Stock (*Reading the Cantos*, p. 111) Pardi discovered underground pre-Roman canals in Italy, and it is this discovery Pound refers to. I do not know just what significance Pound attaches to them, but it is typical of his use of semi-private information that they should recur without provenance in

canto 116 in apposition with 'the record', that is the *Cantos* themselves, which are therefore perceived as a network of underground passages, as it were, mining underneath the superficial appearances of the world and its history. In this case the private associations of 'cuniculi' are of little importance to the reader. The word functions autonomously in its local context. Pound achieves this kind of local autonomy of text in conjunction with a reference to some other part of the poem all too rarely.

2. For a rather hopeful study of Pound's post-Gutenbergian mental apparatus see Max Nänny, *Ezra Pound: Poetics for an Electric Age*, Berne: Francke Verlag, 1973.
3. Walter Baumann, 'Secretary of Nature: J. Heydon', in Hesse, *New Approaches*, pp. 303–18.
4. John Heydon, *The Holy Guide*, London, 1662. I, pp. 33–4.
5. John Heydon, *The Holy Guide*, III, p. 87.
6. Baumann cites Pound's remark in *Gaudier-Brzeska: A Memoir* (p. 127), 'And John Heydon, long before our present day theorists, had written of the joys of pure form . . . inorganic, geometrical form, in his "Holy Guide".' But I find little in Heydon which fits this description, and Pound apparently found as little when he returned to Heydon.
7. Heydon, *The Holy Guide*, VI, pp. 30–4. Heydon repeats the identical vision in the preface to *The Harmony of the World* (London, 1662). In both cases the goddess is careful to mention Heydon's other books as well as forthcoming ones. In fact, she is little more than a celestial literary agent for Heydon. However, the description of the goddess's appearance possesses great charm—in fact, rather more in *Harmony of the World* than in *The Holy Guide*. But there is no evidence that Pound knew any of Heydon's books other than *The Holy Guide*.

Index